Professional and Public Writing

A Rhetoric and Reader for Advanced Composition

Linda S. Coleman
Eastern Illinois University

Robert Funk
Eastern Illinois University, Emeritus

PEARSON

Prentice
Hall

Upper Saddle River, New Jersey 07458

Library of Congress Cataloging-in-Publication Data

Coleman, Linda S.
Professional and public writing : a rhetoric and reader for advanced composition / Linda
S. Coleman, Robert Funk.
p. cm.
Includes bibliographical references and indexes.
ISBN 0-13-183885-7
1. English language—Rhetoric—Problems, exercises, etc. 2. English language—Business
English—Problems, exercises, etc. 3. English language—Technical English—Problems,
exercises, etc. 4. Business writing—Problems, exercises, etc. 5. Technical writing—
Problems, exercises, etc. 6. College readers. I. Funk, Robert. II. Title.

PE1479.B87C645 2004
808'.042—dc22

2004020148

Editor-in-Chief: Leah Jewell
Acquisitions Editor: Brad Potthoff
Assistant Editor: Jennifer Conklin
Managing Editor: Fran Russello
Marketing Manager: Brandy Dawson
Marketing Assistant: Kara Pottle
Manufacturing Buyer: Mary Ann Gloriande
Cover Art Director: Jayne Conte
Cover Design: Bruce Kenselaar
Manager, Cover Visual Research & Permissions: Karen Sanatar
Cover Illustration/Photo: Jon Lezinsky/Corbis Bettman
Permission Coordinator: Judy Ladendorf, The Permissions Group
Composition/Full-Service Project Management: Jessica Balch/Pine Tree Composition, Inc.
Printer/Binder: Phoenix Book Tech Park
Cover Printer: Phoenix Color Corp.

Credits and acknowledgments for material borrowed from other sources and reproduced, with permission, in this textbook appear on the appropriate pages.

Pearson Education LTD., London
Pearson Education Singapore, Pte. Ltd
Pearson Education, Canada, Ltd
Pearson Education–Japan
Pearson Education Australia PTY, Limited

Pearson Education North Asia Ltd
Pearson Educación de Mexico, S.A. de C.V.
Pearson Education Malaysia, Pte. Ltd
Pearson Education, Upper Saddle River,
    New Jersey

10 9 8 7 6 5 4 3 2 1
ISBN 0-13-183885-7

Contents

Preface

College students are projected to make several career changes within their working lifetimes. These transitions and the challenges of their complex personal and public lives will require informed flexibility. *Professional and Public Writing: A Rhetoric and Reader for Advanced Composition* is designed to guide students through the writing required of them as students, professionals, and citizens. Its two central goals are:

- To help advanced students become confident, refined, and effective writers through an active critique of their undergraduate writing practices and of the writing requirements of their academic majors.
- To prepare students for the work required of professional and public writers in their varied discourse communities, each of which operates from distinct cognitive assumptions and within specific rhetorical contexts.

Two core strategies are used to achieve these goals:

- Review of and in-depth engagement with the rhetorical principles introduced in the students' earlier composition courses
- Introduction to and application of the principles and techniques of discourse analysis necessary for success in academic, professional, and public writing

Instructor Expertise

Because few English teachers are fully familiar with the many styles and genres required of student writers in their various majors, let alone the full range of demands made on all professional and public writers, *Professional and Public Writing* depends primarily on instructor expertise in teaching the fundamental rhetorical and research skills that enable any writer to enter a discourse community and identify its cognitive assumptions (values, interests, etc.) and rhetorical features (genres, style, design, etc.). The book provides guidelines and extensive materials for meeting these instructional goals.

Student Readiness

Although students are introduced to key concepts in freshman writing courses, they come to Advanced Composition actively pursuing a major and consciously moving into their professional and civic lives. This timing provides them with significant motivation and interest in refining their current academic skills and understanding the value of applying these skills to real-life situations. *Professional and Public Writing* is grounded in the assumption that these students can be taught the advanced rhetorical knowledge and research practices needed to write successfully for any discourse community within which they might find themselves. This same proficiency is of immediate use in completing the writing required by their advanced college courses.

Writing Assignments

The text is structured around extensive "Writing Activities" and sequenced assignments that meet the needs of students from a range of disciplines and with diverse learning styles and interests. As part of the process, students are asked to keep a "Writer's Notebook" and to engage in collaboration, peer review, and both primary and secondary research. Formal assignments include three increasingly complex and comprehensive "Writer's Profiles," a critical discourse analysis of a student-selected professional essay, and an argument based on a researched literature review. Each chapter also contains genre- and theme-based "Writer's Workshops" that provide additional writing opportunities.

Genre Modeling

Samples of academic writing from a range of disciplines are used throughout the text for purposes of illustration and practice. In addition, two casebook chapters provide students the opportunity to read and analyze thematically linked readings:

> *Professional Writing:* "Privacy in the Information Age" and "Weight, Body Image, and Identity"
> *Public Writing:* "Targeting Discrimination"and "Responding to Homelessness"

The readings represent genres employed by public and professional writers from diverse discourse communities—for example, a proposal by a grassroots community organization, a case study by a sociologist, fact sheets prepared by the government for educators, a Web site for homeless advocates, a position paper by a professional nursing organization, a literary essay published in an interdisciplinary humanities journal, and a researched journal article written for a law journal. Extensive reading apparatus prompts students to apply the concepts of discourse and genre analysis introduced in the opening chapters.

Additional Features

- Frequent activities that encourage students to explore the correlation between their personal skills and those required of professionals in the careers to which they aspire
- Illustrations and readings from Across the Curriculum, including illustrative "Writers on Writing" selections in Chapters 1–3
- An opportunity for students without a major to explore possible careers through research and writing
- An appendix on basic Web use and site construction that offers students and instructors options for research and publishing
- The nuts and bolts of both print and electronic research from project start to finish, including the skills necessary to evaluate and select appropriate sources
- Two complete sample student research projects illustrating MLA and APA styles and varied structures for argument
- Suggestions for formal oral presentations
- An appendix that describes the basic procedures and forms for citing and documenting sources according to MLA, APA, CMS, and CSE styles

Although *Professional and Public Writing* is indebted to research in the areas of advanced composition, writing across the curriculum, ethnography, genre theory, discourse community analysis, and multiple literacies, chapters are written in a clear and engaging tone, introducing appropriate jargon only when it supports more conscious understanding of a practice or concept.

Acknowledgments

This book grew out of our work with advanced composition classes at Eastern Illinois University. We want to thank our students of English 3001 for field-testing the assignments and for providing us with inspiration and insights as well as writing samples. Special thanks go to our editor, Brad Potthoff, for his support and thoughtful advice, and to his assistant, Steve Kyritz, and assistant editor, Jennifer Conklin, for their invaluable help. We are also grateful to Julie Brown of the Permissions Group and to Jessica Balch, our production editor, for shepherding us through the complicated process of getting this book into print. We would also like to thank our reviewers for their perceptive criticisms and useful suggestions: Meg Morgan, UNC Charlotte; Pat Panzarella, St. Bonaventure's University; Stephanie Mood, Grossmont College; Christy Desmet, University of Georgia; Mary Beth Simmons, Villanova University; Elizabeth Larsen, West Chester University; Thomas Dukes, University of Akron; Gary Hatch, Brigham Young University; Diana Reep, University of Akron; Dan Royer, Grand Valley State University; Sandra Stephan, Youngstown University-Metro College; Wendy Bishop, Florida State University. Finally, we must thank our life partners, Casey Sutherland and Bill Weber, for their encouragement, understanding, and extraordinary patience.

Linda S. Coleman
Robert Funk

Chapter 1
Being Aware of Your Writing Practices

Chapter Preview

Professional and Public Writing begins with a review of what most practicing writers regard as essential elements for a successful piece of writing: a viable purpose, an adequate understanding of one's readers and their needs, a focused message, and an appropriate voice. This chapter will help you to think more purposefully about your current approach to writing. As you read this chapter and the next, consider the following points: What kinds of questions do I ask myself as I write? Do I follow a typical sequence of activities when I write? What situations cause my habits to vary and with what differing effects or levels of success? Do my skills provide me with the control and choices I need or would like to have as a writer? You might want to get an early start on the Writer's Notebook you will be asked to keep, informally recording answers to these questions as you read.

You are, of course, an active writer already. You send letters to friends and family, apply for jobs, and write papers and exams for your classes. Your writing practices—the ways you approach the various writing situations you encounter—are the result both of the task before you and of your many years of experience as a writer. You tend to answer e-mails as soon as they arrive, or perhaps you prefer to put off responding until you have time to go into detail about the events of your week. You love the crowded student union as a place to brainstorm essays on your laptop, or you simply cannot begin writing until everyone else has gone to bed and the cats are napping quietly at your feet. And you may worry endlessly about what your readers will think of you, or you are confident that you can make any audience see your point of view.

Our writing procedures are as varied as our personalities and lives. This chapter's purpose, therefore, is not to radically alter your current writing process. There is no one-size-fits-all approach. There are, however, flexible building blocks for success that all active writers need to be aware of and proficient with. Even accomplished athletes and artists are self-critical, seeking feedback from coaches and advisors. Sammy Sosa, for example, is the first Chicago Cub in the batter's cage at practice time. He recognizes that natural talent is seldom sufficient to meet all challenges.

Reviewing the Core Elements: Purpose, Audience, Thesis, and Persona

Although we might not pose them directly, a few essential questions must be considered throughout the process of preparing for and completing any writing project:

- What do I want to accomplish?
- What readers do I want to reach?
- What point do I want to make?
- How should I say it?

Most of the time, the answer to one of these questions is what stimulates us to write in the first place.

From a U.S. Government class, for example, you might develop an awareness of the extent and effects of voter apathy and might, in turn, be inspired to start locally with a campus voter registration drive. Your persuasive **purpose** is clear, but next you begin to narrow the focus by identifying one of a few possible **audiences.** You could either write to the administration, asking to be to allowed to conduct a drive, or, perhaps, to fellow students, to join you in the project. With a quick e-mail to your student government, you discover it already has an established subcommittee that can conduct bipartisan political activities on campus, so you decide to write a formal proposal asking for their help to set up a series of events. Knowing that these student government representatives are busy people, with several other proposals vying for their time and money, you e-mail friends asking for volunteers to staff the drive. Next, you start to gather supporting detail and evidence for your proposal, including checking for available dates in the campus schedule of events. In the process, you discover there are a significant number of programs already planned for the months before the next election, so you cut back that part of your **thesis** and decide to ask for only two dates rather than the four for which you had planned. Having done all of this preparation, you are ready to write. In your proposal your **persona** will appear as a serious, committed constituent who deserves student government support.

In another case you might begin with a **thesis**—for example, an assignment to write a position paper against government intervention into business practices for a class debate on global warming. Though you have a personal view on the topic, you realize that you have been asked to put it aside. Instead, you must successfully argue for one of the two major sides of the debate, so you begin by completing the extensive research needed to gain a credible **persona,** looking not just at the arguments against but also those for government action. Your **audience,** you recognize, will be equally well prepared and set in their points of view, so you limit your **purpose** to informing them about new and even rarely used arguments for your position, hoping to catch the other side off guard.

Purpose, audience, persona, and **thesis,** then, are core elements in completing and polishing any kind of writing activity, from setting up a Web site to completing a report at work. The order in which you determine your answers to the various questions may vary, and, very likely, those answers will change and evolve over the course of finishing the project, but by the end of the process you must feel comfortably aware of and in control of each element and see the logic of the relationships among them.

Refining Your Purpose

Writing is easier and more productive when you have a clear *purpose* in mind. The purpose for writing is not the same as the reason for writing. An error in your telephone bill gives you a reason, or motive, to write to the telephone company, but the purpose of your letter is to *inform* the company that it has made a mistake and to *persuade* it to make a correction in your favor. This distinction also applies to academic and professional situations. Instructors give exams in order to evaluate what you have learned, but they give you a more exact purpose in the questions they ask: *define* the following literary terms, *analyze* the structure of DNA, *argue* for or against corporate ethical reform. The reason for writing a report is that your boss assigned it, but your purpose in writing the report must go beyond that limited motive if you want to show that you understand the goals of the business.

Deciding what you want to accomplish in your writing will help focus your efforts. Indeed, your purpose will affect your whole approach to writing: how to begin, whether to state or imply the main idea, which details to include, how to arrange the material, how to conclude, even what level of language to use. In writing that report for your boss, for example, you would probably take an informative, businesslike approach: you'd get right to the point and not worry about entertaining your readers or engaging their interest; you'd be sure to include all the pertinent details but leave out anything that might be distracting or irrelevant. You'd also want to use clear, direct language. In the conclusion, you might offer a recommendation or express your opinion, especially if you wanted to persuade the management to make a decision or take some action.

In determining your purpose for writing, you may choose to do any of the following:

- To inform: sharing facts, explanations, and ideas—as in articles, reports, memos, and research papers
- To instruct: telling someone how to perform a task—for example, connecting a printer to a computer
- To analyze: examining a topic, such as an economic theory or a marketing strategy, and pointing out how its various parts work together
- To persuade: trying to change someone's mind or behavior—as in letters to the editor, advertisements, and feasibility studies
- To argue: presenting your opinion on an issue that has differing viewpoints, supporting your position with reasoning and information, and urging acceptance of your view—as in a position paper or a research study
- To evaluate: criticizing a performance, an experience, or a work of art—as in a review or recommendation

Of course, these aims overlap. You might write a business report full of information designed to persuade management to increase the budget for a long-range project, or you might analyze a proposal or situation in order to evaluate it or argue against it. But you will probably find it most helpful to select a single purpose and let it serve as the primary goal while you develop your ideas.

It's always a good idea to read through your first draft to evaluate whether you've completed and kept to your assigned or chosen purpose. If a teacher asks you to *evaluate* the relative importance of the causes of the American Civil War but instead you simply state those causes, you are sure to lose points on the exam. And if you mean to *persuade* an employer to hire you but provide little more than what is already clear from a quick review of your résumé, you are unlikely to stand out from the other applicants.

Writing Activity

Read the following excerpts on soap operas and then answer the questions that follow the passages:

A. The soap opera is a broadcast dramatic serial program, so called in the United States because most of its major sponsors for many years were manufacturers of soap and detergents. It is characterized by a permanent cast of actors, a continuing story, emphasis on dialogue instead of action, a slower-than-life pace, and a consistently sentimental or melodramatic treatment. The soap opera began in the early 1930s with 15-minute daytime radio episodes and was inherited by television in the early 1950s and expanded to 30 minutes. By the mid-1950s soap operas dominated late morning and early afternoon weekday television programming. . . . By the 1970s the style and content of soap operas had undergone a revolution. There was open discussion of such matters as abortion, drug abuse, wife abuse, and sexually transmitted diseases. Characters of various racial and ethnic backgrounds were introduced into a previously all-white, Anglo-Saxon population. The traditional emphasis on romantic and marital problems remained, but promiscuous behavior, violence, and criminal activity came to be treated more directly. (*Encyclopaedia Britannica Online*)

B. The surface realism of the soap opera conjures up an illusion of "liveness." The domestic settings and easygoing rhythms encourage the viewer to believe that the drama, however ridiculous, is simply an extension of daily life. The conversation is so slow that some have called it "radio with pictures." (Advertisers have always assumed that busy housewives would listen, rather than watch.) Conversation is casual and colloquial, as though one were eavesdropping on neighbors. There is plenty of time to "read" the character's face; close-ups establish intimacy. The sets are comfortably familiar: well-lit interiors of living rooms, restaurants, offices, and hospitals. Daytime soaps have little of the glamour of their prime-time relations. The viewer easily imagines that the conversation is taking place in real time. (Ruth Rosen, "Search for Yesterday")

1. What is the primary purpose of each passage? Are there any secondary purposes?
2. How would you compare the purposes of the two selections?
3. How does the use of language and examples help you to determine the purpose of each selection?

Knowing Your Audience

One of the best ways to establish your purpose is to identify your *audience.* You cannot easily determine *why* you are writing without also determining *who* is going to read what you write. Your audience may be just one person—your history professor, your project manager, your senator. But most of the time you will want to reach a wider audience—your city council, other students in your major, the readership of your local newspaper.

These larger audiences are called *discourse communities*—groups of people who have similar interests and shared knowledge. Your writing class, for example, forms a discourse community, as does the special interest group you chat with on the Internet or the people you write memos to and reports with at work. The discourse (the ideas, information, and opinions expressed) will change considerably from group to group, as will the language and the format you choose to use.

Suppose you are writing an article for a running magazine. Since you'll be addressing a group of running enthusiasts who share a great deal of technical information about running, you won't need to simplify your presentation. In fact, you can rely on their expertise and avoid the need to define terms and explain basic concepts. You can also assume that these readers have an interest in your topic. But if you're writing the same article for a general publication, like your school newspaper, then you'll have to adjust your approach. You will probably want to avoid specialized language, supply background information, use concrete examples to explain basic concepts, and point out the value and importance of the material to the general reader.

In thinking about audience and purpose, you'll find it especially helpful to identify your relationship to your readers. Consider these questions:

- Are you writing for people who belong to a specific discourse community?
- Are you a member of that community?
- Can you assume these readers will know a lot about the topic and accept the language and format you use?
- Or are you writing for an audience that does not share your expertise and may not be familiar with the way you write?
- Are you writing to equals, experts, or beginners?

Considering these questions will help you to focus your thinking and to make important decisions about content, organization, language, and format.

In many professional and public writing situations, you will be writing to a general audience. Successful newspaper columnists like Ellen Goodman and Dave Barry, along with hundreds of their colleagues nationwide, reach millions of readers every day. They direct their writing to the *general reader,* an individual who knows a little about many things but lacks the specific information on the topic the writer wants to present. Writing for general readers is challenging because you can't always pinpoint their needs and predict their responses. Even professional writers misjudge their audience, offering material that confuses or bores their readers. But difficult as it may be, writing for a general audience can be exciting and rewarding, mainly because you have an opportunity to inform and influence a wide range of people.

Writing Activities

1. Find several examples of newspaper columns that were written to a general audience. Use Google or some other search engine to find columns by Ellen Goodman, Dave Barry, Molly Ivins, Clarence Page, Maureen Dowd, or William Safire. How can you tell that the writers were addressing a general reader?
2. The following definition comes from an economics textbook written for college students. What assumptions did the author make about his readers? Rewrite the paragraph to address high school readers.

The basic notion behind the concept of a market economy is that the individuals and business firms in such an economy respond to the dictates of impersonal markets over which they have little or no control. We now define such an economy as one in which *perfect competition* prevails. By "perfect competition," we refer to a market structure in which all decisions are decentralized in the hands of individual consumers, owners of the factors of production, and private business firms, and in which none of these units is large enough to control or monopolize any significant area of economic life. All the actors on the economic scene simply respond to signals generated by impersonal markets. (Richard T. Gill, *Economics: A Concise Micro/Macro Text*)

3. The following definition comes from a specialized reference work used by linguists and other students of the English language. Write a paragraph identifying and analyzing the ways the passage addresses the needs of readers who are specialists.

   Grammar: a term for the syntactic and morphological system which every unimpaired person acquires from infancy when learning a language. In this sense, grammar is part of a Janus-faced psychological and neurological process: each person learns and uses a private system which blends into a social consensus. All speakers of a language like English "know" this grammar in the sense that they use it to produce more or less viable utterances. Their knowledge is implicit, however, and the use of this natural grammar does not depend on the acquisition of a set of rules and proscriptions. (*The Oxford Companion to the English Language*)

4. Using a general article index (pp. 223 and 226), find two articles on the same topic; choose articles from two different publications. Examine each article and, if possible, the entire issue in which the article appears. What is the intended audience of each article? How do the articles differ? How does each writer target the specific readership of the publication?

Focusing Your Thesis

Good writing makes a clear point. You don't want your readers to finish what you've written and ask, "So what?" The "so what" is your point. It's often called a *thesis*. It may appear explicitly somewhere in the essay or it may simply function as the controlling idea, but it's always a good idea to have a working thesis in mind as your write.

Your thesis is the central idea that ties the rest of your material together. Even if you're composing something for the World Wide Web, you will have a basic concept that validates the links among the pages and sites. Most of the time writers develop a **thesis statement** in the early stages of a writing project. Although they refine this statement as they write and revise, it gives them a vehicle for focusing their thinking and organizing their materials. In some cases, especially in speculative projects, writers need to write in order to identify a position, and so they delay forming a thesis until later in the drafting process.

A good thesis statement makes a claim or an assertion. It names the topic and declares something specific and significant about it. It may also convey your reasons for writing and provide a concise preview of how you plan to arrange your ideas. Here are some examples of topics and their corresponding thesis statements (with the claims or assertions in italics):

Topic	**Thesis**
Ozone depletion	The developed world's efforts to reduce the rate of ozone depletion *have been largely unsuccessful.*
Public aid to education	If the United States wants to compete effectively on the global market, federal and state governments *must make affordable higher education available to all qualified students.*
Benefits of daycare for children	Children who attend good daycare centers *develop communications skills, learn to share with others, become self-sufficient, and build immunity to diseases.*

You shouldn't assume that your thesis statement is a fixture. If working on your topic reveals that the assertion is indefensible or not appropriate for the audience, or that some other claim is more accurate or more interesting, you can always restate your thesis to meet these new developments.

Writing Activity

Revise and refine the following thesis statements to make them more effective:

1. People shouldn't go on fad diets.
2. Our new marketing campaign was a huge success.
3. American children watch too much television.
4. School vouchers are a terrible idea.
5. Freud's theories have been influential.

Controlling Your Persona

Having discovered a purpose, identified an audience, and articulated a thesis, the writer is left with creating the appropriate *persona*. In your everyday life, you shift fluidly among the many aspects of your personality, not giving it much thought. With your friends, for example, you relax and let the extroverted side they love entertain them. At work, on the other hand, you might be required to rein in that humor a bit, calling instead on your extensive knowledge of computers to create trust in buyers who are spending large sums of money. Knowledge of how to respond with friends and clients comes from a combination of past experiences and immediate feedback from those who are interacting with you. **Persona,** then, is the part of yourself you call upon at any one moment to best accommodate the situation before you.

Writing presents unique challenges for choosing and creating an appropriate persona. Because you can't be sure how well your readers know you (often they don't know you at all), you must establish your credibility through the writing alone and make your attitudes clear through the language and, in some cases, through supporting images. Writers prepare by considering the following questions:

- What level of expertise can I or must I bring to the subject?
- What attitude do I wish to convey toward the topic?
- What relationship do I hope to establish with my readers?

For example, a personal philosophy statement to be shared with the other members of the class presents a student taking "Philosophical Foundations of Education" with several opportunities to construct a suitable persona. Although the instructor and classmates will not assume the writer is familiar with the different philosophies to be studied, they will expect an education major to have reflected informally on the many teaching styles she or he has encountered. The student can establish credibility by recounting memories of particularly effective and obviously failed approaches to teaching. And, because it is early in the semester, the student will likely try to write a statement that conveys some mix of interest, seriousness, dedication, and excitement. If successful, this persona will yield respect from teachers and perhaps even carve out a leadership role among fellow students.

Three concepts closely related to persona are **tone, voice,** and **style.** Tone is the attitude you have toward your subject. You might, for example, want to be serious, sympathetic, or affectionate. Both what you say and how you say it are essential here. You will be seen as serious only if you show that you have done all the groundwork and then taken time to prepare a carefully designed paper. An editorial in the student paper opposing student money for fraternity activities appears serious only if fully supported with sufficient evidence and logical arguments, for example. Voice, an expression of the writer's personality, also helps to achieve the proper tone. The student editorial writer, hoping to keep the goodwill of fraternity members, may wish to appear personal rather than professional, and perhaps casual instead of formal.

Finally, style is the writer's distinct or individual way of expressing message, tone, and voice. Different writers, focusing on the same topic, aiming for the same tone, and even taking the same position and using similar evidence and arguments, will produce unique documents because of their styles—the vocabulary they select, the cadence and length of their sentences, and even the ways in which they put together their paragraphs.

Writing Activities

1. Read the following excerpts on why leaves change color in the fall, and then answer the questions that follow the passages:

A. During summer, the leaves of trees are factories producing sugar from carbon dioxide and water by the action of light on chlorophyll. Chlorophyll causes the leaves to appear green. . . . The shortening days and cool nights of autumn trigger changes in the tree. One of these changes is the growth of a corky membrane between the branch and the leaf stem. This membrane interferes with the flow of nutrients into the leaf. Because the nutrient flow is interrupted, the production of chlorophyll in the leaf declines, and the green color of the leaf fades. If the leaf contains carotene . . . it will change from green to bright yellow as the chlorophyll disappears. In some trees, as the concentration of sugar in the leaf increases, the sugar reacts to form anthocyanins. These pigments cause the yellowing leaves to turn red. (Professor Bassam Shakhashiri, "The Chemistry of Autumn Colors")

B. A turning leaf stays partly green at first, then reveals splotches of yellow and red as the chlorophyll gradually breaks down. Dark green seems to stay longest in the veins, outlining and defining them. During the summer, chlorophyll dissolves in the heat and light, but it is also being steadily replaced. In the fall, on the other hand, no new pigment is produced, and so we notice the other colors that were always there, right in the leaf, although chlorophyll's shocking green hid them from view. With their camouflage gone, we see these colors for the first time all year, and marvel, but they were always there, hidden like a vivid secret beneath the hot glowing greens of summer. (Diane Ackerman, "Why Leaves Turn Color in the Fall")

1. How would you describe the persona of each passage?
2. What tone did the authors try to establish? Did they succeed?
3. What features of the styles of the two passages stand out to you?

2. Read the following definitions of *anorexia,* and then answer the questions that follow the passages:

A. Anorexia nervosa is an eating disorder characterized by severe weight loss to the point of significant physiologic consequences. Diagnostic criteria include an intense fear of obesity despite slenderness, an overwhelming body-image perception of being fat, weight loss of at least

25% from baseline or failure to gain weight appropriately (resulting in weight 25% less than would be expected from the patient's previous growth curve), absence of other physical illnesses to explain the weight loss or altered body-image perception, and at least 3 weeks of secondary amenorrhea or primary amenorrhea in a prepubescent adolescent. Associated physical characteristics include excessive physical activity, denial of hunger in the face of starvation, academic success, asexual behavior, and a history of extreme weight loss methods (e.g., diuretics, laxatives, amphetamines, emetics). Psychiatric characteristics include excessive dependency needs, developmental immaturity, behavior favoring isolation, obsessive-compulsive behavior, and constriction of affect.

B. Anorexia usually starts in the mid-teens and affects one fifteen-year-old girl in every 150. Occasionally it may start earlier, in childhood, or later, in the 30s or 40s. Girls from professional or managerial families are perhaps more likely to develop it than girls from working-class backgrounds. Other members of the family have often had similar symptoms.

Nearly always, anorexia begins with the everyday dieting that is so much a part of teenage life. About a third of anorexia sufferers have been overweight before starting to diet. Unlike normal dieting, which stops when the desired weight is reached, in anorexia the dieting and the loss of weight continue until the sufferer is well below the normal limit for her age and height. The tiny amount of calories that she is taking in may be disguised by the quantities of fruit, vegetables and salads that she eats. Also, she will often exercise vigorously or take slimming pills to keep her weight low. Moreover, in spite of her own attitude to eating, she may take an avid interest in buying food and cooking for others.

1. How would you describe the persona conveyed by each passage?
2. What kind of publication did each of these definitions appear in?
3. Describe the readers that each passage is aimed at.

Conclusion

As you work with purpose, audience, thesis, and persona, imagine the relationship among them as being like a spider web. As one element shifts, the other three change as well. The four together, finally, provide the design and the foundation for all effective writing.

Checklist for Analyzing the Core Elements of Writing

The following questions about your readers will assist you in making decisions about the purpose, thesis, and persona of your writing:

☐ 1. What group of readers do I want to reach? What is my purpose in regard to these readers?

☐ 2. Does my thesis suit this audience and purpose?

☐ 3. How much do my readers know about the topic? What new or additional information will I need to supply? What questions will they have? What terms will I have to define and explain?

☐ 4. Will my readers be interested in the topic? If not, how can I get them interested? Will they be in agreement with my ideas? Do I have to be careful not to offend them?

☐ 5. What relationship do I want to establish with my readers? What persona do I want to project to them?

☐ 6. How will my readers treat my writing? Will they read it carefully, evaluate it, scan it for information, look for conclusions and recommendations? What features (headings, lists, summaries, charts, transitions, etc.) should I include to help my readers with their reading?

Writer's Workshop

1. Because you will be writing with and for your classmates in this course, use small group discussion, in-class or electronic, to get to know one another. Begin by asking and answering questions about your majors and career choices. Introduce yourselves and tell the group your majors and intended careers. If you haven't yet decided on a major, discuss your options with the group and select one possible major to ask questions about. Next, stop and individually write out at least two questions that would lead to information you would like to gather about the group's attitude toward your major. Try to be specific here. For example, if you are a Special Education major, you might ask your classmates, "Did you have Special Education students in your grade school classes and, if so, how did you respond to that experience?" Or if you plan to be an attorney, you could ask, "Have you been in a courtroom or visited a lawyer's office? How did that experience confirm or conflict with the image of lawyers on television?" Finally, exchange and discuss the questions.

2. Select one of the following advertisements or go online to www.adcouncil.org and watch one of the campaign ads there (for example, the seat belt dummies or "Friends Don't Let Friends Drive Drunk"). Then answer these questions about one of the ads:

a. What responses does the company that created the ad hope to provoke? How do you know?

b. What types of consumers did the ad target and why? Was it successful?

c. Is there an assertion or even an argument made by the advertisement? What it is and what features of the ad led you to this conclusion?

d. How would you describe the tone and style of the ad? Were they appropriate to the advertiser's intended audience and goals?

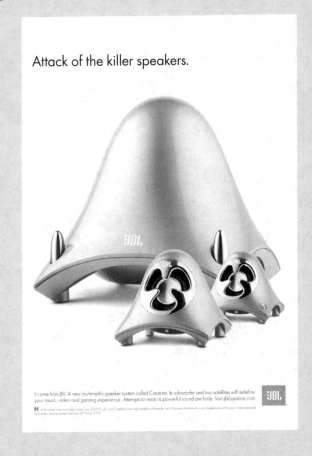

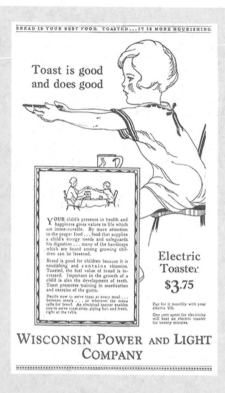

3. Examine a paper that you wrote in the recent past—perhaps an application essay or a paper for a course in your major or minor. Answer the following questions and try the suggested revisions:

   a. What purpose did you have for writing the paper? Did your motives for writing change over the course of the project? Do you feel you achieved your purpose?

   b. What role did audience play? Who were your readers? Did you consciously tailor your writing to meet their needs? How did your awareness of them affect your choice of information, your language, and your presentation?

   c. Was the paper focused on a central idea or thesis? Did you state your thesis in the paper? Could you rewrite the paper using a different thesis? How would that change the paper?

   d. How would you describe your persona? The tone? The style? Now rewrite those paragraphs with a different persona, tone, and style.

   e. Try rewriting your introduction to the paper after you select a different audience and persona for the paper.

4. Using a general and a specialized article index, find two published pieces of writing, one written for knowledgeable readers in a specific discourse community and one written for general readers. Write a brief analysis of each that explains what you see as the author's purpose, intended audience, thesis (implied or stated), and persona. Pay attention to language and vocabulary, length and complexity of sentences, types of examples, amount of detail, and features of formatting. What assumptions does each piece make about the readers' knowledge and interest in the topic?

Writers on Writing

President in Search of a Publisher
Jimmy Carter

Jimmy Carter was the 39th President of the United States. Since writing this essay in 1995, he has published two enormously popular memoirs, An Hour before Daylight: Memories of a Rural Boyhood *and* Christmas in Plains, *and a novel about the Revolutionary War,* The Hornet's Nest.

As a high school student I read voraciously and competed in writing contests. In college, while studying to be an engineer, I was taught to write as crisply and clearly as possible. Since then, in a late-blooming writing career, I have progressed from dutifully producing books that have promoted my political aspirations or met my financial obligations, to writing just for the enjoyment of it. From the pragmatic to the poetic, it has been a continuous learning experience.

My first book was a campaign autobiography, *Why Not the Best?* It was written on yellow scratch pads on airplanes and in hotel rooms. It was early 1975, and I was traveling around the country looking for voters, but with little attention from the public or news media. I had plenty of time to write. . . .

As president, I placed my business in a blind trust, and heard no more about it during my term in office. After my defeat in November 1980, the trustee told me that my farm operation had had some bad years and was almost a million dollars in debt. We were lucky enough to sell the entire business, and Rosalynn and I signed book contracts for our memoirs that would provide the much-needed cash to save our home and land.

Writing the memoirs as a defeated incumbent was a somewhat bitter and difficult task for me, and I was soon in a quandary about how to address some of the more politically sensitive or personal issues. The historian Arthur S. Link offered to assemble at Princeton University about a dozen authorities on presidential biographies and memoirs, and Rosalynn and I spent a very fruitful day with them.

Their advice was not to be defensive, not to distort the facts or try to write a complete history of my administration, but to tell about the personal and interesting things that had not previously been published. . . .

Why Not the Best? and *Keeping Faith* were written as a matter of duty, to further my political career or for income, but most of my other books have been for my own pleasure. I learned a great deal about myself in *Outdoor Journal* as I struggled to describe what motivates me to climb a mountain, spend hours in the total isolation of woods and swamps, attempt to master the technique of flyfishing, or to balance the interests of a conservationist with those of a hunter. . . .

I wrote *Talking Peace* for young people of high school and college age; my purpose was to describe the causes of conflicts and how they might be prevented or resolved. It gave me a chance to report some of my personal experiences in the field, and to tell something about the work that the Carter Center does in peacekeeping, promoting human rights and monitoring elections worldwide. Having taught at Emory University as a distinguished professor for almost a dozen years, I have enjoyed seeing this book (as well as *Keeping Faith* and *Blood of Abraham*) used extensively in high school and college classrooms. . . .

Every book has its own challenges and particular pleasures, and each has taught me something important about myself and the magic of words. I have come a long way, but I still have much to learn. That's what makes the journey worthwhile.

Practicing History
Barbara Tuchman

Barbara Tuchman began writing professionally as a reporter for The Nation *magazine, covering the Spanish Civil War in the 1930s. Although she was not academically trained, Tuchman won two Pulitzer Prizes for history and wrote about everything from the Trojan War to the Vietnam War, from a description of medieval daily life to the portraits of world leaders during the First World War.*

To write history so as to enthrall the reader and make the subject as captivating and exciting to him as it is to me has been my goal. . . . A prerequisite, as I have said, is to be enthralled one's self and to feel a compulsion to communicate the magic. Communicate to whom? We arrive now at the reader, a person whom I keep constantly in mind.

Catherine Drinker Bowen has said that she writes her books with a sign pinned over her desk asking, "Will the reader turn the page?" The writer of history, I believe, has a number of duties, vis-à-vis the reader, if he wants to keep him reading. The first is to distill. He must do the preliminary work for the reader, assemble the information, make sense of it, select the essential, discard the irrelevant—above all, discard the irrelevant—and put the rest together so that it forms a developing dramatic narrative. Narrative, it has been said, is the lifeblood of history. To offer a mass of undigested facts, of names not identified and places not located, is of no use to the reader and is simple laziness on the part of the author, or pedantry to show how much he has read. To discard the unnecessary requires courage and also extra work, as exemplified by Pascal's effort to explain an idea to a friend in a letter which rambled on for pages and ended, "I'm sorry to have wearied you with so long a letter but I did not have time to write you a short one." The historian is continually being beguiled down fascinating byways and sidetracks. But the art of writing—the test of the artist—is to resist the beguilement and cleave to the subject.

Making the Truth Believable
Tracy Kidder

A writer of nonfiction bestsellers, Tracy Kidder has become known as an astute and sensitive observer of ordinary people. His detailed look at the computer industry, The Soul of a New Machine, *won the Pulitzer Prize in 1982. He has since written about the building of a new home, the life of an elementary school teacher, the residents of a nursing home, and the changing demographics of a New England town.*

When I started writing nonfiction a couple of decades ago there was an idea in the air, which for me had the force of a revelation: that all journalism was inevitably subjective. I was in my 20s then, and although my behavior was somewhat worse than it has been recently, I was quite a moralist. I decided that writers of nonfiction had a moral obligation to write in the first person—really write in the first person, making themselves characters on the page. In this way, I would disclose my biases. I would not hide the truth from the reader. I would proclaim that what I wrote was just my own impression of events. In retrospect it seems clear that this prescription for honesty often served as a license for self-absorption on the page. I was too young and self-absorbed to realize what should have been obvious: that I was less likely to write honestly about myself than about anyone else on earth.

   I wrote a book about a murder case in a swashbuckling first person. After it was published and disappeared without a trace, I went back to writing nonfiction articles for the *Atlantic Monthly,* under the tutelage of Richard Todd, then a young editor there. For about five years, during which I didn't dare attempt another book, I worked on creating what many writer friends of mine call "voice." I didn't do this consciously. If I had, I probably wouldn't have gotten anywhere.

   But gradually, I think, I found a writing voice, the voice of a person who was informed, fair-minded, and always temperate—the voice, not of the person I was, but of the person I wanted to be. Then I went back to writing books, and discovered other points of view besides the first person.

Choosing a point of view is a matter of finding the best place to stand, from which to tell a story. The process shouldn't be determined by theory, but driven by immersion in the material itself. The choice of point of view, I've come to think, has nothing to do with morality. It's a choice among tools. On the other hand, the wrong choice can lead to dishonesty. Point of view is primary; it affects everything else, including voice. I've made my choices by instinct sometimes and sometimes by experiment. Most of my memories of time spent writing have merged together in a blur, but I remember vividly my first attempts to find a way to write *Among Schoolchildren,* a book about an inner-city teacher. I had spent a year inside her classroom. I intended, vaguely, to fold into my account of events I'd witnessed there a great deal about the lives of particular children and about the problems of education in America. I tried every point of view that I'd used in previous books, and every page I wrote felt lifeless and remote. Finally, I hit on a restricted third-person narration.

That approach seemed to work. The world of that classroom seemed to come alive when the view of it was restricted mainly to observations of the teacher and to accounts of what the teacher saw and heard and smelled and felt. This choice narrowed my options. I ended up writing something less comprehensive than I'd planned. The book became essentially an account of a year in the emotional life of a schoolteacher. . . .

For me, part of the pleasure of reading comes from the awareness that an author stands behind the scenes adroitly pulling the strings. But the pleasure quickly palls at painful reminders of that presence—the times when, for instance, I sense that the author strains to produce yet another clever metaphor. Then I stop believing in what I read, and usually stop reading. Belief is what a reader offers an author, what Coleridge famously called "That willing suspension of disbelief for the moment, which constitutes poetic faith." All writers have to find ways to do their work without disappointing readers into withdrawing belief.

Writer's Notebook

Active writers are also keen observers who have developed the habit of recording their experiences and insights on a regular basis. Some gather random scraps of paper in topical files, others keep notebooks, and many now use computer files, cell phones, or Palm Pilots. If you are not yet keeping such a notebook, you can begin one by recording your responses to the ideas suggested at the end of the chapters in this text, by making note of your reactions to the readings, and by writing down any random experiences and observations that seem somehow relevant to your development as a writer.

What was the best or worst writing experience you have had since starting college? As you completed that project, how aware were you of your purpose, audience, thesis, and persona? Looking back, do you think your attention to these elements affected the outcome of that experience?

Chapter 2

Being Aware of Your Rituals, Practices, and Habits

Chapter Preview

This chapter outlines typical sequences of activities for completing your writing goals and offers you an opportunity to review and evaluate your current writing rituals, composing practices, and working habits. Before starting this chapter, reread your Writer's Notebook entry from Chapter 1; then write a second entry in which you describe how you went about actually writing that best or most challenging project. For example, how, when, and where did you get started? How many versions did you write? What kinds of changes did you make along the way or just before turning the project in? Did you ask anyone for ideas or other kinds of input? Was your method of working on this project typical of how you approach most writing tasks?

In his book *On Writing*, author Stephen King makes this recommendation to would-be writers:

> [T]o write to your best abilities, it behooves you to construct your own toolbox and then build up enough muscles so you can carry it with you. Then, instead of looking at a hard job and getting discouraged, you will perhaps seize the correct tool and get immediately to work.

As a student you've been constructing your own writer's toolbox for several years, developing a repertoire of strategies and techniques for completing the writing tasks you've come across inside the classroom, on the job, and out in public.

Writing Rituals

The pen is the writing instrument most congenial to my hand. It has the same length and heft as a scalpel, though one is round and the other flat. Ply either one, and something is shed.

Physician Richard Selzer, "Writing with Scalpel"

The situations and rituals that make you comfortable or effective as a writer are as individual as the styles that distinguish your voice in the things you create. Sitting at a favorite computer, wearing a good luck sweatshirt, and revising with a No. 2 pencil are just a few examples of the physical circumstances you might require to begin thinking about and writing a paper. Do you really need these things to complete a project? Probably not. But do they get you in the right mood and provide confidence? Absolutely. In fact, these rituals become a kind of automatic trigger for the state of mind and activities you associate with writing. It's much like the experience of seeing the first road sign for your home city after being on a long road trip: you imagine yourself in your favorite chair or sleeping in your own bed and you begin to relax. Similarly, when you slip on that sweatshirt, you start to take on the writer's role, shutting out distractions and committing a certain amount of time and energy to thinking and working in a concentrated way.

It is important to pay attention to your writing rituals and to try to plan your sequence of writing steps to allow for them. If you need to work in the quiet of the night, don't wait until the morning a paper is due to get to work. And be sure you bring that sweatshirt from home on the weekend you have to write a research paper.

Equally important to finding helpful and effective rituals is the ability to be flexible and to adapt those rituals when they are no longer helpful or when you must work in new or different circumstances. Although you love working in a noisy, stimulating environment, you may have to abandon your dorm computer lab in favor of the library's lab if friends keep interrupting you. You know, too, that except for casual Fridays, few employers will allow you to wear a frayed old sweatshirt to work, and someday much of your writing will be done on the fly using a laptop. In these situations, you will want to consciously create new rituals, ones that fit into changing work environments but provide some of the same focus and creative energy you got from the old rituals.

Writing Activity

What rituals do you practice when you write? How do you think they got started? Have they changed over time or do they change in different places or when doing different kinds of writing? For example, has your use of the computer formed or changed your rituals? What writing rituals do your roommates and friends have?

Composing Practices

A finished piece of writing is the product of a series of interrelated activities, both mental and physical, known collectively as a *process*. This process is complex and unpredictable; it shapes itself as it goes and may loop back or even change direction altogether. It is somewhat misleading, then, to describe writing as a sequence of steps that you complete in a fixed and uniform order. But familiarity with the steps will help you to understand your process and give you freedom to apply it as you need to. The activities you use most frequently in the process of writing are *prewriting, drafting, revising,* and *editing*.

Prewriting: Generating Content

When thinking about writing, you usually think about the finished product. But you also know that a successful product is the result of planning and preparation. This stage of your writing process is called *prewriting;* it involves various activities that enable you to focus on a subject and generate material to support and explain that subject.

One of the first things you have to decide is what to write about. In many situations the topic is decided for you: your employer asks for a memo or report; you need to write for information or request an action; you feel compelled to express your opinion on an issue. If your history professor assigns a paper on a broad topic like the Great Depression or your project manager asks you to suggest ways to increase funding and improve efficiency, you then have to find a way of turning that assignment into a manageable task, one that will allow you to develop interesting information and useful insights.

Instead of waiting around for inspiration, most writers try to get something down on paper, in one form or another. If you like to draw pictures or take photographs, you can try that—and the images may even be useful in the final document. But eventually you want to put your ideas into words. Then you have a record of your work, and the act of writing will focus your thinking and lead you to new material. Prewriting also allows you to test and challenge your ideas, as economist Deirdre McCloskey has discovered:

> Good writers in economics write self-critically and honestly, trying to say what they mean. They often find out that what looked persuasive when floating vaguely in the mind looks foolish when moored to the page. Better, they find truths they didn't know they had. They sharpen their fuzzy notion of an obstacle to trade by finding the right words to describe it; they see the other side of a market by writing about the demand side with clarity.

There are a number of ways to explore a subject and generate ideas. If you have an assigned task or have chosen a topic of your own, these techniques will help to clarify and develop your thinking; if you are still not sure what to write about, these prewriting activities can help you to decide.

In completing the Writer's Notebook assignments for this book, you have already been using one of the most common prewriting techniques—*journal writing*.

You may even be keeping an Internet journal known as a weblog, or blog (see, for example, www.rebeccablood.net/essays/weblog_history.html or www.blogger .com/tour_start.g). You also know that *reading* frequently accompanies writing: you read to investigate new ideas and to expand on what you already know. In previous writing classes you may have used *freewriting* or *brainstorming* to explore topics, dredge up details, and make connections. And you are probably familiar with the set of questions that journalists use—*who? what? when? where? why? how?*—to look at a topic from all angles and see fresh possibilities in it.

Here are two more methods for you to consider. As with the other prewriting practices, these may help you during the early stages of writing or may be used later on when you get stalled and need to reactivate your thinking. Essayist and novelist E. M. Forster once said, "How do I know what I think until I see what I say?" These activities give you a chance to see what you think.

1. *Clustering.* Like freewriting and brainstorming, this commonly used technique relies on free association and rapid, unedited thinking. You begin by writing down a word or phrase in the center of a piece of paper and circling it. This word or phrase should indicate the general subject you intend to write about. As ideas that relate to the topic occur to you, place them randomly around the topic. Try to visualize your ideas as radiating out from the central topic, and use circles and arrows to connect the points to each other. Clustering encourages you to gather the specifics about a topic as fast as you can and to lay them out where you can look at their relationships. The example in Figure 2.1 will show you how a

Figure 2.1   Sample Clustering

student writer used clustering to generate material for her article on the historical attractions of the Mississippi River near her hometown.

2. *Cubing.* This method of exploring a topic combines freewriting with most of the journalist's questions. It gets its name from the six steps involved in the system, equivalent to the six sides of a cube. In this procedure you look at a topic from all angles and explore various approaches for writing about it. Cubing is also an excellent study technique and can help you answer questions on essay exams. Try to write for three to five minutes for each part of the cube.

Describe how your subject looks, sounds, feels, smells, tastes.

Compare your subject to other ideas, objects, people, places, and so on.

Associate your subject with events, ideas, concepts, persons, times, and places.

Analyze the parts of your subject and explain how they relate to each other.

Apply your subject, explaining how it might be used.

Argue for or against your subject and defend your position.

Each of these activities can be done freehand or on a computer. In fact, keyboards can be a great way to generate thoughts quickly. You might even try adjusting the contrast on the monitor or turning it off; this helps you concentrate on ideas, not editing. Draw and paint programs and bold and italics codes are other useful ways to create and visually manipulate ideas at the invention stage of the process.

Writing Activities

1. Get into groups of four. In each group, select two people to be observers and two to complete the assigned task. The task is to brainstorm on one of the following topics and come up with a description of something that might be written on that topic—a paper, an editorial, or a personal letter, for example.

   - finishing college in four years
   - maintaining friendships
   - voting

   The description should specify a message, an audience, and a persona.
       Each observer should record the actions of the brainstorming pair, including all the details of how the group gets its task accomplished. After the description for the project is completed, the observers should read their reports aloud and then the group can discuss how the two observations compare, including where they overlap and why they might differ.

Also evaluate how successful the brainstorming pair was in generating their description. Finally, if you have time, compare how this group experience compares to others each of you has had.

2. Use *clustering* to explore one of the following topics:

   a. the values and benefits of part-time work for students

   b. how campus safety can be improved

   c. why students cheat

3. Choose an object like a pen, a comb, or an oatmeal cookie, and prepare to write an essay about it by using the steps in *cubing* to generate material: describe it, compare it, associate it, analyze it, apply it, argue for or against it.

   What did you discover about your knowledge of this object? Would you be able to write an essay about it? Although the object is trivial, you probably found that you were able to say quite a lot about it. Practicing with something small and concrete is a good way to get the feel for this technique.

Prewriting: Organizing Your Material

Painters make sketches, architects draw up blueprints, therapists map out treatment programs. These people plan their work ahead, projecting the outcome early on, when changes can still be made quickly and inexpensively. Writers do the same thing. After exploring ideas and generating details, they take steps to organize their efforts. Although some writers plunge right in and begin drafting to discover what they want to say, others identify a central idea and map out a plan. Even if you're not much of a planner, you have probably found that a thesis and an outline of some kind enable you to gain control of a writing project and save time under the constraint of project deadlines.

Finding a Center. Formulating a central idea, or *thesis,* can lead you to make important decisions about the scope and direction of your writing. A useful thesis statement explicitly identifies the point you want to make or summarizes your main ideas. For example, you may begin a marketing report with a general observation:

> This new product brought in over $500,000 last year.

This is an interesting statement of fact, but is that the point you want to make? Will it satisfy your employer's needs? What stand can you take about this fact? Perhaps you need to add a claim or an assertion:

> This new product succeeded last year because of an inventive and diversified marketing strategy.

This statement gives you an idea to explain and defend. You can also expand it to indicate the main subpoints you expect to write about:

> This new product succeeded last year because of an inventive and diversified marketing strategy, especially the extensive television coverage and the interactive online promotion.

The statement now provides you and your readers with a concise preview of how you will present your material.

If you want to sharpen a vague or uncertain thesis, you can try a technique called *looping*, a form of structured freewriting that pushes you to formulate a clear central idea.

1. In the first loop, put your topic or tentative thesis at the top of the page and write about it for several minutes. At the end of the time, stop and read what you have written. Then write a sentence that summarizes your main idea. This is called a *center of gravity sentence*; it is meant to capture the essence of your thinking in a single, clear statement. Take a little time so that you are satisfied with this sentence.

2. In the second loop, respond to the center of gravity sentence. You can expand on it, or you may want to examine any contradictions or problems you see in this first sentence. At the end of your second loop, read what you have written and prepare another center of gravity sentence.

The third loop works the same way as the first two. By this time, you should have produced a useful statement of your central idea. If not, try another loop or two. You may need to return to your prewriting to reconsider your topic, purpose, audience, or persona. For those who dive in and begin drafting without a thesis, looping can be a way to pull a focused idea from the many possibilities generated in the draft.

Writing Activity

Use looping to formulate a useful thesis for one of the following topics:
   a. the causes and treatment of depression
   b. the origins of prejudice
   c. televised sports vs. live sports
   d. the appeal of talk radio
   e. the drawbacks to fad diets
   f. the effect of TV on voting

Mapping a Plan. Even professional writers disagree about the value of outlining. Author and philosopher Jacques Barzun finds outlines "useless and fettering," and critic John Ciardi says the "only workable outline I know anything about is something called a first draft, which can then be developed into a better outline called a second draft." On the other hand, journalist and essayist Tom Wolfe sees a close connection between outlining and composing:

> I make a very tight outline of everything I write before I write it. . . . By writing an outline you really are writing in a way, because you're creating the structure of what you're going to do.

Nature writer Annie Dillard describes a similar interaction: "You are always going back and forth between the outline and the writing, bringing them closer together, or just throwing out the outline and making a new one."

Whatever thoughts and feelings you have about outlines, you might consider their advantages as an efficient way to create and evaluate your organization. Sometimes an outline is a good way to move from prewriting to drafting. It can also focus your thinking, keep you on track, and get you to think about how your points fit together. After you draft, you can use an outline to check for inadequate and inconsistent coverage, as well as for the logic of your plan.

You should also realize that outlines come in many forms, some more flexible than others. Sometimes a simple listing of main points and their relevant supporting details will give you all the direction you need. For more complicated projects you may want to construct a formal outline that lays out the main ideas in full sentences and breaks them down into detailed subdivisions. You should also remember that any outline you use is a tentative sketch that can be revised as you draft and redraft your writing.

Most word processors include an outlining program that may help you to organize your writing. You can view almost any document in outline form; the buttons on the toolbar allow you to move text and headings easily throughout the document. With this "outline view" feature you can check the organization in a draft or experiment with different patterns and arrangements as you compose.

Writing Activity

What advice would you give to freshmen writing students about using outlines? Drawing on your own experiences to support and explain your advice, write a letter or prepare a handout for these students. Compare your views with several members of your writing class, either online or in class.

Working Habits

The difference between prewriting and writing is somewhat arbitrary, since these stages frequently overlap. But at some point you will sit down and put the ideas and details you have generated into a text of connected sentences and paragraphs. This part of the process—*drafting* and *revising*—goes more smoothly if you can call on a variety of strategies for getting started and staying on track.

Drafting

As with all aspects of writing, the drafting behavior of writers varies. Some need to turn out a complete draft in one sitting, if at all possible. Others produce their drafts in sections, over a period of time. Some writers like to move forward as quickly as possible so they don't lose momentum, while other writers ponder their words and make textual changes as they draft. The only correct drafting style is the one that works for you, but it's important to do a regular and honest analysis of its success.

Getting started is often the hardest part. Most writers, students and professionals alike, find ways to procrastinate. And sometimes procrastination can actually help if you keep your ideas simmering. Teacher and writer Donald Murray explains his use of this strategy:

> Often I write by not writing. I assign a task to my subconscious, then take a nap or go for a walk, do errands, and let my mind work on the problem.

At some point, however, you have to face the blank page and get started. You may already have your own routine for getting down to work, but here are some suggestions that might help you, especially if you're having trouble getting started:

- Create a working environment that suits your writing rituals. Find a place to write and gather the materials you need.
- Review your prewriting materials and start your draft with whatever comes to mind.
- Freewrite or type nonsense until something you can use starts coming.
- Draw a diagram or a picture of what your final paper will look like.
- Skip the opening and start in the middle, or write a tentative conclusion first.
- Divide your topic into manageable chunks and start writing the one that seems easiest.

Once you've started writing, you should gather momentum and the words will begin to flow. If not, or if you find yourself stalled at some point, here are some things to try:

- Reread what you've already written. Many writers repeatedly scan what they've just written as a way to keep moving forward.

- Try to keep writing. Follow the advice of Garrison Keillor: "Don't tear up the page and start over again when you write a bad line—try to write your way out of it. Make mistakes and plunge on."
- Leave blank spaces if you can't think of the right word; put brackets around sentences that you're not satisfied with; use question marks to indicate points that need to be looked at again.
- Use a separate sheet of paper, the insert feature of your word processing program, or even a different computer file to record new ideas that pop up but don't seem to fit in—and deal with them later.
- Put off making corrections in grammar and mechanics. Focusing too much on these details at an early stage can suppress your creativity and divert your attention from larger issues. Save them for revision.
- Get feedback from others. Ask for reactions to what you've written and for suggestions about what to write next.
- Take a break and let your subconscious mind work for a while.

You might decide to stop drafting for any number of reasons: when you feel you've made your point, when you've reached the assigned word limit, when you've run out of things to say, when your deadline is getting too close for comfort. But the most important thing to keep in mind is that you must have time to revise. A first draft is often an exploration, a place where you test your ideas, work out your organization, and discover your voice. You should always plan on revising.

Writing Activities

1. Interview several people outside your writing class about their approach to writing a first draft. Talk to roommates, teachers, friends, co-workers, anyone who does writing. Ask them these questions: Do you do a great deal of planning before you begin a draft? Do you prefer to draft in one sitting or in several sessions? What do you do when you get stuck? How do you feel when are drafting? Write up a brief summary of your findings and report back to your class.
2. Create a metaphor to describe your drafting behavior. You might compare yourself, for example, to an animal, an athlete, or a vehicle—anything that accurately conveys the essence of your writing style.
3. Read the interview with popular humorist Dave Barry that appeared in *Contemporary Authors, New Revision Series*, Vol. 134 (1992). Then write a brief description of his composing and drafting habits. Were you surprised by anything he said? How do his writing practices compare with yours?

Drafting Collaboratively

Writing in groups is a common practice, especially in the workplace. For example, a company may assemble a team of experts—an architect, an engineer, a biologist, a legal consultant—to prepare an environmental impact statement in preparation for building a new plant. In college, a group of students may undertake a research project that is too big for an individual to complete. And a community group will probably work jointly to produce its mission statement. The Internet has made it possible for many groups to collaborate online, using electronic mail, listservs, class or company Web sites, FTP (file transfer protocol) sites, and synchronous discussions.

The advantages of working in a group are that group members may bring different skills to the project and that you are likely to discover ideas and perspectives you might have overlooked working alone. The collaborative process can also reduce the stress of writing and help you to develop your interpersonal communication skills. The downside is that groups sometimes digress and get slowed down by conflicts. Working with others demands special care and attention. There are some steps you can take to avoid problems later on in the group process:

1. Decide on the goals for your project.
2. Establish ground rules for your work—for example, that all members have an equal opportunity to contribute.
3. Address disagreements promptly.
4. Set deadlines for completed work.
5. Choose a coordinator who can keep the group focused.
6. Schedule frequent review sessions.
7. Set up a procedure for seeking outside advice—from your instructor or project supervisor, for example.

In the actual drafting of a document, your group can choose one of several approaches:

1. You can divide the work and assign separate parts to each member. This is the quickest way to complete a group writing project. But if you divide the work up, you'll also need to set aside plenty of time to revise the final document to eliminate overlaps, fill in gaps, and achieve a consistent style.
2. You can draft the document as a group. Word processors make such close collaboration possible: one person controls the keyboard as others read the screen and participate directly in composing the text; or a text file circulates using the track changes tool. Although this method allows group members to give immediate feedback on every point, it can be time consuming and is usually reserved for small projects.

3. You can divide the research and collaboratively construct an outline but have one person write a complete rough draft that everyone in the group then revises and edits. This method produces a uniformity of style, but it may lead to an unfair distribution of work.

Collaboration is also useful for revising and editing. People working in groups can often see problems—and suggest solutions to those problems—that someone working alone might not see.

Writing Activity

Working with two or three classmates, draft a mini-review (100–200 words) of a current movie or TV show. Decide collaboratively what to write about, how to approach the topic, and how to handle the actual drafting. When you're finished, exchange your draft with another group, and make suggestions for revisions in each other's reviews.

Revising

"The beautiful part of writing," says novelist and newspaperman Robert Cormier, "is that you don't have to get it right the first time—unlike, say, brain surgery." To most writers revising is the key to good writing. They almost never say what they want to say the first time. Teacher and writer Anne Lamott says that every piece of writing should go through at least three drafts:

> [T]he first draft is the down draft—you just get it down. The second draft is the up draft—you fix it up. You try to say what you have to say more accurately. And the third draft is the dental draft, where you check every tooth, to see if it's loose or cramped or decayed, or even, God help us, healthy.

Revising from the Top Down. As Lamott's comments suggest, not all revising is the same. One kind of revision involves large-scale changes, ones that significantly affect the content and structure of your writing. Such changes might include enlarging or narrowing your thesis, adding more examples or cutting irrelevant ones, and reorganizing material to improve logic or gain emphasis. A second kind of revision focuses on improving style: checking paragraph unity, strengthening transitions, combining and refining sentences, finding more effective words, adjusting tone. It's usually more efficient and productive to take a top-down approach to revising: start with the large-scale issues and work down to the smaller elements. If you try to do the fine-tuning and polishing first, you will use up valuable time and energy and might not get around to the main problems.

Getting Perspective on Your Work. The biggest obstacle you face when revising your work is your familiarity with it. You *know* what it says—or at least what it's supposed to say. To revise effectively, you need to become a stranger to your own words, to anticipate how your readers will see them. That's not an easy task. It means developing strategies for putting distance between yourself and your writing so you can evaluate what you have actually *done* rather than what you *intended* to do.

You've probably learned from experience to put some time between drafting and revising. It is hard to overestimate the difference a good night's sleep will make in your ability to look at your writing as a reader would. You also know that it's not a good idea to revise everything at once, that it's helpful to set an agenda and spread your work out over the time you have available. Here are a few other revising strategies to consider:

- Change the look of your work. If you wrote your draft by hand, type it. If you composed on a computer, print it out. The different medium may reveal problems or weaknesses you didn't see in the original form.
- Listen to what you've written. Read your draft aloud to yourself or into a tape recorder, or get someone to read it to you. Hearing your words, instead of seeing them, can alter your perspective.
- Make full use of the editing function of your word processing program: spell and grammar check, block and move, track changes, word count, and find (for repetition or spelling, for example). If you're unfamiliar with these functions, use the program's "Help" option on the toolbar to learn about them.

Outlining Your Draft. One way to focus your attention on what you've actually written is to make a brief outline of your draft. This kind of after-the-fact outlining is not a waste of time; it allows you to detect flaws in your arrangement and to review the development of your main ideas at the same time. First, write down your thesis statement. Next, read through the draft, highlight the main points supporting the thesis, and write these sentences down in outline form. Then review the outline to check for logical order, gaps, and digressions.

Getting Feedback: Peer Review. Practicing writers routinely seek the help of potential readers to find out what is working and what is not working in their drafts. Someone else can often see places where you *thought* you were being clear but were actually filling in details in your head, not on the page. Even professional writers ask for suggestions from editors, reviewers, teachers, colleagues, and friends. In the workplace or when working with community groups, much of the writing that you do will be passed around, with various writers adding their sections and making suggestions about yours.

In college classes, as you've discovered, students sometimes meet in small groups, read photocopies of one another's drafts, and provide suggestions for improvement. In other cases they post their drafts on a class Web site or submit them electronically on a computer bulletin board. Many word processors include a review feature that allows teachers, editors, coauthors, and other reviewers to make suggested revisions on the draft document itself. These comments are marked in different colors, with one color for each person who reviews the document; the writer can then accept or reject these suggestions simply by clicking on a button on the program toolbar.

If your instructor doesn't set up a peer review system, form one of your own to get reactions to your drafts. You can meet together outside of class or use an Internet mailing list. Here are some questions to use in asking for feedback:

Have I accomplished my purpose? Does the main idea come through clearly?

Does the introduction capture your attention?

Are there any points you don't understand?

Do I need to supply more reasons, explanations, details, or examples?

Does the conclusion tie everything together for you?

How appropriate is the tone?

Are the sentences clear and readable? Do you notice any problems with grammar, usage, and mechanics?

Writing Activities

1. Search for some writing groups on the Internet. For example, visit the site at www.forwriters.com. Write a brief assessment of what you find. What resources do they provide for their members? Do you think it would be helpful to join such a group?
2. Discuss the difficulties you have had with revision. What's your biggest problem when revising? What suggestions have your teachers and peers given you? Can you think of other ways to resolve the problem?

Editing and Proofreading

Editing and proofreading are the final steps in getting a written document ready for your audience. Even if you make corrections and changes while composing your drafts, as many writers do, you'll still find it helpful to think about revising, editing, and proofreading as separate operations. When you revise, you focus on *what* you're saying—on ideas, content, purpose, audience, and organization. But when you edit, you shift gears and concentrate on *how* you're saying it—on clarity, style, and tone. It's a good idea to postpone most of your editing and proofreading until the end of a project. If you start making small-scale changes too soon, you could waste time on material that gets deleted during the revision stage.

The goal of editing is to make your writing more readable. Although each discourse community you will participate in has unique assumptions about what makes writing appropriate for your audience, purpose, and persona, here are some common points to look at when you edit:

- *Sentences:* Do they express their intended meanings? Are they smooth, or do them seem choppy and dull? Are they varied in length and structure?
- *Word choice:* Is your language accurate and engaging? Does your vocabulary suit your audience and purpose? Do you use the terminology your readers expect and understand?
- *Tone:* Do you convey a suitable amount of seriousness and competence? Are you too personal, or too impersonal, in your approach? Do you avoid language that might offend your readers or strike them as excessive?
- *Transitions:* Do you provide adequate signposts for your readers? Does your prose flow smoothly from one sentence to the next? Can you improve the connections between paragraphs or sections?
- *Introduction and conclusion:* Does your opening give your readers the information they expect? Does it fit the typical pattern for the kind of writing you're doing? Does your conclusion pull your ideas together and leave your readers with a sense of completion?

If you have doubts about any of these elements, take a look at similar pieces of writing. For example, if you are putting together a brief reference guide to infectious diseases in preschoolers for a health studies class, look at similar documents to see what kind of openings they have or whether the authors use *I* and address the readers directly with *you.*

When you proofread, you look for errors in mechanics, format, and appearance. As you undoubtedly know, this final check is noncreative and mechanical. You may need to use some method for keeping the content from distracting you, such as reading aloud or placing a ruler under each line as you read. Another strategy is to read backwards in search of spelling or mechanical problems of a kind that commonly surface in your drafts. Professional proofreaders sometimes read "against copy," comparing the final draft, one sentence at a time, against the previously edited version. Tedious as it may seem, proofreading is important. The appearance of your work is the first impression you make on your readers, and a pattern of errors can undermine your credibility. As journalist and author Jessica Mitford says, "failure to proofread is like preparing a magnificent dinner and forgetting to set the table."

Fortunately, you can call on a number of resources to assist you in checking and correcting your written work. In addition to your dictionary, you might want to have a thesaurus on hand, along with a handbook of grammar and usage. You can also use your word processing program's grammar and spell-checking programs, and find help online. For example, you can get editing and proofreading tips from the Guide to Grammar and Writing (http://webster.commnet.edu/grammar/composition/editing.htm); and the Writer's Web offers guidance on editing for clarity and style along with help with punctuation, sentence structure, and mechanics (http://writing2.richmond.edu/writing/wweb.html). If you need advice on style and formatting for a particular academic discipline, the Purdue Online Writing Lab has links to twenty subject areas (http://owl.english.purdue.edu/handouts/research/r_docsources.html). These include both official Web sites and sites that explain in detail how to follow each style.

Writing Activity

Write a description of your past experiences with editing and proofreading. How do you find what needs to be edited in your drafts? What changes do you usually look for? Do you keep a record of the errors you tend to make? What kind of help do you get in editing your writing? What techniques do you use to help you proofread?

Checklist for Analyzing Writing Rituals, Composing Practices, and Working Habits

☐ 1. Are my writing rituals useful and supportive? Can I adapt them when I need to?

☐ 2. Am I able to employ a range of effective strategies for exploring topics and generating material? Do I need to try some new techniques and quit using others?

☐ 3. How much planning do I do? What additional steps might I add?

☐ 4. Are my drafting habits efficient and productive? What can I do to improve them?

☐ 5. Do I leave enough time between drafting and revising?

☐ 6. Do I have a clear revising agenda? Do I revise from the top down? Do I get feedback from others? What can I do to make my revising efforts more successful?

☐ 7. Do I distinguish among revising, editing, and proofreading? Do I take the time to edit and proofread carefully?

Writer's Workshop

1. Do you remember learning to write? Who or what had the biggest influence on how you compose? For example, what were your parents' or siblings' composing practices?

2. One especially helpful way to learn about your composing practices is to observe yourself write. It seems a bit awkward at first but, like freewriting or brainstorming, it feels more natural as you go along. If you have a

specific assignment for another class, use that as your observation subject. Otherwise, take this opportunity to write a letter to the editor on some topic you've been thinking about for a while, for example, the biggest challenge facing your student government or a problem in the community in which your campus is located. As you write, stop after each step you take, starting with your very first response to the assignment or topic. Quickly jot down a brief description of what you do, why you do it when you do it, and how it seems to further your thinking or progress on the assignment or letter you are writing. Take note of downtimes, roadblocks, strategies for overcoming problems. Pay attention to ideas that come easily and those that need to be sparked through some form of prewriting. If you stop to reread, note that and then record the effects. Has reviewing your work changed your thinking on the topic or simply given you a new approach to organizing or expressing your ideas? When you've finished your observations, read them through, expanding for clarity's sake and jotting down any additional insights into your composing practices.

Writers on Writing

Strengthened by a Pale Green Light
Reynolds Price

The James B. Duke Professor of English at Duke University, Reynolds Price has published several dozen titles in many different genres: fiction, poetry, drama, and several categories of nonfiction. His novel Kate Vaiden *won the National Book Critics Circle Award in 1986, and his memoir of his bout with spinal cancer,* A Whole New Life *(1994), became a best seller.*

As an American, born in rural North Carolina in 1933, I've been given, in the past decade, two enormous boons from the realm of hard new technology. In the spring of 1984 an enormous malignant tumor was discovered in the midst of my spinal cord. Even in a world-class medical center like that at Duke University, the therapies available to radiologists and neurosurgeons in the early eighties did not allow them to remove, or substantially reduce, that tumor. After an initial abortive surgery I was, in a matter of weeks, paraplegic. My body was paralyzed from the upper chest downward; my arms and hands were spared, but my very existence was still the target of a hungry and rapidly growing cancer.

However, by the time that tumor became imminently life-threatening in the spring of 1986, my surgeon had mastered a brand-new tool of medical technology—an ultrasonic laser scalpel. With that sophisticated instrument in hand, and over a period of five months in two lengthy procedures, he re-entered my spinal cord and removed all visible traces of the tumor—sparing my hands and arms again. And my life. A decade later—checked annually by the magnetic resonance imager, another tool that was unavailable in 1984—I've had no further losses or symptoms of the tumor.

At the same time, my career was profoundly changed by yet another new machine. In 1983, a year before I was aware of the threat of illness, I'd acquired my first word processor, an IBM Displaywriter. As a man with a long record of not understanding the workings of any tool more complicated than the hammer, I faced a new computer with considerable qualms. Once I'd learned my superficial way around its cryptic keyboard, I began to use the computer to transcribe, every day or so, the just-written pages of a new novel called *Kate Vaiden*. For the actual writing, I continued to practice my lifelong method—the setting down, and steady correction, of words and sentences by hand and fountain pen (I'd never been able to compose with any degree of success on a typewriter—too much noise and too cumbersome a process when it came to inserting the constant changes I make in my first and second thoughts).

After a few weeks of the new procedure—gingerly entering handwritten prose into the computer while I could still decipher my own script—it began to dawn on me that I was failing to accept a large opportunity. As I watched the blessedly silent transformation of my manuscript into pale green lights on a sizable screen—and as I revised them there with so little expense of time and effort—I began to suspect that the computer might revolutionize not only my time-hallowed and strictly manual method of writing but the final product as well.

And within a matter of a few days, I was off and streaking—a confirmed computer-keyboard compositor. In the thirteen years since that discovery—a truly momentous time for me and my work—I've completed and published fifteen full-length volumes of fiction, poetry, drama, essays, and translations. In the previous twenty-one years of publication, I'd completed twelve volumes. What, other than unconscious psychic factors, explains such a midlife doubling of one's rate of work?

I have to assume that my own ability to conceive and transcribe my work has been powerfully strengthened by my daily access to a machine that's been available to American writers for little more than a decade (in the past four years I've worked on the uncannily simple and resourceful Macintosh IIsi computer and a Mac PowerBook 145 when traveling). I've discussed my experience with numerous writing colleagues and find that their responses to computer work are remarkably similar to mine. I've encountered no one who has seriously attempted and then rejected computer writing.

In general the ease of revision, even the radical reorganization and transfer of sentences and paragraphs, has made it possible for our mental faculties to secrete and deliver the words a good deal more rapidly than was previously possible to most of us in the grip of ponderous typewriters, pencils, or pens. Virtually all computer writers confirm another finding of my own. Given the speed available to one's fingers and mind, and the quiet seductiveness of seeing one's words materialize on a lighted screen, the always laborious process of composition has been considerably sweetened and lightened by more than a hint of sheer play.

To a same and easily controllable extent, writing now often becomes a higher and far more rewarding branch of the videogame. The only detectable drawback, for me, of the games aspect of word processing has been my discovery that I cannot achieve a rigorous final edit on-screen. Something in the nature of the lighted screen itself convinces me that the work is finished when, in fact, it's not. Perhaps it's only the result of my years of experience with handwriting, but I've now learned that, at the final stage, I must print out hard copy and insert my final revisions by hand. I and any consumer—any serious reader of my work and the work of other computer craftsmen—should obviously ask the next question. Has this new and cheerfully submissive tool of contemporary technology merely provided me and my colleagues with a toil-saving device that results, or will come to result, in a diluted and inferior product—a written version of prepackaged, denatured, and characterless food? The reader must answer this for himself, of course, as he consumes or rejects the new work.

As for me, though I seldom reread my work once I have seen it through the press, I claim to have added new levels of emotional complexity and honesty to a prose and verse that's grown increasingly lucid and thus more accessible. Convinced of that, I face the millennium as a writer in his early sixties who works all day, six days a week, with the blessings of contemporary technology—a writer who hopes to work for many years more with the aid of increasingly intelligent and elegant devices, all invented and made by what I suspect is the ultimate magician: the human brain and the hands it moves.

Writer's Notebook

How have your rituals, practices, and habits changed since you started college? Which changes have been requested or suggested by others and which have come naturally as you've adapted to new environments? How difficult have the changes been? Which ones seem to have had a significant impact on your success as a writer?

Writer's Profile One: How Did I Become the Writer I Am?

Throughout Chapters 1 and 2 you have been thinking and writing about yourself as a writer, from where you like to write to your best and most challenging writing experiences. This first "Writer's Profile" is an opportunity to bring those varied reflections together into a coherent portrait, focusing only on that part of you that is a writer. Your audience is your instructor and classmates.

Possible material for this essay includes:

- Memories of past writing experiences, especially since beginning college—what you've written, when you succeeded and failed and why, where and from whom you learned what you learned, the range of styles to which you've been exposed
- Insights into your established writing rituals, composing practices, and working habits.

You can select one of two familiar essay forms as the primary way to present your ideas:

- A narration of an illustrative writing experience in which you reveal and critique your process, or
- A more direct analysis of your usual writing process in which you reference past and current experiences.

In either format, as part of constructing your writer's self-portrait, you will also be in a position to evaluate your writing rituals, practices, and habits and speculate on things that might need to be changed or adjusted, either in general or to suit new and varied writing situations. In short, how successful is your current writing self?

The following sequence of activities might help you to make decisions about this assignment:

- First, review the "Writer's Workshop" responses and "Writing Notebook" entries you completed for Chapters 1 and 2. Concentrate on those responses that target college-level writing experiences and insights into current practices.

The next two steps can be completed in this order or, more likely, will be made alongside one another, with your decisions changing and evolving as you go along:

- Using the *Checklist for Analyzing Core Elements of Writing* (p. 12), evaluate and make choices about your writing situation (persona, audience, purpose).
- Decide upon a format—either a narration or an analysis—and make note of the features that are typical of that form. What do readers expect from an effective narration? From a successful analysis? What voices are appropriate? What choices do you have for organizing the material?

Next,

- Review your prewriting exercises, selecting material that will support the goals you have set and identifying areas where you will need to discover and develop new supporting ideas.

Consult the *Checklist for Analyzing Writing Rituals, Composing Practices, and Working Habits* (p. 34) for additional advice on completing the process, including the possibility of working with your peers (who, in this case, are also your readers) through the discovery, drafting, revising, and editing stages.

Chapter 3
Becoming Aware of Professional Writing Practices

Chapter Preview

This chapter introduces a set of strategies for analyzing a professional discourse community through observing its rhetorical practices and analyzing the documents it produces. As a freshman, no doubt, you were confused by your teachers' differing responses to your writing. Your English teacher may have valued originality of interpretation and subtlety of expression, but your sociology professor expressed frustration when you buried your highly subjective thesis on page two or, worse yet, implied rather than stated it upfront. "What do they want?" is a common student response. The answer, as you have since discovered, is that each is, in fact, looking for something different. The definition of good writing is context specific.

This chapter will provide critical thinking strategies that complement the content and method being taught to you in your general education and major classes. It will take you beyond simply recognizing differences among discourse communities, and make you less dependent on others to guide you in developing the style, form, and vocabulary required in class assignments and professional projects.

The key to independence and flexibility as a writer is to understand that disciplinary differences are manifestations of different ways of knowing and thinking. Each discourse community has a distinct purpose and set of interests and operates from its own set of negotiated and agreed upon norms and values. And the forms of communication that a community uses for producing and sharing knowledge offer an effective window into that group's way of thinking.

Investigating the Profession

Current research conjectures that today's college graduates can expect to have several careers, not just individual jobs, in the course of their working lives. Even within a single career, writing responsibilities evolve. Law enforcement is just one example:

> As employees advance through the ranks of an agency, the nature of their writing changes. Sergeants write fewer incident reports and more performance evaluations; lieutenants and captains respond to letters from the public, propose new programs, submit grant requests and the like; even chiefs and sheriffs find themselves writing unfamiliar documents for new audiences. . . . As one student at the FBI National Academy recently said, "In law enforcement, there is a point where the gun becomes less of a weapon and writing becomes more of one." (*FBI Law Enforcement Bulletin*, Feb. 2003)

While job-related experience and continuing education will be necessary for you to flourish in such transitions, being an observant and flexible writer is critical to your success.

In Chapter 1 you were introduced to discourse communities as a way to understand the needs of your audience. If you place readers into some identifiable category—members of your family, university students, amateur photographers—you can begin to determine, among other things, what interests they share and what level of knowledge they might have about your topic. You can assume that most members of a photography club scan the latest issues of the relevant specialty magazines, and you won't need to explain terms like *aperture* and *shutter speed* when you send out a newsletter article on a new digital camera. Seeing your writing as taking place within discourse groups offers you useful insights into the various communities where you will live and work, as well as strategies for succeeding within these environments, especially as a writer.

A discourse community operates as a culture. Its interests and shared knowledge create and are created by its ideologies, values, and norms. The United States, for example, was founded as a democracy with a set of related core assumptions, including the belief that all people are created equal. As a result, we value open access to education and have created laws that allow us to exercise certain rights, such as freedom of speech. Discourse communities, though, are dynamic entities; they change across place and time. When the Founding Fathers said "All men are created equal," they excluded many groups from full participation in our democracy. Our current more inclusive definition of "all men" is the result of ongoing negotiations for change. As the definition changed, so have the practices that support the values. Those who were once enslaved were eventually given rights associated with full citizenship, and their underground dissent, expressed through spirituals and slave narratives, has come to the surface in forms as diverse as novels, journalism, and rap music.

For writers, a discourse community is a context, an environment in which they think, work, and communicate. To succeed, whether simply to function within the community or to change it, they must understand the complex dynamics at work.

Analyzing a Discourse Community

Take the simple rose. To the master gardener, it's a source of professional pride and aesthetic joy. To the botanist, it's an object of study, a shrub or vine that belongs to the genus *Rosa*. And to the reader or student of literature, it's a common symbol, bringing to mind lines from Shakespeare and Gertrude Stein. You can better understand these varied responses by closely analyzing the group to which each observer belongs.

Reflecting on Your Experiences: Asking Questions

One easily remembered way to begin to look for and understand the assumptions at work within any given discourse community is by asking and expanding on the journalist's core questions:

- *Who:* Who are the typical participants? What personality and interests seem to make someone more or less successful in the group? What personas are they asked to adopt?
- *What:* What do participants need to know to work effectively in this community? What kinds and depth of knowledge are expected? What topics are appropriate for discussion, reading, and communication? What critical assumptions lie behind the actions and communications of participants?
- *When and Where:* When and where do people accomplish the work of the group? Are there recognizable rituals and working habits—a "workplace culture"—in this community? Are there rules and regulations that must be followed, for example? Do people work alone or mainly in groups?
- *How:* How are questions asked, answers found, and results conveyed within this group? How are problems resolved? What forms of communication are most common? Do writers usually know their readers personally?
- *Why:* Why does this group exist or why was it formed? Given your other observations, what beliefs or values seem to guide the people and practices of this community?

Observing a Discourse Community

A classroom is as good an example as any of a working discourse community. Each class is one of many offered by your university and is, more narrowly, a course within a particular department or discipline of study. It shares many traits with other courses in the university. Briefly, the participants are students or teachers; students are expected to have a set of writing, thinking, and speaking skills, and professors have earned advanced degrees, giving them an extensive body of knowledge in their field; classes generally meet on a regular schedule and in the same place (a classroom, lab, or studio); class formats may include laboratories, lectures, and/or discussions; both objective and essay tests are administered and research papers required; everyone expects that professors and students will act respectfully toward one another, that students will advance their understanding and skills, and that such accomplishments will be fairly evaluated for a course grade that will become part of the student's college transcript.

Although courses within individual departments share many traits, each department further reflects the specific ideology, values, and norms of its discipline. In an English Department, for example, most professors expect active discussion, require close reading of texts, and offer opportunities for original thinking in the completion of assignments. Course content and class practices suggest a high regard for critical thinking, personal experience, and creativity.

Writing Activity

It's your turn to take our analysis of university classes one step further. Using the questions listed above, write an informal description of the writing class you're now in. Feel free to add information and shape the questions as necessary. For example, *Who* should include both students and teachers. And under *What* you might want to ask, "What critical assumptions has the teacher made in designing the course or handling of class discussion?" For *How* you could personalize the question to ask, "How have problem-solving techniques been most helpful to me in this class?" Be sure to include any changes you have seen over the course of the semester so far, both in yourself as a participant or in the class as a whole.

Bring your description to class and break into small groups, or circulate your findings electronically. Compare your observations and, if there is time, complete a final report based on the results of your discussion and exchange copies with other groups in the class.

Writer's Notebook

After discussing the "Writing Activity" in class, prepare a notebook entry in which you consider the insights you gained from completing the exercise, including what you discovered through your own observations and in discussion with classmates. How might what you have learned be put to immediate use in the class? In other classes?

Studying Forms of Communication

As the expanded definition of discourse community might imply, all aspects of writing, from persona to purpose, from habits to rituals, are, in fact, shaped by your working environment. Analyzing a discourse community's typical documents and undertaking primary research within the community are two ways to expand your answers to the journalist's questions. These activities yield a fuller understanding of the nature of a group and especially the ways its members think about, solve, and communicate answers to problems.

Genre

Writers working within a particular discourse group assume that certain acts of writing, known as *genres*, are commonly used and expected in that community. There are many different forms of reports, Web sites, essays, articles, case studies, charts, memos, FAQs, proposals, reviews, press releases, and letters that satisfy the needs of the various personal, public, and professional discourse communities you will participate in. For example, your family might enjoy frequently exchanging brief, funny e-mails, and students at your university are used to finding thick stacks of informational flyers in their daily mail. Writers hoping to join or communicate with a discourse group can become familiar with the typical genres by learning and practicing their features. New members of your family might, at first, be put off by the abrupt and barbed notes showing up in their e-mail inboxes, but they will probably join the conversation if they really want to fit into your clan, perhaps even adding new and unexpected twists to their messages!

There can be both great satisfaction and significant challenges to becoming part of a community. For example, although you probably thought long and hard about the career you would pursue, your knowledge of what it would mean to participate in that major was gained as an *outside observer*. In the process of taking your first courses in your field, however, you have begun to take on the identity of a major, in part because you have been asked to learn and practice the special and sometimes unusual ways in which writers in your field typically present their ideas and research findings. As a *participant-observer*, you may have been asked, for example, to write formal essays on works of literature, prepare Power-Point presentations of annual reports, or assemble colorful brochures on the new fall clothing line. And as you have gained experience and expertise—that is, as you have become a part of the community—you have very likely gained the skills necessary to refine your use of these genres by tweaking, expanding, or excluding features of the medium to suit your specific writing situations.

Writing Situation and Medium

One genre that science majors must practice and perfect is the laboratory report. Like all genres, this form consists of two primary elements, a commonly occurring writing *situation* and a consistently used *medium*. The writing situation for college laboratory reports is often the same from report to report. In an introductory course, for example, the audience is the knowledgeable and interested instructor, the persona is a serious and objective student, and the purpose is to record and convey the results of a specific experiment. The student also wants to demonstrate an ability to complete a standard experiment and report the outcome in the style and form required by the teacher. A variation on this genre is the lab report produced by a practicing scientist who is writing for other scientists about new discoveries. The writing situation shifts a bit, still reflecting the science community's regard for objectivity, but also adding an emphasis on originality and creativity, combined with more extensive knowledge of the existing research on the topic.

The basic form employed within a situation to create a genre is the *medium*, a set of required and, in fact, expected verbal and sometimes visual components. Once familiar with these cues, we can often simply look at a piece of writing and name the medium. A "Dear Sandra" greeting and "Love, Ellen" closing tell us we are reading a letter, and more specifically, the genre of the personal letter. If, however, it turns out that Ellen doesn't really know Sandra and this letter is, in fact, a sales letter, the violation of the norm is likely to create ill feelings, frustrating the writer's purpose to create a receptive audience.

Returning to the lab report, we know that the report medium is used in any number of writing situations—a community group's end-of-the-year report to contributors, an employee's report to the company on the results of a study of product options, and, of course, a biology student's lab report of findings. All of these communications share certain features: a logically organized, carefully researched presentation in an objective voice and style. Dates, figures, and illustrations are frequently used to clarify and efficiently present results. The expected features of the format, however, are further refined by a discourse community to suit its specific needs and create a genre. Medium + Situation = Genre.

In the introductory biology class, for example, students are taught both the content and process of this particular kind of science. In order to teach the process and, in turn, to evaluate the students' understanding of the topic and method, the teacher usually requires that students use the science lab report genre and, more specifically, mandates the following features:

- Title Page (a separate page containing an accurate title plus information that identifies the student and the course)
- Introduction (an abstract of the hypothesis or a summary of objectives, along with a short overview of methods, results, and discussion)
- Apparatus, Materials, and Methods (usually a list of equipment, supplies, and a summary, outline, or flow chart of the procedure used)
- Results (an objective, organized summary of data, usually including clearly labeled graphs, charts, and tables)
- Discussion (a narrative presentation of conclusions drawn, including an analysis of the value and validity of the results and an explanation of any problems or errors)

Students are often given a set template such as this for reporting their results, including suggestions for maintaining an objective voice and accomplishing expected goals.

The structure and style of the lab report have been agreed upon by members of the biology community. The genre's purposes—to inform, analyze, and evaluate—are all well served by its careful structure and predictability. Readers know exactly where to go in the report for any one piece of information, and the inclusion of visual elements (charts, graphs, etc.) ensures both ease and clarity of understanding.

It is important to remember that genres, like discourse communities, are dynamic structures created to serve specific needs. As those needs change or evolve, so do the genres. Its features, perhaps its organization or style, may change over time in response to shifts in values or practices among the members of the community. With the introduction of the computer, for example, e-mail has largely replaced the memo as the format for office communication. While still largely an objective and information-based form of communication, e-mail is more spontaneous, and thus the tone of the intra-office genre is now commonly less formal.

Expanding the Definition: Oral and Visual Genres

Genres are not unique to writing, of course. There are many oral and visual genres that we just as easily recognize and generate. The protest poster, the Kiwanis's Club speech, and the political cartoon, although similar in purpose to the letter to the editor, are easily distinguished genres. Oral, written, and visual genres are often combined, as well, either in one or linked documents, to serve overlapping purposes. CEOs keep stockholders informed through annual speeches as well as annual reports, with the briefer, persuasive speech containing the gist of the fuller, more objective report. Because of the medium, stockholders expect full charts, complete figures, and extensive explanations in the report. But the speaker who provides such inclusive detail is likely to lose or bore an audience. A brief PowerPoint presentation will meet their needs and keep their attention.

Buildings, sculptures, and other works of art are combined functional and aesthetic mediums that we call upon in particular situations to create a wide range of genres. The grave marker, for example, is a form of monument, a sculpture created to meet the practical, aesthetic, and emotional needs of mourners. There are cues that tell us that an object is a cemetery marker: its location in a cemetery or mausoleum and at least one name and the dates of birth and death written upon the wood or etched into the stone. The individual being memorialized or those remembering distinguish their marker with varying shapes and sizes, simple or elaborate forms, and additional details about the person's life.

Writing Activities

1. Study these four sample genres and then answer the questions that follow.

   "Identify the major and minor plots in Richardson's novel *Clarissa*. Outline and analyze the relationships among these plots."

   a. What genre is exemplified here?

b. What medium does it illustrate?

c. What does the genre assume of its readers?

d. How does the genre reflect the values of its community?

SAGE AND ROSEMARY'S

Eat Healthy at the Intersection of Frenchman St. and Willis Ave.

Today's Dinner Specials

**Rosemary's Tempeh Cacciatore
Tempeh, mushrooms, and peppers in a red wine sauce over whole wheat pasta and served with our freshly baked sourdough bread

**Sage's Marinated and Grilled Red Curry Tofu
Served with grilled vegetables and pineapple over saffron rice

Salads
Baby greens, goat cheese, roasted pepper,
toasted walnuts, and raspberry vinaigrette

Bibb lettuce, carrots, cherry tomatoes, and garlic croutons

Soups
(served with our freshly baked sourdough bread)

Okra Gumbo	bowl
	cup
Minestrone	bowl
	cup
Carrot, Leek, & Thyme	bowl
	cup

Beverages
peach, lime, or papaya mineral water

chai teas

tropical fruit smoothies
(Wine List Available from Server)

---

a. What genre does this sample illustrate?

b. What features of the medium led you to identify the genre? Are any features missing?

c. What can you gather about the writing situation from the sample? For example, what knowledge and habits does it assume in its readers? Does it imply anything about the values or beliefs of its creators?

a. What genre is exemplified by the object in this photograph?

b. What features of the medium led you to identify the genre?

c. What habits and practices does the genre assume of its users? Does it imply anything about the values or beliefs of its creators?

Frasier

9 pm/ET, NBC

Christmas at the Cranes isn't very merry as the siblings squabble over who'll host the big day's festivities.

    Frasier (Kelsey Grammar) claims the honor, since he's held it at his home for the last nine years. However, Niles (David Hyde Pierce) believes "it's time to start a new tradition" and that his brother is "just being a churl." Their tiff turns off Martin, who refuses to choose sides, deciding to work on the holiday instead. His shamed sons then set out—with chaotic results—to take the celebration to their dad at his workplace.

    In another storyline, Roz (Peri Gilpin) gets a job as an elf at a department store, where she fancies the Santa (Dean Cain).—*Skip Carrington*

a. What genre is exemplified in this example?

b. What features of the medium led you to identify the genre?

c. What habits and knowledge does the genre assume of its users?

d. What features of the style particularly suit the content of the example?

2. Find a short sample of writing from your major, or from a favorite class, that represents what you believe is a typical genre for that discipline—for example, a certain kind of case study, report, letter, proposal, or advertisement.

a. Analyze the sample as a piece of successful writing based on its handling of audience, persona, message, and purpose. Consider the format of the document (including any visual elements).

b. Review the journalist's questions for understanding discourse communities. If you were to analyze the discipline from which the sample comes as a discourse community, what answers would this genre provide?

Style

Style is a significant component of a community's discourse. While the term *style* may be difficult to define, you can usually recognize the most common writing styles when you see them. Look at the following excerpts and identify the genre that each represents:

> And he said unto him, it was meet that we should make merry and be glad: for this thy brother was dead, and is alive again: and was lost, and is found.

> anyone lived in a pretty how town
> (with up so floating many bells down)

> Once upon a time in the middle of winter, when the flakes of snow were falling like feathers from the sky, a queen sat at a window sewing, and the frame of the window was made of black ebony.

> Any person who willfully, maliciously and repeatedly follows or harasses another person or who repeatedly makes a credible threat with the intent to place that person in reasonable fear of death or serious physical injury is guilty of the crime of stalking.

> He's a dinosaur and he knows it.
> He's an old-fashioned shooter in a slam-jam, alley-oop world, and he embraces it.
> He's soft-spoken, intelligent and as flashy as his crewcut.
> But don't make the mistake of ignoring him.

Although these excerpts are brief, you probably had little trouble recognizing the genre of each one: bible verse, lines of poetry, fairy tale, criminal statute, and sports writing. Perhaps you could even identify the specific source of the first three: the King James version of the Bible, a poem by E. E. Cummings, and the opening of "Snow White and the Seven Dwarfs" by the brothers Grimm. The content provides some clues, but it's the language and format that set each of these passages apart and tell you what kind of writing you are reading. In other words, you read the style as well as the content.

You already know that different kinds of writing require different styles. You don't write a letter applying for an internship in the same way you write a letter to a friend back home. You adapt your writing style to meet the needs and expectations of your audience. And you do the same when you enter a new discipline or profession: you try to develop a clear sense of your readers and discover the stylistic features for the various genres that are standard in that field. Much of your learning will take place automatically as you participate in the new discourse community. According to a study of disciplinary writing in college, the biology students who got involved in collecting data, conducting an experiment, and consulting experts for responses to their drafts were far more successful at creating their voice and persona than the students who tried to write their research reports without getting involved in the scientific process.[1]

You can also consciously study the features that characterize the style of the writing you'll be doing. If you're going to write an engineering design report or a proposal for a childhood education initiative, for example, you want to be sure you study a number of models or examples of how these documents are written. Your style will involve voice and tone, but most of your decisions will be about the language you use or avoid. The following list summarizes the most frequently asked questions about style. This list is not exhaustive, and the relative importance of each feature varies from situation to situation; but these are the stylistic choices you will need to consider when deciding how to adapt your writing to the demands and expectations of a particular discourse.

POINT OF VIEW: Can I write from my own personal point of view using *I, me, we,* and *our*? Or should I use *one* or avoid referring to myself at all? Can I address the readers directly as *you*?

VERBS: Should I use the active voice ("I collected samples") or the passive voice ("Samples were collected")? Do I need to use the historical present to refer to the research of others ("Langer's study *demonstrates* the faulty nature of opinion research") or to recount what happens in a work of literature or art ("Antigone *declares* her defiance of the law")? What tense do I use to describe my own work and to set forth my claims?

WORD CHOICE: Should I use specialized terms and polysyllabic words ("thermally elevated"), or do I need to use common words and accessible language ("hotter")? Am I expected to use the jargon and terminology of the discipline or profession? Will my readers prefer general, abstract words ("post-secondary education") or expect specific, concrete language ("college")?

LEVEL OF USAGE: Can I use contractions, abbreviations, and colloquial expressions? Are figures of speech and colorful language acceptable? Do I write numbers out or use numerals? Do I refer to people by first name, last name, or both? Should I include titles (like Dr. and Ms.)?

SENTENCES: Should I try to keep my sentences short and simple, or will my readers expect longer, more complicated syntax? Can I use incomplete sentences, rhetorical questions, or exclamations?

---

[1]Walvoord, Barbara E., et al. *Thinking and Writing in College: A Naturalistic Study of Students in Four Disciplines.* Urbana: NCTE, 1990.

PARAGRAPHS: Do I need to use frequent paragraph breaks (as journalists do), or are longer, fully developed paragraphs more appropriate? Can I use one-sentence paragraphs for effect?

TONE: Should I use an objective, impersonal voice, or can I reveal my own feelings about the subject? Will humor and personal anecdotes be appropriate? Do I want to come across as an expert, a colleague, or a neutral observer?

Writing Activity

1. What is the tone of the following selection (which was taken from *Parade Magazine*)? What details support your conclusion? Rewrite the piece in a neutral tone, as the Bureau of Labor Statistics might have done in a news release. (To see a model of this genre, visit http://www.bls.gov/.)

    Social Security Snafu

    The federal government had to cough up cash last month and mail a "letter of explanation" to 51 million Americans who were short-changed on their Social Security checks. It seems the Bureau of Labor Statistics was supposed to give them 2.5% cost-of-living increases but only added 2.4%, due to faulty math. Recipients won't get rich: It's about $12 to $19 more. (We wonder what it cost to calculate the difference, then print and mail all those letters.) But the blunders didn't stop there: Some folks were sent financial data about their neighbors.

2. The following is part of an actual recall letter that a car manufacturer sent to owners of possibly defective automobiles. Rewrite the letter to make it clearer and more reader-friendly. Keep in mind the intended audience.

    A defect which involves the possible failure of a frame support plate may exist on your vehicle. This plate connects a portion of the front suspension to the vehicle frame, and its failure could affect vehicle directional control, particularly during heavy brake application. In addition, your vehicle may require adjustment service to the hood secondary catch system. The secondary catch may be misaligned so that the hood may not be adequately restrained to prevent hood fly-up in the event the primary catch is inadvertently left unengaged. Sudden hood fly-up beyond the secondary catch while driving could impair driver visibility.

Design

"Some people think design means how it looks," says Apple computer guru Steve Jobs. "But of course, if you dig deeper, it's really how it works." These two principles of *design*—how it looks and how it works—play an important role in writing. The arrangement of ideas and the presentation of information affect the way your readers perceive and process your writing. Whether you're preparing a research paper, a set of instructions, a hospital newsletter, a political ad, or a ré-sumé, you want a design that not only captures your readers' attention and meets their expectations but also helps them to understand your message.

Design is closely allied to purpose. *The New Oxford American Dictionary*, in fact, defines *design* as "purpose, planning, or intention that exists or is thought to exist behind an action, fact, or material object." An argument, for example, is designed to convince your readers to accept your point of view; it includes certain basic components—claims, evidence, refutation—and adheres to a particular structure. If you leave out the evidence or fail to refute the opposition or don't present your case in a clear and logical order, your argument probably won't accomplish its purpose. You will find that most documents have a *rhetorical design.* A recommendation report or feasibility study, for instance, contains several standard features presented in a customary format. Such reports present data, draw conclusions, and make recommendations based on the data and the conclusions. But the conclusions and recommendations are usually given up front, followed by the field observations and the findings that support the conclusions. That's how this kind of report works, and a writer will be expected to follow its conventional design.

Writers also use visual signals to clarify the rhetorical design and reinforce their verbal messages. You already follow a number of typographical and spatial conventions that make your writing easier to read: spaces between words and sentences, capital letters, paragraph breaks, margins, page numbers, and the like. The ever-changing capabilities of computer software make it easy for you to further alter the appearance of the text, incorporate graphics and illustrations, and improve the layout of pages. With a few simple key strokes or mouse moves, you can vary type fonts and sizes, modify line spacing, change typeface (like *italics* or **boldface**), add headings, create bulleted or numbered lists, draw a box around key material, put in charts and tables, set up columns, include headers and footers, and even use color and clip art to increase the visual impact of your documents. Your word processor may provide *wizards* or *templates* for many kinds of documents, such as letters, memos, reports, agendas, résumés, and brochures. These can be useful, but not if you turn out the same cookie-cutter document for every writing situation.

These design options, however, will not guarantee a more effective document or make up for mediocre writing and inadequate content. As you design your documents, you want to think carefully about your purpose, the expectations of your readers, and how they will approach your text. Here are some goals to consider when selecting visual elements:

- Create a flow that takes your reader through the document.
- Use space to ease crowding and focus reader attention.
- Break information into accessible units.
- Highlight key points and important ideas.
- Deploy elements consistently and avoid confusing variations.
- Don't make the document more complex than the situation requires.

You can learn to produce effective, appropriate documents by studying the conventions of visual design for different genres and writing situations.

Writing Activity

Get a copy of *USA Today, Time, Newsweek,* or some popular publication that uses format and other visual elements to present information and make its points. Write a brief analysis of the presentation. How effective is it? Do the visuals promote understanding of the written text? Do they oversimplify or mislead the reader in any way?

Studying Writers in Their Environments: Primary Research

Although impressionist answers to the journalist's question can supply useful preliminary insights into a discourse community, a more accurate and complete analysis requires a closer look. *Note taking, interviewing,* and *observation* are among the skills necessary to undertake such primary or direct research. They also help you to develop and refine related skills, including close and objective *listening,* clear and effective *speaking,* and thoughtful and purposeful *synthesis* and *analysis.* The experience of studying or interviewing members of the discourse community, or even actually working within the group, will deepen your understanding. You might, for example, be under the impression that most of the writing done by a librarian is accomplished within working hours and alone. On-site observation, however, would show that that much of the day-to-day report writing is done collaboratively, by committee, and that many librarians complete research writing for professional journals after their formal working day. If you are considering a career in the information sciences, clearing up such misconceptions would help you to make a more informed decision.

Ethnographic Research

One particular style of primary research has become common within the field of writing and discourse community studies, though its origins are in anthropology. *Ethnography* looks at a situation from as many angles as possible in order to understand how it functions as a whole. More specifically, researchers enter into their studies with the intention of being active participant-observers. Their goal is to see things from the inside, at the same time recognizing the realistic limits of being able to do so. In reporting their findings, they foreground their personal responses to what they see and do and hear. The results are presented in a way that makes readers part of the experience rather than asking them to stand off at an evaluative and objective distance.

Ethnography has been described as offering a "window on culture," a phrase that captures why this approach can be of immediate and long-term use to you in a variety of personal, public, and professional situations. Whether you are already in a community or just entering into one, careful and engaged observation opens new opportunities by giving you insight into the group's knowledge, values, and norms, including its communication practices. Logically, most ethnographic studies take place over extended periods of time to allow the observer to become a meaningful participant and to gather as much knowledge and experience as possible. Karen Honeycutt, for example, spent six years and interviewed close to a hundred women to complete her study of the social construction of obesity (pp. 125–139). Although you will not always have the time or inclination to complete such a full study of a discourse community, you can make use of ethnographic methods in many situations. For example, when you walk into a room full of strangers or travel to a new country, your successful integration into that group depends on how carefully you observe, how skillfully you ask questions, and how thoughtfully you act on the things you learn.

As you complete your major, you can use an ethnographic approach to make this period of apprenticeship more meaningful. Its techniques make you more alert to the future value of each step you take—listening to lectures, reading assignments, completing projects—and guide you to continuously weave together the many different things you experience and learn into a comprehensive understanding of your discipline, of your reactions to it, and, in turn, of the profession you hope to enter.

Writer's Notebook

What observations or interviews have you been asked to complete for courses in your major? Examples might include habitat observations in an ecology course or interviews with elementary students for an education practicum. Select one or two assignments and write about the following aspects of the experiences. If you haven't yet selected a major, write about any observation or interview you have been required to complete in a college course, perhaps in an area you are considering as a major. In fact, these exercises might assist you in your decision-making process.

a. *What specific instructions or advice were you given about conducting this research?*

b. *What did you learn about observation and interviewing from the experience?*

c. *What insights did you gain into your major, future career, or the department as a discourse community from preparing for and completing the research? Does the choice of research style reflect a general concern in this field of study for a certain kind of professional practice or approach to knowledge? For a particular personality or persona?*

Getting Started on Primary Research

All research is a kind of conversation between writers, their topics, and others interested in the topics. One of the challenges for writers undertaking this task is to define their part in the larger conversation accurately and ethically. A second challenge is to feel comfortable with the persona that this work requires, being both an observer of the larger dialogue and a participant in it.

Ethical Considerations

You were introduced to the idea of ethics in research at an early stage in your education when your teachers emphasized the importance of adequately acknowledging your sources when presenting your results. *Plagiarism* is the term for failing to do so. You've learned that it is not enough to change a few words or to skip the quotation marks and just cite something in the *Works Cited* list when you have, in fact, quoted directly.

The core operating principle behind avoiding plagiarism and adhering to all research-related ethical standards is respect: for the person whose ideas you are employing, for your own voice and credibility, and for your audience. No one wants to do the hard work of creating ideas and shaping an appropriate language only to have someone else take credit for it.

Approaches to avoiding plagiarism in secondary research are covered in more detail in Chapter 6, but there are a few specific ethical concerns that must be addressed when undertaking primary research. When you conduct interviews and make observations, you need to understand the specific ethical guidelines or practices of your own group and of the community you are studying. A good general starting point is to be as straightforward as possible. Tell your participants:

- who you are (including your qualifications for conducting this research)
- what you will be doing
- what you expect of the participants
- what you hope to accomplish.

In some cases operating honestly is simply a matter of personal ethics; in others it is a legal requirement. Most universities, for example, have strict guidelines for conducting research, as do professional associations such as the American Chemical Society and the American Psychological Association. APA's extensive *Ethical Principles of Psychologists and Code of Conduct* details such issues as securing the informed consent of the participants and the very narrow circumstances when such consent may be suspended because of the nature of the research. Be sure that you investigate the existence of such documents for the group you belong to and any groups you might be working with. A quick Internet search of the sites for your professional organizations or associations can usually lead you to this information.

Writing Activity

The following is excerpted from the Code of Ethics of the American Academy of Audiology:

> **PRINCIPLE 5:** Members shall provide accurate information about the nature and management of communicative disorders and about the services and products offered. **Rule 5a:** Individuals shall provide persons served with the information a reasonable person would want to know about the nature and possible effects of services rendered, or products provided. **Rule 5b:** Individuals may make a statement of prognosis, but shall not guarantee results, mislead, or misinform persons served. **Rule 5c:** Individuals shall not carry out teaching or research activities in a manner that constitutes an invasion of privacy, or that fails to inform persons fully about the nature and possible effects of these activities, affording all persons informed free choice of participation. **Rule 5d:** Individuals shall maintain documentation of professional services rendered. **PRINCIPLE 6:** Members shall comply with the ethical standards of the Academy with regard to public statements.

1. What do you learn about the values and norms of audiologists from reading these guidelines? Jot down your responses and then get into small groups and compare conclusions with fellow students.
2. Search the Internet or identify a published version of the code of conduct for a major or profession you're interested in. These codes are sometimes included in published style manuals. (See pages 230–231 in Chapter 6 for a list of the most frequently used style sheets.) Analyze the content, genre, and style of the code of conduct to generate additional answers to your ongoing analysis of the discourse communities in your chosen or possible profession.

Making Contacts

Successful observations and interviews take care and planning—and courtesy. Before you contact someone, consider the following questions and guidelines:

- What are your exact goals? You want to be certain that it is necessary to conduct this research to accomplish those goals. For example, avoid requesting an interview with someone if all of what you need to know can be found in that person's published work. Interviews are not a shortcut to completing secondary research.
- Have you identified the best and most appropriate people or groups to accomplish the goals of your project? Try to select your subjects *randomly* and in *sufficient* number. If this is not possible or appropriate, be sure to modify your conclusions to reflect the limits of your choices. Also, although it may sometimes be necessary to make preliminary contact to determine a subject's

viability, you want to narrow your possibilities as fully as possible before setting up interviews.

- Is there sufficient time to complete the project? Avoid waiting until the last minute to ask people with their own busy lives to cooperate in your research project. Plan ahead and allow for negotiation between your schedules.
- Is there a component of the interview or observation that you do not intend to reveal? Be prepared to explain this in advance and to satisfy any questions or worries this might create.
- What will you require of the person or group you are researching? For an observation, for example, will they need to allot time to meet with you or will you simply follow them through their normal routines?
- Are there any required formal permission forms to prepare?
- Do you need to prepare a working script for your initial contact so you have all your requests and information at hand?

Keeping Things Organized

For many writers, especially those used to an informal style of drafting, the transition to complicated, long-term professional projects is challenging. Ruffling through scattered highlighted passages and recalling conversations from memory become unworkable strategies for controlling large amounts of complex and perhaps unfamiliar information. Additionally, keeping track of your own thoughts, as they evolve over the course of the research, becomes more difficult. A project notebook or dedicated computer file is an excellent way to resolve such problems.

The Project Notebook

Think of your project notebook as a history of your actions and thinking during a research project. It should be the site of all your ideas, goals, gatherings, references, reflections, and conclusions. Here is a model for such a notebook:

1. Begin with a narrative presentation of your topic or research project:
   - How did you come up with your idea?
   - What do you already know about the topic or community you wish to study?
   - Do you have any preconception about the people, place, or topic that might affect your study? For example, have you worked in a similar environment and established biases? Is your education level different from those with whom you will interact? Are there relevant differences of class, race, or age? How will you handle these biases as you structure, undertake, and analyze your study?

2. Create a proposal for your study:

- What hypotheses are you working with, if any? Try to put these points in the form of working questions to guide the study. Analyze what makes the questions *valid* and *relevant*. What information will you need to gather to complete the research? What techniques (interviews, etc.) will be used? In what order will the steps be taken?

- Identify the people you will interview or survey and the places you will observe. Describe the type of relationship you hope to establish with the people or environment. For example, will you observe as an outsider or work within the environment to achieve a participant-observer relationship? Obtain as much background information as possible (through Web sites, brochures, publications) and get phone numbers, e-mail addresses, and mailing addresses.

- Create a plan for analyzing any documents that are provided during an interview or that you collect during your observation. Consult the journalist's questions and the discussions of style and genre for advice on this part of the plan.

- Set a tentative schedule with a flexible arrangement to allow for time conflicts and changes in your plan. When must the project be completed? How many visits or contacts will be needed? What changes might be anticipated?

3. Once the interviews and observations have begun, record them in the notebook and arrange some form of divided page so that you can write comments and observations alongside the recorded information.

- You can either draw a line down the center of the page, use opposite pages in a spiral notebook, or divide a computer document page in half.

- Your comments and observations can be both objective (analytically drawing comparisons among responders or noting differences, for example) and subjective (connecting your experiences to those being recorded, for example).

- Also include a kind of running version of your thesis. In short, record how you are seeing your idea take shape and evolve at each stage of the project. (See Figure 3.1 for a sample entry from a divided-page notebook.)

4. Somewhere in the notebook or file, very specifically record any analysis of readings or other data collected, any additional suggestions you receive from others, and any future projects that the research inspires. In fact, in some professions, where the results of your research might have significant legal or social significance, careful recording of all details is required as part of the standard practices of the profession.

Interview	Reflections
My interview with Dr. Sutherland began at 2:30 on 2/2/03 and was conducted in her office.	Although she seemed busy, Dr. S closed the door and gave me her full attention during the interview. She seemed pleased at my interest in her profession.
Me: As I indicated when I contacted you for this interview, I am interested in the kind of research you conduct as a Library professional—not the subjects of your research but the methods you use. Is it quantitative or qualitative, for example?	I learned from the interview with Dr. Weber that I need to be more specific with this question—and it worked!
Dr. Sutherland: Well, most of my everyday research would be called quantitative, I guess. As a cataloguer, I troubleshoot problems with our automated system and publish the results on our Web page. This requires defining the problem, framing a possible solution, outlining steps to testing that solution, conducting tests, and, if it works, putting the results into a form our users can understand and use. Me: Did you expect to do this type of research when you decided to become a librarian?	Hmm. I guess I'd expected most librarians to order and shelve books! But this makes sense given the increased use of computers in libraries.

Figure 3.1   Sample entry from a divided-page notebook

Note Taking When Interviewing and Observing

As you have discovered when reviewing class lecture notes for an exam, good note taking is an invaluable skill. In professional and research environments, it can make the difference between staying in control of the information and making a significant error that skews the research or affects your credibility with your peers and employer. In a worst case scenario, you may be accused of plagiarism or libel if you mishandle quotations or misrepresent situations.

Many professionals take notes on a regular basis. Accountants and lawyers meet with their clients, doctors participate in conferences, and park rangers interact with tourists and government agencies. These situations require them to record observations, impressions, and dialogue. Lawyers, for example, might be as interested in how their clients say things as in what they say. These can be challenging listening and writing environments.

The key to good listening and observing is freeing your mind as much as is realistically possible of all distractions. Although you may want to include your reactions to the things people do and say, your first goal is to record the actual words and actions as objectively as possible in order to have an accurate base of information to which you can add your responses. The double entry research notebook allows you to record and react at the same time or at different times.

- In an interview or observation where you are primarily listening, take exact notes and record precise details. If you find it easier, and if the participant agrees, you might want to tape record for accuracy. Include time, place, and specific names for later use. You may even want to make a sketch of the physical situation.
- In situations where you are a participant, exact notes become more difficult to manage. You will need to develop and practice a system of shorthand references (abbreviations and symbols help) and learn to use key words or phrases to record dialogue or capture impressions. You can return to these notes immediately after the meeting to expand, clarify, and react. In these circumstances, there may still be a need for selective exact quotations. If a point is especially important and if it seems appropriate, you can also ask that comments be repeated or clarified.

Getting Ready to Take Notes

Being fully prepared for the note-taking experience is an additional strategy for success. Precise questions, adequate knowledge of your topic and the people you will be working with, and clear project and session goals will make the process easier and the results more useful. In an observation environment, for example, you will need to select among many things that may be happening simultaneously. You want to record as much as possible, even things that might not seem relevant at the time, but if you know your exact purposes, making tough decisions about what to record will come more readily. This does not mean you should be closed to expanding your goals as you observe, only that you need some filters to help you make on-the-spot decisions.

If your notes become part of a research notebook, take the time after your interview or observation to respond and analyze. In addition, include *synthesis,* in which you compare what you learned and saw with your expectations and past experiences. After several interviews with witnesses to a crime, for example, an investigator begins to construct a scenario based on the various threads offered by each witness. This becomes a working theory to be used in asking follow-up questions or revisiting the crime scene to test the theory in a different way.

Although these suggestions outline note taking as a medium, discourse communities often have distinct genres of note taking with specific purposes and methodologies. Some practice an informal style of recording, leaving the details to the individual writer. These notes are usually meant only for the use of the author. Others have exact requirements down to using permanent ink rather than pencil to ensure a legal record of the activity. The science laboratory notebook, for example, is the site of both discovery and a resource for publication. And a note-taking genre much used by nurses—charting—is described in a text on clinical nursing as having several purposes: "communicating information, assisting evaluation, and providing a legal record."[2] Again, consult your community's style manuals (see a list of common style manuals in Chapter 6, pp. 230–231) or other writers in the field for suggestions.

Writing Activities

1. Take five minutes to write an observation of a familiar environment where people are active and will not notice your activity—a library study room, for example. Use a divided-page entry to record your observations and, when you have finished, add your reactions to the experience and to the notes you have taken.
2. Get into small groups in class and select a topic of conversation that is of interest to all members of the group. Again using the divided-page style, each member should take notes as the group conducts its conversation. After 5 to 10 minutes, stop and allow time for written reflection. Then compare your notes: discuss any contrasting results and compare your reflections.

Preparing for an Interview

In addition to the usual preparation and note-taking skills required by primary research, interviewing preparation involves making a number of important decisions about the questions you will ask and the style of interview you will conduct.

- You can ask narrowly focused questions to elicit specific answers or open-ended questions to expand the scope of the topic and the direction of the interview. "When did you decide to become a teacher?" and "Did specific people influence your decision to go into education?" are focused questions. "Can you talk about deciding to be a teacher?" is open-ended. In either style, you should be prepared with a set of follow-up questions that return the informant to your intended direction or develop the topic further.
- Be open to pursuing an interview that takes an unexpected direction. If you can see that the informant has introduced an angle that you had not considered, you might briefly follow up that line of thought to see if it is, in fact, relevant to your purpose.

---

[2]S. F. Smith et al. *Clinical Nursing Skills.* Upper Saddle River: Prentice, 2000: 45.

- The number of questions you will need is determined by the amount of time you've scheduled and the style of the questions you ask (open-ended questions will require more time to answer). Arrange your questions so that those that you absolutely want answered will be asked, and then turn to a secondary set of questions if time remains.
- Consider issues of persona, audience, and purpose as you design your questions. In general, be polite, clear, and to the point. Try to keep the focus of the interview on the informant, not on yourself.
- Practice your interview if possible. It will give you an opportunity to practice your note-taking skills, and the person helping you can provide feedback on the questions you plan to use. You will also become more comfortable with the role of the interviewer, especially if you know whether the interview will be formal or informal in tone and you conduct your practice session in the same style.
- As soon as possible after the interview concludes, review and complete your notes or transcribe your tape.

Writing Activity

Using the suggestions for creating interview questions, construct a brief series of questions for ten-minute interviews with other members of the class about their reasons for pursuing their intended careers, or, for those still undecided, for their potential choices. Conduct one or two of the interviews as time allows. Give a copy of the notes that you take to the person you interview.

Writer's Workshop

1. Conduct an interview with two professors who teach courses in your major or an area you think you might major in. The initial goal is to collect information about the genres used by people in your major and, if possible, by people who pursue the career you are considering. Fully prepare for the interviews by using the guidelines for interviewing and note taking. In addition, review the journalist's questions for analyzing discourse communities and the discussion of genre to create your questions. Other members of the class might be willing to practice with you in exchange for practicing their own interviews. When you have completed the interviews, prepare transcripts of them. Then, based on your analysis of the interviews, write an objective article on the kinds of writing to be

encountered in this discipline. The article should be one that could be included in a department brochure for students considering enrolling in your major.

2. Identify a class in your chosen or probable major that you would like to observe. If you are currently enrolled in the class, you can approach the task as a participant-observer. Otherwise, identify a class and request permission to attend a session as an outside observer. Prepare a formal proposal for observing the class with the goal of deepening your ongoing analysis of the *Who, What, When, Where, How,* and *Why* of your discourse community. After your instructor has approved the proposal, conduct the observation and complete a divided-page transcript of your notes that includes reflections, analysis, and synthesis.

Writers on Writing

Natural Selections

E. O. Wilson

A world-renowned entomologist, E. O. Wilson is also an acclaimed author and a philosopher. His two Pulitzer Prize–winning books demonstrate the range of his expertise: The Ants *(1990) is a detailed study of insect life, and* On Human Nature *(1978) examines the influence of biology on human behavior. His most recent work,* The Future of Life *(2002), argues that only technology and science can save the natural world.*

In 1954, as a newly minted 25-year-old Ph.D. in biology, my dream was to hunt for ants in remote, unexplored rain forests. The dream—scientific thema might be the better phrase—was an extension of my experience as a teenage entomologist in the forests and swamps of my native Alabama. To trek across wide, unmapped terrain searching for new species was for me the greatest imaginable adventure. The tropical forests were the wildlands of Alabama writ large. That image was fixed in my mind; it still is. I have followed many goals in my professional life, many of them sublimations of the dream, but if I were given free reign in an afterworld, that is what I would choose to do forever.

It all began in my childhood bug period. My first excursion was in 1939 in Washington, D.C., where my father, a federal employee, had been called for a brief tour of duty. With an excitement I can still summon, I went forth one day from our apartment on Fairmont Street, bottle in hand, to explore the wilderness of nearby Rock Creek Park and bring back specimens of ants, beetles, spiders, anything that moved, for my first collection. Soon I discovered the National Zoo, also within walking distance, and the National Museum of Natural History, a 5-cent streetcar ride away, and began to haunt both. Then I narrowed my focus to butterflies, and with a homemade net began a pursuit of the red admiral, the great spangled fritillary, the tiger swallowtail and the elusive and prized mourning cloak. At this time, thanks to a *National Geographic* article on the subject, I also acquired a fascination for ants.

Returning to Alabama, I escalated my bug period by shifting to snakes. Now I hunted the black racer, the ribbon snake, the coach-whip, and the pygmy rattlesnake. In time I caught, studied and released nearly all of the 40 species native to southern Alabama, though a few I kept for a while in cages I constructed in the backyard. In my senior year in high school, I switched to ants, to my parents' undoubted relief. I had always wanted to be an entomologist. College is coming, I thought. Now is the time to get serious.

At the University of Alabama and later, in graduate studies at Harvard University, I continued to spend as much time as possible outdoors. Then came the golden opportunity that turned dream into reality. I was elected to Harvard's Society of Fellows for a three-year term, with full (well, reasonable) financial support to go anywhere, pursue any subject. So off I went and was rarely seen thereafter at Harvard. At last I could reach the tropical forests—my Louvre, my Library of Congress! After trips to Cuba and Mexico, I departed for a lengthy tour of the South Pacific: Fiji, New Caledonia, Vanuatu, Australia and finally the splendid naturalist paradise of New Guinea.

In the mid-1950s very few young biologists had the means to undertake such   5
a distant expedition. I liked being alone. I savored pristine wilderness, climbed the unexplored center of a mountain range (on the Huon Peninsula of New Guinea), discovered scores of new species and filled my journal with notes on the behavior and ecology of ants. Returning to Harvard, I converted the information into a stream of technical articles. Most were strictly factual or theoretical, their data squeezed into the mandatory straitjacket of scientific writing.

Descriptive field research is sometimes dismissed by laboratory scientists as "stamp collecting." There is truth in the label. Natural history is primitive and simple, motivated, I believe, by an innate human urge to find, name and classify, going back to Aristotle and beyond. The naturalist is a civilized hunter. But there is much more to the science than muddy boots, mosquito bites and new species. While I was in the South Pacific, my mind was turning over the rich theories of ecology and evolution I had learned in reading and formal study. I was especially fascinated by the idea of faunal dominance. That sweeping concept was developed during the first half of the 20th century, first by the paleontologists William Diller Matthew and George G. Simpson and then, most thoroughly, by Harvard's curator of entomology Philip J. Darlington—whose position I was eventually to inherit. . . .

None of my reports and theory hinted of motivation, and very little emotion was expressed beyond the occasional "I was interested in the problem of . . ." or "It turned out, to my surprise, that. . . ." I played by the aforementioned rules: Humanistic excursions are not relevant; confession is a sign of weakness and self-indulgence. The audience of a scientific communication is other scientists, and not just any other scientists but fellow specialists working in and around a narrowly defined topic. I doubt that more than a dozen fellow entomologists read my article announcing the discovery of cerapachyine ants on New Caledonia, although the data are still used. The taxon cycle and island biogeography became familiar to a wider circle of biologists but still are unknown to the lay public, and for that matter a majority of scientists, who are preoccupied with their own sectors of the frontier.

Only later did it occur to me to write about these early efforts as a personal history, in a narrative that includes motive and emotion. When I decided to try it, in *Biophilia* (1984) and *Naturalist* (1994), I discovered how difficult it is to compose this form of literature. Not only difficult but risky, opening the author to the indignity of being all too clearly understood. The vast majority of scientists would rather stay inside the guild, so that attempts to cross over from their own research directly to the arts (as opposed to merely playing the cello or admiring modern art) are correspondingly rare.

But the rewards to the broader culture, if the effort has quality, are potentially great. I hope others will try. Thanks to the continuing exponential growth of scientific knowledge as well as the innovative thrust of the creative arts, the bridging of the two cultures is now in sight as a frontier of its own. Among its greatest challenges, still largely unmet, is the conversion of the scientific creative process and world view into literature.

To wring literature from science is to join two radically different modes of thought. The technical reports of pure science are not meant to be and cannot be reader-friendly. They are humanity's tested factual knowledge, open to verification, framed by theory, couched in specialized language for exactitude, trimmed for brevity and delivered raw. Metaphor is unwelcome except in cautious, homeopathic doses. Hyperbole, no matter how brilliant, is anathema. In pure science, discovery counts for everything, and personal style next to nothing.

In literature metaphor and personal style are, in polar contrast, everything. The most successful innovator is an honest illusionist: His product, as Picasso said of visual art, is the lie that helps us see the truth. Imagery, phrasing and analogy in literature are not crafted to establish empirical facts, and even less are they meant to be put into a general theory. Rather, they are the vehicles by which the writer conveys his feelings directly to his audience.

The central role of literature is the transmission of the details of human experience by artifice that intensifies aesthetic and emotional response. Originality and power of metaphor are coin of the realm. Their source is an intuitive understanding of human nature, not an accurate knowledge of the material world; in this respect literature is the exact opposite of pure science. The linkage of science and literature is a premier challenge of the 21st century, for the following reason: The scientific method has expanded our understanding of life and the universe in spectacular fashion across the entire scale of space and time, in every sensory modality, and beyond the farthest dreams of the pre-scientific mind. It is as though humanity, after wandering for millennia in a great dark cavern with only the light of a candle (to use a metaphor!), can now find its way with a searchlight.

No matter how much we see, or how beautifully theory falls out to however many decimal places, all of experience is still processed by the sensory and nervous systems peculiar to our species, and all of knowledge is still evaluated by our idiosyncratically evolved emotions. Both the research scientist and the creative writer are members of Homo sapiens, in the family Hominidae of the order Primates, and a biological species exquisitely adapted to planet Earth. Art is in our bones: We all live by narrative and metaphor.

The successful scientist is a poet who works like a bookkeeper. When his bookkeeper's work is done and duly registered in peer-reviewed technical journals, he can if he wishes return to the poetic mode and pour human life into the freeze-dried database. But chastely so, taking care never to misstate facts, never to misrepresent theory, never to betray Nature.

Chapter 4

Learning from Professional Writing

Chapter Preview

This chapter provides two thematic casebooks of readings from the humanities, social sciences, arts, and the various professions, including business, education, consumer sciences, and technology. The goal of the chapter is to introduce you to conversations going on in several professional discourse communities; you will also have the opportunity to use the discourse analysis skills you have learned so that you can recognize, critique, and employ the methods of communication going on in these communities.

Tracing the Genealogy of a Profession

> If it's green, it's biology
> If it smells, it's chemistry
> If it's broken, it's physics

As this bumper sticker playfully suggests, professions involve many levels of specialization. Your university is divided into several schools or colleges which reflect broad disciplinary differences in interests and approaches. Typically these divisions are the arts and humanities, social sciences, sciences, and the professions (education, business, technology, consumer sciences, to name a few). The sciences attempt to explain the phenomena of our physical world. The style is objective, and practitioners use the quantitative scientific method within carefully proscribed procedures and genres, such as the lab report or scientific essay. Social scientists, too, primarily generate explanations, but they employ both quantitative and qualitative methodologies, focusing their attention on the social world—

on people and their natures and behaviors. The documents they produce include case studies and problem-solution articles.

The creation and interpretation of meaning define the arts and humanities. Students in these areas are taught to reflect, analyze, interpret, and create with the goal of more fully understanding our personal, social, and aesthetic lives. Research in this field is usually qualitative. Genres range from literary criticism to nonfiction personal essays. Finally, in the professional colleges—education, business, technology, and consumer sciences, for example—topics and methods from a variety of related disciplines are studied in the context of a particular application or practice. Consumer science, for example, draws from art, business, and technology. Lessons plans, project designs, and business letters serve the purposes of these communities.

Within these colleges and schools there are further divisions. In the sciences you can choose to study chemistry, physics, biology, zoology, geology, mathematics, or engineering. In social science you might major in sociology, political science, or anthropology. English, philosophy, speech, history, art, and music generally are housed in the arts and humanities college. That some subjects are harder to place reveals the difficulty of making clear-cut distinctions among the disciplines. Descriptions in these cases must be based on the methods and goals of a particular program. Economics, for example, is sometimes found in a college of science and sometimes in a school of business. Journalism can be a separate professional school or part of the humanities. Psychology is usually a part of the sciences, but can be found among the social sciences or as part of a school of education.

The specialization continues when you select a career. As an English major, you might choose to teach or to write. And if you choose to write, you still narrow the choices, perhaps becoming a technical writer for a corporation or a freelance writer. In the sciences, you can spend your day doing experiments in a corporate or university laboratory and producing scientific reports, or you can combine your biology degree with an interest in writing to become a science essayist for a popular magazine or a public relations specialist for an environmental interest group. Your decisions about your major and ultimately your profession should reflect both an affinity for a broad discipline and your unique set of interests, abilities, skills, personality traits, and goals.

Writer's Notebook

What is it that interests you about the readings you do for courses in your major or favorite classes? Are there other readings with similar topics, in magazines or on Web sites, for example, that easily draw and hold your interest? Is there a typical persona or purpose for these readings? What genres do these readings represent? Is there a style you especially like and might try to use as a model for your own professional writing?

Putting Your Discourse Analysis Skills to Work

Through your college readings, lectures, and assignments, you have learned a great deal about the various academic communities. If you have yet to determine a major, you can make more informed decisions about your future by looking more closely at the qualities of each discourse community and by practicing the genres common to each. Once in the major, you have the opportunity to move from outside observer to active and self-confident participant by deepening and expanding this interrogation.

This chapter contains two thematically arranged casebooks: "Privacy in the Information Age" and "Weight, Body Image, and Identity." While these topics can be found in both professional and public writing, the readings here illustrate disciplinary differences and model the genres employed by various professional communities to reach their particular audiences. As you read the selections, you will be asked to see each selection as representative of its discourse community in content and form. The investigative skills learned and practiced in Chapters 1, 2, and 3 will guide your reading and analysis. Although you may want to consult the checklists and guides on pages 12 (Chapter 1 checklist), 34 (Chapter 2 checklist), 43 (journalist questions), and 51 (style checklist), you should keep the following questions in mind as you read:

- How has the author handled the rhetorical issues of audience, message, purpose, and persona?
- What insights into the author's writing practices are evident in the finished product?
- What does the selection reveal about the *who, what, where, when, why,* and *how* of the discourse community? For example,
  - What kinds of previous knowledge and experience does the author assume?
  - If research is involved, is it quantitative or qualitative?
  - How, exactly, does the piece define the problem and suggest solving it?
  - Does the author consider conflicting approaches from within the community?
- To what genre does the selection belong? What are the writing situation and the medium?
- What particular features of style and design are illustrated?

Casebook of Readings: Privacy in the Information Age

Writer's Notebook

Before reading the casebook on privacy in the information age, take a few minutes to write about your opinions on and past experiences with the topic. How do you define the term privacy? To what extent have you been aware of technology-related privacy concerns in your everyday life? For example, have you used a firewall on your computer? Downloaded from Napster or a similar site? Had your e-mail monitored at work? Can you project what privacy issues might be relevant to your future as a professional?

Is Privacy Still Possible in the Twenty-First Century?
Jerry Berman and Paula Bruening

This article from the interdisciplinary journal Social Research *is part of a special issue on privacy. As social scientists, the journal's editors convene topical conferences and publish the presentations in order "to foster discussion of matters of grave public interest in light of their often neglected and generally illuminating historical and cultural contexts." Jerry Berman and Paula Bruening are well positioned to take up this purpose. Both are lawyers who specialize in technology-related public policy at the nonprofit Center for Democracy and Technology. Berman is the organization's founder and president and Bruening serves as the staff counsel.*

Is privacy a realistic possibility in the twenty-first century? Will the "Digital Age" be one in which individuals maintain, lose, or gain control over information about themselves? Will it be possible to preserve a protected sphere from unreasonable government and private sector intrusion?

Without question, the growth of government and commercial transactions and the increase in technological developments over the last fifty years have heightened threats to privacy. Today the Internet accelerates the trend toward increased information collection and facilitates unprecedented flows of personal information. Cellular telephones and other wireless communication technologies generate information about an individual's location and movements in a manner not possible until now. Electronic communication systems generate vast quantities of transactional data that can be readily collected and analyzed. And law enforcement agencies, particularly at the federal level, place increasing emphasis on electronic surveillance.

Confronted by these challenges, there are still grounds for optimism. While dangers to privacy capture our attention, they sometimes lead us to understate the unprecedented gains in privacy protection that have also been achieved over the last half of the twentieth century. In many cases the legal system has laid a foundation for privacy protection through court decisions, state and federal legislation, and self-regulation. For example:

- tapping personal telephone calls without a warrant was not considered unconstitutional until 1967;
- national security surveillance gained considerable oversight in the post-Watergate era; during the Vietnam era millions of citizens were watched by federal authorities;
- important privacy protections were provided for electronic communications in 1986; and
- although records have never been given constitutional protections, Congress has stepped in to protect privacy by passing legislation that includes the Fair Credit Reporting Act, the Privacy Act, and the Video Privacy Protection Act.

In many instances, users of new technologies have taken their privacy into their own hands. They have demanded and availed themselves of powerful new technologies to protect their privacy. And individuals have found—and used—the avenues afforded them by new communications media to make vocal their demands for privacy. New technologies and standards that enable users to protect their privacy are on the way.

These privacy gains can be augmented and many threats to privacy can be 5 overcome if citizens band together for reform and enlightened policy. The hope for progress, in sum, lies in the hands of engaged citizens who avail themselves of the legal, technological, and political opportunities to act in the marketplace and the political arena. Advocates, committed to reform, must communicate that promise to the public. To do otherwise risks convincing individuals that they are powerless in the face of the rise of digital technology and that their only choice in the era of information is to do nothing. Recent history, technological developments, and the action of an informed public make the case for something different: given the necessary legal and technological tools and a clear voice, citizens can demand and achieve good privacy protection. The answer to whether privacy can still be protected is an emphatic *yes*. What is critical in making privacy a reality in the twenty-first century is the conviction of citizens that privacy is possible.

What Do We Talk About When We Talk About Privacy?

In the United States, the concept of privacy has evolved since it was first articulated by Justice Brandeis in 1898. His definition of privacy—"The right to be let alone" (Brandeis and Warren, 1890)—has been influential for nearly a century. In the 1960s, 1970s, and 1980s, the proliferation of information technology (and concurrent developments in the law of reproductive and sexual liberties) prompted further and more sophisticated legal inquiry into the meaning of privacy. Justice Brandeis's vision of being "let alone" no longer suffices to define the concept of privacy in today's digital environment, where personal information can be transported and distributed around the world in seconds.

At the end of 2000, ideas about privacy are more complex, reflecting the rapid and remarkable advances in computing that have made possible both unprecedented monitoring and the unprecedented collection, storage, manipulation, and sharing of data.

Today, when we talk about privacy, we are often talking about personal autonomy as it relates to information about an individual. Privacy entails an individual's right to control the collection and use of his or her personal information, even after he or she discloses it to others. When individuals provide information to a doctor, a merchant, or a bank, they expect that those professionals or companies will collect the information they need to deliver a service and use it for that sole purpose. Individuals expect that they have the right to object to any further use. Implementation of principles of fair information practices—notice, choice, access, security, and enforcement—is key to preserving this autonomy by ensuring that an individual's privacy interests in his or her personal information are protected.[1]

Privacy today also refers to protection from government surveillance. The Fourth Amendment, originally intended to protect citizens from physical searches and seizures, establishes an expectation of privacy in communications as well. New technologies that enhance the ability of law enforcement to monitor communications and compile an array of information about an individual test the limits of Fourth Amendment protections and require that we revisit and redefine our established ideas about this constitutional protection.

Threats to Privacy

Advances in communications technologies over the last half century significantly challenge individual privacy. Deployment of rapid and powerful computing technologies has vastly enhanced the ability to collect, store, link, and share personal information. This ability to manipulate information has played a critical role in reshaping the American economy, making it possible to predict consumer demand, manage inventories, serve individual consumer requirements, and tailor marketing techniques. But to do this successfully, businesses require and use information about individuals, which means that the demand for personal information, and business efforts to acquire it from customers, constantly increase.

Undoubtedly, the Internet has made this kind of data collection and analysis easier and more efficient. Rather than rely on secondary sources of consumer information, or engage in cumbersome telephone and mail-in information collection practices, companies can collect data online, through registration and as a transaction is carried out. Technologies such as "cookies," written directly onto a user's hard drive, enable websites to collect information about online activities and store it for future use. Using cookies, companies can track a consumer's online activities, creating a wealth of behavioral and preference information. This information can be collected over multiple websites, potentially creating a rich dossier about consumers, including their preferences and their online behavior.

Cellular networks generate data by collecting information about the cell site and location of the person making or receiving a call. Location information may be captured when the phone is merely on—that is, even if it is not handling a call. Both government and the private sector are interested in this location information. While the government seeks to build added surveillance features into the network and ensure that it can access the increasingly detailed data the network captures, the private sector is using this new information to provide emergency "911" services and is considering its potential for advertising.

Enhancements to law enforcement surveillance capabilities also raise serious privacy concerns. Wireless services provide phones that are readily tapped at central switches. Wireless phone location information generated when a person makes or receives a call can be obtained by law enforcement by subpoena or court order. Email messages are in some respects easier to intercept than regular mail. Technology has freed law enforcement intercepts from the constraints of geography, allowing intercepted communications to be transported hundreds or thousands of miles to a monitoring facility. And computer analysis allows agencies to review vast amounts of information about personal communications patterns far more easily.

A Look at History

Although threats to privacy have loomed large in recent decades, advances in privacy have also been significant. If, when we talk about privacy, we mean personal autonomy and protection against unwarranted government surveillance, recent history gives us reason to be hopeful about the future of privacy.

Limits on Electronic Surveillance

In the landmark *Berger v. New York* (1967) and *Katz v. United States* (1967) 15 cases, the Supreme Court ruled that electronic surveillance constituted search and seizure and was covered by the privacy protections of the Fourth Amendment. In Berger, the court condemned lengthy, continuous, or indiscriminate electronic surveillance,[2] but in Katz, the court indicated that a short surveillance, narrowly focused on interception of a few conversations, was constitutionally acceptable if approved by a judge in advance and based on a special showing of need. Congress responded to these rulings by regulating wiretapping, establishing a system of protections intended to compensate for the intrusive aspects of electronic surveillance. According to the Senate report, the legislation had "as its dual purpose (1) protecting the privacy of wire and oral communications, and (2) delineating on a uniform basis the circumstances and conditions under which the interception of wire and oral communications may be authorized" (U.S. Senate, 1968: 66).

In 1972, the government took first steps to address the collection and storage of information through computer technologies. Elliot L. Richardson, secretary of the Department of Health Education and Welfare, appointed an Advisory Committee on Automated Personal Data Systems to explore the impact of computerized record keeping on individuals. In the committee's report, published a year later, the advisory committee proposed a code of fair information practices. These principles form the basis of the Privacy Act of 1974, a response to privacy concerns raised by Watergate-era abuses that addressed collection of information by the federal government. Creating the principles of fair reformation practices proved to be seminal work; they have formed the basis for all subsequent codes and laws related to information collection at the state and federal level and in international agreements and treaties.

Congress acted to regulate wiretapping in national security cases in 1978 through another statute, the Foreign Intelligence Surveillance Act (FISA). In 1986 Congress addressed the challenges to privacy presented by the emergence of wireless services and the digital era with the adoption of the Electronic Communications Privacy Act (ECPA). ECPA addressed wireless voice communications and electronic communications of a nonvoice nature, such as email or other computer-to-computer transmissions. ECPA was intended to reestablish the balance between privacy and law enforcement, which had been tipped by the development of communications and computer technology and changes in the structure of the communications industry.

Legislative Advances in Information Privacy

While gains in privacy protection in the 1970s focused on limiting government surveillance, the rapid advances in computing and in Internet communications and commerce have turned the focus toward information privacy. In the late 1990s, individuals achieved new gains in the privacy of personal information. More work toward legislative protection remains to be done.

Medical Information. In the early 1990s society witnessed tremendous changes in both the collection and the use of health information. The transition from fee-for-service health care to managed care led to demand for unprecedented depth and breadth of personal information. At the same time the environment for information began to move rapidly from paper forms to electronic media, giving organizations a greater ability to tie formerly distinct information together and send it easily through different sources. To address theses concerns, the Clinton administration issued new rules under the 1996 Health Insurance Portability and Accountability Act to protect the privacy of medical records. This set the first comprehensive federal standards for transactions that, until then, were regulated by a patchwork of state laws.

Children. Congress passed the Children's Online Privacy Protection Act (COPPA) to protect children's personal information from its collection and misuse by commercial websites.[3] COPPA, which went into effect on April 21, 2000, requires commercial websites and other online services directed at children 12 and under, or that collect information regarding users' ages, to provide parents with notice of their information practices and obtain parental consent prior to the collection of personal information from children.

Consumer Information. The late 1990s brought the first steps toward protection of information collected from consumers online. Efforts on the part of government and business to require that companies doing business online comply with fair information practices represent an unprecedented step toward empowering consumers to protect the privacy of their personal information. In the past, information collected from consumers online or offline was not subject to fair information practices—consumers received no notice about a company's information policy, were afforded no choice about how the information might be used, and had no recourse when the privacy of their information was not respected. Importantly, consumers had no avenue for redress when information about them had been used improperly. The advent of the Internet brought a new focus on information collection practices and new self-regulatory oversight.

As the debate continues about protecting consumer information, growing effort is being directed toward baseline legislation requiring companies to comply with fair information practices and to submit to a dispute resolution process. For the first time, we are on the way to investing individuals with rights in their information and with an avenue of recourse for privacy violations.

The Promise of Technological Tools for Privacy

Progress in law is only one area in which privacy has been enhanced in the last century. Applications of technology that limit the collection of transactional information that can be tied to individuals have proliferated, giving individuals tools to protect their own privacy. From anonymous mailers and web browsers that allow individuals to interact anonymously to encryption programs that protect email messages as they pass through the network, individuals can harness the technology to promote their privacy.

Some tools developed to protect privacy exploit the decentralized and open nature of the Internet. These tools may limit the disclosure of information likely to reveal identity, or decouple this identity from other information. Others create cashlike payment mechanisms that provide anonymity to individual users, vastly reducing the need to collect and reveal identity information.

Encryption. Encryption tools provide an easy and inexpensive way for a 25
sender to protect information by encoding information so that only a recipient with the proper key can decode it.

Encryption is particularly important because of the inherent difficulties of securing the new digital media. The open decentralized architecture that is the Internet's greatest strength also makes it hard to secure. Internet communications often travel "in the clear" over many different computers in an unpredictable path, leaving them open for interception. An email message from Washington to Geneva might pass through New York one day or Nairobi the next—making it susceptible to interception in any country where lax privacy standards leave it unprotected. Encryption provides one of the only ways for computer users to guarantee that their sensitive data remains secure regardless of what network—or what country—it might pass through.

The recent relaxation of export laws in the United States should ensure that stronger encryption technologies will be built into commercial products. As this begins to occur, it will be important to educate consumers on how they can protect themselves using these tools.

The Platform for Privacy Preferences. Developed by the World Wide Web Consortium, the Platform for Privacy Preferences (P3P) is emerging as an industry standard that provides a simple, automated way for users to gain more control over the use of personal information on websites they visit. P3P-enabled websites make information about a site's privacy policies available in a standard, machine-readable format. The P3P standard is designed to automatically communicate to users a website's stated privacy policies and how they compare with the user's own policy preferences. Users are then able to make choices about whether to visit a website on the basis of the site's privacy policy.

P3P does not set minimum standards for privacy, nor can it monitor whether sites adhere to their own stated procedures. However, P3P technologies give control to web users who want to decide whether and under what circumstances to disclose personal information.

The Voice of Empowered Individuals

Equally important to the strides in privacy is the voice of individuals. Using email, websites, listservers, and newsgroups, individuals connected to the Internet are able to quickly respond to perceived threats to privacy. Individuals protested when Internet advertising company DoubleClick's plan to link personally identifiable information collected offline with that collected online was revealed. Negative media coverage, coupled with plummeting stock prices, forced DoubleClick to pull back from its plan. Similarly, when Intel released its Pentium III microprocessor with technology that facilitates the tracking of individuals across the World Wide Web, outcry in the Internet community prompted Intel not only to install a software patch that disabled the technology but also to discontinue its installation in the next model, Pentium IV. Clearly the Internet provides users with a wide forum for discussion and a powerful platform from which to spread their message. Through the Internet and other media, the active vigilance of individuals can and does force the government and the private sector to reckon with a growing and vocal privacy constituency.

Conclusion

Recent history has presented enormous threats to privacy, but the public has also made significant gains in privacy protection through legislation, technological tools, and action in the marketplace and the political arena. Privacy is a work in progress, and more work remains to be done. In particular, baseline legislation to address the collection of consumer data is a critical resource that would assure individuals consistent application of principles of fair information practices and an effective redress mechanism. Industry must continue to develop and refine privacy-enhancing software so that they keep pace with new business models and new technologies. In the debate about privacy, individuals must continue to use the Internet and new communications technologies to make their views clearly heard and understood.

Is privacy something we can reasonably hope for in the twenty-first century? If recent history is any indicator, it is. But whether or not we achieve the kind of privacy we want ultimately depends on whether citizens are willing to organize and act as they have in the past. That will happen only if the public believes privacy is possible.

Equally important is the newfound voice of individuals. Through the use of email, websites, listservers, and newsgroups, individuals on the Internet can quickly respond to perceived threats to privacy. Whether it is a proposal before the Federal Reserve Board requiring banks to "Know Your Customers," or the release of a product like Intel's Pentium III that could facilitate the tracking of individuals across the World Wide Web, Internet users have a forum for discussion, and a platform from which to spread their message. This active vigilance can and does force the government and the private sector to contend with a growing and vocal privacy constituency.

Notes

1. Under principles of fair information practice, an individual must first receive adequate notice about what information is being collected about him and how it is to be used. Second, the individual must be able to make choices about the use of information collected about him. Third, the individual must be allowed reasonable access to information maintained about her. Fourth, information about an individual must be secured, so that its accuracy and integrity is maintained. Finally, collectors of information must be subject to an enforcement mechanism that assures their compliance with fair information practices and provides individuals with a means of recourse when their rights in their data have not been respected.
2. See *Berger v. New York* 388 U.S. 59 (1967); *Katz v. United States,* 389 U.S. 354–59 (1967)
3. The Federal Trade Commission promulgated the Children's Online Privacy Protection Rule in 1998.

References

Brandeis, Louis D. and Samuel D. Warren. "The Right to Privacy." *Harvard Law Review* 4 (1890).

U.S. Senate. *Omnibus Crime Control and Safe Streets Act.* Rept. No. 90-1097 (1968).

Exploring the Message

1. How many definitions of privacy are included in the article? What are they?
2. What threats to privacy are discussed?

3. How much of the information in this article was familiar to you? What was new or even surprising to you?

4. How might the events of 9/11 and its aftermath have changed Berman and Bruening's message?

5. After reading this article, how would you answer the question "Is privacy still possible in the twenty-first century?" Which of Berman and Bruening's points persuaded you to take that position?

Investigating the Discourse Community

1. What aspects of the authors' discourse community are revealed in paragraph 5? For example, what assumptions do they make about the attitudes and behaviors of their readers? How do they propose that social problems should be solved? Locate two or three other places in the article where you see further evidence of these traits and assumptions.

2. How does the article help to explain why these writers decided to use their legal training to pursue careers with the Center for Democracy and Technology? Visit the Center's Web site to learn more about its purpose and activities: www.cdt.org.

Understanding the Genre

1. Define Berman and Bruening's writing situation.

2. How would you describe the writers' collaborative persona? How is it reflected in the article's style, especially the point of view, word choice, and tone? Collect examples from the essay to support your views.

3. How does this use of the research medium compare to the genres you were assigned in your social science classes—sociology and political science, for example? Consider how the essay is organized and designed, as well as how the authors use evidence to present their argument. For additional examples of the genre, visit the *Social Research* Web site: www.socres.org.

Writing Activity

In paragraph 3 of "Is Privacy Still Possible in the Twenty-First Century?" the authors give four examples of policies and laws enacted to protect individuals from technological intrusion. Pick two of the policies or laws, and use

the Internet or library to research their current status, especially in light of
the Patriot Act. Use your research, your responses to the article, and your
personal experiences to write a brief article for your classmates in which
you suggest a change in the assumptions, purpose, or message of the original article.

Technology as Security
Declan McCullagh

*The chief political correspondent for CNET's News.com, Declan McCullagh lives and works
in Washington, D.C. He has written for numerous publications, including* The New Re-
public *and the* Wall Street Journal, *and has appeared on National Public Radio, ABC's
"Good Morning, America," the NBC evening news, Court TV, and CNN. In 1994 McCullagh founded* Politech, *an electronic mailing list that looks broadly at politics and technology
(www.politechbot.com). He is also an adjunct faculty member at the law school of Case Western Reserve University.*

The following article, which appeared in the Harvard Journal of Law & Public Policy, *is a revised version of remarks McCullagh made at the Federalist Society Student Symposium on "Is Technology Changing the Law?" at Boalt Hall School of Law, March 9–10,
2001.*

I. Introduction

It has become fashionable to fret about whether developments in technology
have outpaced the law. To continue the metaphor, athletic Internet entrepreneurs
are racing against stately, but plodding, courts and legislatures. The University
of Michigan Law School has sponsored a symposium subtitled "Is Technology
Outpacing the Law?"[1] Former Attorney General Janet Reno claimed in June 2000
that the Microsoft antitrust case proved to be a "strong reaffirmation" of antitrust law's ability to keep up with technology.[2] A commentator has described
the 1998 Digital Millennium Copyright Act as "only about keeping up with
technology."[3]

---

[1]Audio tape: Symposium, *Challenging Legal Paradigms: Is Technology Outpacing the Law?*, held by Michigan Telecommunications & Technology Law Review (Mar. 12–13, 1999), *available at*
http://www.mttlr.org/ html/body_audio_archive.html.

[2]Declan McCullagh & Nicholas Morehead, *Reno Says: Beware Technology*, WIRED NEWS (June 15, 2000),
at http://www.wired.com/news/politics/0,1283, 37016,00.html.

[3]Robert Lemos, *Copyright Bill Unites Foes*, ZDNET NEWS (August 3, 1998), *at* http://www.zdnet.com/
zdnn/stories/news/0,4586,2124816,00.html.

But truthfully, technology has begun to supplant law, and at an accelerated pace.[4] Contrary to conventional wisdom, this may be a welcome and inevitable development. Instead of protecting rights such as privacy, free speech, and copyright through legal means, more people are turning to technological protection methods. To guarantee liberty, mechanisms such as public key encryption and anonymity-providing "dc-nets"[5] rely on the equations of mathematics and not the whims of courts and legislatures.

Congress may, for instance, allow police to wiretap more easily or reduce the requirements for warrants. Judges may rule works like James Joyce's *Ulysses* to be obscene, then reverse positions a generation later.[6] But the laws of mathematics do not vary based on the whims of government officials or shifts in public opinion.

This view is somewhat controversial. Freedom fighters using encryption to conceal their communications from Burma's brutal military junta may applaud technology's rule, but the FBI warns that the widespread use of encryption allows terrorists, drug smugglers, and child pornographers to evade law enforcement.[7] Anonymous publishing tools may cheer whistleblowers, yet provide little legal recourse when malicious lies are spread anonymously. Although copyright protection mechanisms may hinder piracy and reduce costs to consumers, librarians and civil libertarians argue that fair use rights will be lost in the process.[8]

A loosely organized group of essayists, activists, and programmers called the "cypherpunks" has been a fierce champion of a technology-over-law approach. Using a mailing list[9] and a smattering of physical meetings around the globe, they have developed technological tools to protect privacy and free expression in areas where they feel the law does not.[10] A 1988 essay written by "cypherpunks" co-founder Tim May explains it well:

> Computer technology is on the verge of providing the ability for individuals and groups to communicate and interact with each other in a totally anonymous manner. These developments will alter completely the nature of government regula-

---

[4]This article deals primarily with how advances in technology affect the ability of individuals to protect their rights. It does not, for instance, cover how advances in technology allow greater police surveillance.

[5]*See* David Chaum, *The Dining Cryptographers Problem: Unconditional Sender and Recipient Untraceability,* 1 J. CRYPTOLOGY 1, 65 (1988) (describing a mathematical technique called a "dc-net" that allows participants to send and receive messages anonymously over a network).

[6]See generally Robert Spoo, *Copyright Protectionism and Its Discontents: The Case of James Joyce's* Ulysses *in America,* 108 YALE L.J. 633 (1998).

[7]John Hanchette, *Looking at Growing Threats to Personal Privacy,* Gannett News Service, Aug. 30, 1999, LEXIS, Nexis Library, News Group File.

[8]*See* Neil Munro & Drew Clark, *Digital Dilemma,* NAT'L JOURNAL, July 28, 2001, at 2386 (discussing the balancing involved in "protect[ing] copyrighted property . . . and at the same time preserv[ing] such fundamental rights as freedom of speech and of the press").

[9]*See* Cypherpunks HyperArchive, *at* http://www.inet-one.com/cypherpunks (last visited Dec. 29, 2001).

[10]*See* David Honigmann, *Books: Hot Secrets of Cyberati: US Government Versus the 'Cypherpunks': David Honigmann Reports on a Long Running Battle,* FIN. TIMES (London), Feb. 3, 2001, at 4.

tion, the ability to tax and control economic interactions, the ability to keep information secret, and will even alter the nature of trust and reputation.[11]

As it turns out, May's prediction was premature. Technology has not forced governments to rethink their tax systems, and government regulation has not changed dramatically in the last ten years. But, May was one of the first to point out the powerful possibilities of protecting rights through technologies such as encryption and anonymity.[12]

II. Copyright

Consider copy protection technology. Content owners, distributors, and publishers fret about how relatively easy online distribution methods will encourage copyright infringement and reduce sales.[13] They have reason to worry. As bandwidth increases and distribution technology improves, the cost of reproducing intellectual property could begin to edge toward zero. Everyone likes getting something for free, and piracy has always nibbled at the edges of publishers' and distributors' profits. But it is far easier and cheaper to copy an MP3 file than to photocopy a Tom Clancy novel, and digital copies—unlike their analog counterparts—do not diminish in value. Every digital copy has the same quality, which means that, if taken to its logical conclusion, widespread piracy will destroy the incentives to create valuable content.

The law, standing alone, has not been able to protect copyrighted works effectively. Teenage pirates flout legal restrictions, secure in the knowledge that there are too many judgment-proof youth to fight with a civil suit. In the United States, trading copyrighted works is a felony under the No Electronic Theft Act of 1997.[14] But the prospect of becoming federal felons did not stop some 50 million Napster aficionados, whom the Justice Department has yet to force into compliance.[15] Overseas pirates are even less likely to be concerned about copyright laws, because foreign piracy laws are generally not as strict as those in the United States.

Just as tangible property holders rely on technology in the form of fences, locks, and safes to guard their property, copyright holders have started to do the same. Unhappy with the limited number of criminal prosecutions and recognizing the futility of suing millions of potential customers, companies like Adobe, Microsoft, and Verance are turning to technology instead of the law. They are

---

[11]Timothy C. May, *The Crypto Anarchist Manifesto*, at http://www.csua.berkeley.edu/cypherpunks/rants/.crypto-anarchy.html (Nov. 22, 1992).

[12]*See id.*

[13]*See* Munro & Clark, *supra* note 8, at 2386.

[14]17 U.S.C. § 506(a) (Supp. 1998). The law's criminal provisions apply to "[a]ny person who infringes a copyright willfully either . . . for purposes of commercial advantage or private financial gain" or if the value reaches a $1,000 threshold. *Id.* The Act defines financial gain as "receipt, or expectation of receipt, of anything of value, including the receipt of other copyrighted works." *Id.* at § 101.

[15]Neil Strauss, *Foraging for Music in the Digital Jungle*, N.Y. TIMES, Aug. 20, 2001, at E1.

testing copy-protection systems and watermarking methods that may become widely used as technological protection schemes for copyrighted works.[16] It is too early to tell whether they will be successful, which technologies will become standards, what kinds of licenses will emerge as defaults, and whether consumers will tolerate strong copy protection—but the trend is clearly moving towards trusting technology more and the law less.

Unfortunately for copyright holders, another trend is equally apparent: using technology to circumvent copy protection schemes. Hackers who want to play DVDs on a Linux computer for which there is no licensed player, those who want to view Adobe's eBooks on a laptop for which they do not have a license, and those who simply plan to pirate copyrighted material have made a sport of tunneling through content owners' technological schemes. Under the Digital Millennium Copyright Act ("DMCA"), this is a violation of federal law.[17] The DMCA, however, has had scant effect. Eight movie studios sued *2600 Magazine* under the statute to remove a copy of DeCSS, a DVD-descrambling program, from its website.[18] The magazine complied by deleting DeCSS—and replacing it with the web address of where it could be found. A Google search in August 2001 reported 82,700 matches for DeCSS, many of them copies of the program the movie studios would like to erase from the Internet.[19] These facts reveal the other side of technology's coin. If content owners hope to rely on technological protection mechanisms, they had better hope such schemes actually work.

III. Privacy

In the United States, privacy rights depend on an intricate patchwork of state statutes, caselaw, and federal statutes. Federal privacy law has taken a sector-by-sector approach, with data collection and use regulations aimed at activities like banking, video rental, electronic surveillance, and websites that target minors.[20] Therefore, the effective degree of privacy that Americans enjoy is directly related to the current views of legislatures, judges, and bureaucrats. It is reasonable to say that abrupt changes are part of a democratic process, but that argument seemed more persuasive when there was little practical alternative. Now, with the availability of encryption technology online, technology that has existed in theory for the last two decades is slowly becoming more widely deployed. To use

---

[16]*See* Munro & Clark, *supra* note 8, at 2387–91.

[17]*See* Digital Millennium Copyright Act, 17 U.S.C. § § 101, 112, 114, 512, 1201, 1203, at § 1201(a) (Supp. 2000) ("No person shall circumvent a technological measure that effectively controls access to a work protected under this title.").

[18]Declan McCullagh, *Digital Copyright Law on Trial*, WIRED NEWS (Jan. 18, 2000), *at* http://www.wired.com/news/politics/o,l283, 33716,00.html.

[19]*See id.*

[20]*See, e.g.,* Video Privacy Protection Act of 1988, 18 U.S.C. § 2710 (1994); 47 U.S.C. § 551 (1994) (concerning privacy of cable television subscriber information); Children's Online Privacy Protection Act of 1998, 15 US.C. § § 6501–6506 (Supp. 1999).

one example, e-mail encryption that had been slow to gain widespread acceptance because of its originally cumbersome technology is available at Hushmail.com through a simple web interface.[21] Hushmail.com automatically scrambles messages exchanged between its users; all a customer must remember is a pass-phrase. This mechanism guards the privacy of e-mail in transmission and storage. A litigant or prosecutor hoping to gain access to stored Hushmail.com messages via subpoena will find that she needs a pass-phrase to decrypt them. In other words, users can protect their privacy, not through law, but through the self-help methods of technology. . . .

IV. Trust

These developments would be merely interesting but practically inconsequential if we could trust everyone with access to our personal information. But even websites with stellar privacy policies are vulnerable to hackers. For instance, the Code Red worm that infested the Internet in July 2001 revealed a number of vulnerable Microsoft web servers.[22]

Although reasonably strict rules govern how police may conduct wiretaps, the system still lacks effective oversight. In 1998, for example, the Los Angeles Police Department was found to have used hundreds of illegal wiretaps that captured tens of thousands of conversations.[23] The Los Angeles County Public Defender even accused the district attorney's office of covering up police lawlessness.[24]

Although most police are honorable professionals, history tell us it is risky to assume that all are. The FBI, the military, and other law enforcement organizations have ignored the law and spied on Americans illegally on past occasions. The FBI, for example, admitted in 1988 that Justice William O. Douglas had been the target of wiretaps.[25] Agents also overheard conversions of Justices Earl Warren, Abe Fortas, and Potter Stewart.[26]

Opening mail may be an imprecise form of surveillance, but that did not stop   15
the FBI and CIA from surreptitiously reading hundreds of thousands of letters

---

[21]*See* Declan McCullagh, *Shhhh: Hushmail Has Big Plans*, WIRED NEWS (March 6, 2000), *at* http://www.wired.com/news/business/0,1367,34610,00. html.

[22]*See* John Schwartz, *Return of Computer "Worm" Feared Today*, N.Y. TIMES, July 31, 2001, at C2.

[23]*See* Kevin Poulsen, *Wiretapping Abuses Alarm EFF, EPIC*, ZDNET NEWS (October 21, 1999), *at* http//www.zdnet.com/zdnn/stories/news/0,4586,2378 149,00.html.

[24]*See* Jennifer C. Granick, *Illegal Wiretapping: Copper Wiring*, WIRED NEWS (June 9, 1998), *at* http://www.wired.com/wired/archive/6.09/netizen.html?pg=4. The Public Defender's Office has placed a wealth of court documents related to the Wiretapping Investigation, Research, Education, and Defense (W.I.R.E.D) Project on its website, at http://pd.co.la.ca.us/index.htm (last visited Dec. 29, 2001).

[25]*See* Curt Gentry, *J. Edgar Hoover: The Man and the Secrets* 630–31 (1991). In 1970, J. Edgar Hoover sent H. R. Haldeman a detailed report on an intercepted conversation of Justice Douglas's concerning the impeachment of another justice. *See id.*

[26]*See id.*

from 1940 to 1973.[27] Government employees (who took special classes to learn this skill) would stealthily open the envelope and photograph whatever was inside. Included in the agency's dragnet were three United States senators, a congressman, a presidential candidate, and many business and civil rights leaders. Although obstructing the delivery of the mail is a violation of federal law punishable by fine or six months in jail,[28] not one agent appears to have been prosecuted.

V. Anonymous Publishing

Perhaps the most far-reaching impact of technological self-help will be in the area of free speech. Federal courts have generally awarded greater First Amendment protection to political speech, as compared to other forms of expression.[29] Anonymous publishing offers an alternative medium of expression for those whose speech has been regulated in more traditional settings.

At the present time, due to costs and legal barriers, anonymous publishing tools are relatively undeveloped when compared to other privacy technologies. One reason for this difference is that other privacy technologies rely on a one-to-one communications channel, which consumes relatively small amounts of bandwidth and lasts only during the duration of the exchange. Publishing is a more costly venture. Although many people seem to appreciate a privacy-protected Internet experience, fewer are interested in having their thoughts appear anonymously. Since a compensation system has not developed that maintains anonymity, third parties have little incentive to distribute anonymous materials. These impediments are one reason for the slow growth of anonymous publishing.

Anonymous publishing also has more legal barriers than privacy-enhanced web browsing. It is generally legal to download libelous, obscene, or copyright-infringing material but not permissible to distribute it.[30] Nonetheless, controversial material is likely to flood into a system that permits anonymous publishing. Such material might include trade secrets, copyrighted works, libelous material, and child pornography—collections that society has deemed illegal to distribute and, in the case of child pornography, even possess.

---

[27]*See* S. Rep. No. 94-755, at 561 (1976).

[28]*See* 18 U.S.C. § 1701 (1994).

[29]*Compare, e.g.,* Central Hudson v. Public Service Comm'n of NY, 447 U.S. 557, 561–66 (1980) (holding that commercial speech regulation is subject to an intermediate standard of scrutiny where the state must demonstrate a *substantial* government interest in a way that is *reasonably tailored* to achieve that objective), *with* Boos v. Barry, 485 U.S. 312 (1988) (holding that political, content-based speech regulation is subject to strict scrutiny where the state must demonstrate that its statute was *narrowly tailored* to a *compelling* state interest).

[30]*See, e.g.,* 18 U.S.C. § 1465 (1994 & Supp. 1997) (outlawing the *transportation of* obscene matters for sale or distribution); Mary Rasenberger & M. Lorrane Ford, *Untangling the Web of Rights to Film and Video,* N.Y. L. J. Sept. 18, 2000 at s3.

The flip side is that anonymous publishing allows social minorities to express politically unpopular views without incurring retribution. Radicals might circumvent oppressive laws and social constraints with ease, provided the technology works as planned.[31] This technology may provide an opportunity for revolutionaries to express their opposition to repressive regimes, for whistleblowers to reveal corporate and government wrongdoing, and for investigative journalists to take risks without worrying about ruinous libel suits. Because technology does not differentiate between a socially appropriate byte series and one that is deemed illegal, it probably will be difficult for legislators and courts to respond in an effective way.

Currently the most prominent example of an anonymous publishing technology is Freenet.[32] Unlike Napster, Freenet does not include a central directory that opponents can sue to shut down. Freenet's webpage boasts that it "allows information to be published and read without fear of censorship, because individual documents cannot be traced to their source or even to where they are physically stored."[33]

"The fundamental underlying principle behind Freenet is that a third person should not be able to prevent two other people from communicating," says Freenet inventor Ian Clarke.[34] "If that were actually the case today, we would be living in a better world."[35] This consensual-communication concept would challenge copyright law and invalidate other legal prohibitions such as those against publishing trade secrets, libelous or slanderous material, obscenity, child pornography, and military secrets. A 21st-century Pentagon Papers' publisher would not need the Supreme Court's permission to go ahead. This would push the experience of free speech to new limits. Even during the 1970's, an era of expansive First Amendment jurisprudence, Justice William Brennan indicated that United States law could place limits on free speech. "No one would question but that a government might prevent actual obstruction to its recruiting service or the publication of the sailing dates of transports or the number and location of troops."[36]

If Freenet succeeds, technology will have outpaced the law in dramatic fashion. Clarke described his philosophy in this way:

> I see it as a little bit of what it's like in mathematics. . . . If you have an axiom that
> you know to be true and you discover other hypotheses that conflict with that

---

[31]For example, anonymous publication may have allowed novelist Henry Miller to publish THE TROPIC OF CANCER (Grove Press 1961) and THE TROPIC OF CAPRICORN (Grove Press 1961) without worrying about obscenity accusations, which delayed publication of the books in the United States until over 20 years after their publication in Europe.

[32]Freenet advertises itself as a single worldwide information store that stores, caches, and distributes the information based on demand. *See* The Free Network Project, *The Free Network Project: Liberty Through Technology*, at http://freenet.sourceforge.net (last visited Dec. 29, 2001).

[33]The Free Network Project, *Frequently Asked Questions about Freenet*, at http://freenetproject.org/cgi-bin/twiki/view/Main/FAQ (last visited Dec. 29, 2001).

[34]Telephone Interview with Ian Clarke, Inventor of Freenet (Dec. 15, 2000).

[35]*Id.*

[36]New York Times Co. v. United States, 403 U.S. 713, 726 (1971) (Brennan, J., concurring) (citing Near v. Minnesota *ex rel.* Olson, 283 U.S. 697, 716 (1931)).

20

axiom, you know they're false. It may take you a while to realize why they are false, but you nevertheless know that they are. My axiom is that if two people want to communicate, a third person should not be able to stop them.[37]

He has chosen not to rely on Supreme Court justices who may retire, bow to political pressures, or change their views over time to protect free speech rights. Instead, Clarke and the other open-source software developers who are working with him have chosen to rely on technology. . . .

Another implication of anonymous publishing is that, by eliminating government restrictions, technology makes it more difficult to control information, keep secrets, and force people to delete data. For example, in the future an anonymous publisher might be able to sell credit reports containing information older than the seven-year limit established by the Fair Credit Reporting Act.[38] Disgruntled employees might be able to sell trade secrets anonymously. Even national secrets could be exposed with this publishing mechanism. If anonymous technologies successfully defy legal attempts to shut them down, those with secrets to protect will have to find ways outside of the legal system to shield information from disclosure.

VI. Digital Currencies

The biggest obstacle to these emerging technological marketplace networks is the fact that a payment system with comparable anonymity has not been created. Although true digital cash, currency that is as anonymous, as privacy-protected, and as cheap as the humble greenback, is lauded and adored by pundits and technologists, markets stubbornly fail to adopt it. One reason that the market might be lagging is that the important patent holders have experienced financial difficulties while trying to get started. . . .

In addition to the hurdles of marketing and licensing, assuming that there are no real technical problems, looming regulatory obstacles could thwart the deployment of truly anonymous digital cash. Given the threat that anonymous marketplaces pose to much existing government regulation, it should be no surprise that federal agencies have been closely monitoring developments. The Treasury Department has taken the view that digital cash could be used for tax evasion. "Problems could arise from the increasing sophistication of Internet encryption codes that are established for valid reasons of commercial secrecy but can also be used to conceal relevant tax details from tax administrations," former Treasury Secretary Lawrence Summers said in July 2000.[39] ECash CEO John Filby has stressed that "everything that we've done so far has been in consultation with the regulatory authorities." He asserts that he probably only would license the com-

---

[37]Telephone Interview with Ian Clarke, *supra* note 34.

[38]*See* 15 U.S.C. § § 1681(c) (1994).

[39]Declan McCullagh, *Is Encryption Tax-Protective?*, WIRED NEWS (July 15, 2000), *at* http://www.wired.com/news/politics/0,1283,37573,00.html.

pany's patents in a way that preserved the ability to trace for law enforcement purposes.[40]

VII. Law and Technology

Filby's comments show that technology rarely outpaces the law overnight. Instead of being a footrace, the interaction between the law and technology is a ballet with its own nuances, rhythms, and delicate steps. At times, technology advances to evade the law. For example, legal restrictions on publishing spurred the development of Freenet. Developments such as content protection schemes prompt Congress to enact laws such as the Digital Millennium Copyright Act[41] that seek to make bypassing such technology a federal crime. The invention of the Internet, and the markets spawned by it, led Congress to limit sexual content with the Communications Decency Act[42] and regulate it with the Children's Online Privacy Protection Act.[43]

Moreover, advances in technology may encourage lawmakers to repeal laws that become more easily circumvented. For example, Phil Zimmermann created his Pretty Good Privacy encryption program as a response to a bill pending in Congress to ban encryption that would prevent government surveillance. Nearly a decade later, the Clinton Administration relaxed encryption regulations because Pretty Good Privacy and other technologies had become so commonplace.[44]

Larry Lessig of Stanford University Law School has coined the phrase "code is law." Says Lessig: "The architectures of cyberspace are as important as the law in defining and defeating the liberties of the Net. Activists concerned with defending liberty, privacy or access must watch the code coming from the Valley, West Coast Code, as much as the code coming from Congress, East Coast Code."[45] But Lessig's "West Coast Code" does not have the same power of compulsion that the law does. By blurring the boundary between the two, Lessig comes close to equating the government's power to arrest, imprison, and execute a person with a company's right to sell its eBooks in copy-protected form. The difference is that a company has no power to compel the consumer to buy its product. If it makes poor choices and alienates consumers, the market will punish it severely.

As the interaction between law and technology intensifies, there will be increased legal attention paid to socially disruptive technologies in the form of civil

---

[40]Declan McCullagh, *Digging Those Digicash Blues*, WIRED NEWS (June 14, 2001), *at* http://www.wired.com/news/ebiz/0,1272,44507,00.html.

[41]*See* 17 U.S.C. § § 101, 112, 114, 512, 1201, 1203 (Supp. 2000).

[42]*See* Telecommunications Act of 1996, 47 U.S.C. § 223 (Supp. 1997). The Act's "indecent transmission" and "patently offensive display" provisions were struck down by *Reno v. ACLU,* 521 U.S. 844 (1997).

[43]*See* Children's Online Protection Act of 1998, 15 U.S.C. § § 6501-06 (Supp. 1999).

[44]*See Congressman Bob Goodlatte and Zoe Lofgren Become First to Export PGP Encryption under New Rules,* PR NEWSWIRE, Jan. 20, 2000.

[45]Larry Lessig, *The Code Is the Law,* INDUSTRY STANDARD (April 9, 1999), *at* http://www.thestandard.com/article/0,1902,4165,00.html.

suits and perhaps even criminal investigations. Content owners have strong financial incentives to sue anonymous publishing systems, such as Freenet and MojoNation, that illegally distribute copyrighted material. Prosecutors have strong political incentives to imprison operators of re-mailers or servers that are distributing illicit material. No government will want to permit anonymous digital cash if its tax system will be threatened.

The advantages that technology has are simple: it is cheap, it allows unpopular laws to be circumvented, and it is growing more powerful by the day. Without taking draconian steps such as banning encryption or monitoring all Internet traffic, there may be nothing governments can do to prevent the increasing challenge that technology presents to law. In this dance between "East Coast Code" and "West Coast Code," technology has already taken the lead, and the long-term trends are on its side. Let the best code win.

Exploring the Message

1. What is McCullagh's main thesis about law, technology, and privacy? Did you find his arguments persuasive? Which examples were the most convincing? What is controversial about the author's view of technology? Would Berman and Bruening agree with his proposals?
2. Why has it been so difficult for the law to protect copyrighted works effectively?
3. What does McCullagh mean by "technological self-help"? Why does he say it's a necessary means of protecting privacy?
4. What are the benefits and dangers of anonymous publishing? How does the exercise of free speech threaten the right to privacy in this area?
5. What does the phrase "code is law" mean? What are "East Coast Code" and "West Coast Code"? Why are they in conflict and which one is winning?

Investigating the Discourse Community

1. What opinion of the law, lawmakers, and law enforcers does McCullagh assume his audience will have? Does he share this opinion? How does he negotiate between his views and the ones he expects from his audience? Consult the Web sites for the Federalist Society (www.fed-soc.org) and the Harvard Journal of Law & Public Policy (www.law.harvard.edu/studorgs/jlpp/) to help you answer these questions.
2. What does the author's use of examples and quotations reveal about his professional background and experience? How does he establish his expertise in both law and technology?
3. Does McCullagh assume his audience has the same level of knowledge about technology as he does? Cite some examples to support your answer.

Understanding the Genre

1. How can you tell McCullagh is addressing lawyers and law students and not computer experts?
2. This article was originally given as a speech. What elements of spoken discourse are still evident in the written text? What features were probably added for publication in the *Harvard Journal of Law & Public Policy?*
3. How would you describe McCullagh's persona and tone? How do they fit with what you know about his background and his writing situation?

Writing Activity

What forms of "technological self-help" do you use to protect your rights? For instance, what protections do you have for your e-mail account or your computer files? Make a list of the ways you use technology to protect your privacy. Use the Internet to investigate the actual effectiveness of two or three of them. How effective are they? How could they be improved? Write up your findings in a report to share with your classmates. The Web site of the Electronic Privacy Information Center (EPIC) at www.epic.org might help you with this report, especially "EPIC'S Online Guide to Practical Privacy Tools" and "EPIC's Online Guide to Privacy Resources."

Balancing Security & Privacy in the Internet Age
Institute of Management & Administration

HRFocus, *the monthly newsletter from which this article is taken, targets a variety of business professionals: human resources officers, personnel directors, benefits and compensation managers, and vice-presidents for administration. Articles address policies and legislation related to "terminations, performance reviews, workplace policies, and standards." To handle this range of issues knowledgeably, the IOMA hires a writing staff with backgrounds in higher education, business, publishing, journalism, and law. "Balancing Security & Privacy in the Internet Age" appeared in August 2002.*

Of all the high-wire acts HR [Human Resources] must now perform, none is more perilous than balancing the company's need for safety with the employees' desire for privacy.

How can today's organizations protect their vital computer systems, their organizational information, and their legal standing without trampling workers' privacy rights in an age where increased dependence on the Internet invites vast opportunities for misuse and even abuse by employees?

Various approaches to the security/privacy conundrum were suggested at a session at the Society for Human Resource Management's recent annual conference in Philadelphia. Rodney Glover, a partner with the law firm Wiley Rein & Fielding LLP (Washington, D.C.), discussed how to use electronic monitoring to avoid employer liability for employee misuse of company technology and how to balance workplace privacy considerations with monitoring.

To set the scene, Glover offered the following statistics:

- More than 80% of major U.S. companies now monitor employee use of the Internet.
- Fifty-seven percent of U.S. companies use blocking software.
- Forty percent block access to some Internet sites.
- Sixty-seven percent have disciplined employees for Internet misuse, and 31% have discharged people for it.
- Employees spend an average of six hours a week at work surfing the Web for personal reasons.
- Since 1990, legal claims concerning privacy have increased 3,000%.
- Twenty percent of Fortune 500 companies now have a chief privacy officer.

Why Monitor?

There are four reasons to monitor how employees use the Internet at work:

1. Employers are liable for employee misuse of company-provided technology. If employees misuse technology that the company buys or leases and gives them to use, the employer can be held liable. Even worse: Employers are presumed to know how employees are using the technology they provide.

Proper monitoring makes employers aware of employee activities that could be "dangerous." The company can then stop them before they damage the computer system or compromise the company legally by, say, downloading pornography and circulating it through the office.

Monitoring can also help identify external threats such as viruses and hackers. (For more on these challenges, see the section, "Protecting Your Organization from External Threats.")

2. Employers need to protect trade secrets and avoid corporate defamation. Disgruntled workers or former workers have been known to post corporate trade secrets or defamatory information about employers and management on the Internet. Some courts treat such actions as protected speech under the First Amendment, which makes them hard to control.

Although there is little that HR professionals can do to prevent defamation, all employees should sign a non-disclosure agreement concerning corporate trade secrets. 10

3. Employers need to guard against discovery in litigation. Having an effective monitoring system will help discourage inappropriate internal communications, such as e-mail, that can be turned up in the course of investigating a lawsuit.

Employers should implement a document-destruction policy that complies with all applicable laws and includes e-mail.

Glover suggests that HR and employers counsel employees to use what he called the "mom test" concerning e-mail content—send no e-mail you wouldn't want your mother to see.

Monitoring and blocking the sending of materials—sort of a reverse firewall—can also help control the dissemination of certain types of information.

4. Employers need to ensure Internet use does not hurt productivity. Internet 15 misuse or abuse can affect both personnel and systems productivity, Glover said. For instance, 70% of all "hits" to pornography sites occur during work hours. Another frightening statistic: 11% of workers who earn $75,000 to $100,000 search for jobs online while at work.

Although companies can permit some personal use, monitoring to block access to certain sites is possible and advisable. Key: Employees must be informed of this fact.

Glover counseled employers to know their state laws, since courts have taken conflicting positions on whether such monitoring is an invasion of employees' "reasonable expectations" of privacy. In the cases to date, the central issue has been whether the monitoring was reasonable. Informing employees that the employer is monitoring Internet use has been a factor in some, but not all such lawsuits.

Other Issues

Glover cited other privacy- and security-related issues that HR should be aware of. These include:

- Negligent hiring. Information available on the Web can help employers perform background checks on potential hires. Here, too, the reasonableness question comes into play in court cases. Elements to consider are the historic behavior of an individual, what is a reasonable background check under the circumstances, and the limitations under the Fair Credit Reporting Act (if a third party conducts investigations).

  There can also be a legal duty to warn of past employee misconduct under certain circumstances, including public safety and financial issues such as stealing.

  Helpful: Set standard pre-hire background search procedures for your 20 business and maintain files on the results of your background searches.

- Hostile work environment and negligent retention. Employers have been sued on the grounds that they "knew or should have known" that defamatory or other information was downloaded and displayed by an employee on a company chat board. An Internet use policy that is broadcast to all and enforced can keep these issues from turning into lawsuits.
- HIPAA (Health Insurance Portability and Accountability Act of 1996). This legislation includes privacy requirements concerning medical information.
- Global privacy issues. European Union (E.U.) directives restrict information that can be sent to the U.S. about employees working in the E.U. This includes e-mail transmissions.
- Pending legislation. Although Glover thinks it's unlikely that any action will occur in this Congressional term, he suggests keeping track of these bills:
  -- Employer Monitoring Act (HR 4908, S. 2898).
  -- S. 19, S. 318, and HR 602, all of which deal with restricting employer genetic testing.

He also advised keeping an eye on state-level action.

Protecting the Company

To integrate their approach to security and privacy issues, companies should include HR, the legal department, information systems personnel, and senior management. These groups should work together to develop a privacy policy and a monitoring policy. Then:

- Disclose your policy to all employees at the time of hire or even before, and remind them periodically about the policy. Have employees sign written forms acknowledging that they have read and understood the policy.
- Explicitly state that technology is company property and is meant for business purposes. Include specifics on cell phones if your company reimburses workers for their use. Reason: Employers can be held liable if an employee has a car accident while talking on a phone the company pays for.
- Consider a statement banning downloads of large files of music and video—these challenge the system and slow your servers.
- State that there is no expectation of privacy created by permitting employees to use the Internet.
- Consider making a nondisclosure/privacy policy on trade secrets a part of the paperwork to be signed at the start of employment. Spell out which materials must be kept in the office. Consider software that gives "look only" privileges and restricts printing/copying abilities to certain users.
- Be sure that any document destruction policy, electronic or otherwise, is in full compliance with the law, since a range of statutes require document retention for set periods of time.

- Use your monitoring and computer use policy as an opportunity to reiterate your non-harassment and non-discrimination policies.
- Inform workers about the penalties for violating the Internet use policy— and make sure they are enforced. "The only thing worse than no policy," said Glover, "is having one that you don't enforce."

Protecting Your Organization from External Threats

Not only are your computer systems vulnerable to misuse by employees, they are also in danger from the outside world. Viruses, hackers, even a flood of spam can all do damage. HR should be aware of the risks and work with information systems (IS) staff and senior management to institute the appropriate defenses.

The following suggestions on how best to protect your company's systems from external abuses are adapted from a recent presentation by technology consultant Roman Kepczyk, president of InfoTech Partners North America, Inc. (Phoenix, Ariz.).

- Systems security. This refers to having the software, processes, procedures, and hardware in place to ensure that information resources are available only to authorized personnel. Security concerns include: access control, authentication, non-repudiation (is the sender really that person?), authorization, viruses, and hostile acts. Today's computer systems are under constant attack, mostly through the Internet, said Kepczyk. In fact, the number of security vulnerabilities at organizations doubled between 2000 and 2001. Other troublesome statistics:
  -- A 2001 study by the FBI reported that 85% of corporations experienced a security breach during the prior 12 months.
  -- Among companies that had a security breach, 70% found a connection through the Internet to those breaches. But more than 70% of the breaches began from inside the organization.

Further Risks

In addition to the risks cited by Rodney Glover . . . , Kepczyk identified these risks from security breaches:

- Damage to integrity. It's not just the Internet that can be a threat here. How about an office break-in? Or a fire or hurricane that strews paperwork from an HR office all over the neighborhood? Information storage security is an issue for HR, which handles much sensitive data.
- Liability. More than lawsuits are involved if there is an interruption to your business from a natural disaster or even a short-term crisis, such as a blackout.

Protecting Your Systems

A computer use policy is a must. So is explaining and distributing it to employees
at least annually. Make users aware of potential problems and their effects on the
company. To protect against outside interference, Kepczyk recommends that organizations take these steps:

- Physical security. Control access to sensitive files—simple steps such as
  locking file rooms or cabinets can protect the privacy of the data. Secure
  workstations—cable-locked or otherwise attached to heavy furniture—can
  keep the computer itself (and data and systems access) from "walking" out
  of your offices.
- Systems protections. Access at all hours is common today, and so are hackers. You must have firewalls and other protections to keep files and information from being destroyed or stolen.
- Data backups. Backing up HR files should be part of the overall corporate
  backup policy. Be sure that your computerized records are being backed up
  on a regular basis. Discuss the matter with your IS manager. Ask how often
  backups are being made, in what format, where they are stored, and how
  often the IS department tests whether the backups can properly restore
  data if necessary.
- Passwords. Regular changes in passwords are a challenge to remember, but
  they represent a simple and inexpensive way for all employees and managers to help protect the integrity of the systems.
- Digital identification. Digital certificates or encryption are the next level of security above passwords. They can be especially important for HR professionals who work with outsourcers in automating benefits information and
  related applications, since highly private information is traveling over the Internet and must be protected. Discuss these issues with any potential vendors.
- Impact of viruses. Organizations lost $13.2 billion in 2001 because of viruses,
  so take the threat seriously. Report any suspicious incoming messages to
  your IS department. You can check for virus hoaxes at these Web sites:
  -- www.mcafee.com
  -- www.norton.com
  -- www.trusecure.com
- Telecommuter or remote-user issues. Workers who use a computer at home
  or other remote site that connects to the office must use a firewall if they access the Internet via DSL or cable. Without that, their computers are wide
  open to attacks from viruses and hackers—and their computers are direct
  conduits into your organization's servers.

Exploring the Message

1. What major challenges do employers face when creating company policies on computer use and computer safety? Describe the attitudes and ac-

tions that help Human Resources and Information Systems departments meet these challenges.

2. What is the core purpose of this multifaceted article? Is it achieved?

3. Which of the points were familiar to you and which provided new insight into employer privacy and technology practices? For example, did you know that an employer can be liable for an employee who has an accident while talking on a company cell phone? Would these new insights affect your behavior as an employee?

4. What is the "mom test"? Why do you remember this point so easily?

Investigating the Discourse Community

1. Visit the "About Us" link on the Institute of Management & Administration Web site at www.ioma.com/contacts/aboutus.php. In what ways does "Balancing Security & Privacy in the Internet Age" reflect the purposes set out by this organization?

2. What are the professions of the two authorities cited in the article? What makes them particularly good resources for this newsletter?

3. In the "Protecting the Company" section, readers are advised to create an integrated approach to security and privacy issues. What attribute of the corporate workplace is revealed here?

4. Why would IOMA publish *HRFocus* monthly rather than quarterly or semiannually?

5. What is the primary tone of this article? For example, what attitude toward employee/employer relationships does it convey? Find phrases or examples that support your view. Would this same tone be appropriate for a brochure for employees on acceptable computer use?

Understanding the Genre

1. Describe the document's overall design, as well as the various formats used throughout the article. What assumptions does the writer make about the background knowledge and reading practices of the target audience? Would you suggest any changes in the article's organization?

2. In its original published form, the section from "Protecting Your Organization from External Threats" to the end of the article was laid out as a separate sidebar. How does that arrangement serve the purposes of the business newsletter genre?

3. According to the IOMA Web site, *HRFocus* is published "in a vibrant 3-color format." Why include this information in its advertising?

4. What purpose does the section "Protecting the Company" serve? Are there similarly purposed sections in other parts of the article?

Writing Activity

Select any of the major sections of "Balancing Security & Privacy in the Internet Age" and rewrite it in a different genre or in a different tone or style. For example, in the "Protecting Your Organization from External Threats" segment, the phrasing is used to create an image of a besieged employer: systems are "vulnerable" and "in danger from the outside world," which means employers need to construct "appropriate defenses." Could you eliminate this battle metaphor and still achieve the same purpose for the same audience?

American Nursing Association Action Report: Privacy and Confidentiality

Introduced by Beverly L. Malone

The ANA is a Washington, D.C.–based professional organization with a membership of over 180,000. Its goals include promoting positive nursing practices and lobbying for progressive health care legislation. On its Web site, the ANA posts the 1893 "Florence Nightingale Pledge," which includes this promise to patients: "I will . . . hold in confidence all personal matters committed to my keeping and all family affairs coming to my knowledge in the practice of my calling." Maintaining this trusting relationship has become far more complicated in the information age, as the organization acknowledges in the following 1999 report.

1999 ANA House of Delegates
Subject: Privacy and Confidentiality (Action Report)
Introduced by: Beverly L. Malone, PhD, RN, FAAN President

EXECUTIVE SUMMARY: Advances in technology have led to the development of computerized medical databases and telehealth systems and have raised serious concerns about patient privacy and the confidentiality of health care information. Threats to confidentiality of medical records and health care information affect the kinds of care that patients seek and potentially undermine the relationship of trust between health professionals and patients that is essential to quality health care. Nurses play a critical role in preserving patient privacy and confidentiality and should participate in the ongoing debate about and development of Federal laws designed to ensure patient privacy/confidentiality.

Recommendation(s)

That the American Nurses Association:

1. Develop a position statement on patient privacy and the confidentiality of health records/information and the nurse's role in preserving privacy/confidentiality as technological advances affect the transmission and storage of information.
2. Disseminate information to members and other relevant groups to inform and educate them about nursing's role in protecting patient privacy and the confidentiality of health records/information.

Report

Advances in technology, including computerized medical databases, the Internet, and telehealth, have opened the door to potential, unintentional breaches of private/confidential health information. Protection of privacy/confidentiality is essential to the trusting relationship between health care providers and patients. Quality patient care requires the communication of relevant information between health professionals and/or health systems. Nurses and other health professionals who regularly work with patients and their confidential medical records should contribute to the development of standards, policies, and laws that protect patient privacy and the confidentiality of health records/information. This report is intended to both follow up on ANA's activity to date and address emerging privacy/confidentiality issues (such as confidentiality of genetic information).

Background

Recent developments in technology have changed the delivery of health care and the systems used to record and retrieve health information. In addition to using paper medical records, health professionals, hospitals, and insurers routinely use computers, phones, faxes, and other methods of recording and transferring information. In many instances, this information—which could include medical diagnoses, prescriptions, or insurance information—is readily available to anyone (including clerical and other staff) who walks by a fax machine or logs on to a computer. This lack of privacy has the potential to undermine patients' relationships with providers and adversely affect the quality of care. Patients may also fear that the exposure of personal health information, including the results of genetic tests that are becoming increasingly available, could result in the loss or denial of health insurance, job discrimination, or personal embarrassment.

Currently no federal legal protections exist for health care information stored electronically. Federal laws establishing at least a floor of protection are necessary because the Internet, telehealth, and fax/phone communication know no state boundaries. This lack of federal protection has already affected the behavior of some patients. According to Janlori Goldman, Director of the Health Privacy Project,

The numbers document that people are anxious about how their medical information is used. Because there is no federal law to protect that information, people are taking drastic actions to protect their privacy—withholding or providing inadequate information to their doctors, paying out of pocket for covered services, and hopping from doctor to doctor—putting themselves at risk for untreated conditions. At worst, others are avoiding care altogether because of privacy concerns. This is not just about protecting individual privacy but protecting public health as well because if people provide incomplete information or are left out of care, then the data needed for research, monitoring quality of care and other public health functions will be woefully inadequate (Goldman, 1999).

Congress acknowledged this lack of Federal protection in the Health Insurance Portability and Accountability Act of 1996 (HIPAA) (P.L. 104-191). In that law, Congress requires the Secretary of Health and Human Services to: 1) submit to the relevant Senate and Congressional committees "detailed recommendations on standards with respect to the privacy of individually identifiable health information" within one year of HIPAA's enactment; and 2) "promulgate final regulations containing such standards" if Congress has not enacted a privacy law within 3 years of HIPAA's enactment. In his 1999 State of the Union Message, President Clinton reminded the Congress and the American people that he will enact medical privacy protections this year if Congress does not act by August, 1999.

Several House and Senate bills have been introduced or are being drafted to address the requirement of HIPAA. The common framework for all of the major bills includes a right of consumers to see what is in their own record; limits on disclosure through some type of authorization; a requirement for notice about the circumstances of disclosure; provisions dealing with access for research purposes; law enforcement access; remedies and enforcement, possibly including a private right of action and civil and/or criminal penalties for egregious violations; and preemption of state laws. Contentious issues include: the extent of the preemption of state laws; the nature of the authorization and informed consent; possible costs to the private sector; restrictions on adolescent confidentiality; insulating employee health records from employers who provide health benefits; and problems unique to mental health patients, such as involuntary commitments.

ANA has demonstrated its concern about the impact of computerized health records on privacy/confidentiality. In 1995, the ANA House of Delegates approved a Policy/Position on "Privacy and Confidentiality Related to Access to Electronic Data" while the Board of Directors endorsed three position papers put forth by the Computer Based Patient Record Institute: "Authentication in a Computer-Based Patient Record," "Access to Patient Data," and "Computer-Based Patient Record Standards." In March 1998, the ANA Board of Directors endorsed the "Core Principles on Telehealth" drafted by the Interdisciplinary Telehealth Standards Working Group, a group spearheaded by ANA which consists of 41 professional associations and health care organizations. Among the core principles identified by this group is the following: "confidentiality of client visits, client health records and the integrity of information in our health care information system is essential."

Most recently, and in an effort to participate in the formulation of Federal laws addressing privacy/confidentiality, ANA has been participating with the Consumer Coalition for Health Privacy. This group has agreed to a set of principles that should govern the federal legislation called for in HIPAA. The coalition is committed to the development and enactment of public policies and private standards that guarantee the confidentiality of personal health information and promote both access to high quality care and the continued viability of medical research. The coalition's principles address:

- the right to privacy established by law;
- limitations on identifiable information;
- an individual's right to access his or her own health information and to supplement such information;
- the right of individuals to be notified about how their records are used and when their individually identifiable health information is disclosed to third parties;
- a prohibition on use or disclosure of individually identifiable health information absent informed consent;
- protections which do not impede important public health efforts or clinical, medical and quality of care research;
- a requirement for development of security safeguards for the use, disclosure and storage of personal health information;
- strong and enforceable remedies for violations of privacy protections and protections for health care workers from retaliation if they disclose abuses; and
- a national law which provides a floor for the protection of individual privacy rights, not a ceiling.

Discussion

Privacy and confidentiality are key to the trusting relationship between nurses and patients. An expectation that information is private/confidential is frequently what allows patients to share sensitive information with nurses and other health providers. Privacy refers to the right to be left alone and free from intrusions. In health care, the right to privacy includes the right to choose without interference based upon personal beliefs, feelings, or attitudes; and is linked to the right to control bodily integrity (accepting or rejecting treatment, invasion, or exposure of the body) and to control when and how sensitive information is shared. Confidentiality refers to the nondisclosure of information received from or concerning patients.

Protection of patient privacy/confidentiality is not absolute. Communication of information between health providers is essential to quality care. Information about patients is shared on a "need to know" basis. Information that has no bearing on the patient encounter is not shared information. Additional limits on privacy and confidentiality exist because society sometimes deems individual and collective needs more important than any individual's need for privacy or confidentiality. Examples include situations where individual or public health and safety are in danger such as threats to life or the risk of exposure to contagious diseases.

The public recognizes the importance of confidentiality in health care. People are generally concerned about protecting their personal health information. The public expects that nurses will protect confidential and private information. Nurses are often in a position to protect vulnerable patients from unauthorized disclosures. The protection, and conversely, the disclosure of private/confidential health information requires knowledge, discretion, and discernment of ethical and legal issues. Nurses have long recognized that preserving and protecting patient confidentiality and privacy are an integral part of nursing practice. The nurse-patient relationship is based upon fidelity (promise-keeping, trust), a respect for persons, and refraining from harm (non-malfeasance). Privacy and confidentiality have been identified in the ANA *Code for Nurses* as fundamental to the integrity of the nursing profession.

Nurses, like other health providers, are accountable for maintaining standards of privacy and confidentiality. Nurses have an obligation to participate in the development of strategies that will promote patient privacy and the confidentiality of patient health records/information. Nurses are key health care providers who can contribute to the development of standards, policies, and laws that protect patient health information. Given the current federal activity and the imminent legislative deadline codified in the HIPAA law, to the extent that nursing wishes its views to be heard, the time is now.

The increased capability and use of technology such as computers for recording, transmitting and storing sensitive patient information has far exceeded previously established safeguards for privacy and confidentiality. It is now incumbent upon the nursing profession to lead in the development of strategies to address this concern.

References

Goldman, J. (1999, January 29). Statement of Janlori Goldman, Director Health Privacy Project, quoted at http://healthprivacy.org/latest/index.html.

Exploring the Message

1. How does the ANA define privacy, particularly in the context of health care?

2. According to the ANA, in what ways does technology challenge good nursing practices? Has technology been helpful in other ways?

3. What risks to patients are identified in the report? Do you find the ANA's assessment of the situation realistic?

4. How would the existence of this document add to Jerry Berman and Paula Bruening's hopeful position on technology? How does their definition of privacy compare to the ANA's? Would Declan McCullagh agree with the ANA's strategies?

Investigating the Discourse Community

1. Using the "Executive Summary," identify the core values and assumptions supporting the document's recommendations. Do other explicit or implied values and assumptions surface in the expanded report? How do these traits of the discourse community compare to your images and expectations of nurses?

2. In what ways do the "Background" and "Discussion" sections expand your understanding of possible career paths for nursing majors?

3. After studying the list of Consumer Coalition for Health Privacy principles on p. 101, identify a group or groups that might not share the coalition's assumptions about technology and privacy.

4. Were you surprised by the claim that "Protection of patient privacy/confidentiality is not absolute"(paragraph 11)? Is this consistent with other ANA positions? Do you agree with the statement? Identify a few examples that support your position.

Understanding the Genre

1. Describe the function of each of the major sections of this report. How would you explain their order and the overlap among them? Why are no visual elements included? What does the overall design tell you about the habits and expectations of the intended audience?

2. How would you describe the persona and style of the ANA report? Does it reflect the image of nurses conveyed in the report's descriptions of the profession? If not, why not?

3. Visit the American Medical Association's Web site at www.ama-assn.org and surf its ethics and policies links on the Physicians page. Compare the style and voice in the ANA report to those features in the AMA presentations.

Writing Activity

Write a report using the "American Nursing Association Action Report: Privacy and Confidentiality" as your model. Brainstorm topics for your report by recalling actions taken or resolutions made by groups you belong to.

Examples might include your sorority's resolution to increase their participation in local community causes, your running club's position on adding power walking to its endorsed activities, your writing group's project goals, your family's resolution to continue to take annual vacations together. As you plan and draft, use your analysis of the genre and style of the ANA report. Pay special attention to the organization, point of view, level of usage, sentence structure, and tone.

Stop That Face!

Linda Rothstein

The Bulletin of Atomic Scientists *is published by the Educational Foundation for Nuclear Science, whose stated mission is "to educate citizens about global security issues." Linda Rothstein has been an editor at the* Bulletin *since 1988 and managing editor since 1992; in 2000 she took over as editor-in-chief. The following article appeared in the November-December 2001 issue.*

Video cameras and face-recognition technology were used during the January 2001 Super Bowl (now known as the "Snooper Bowl") to search the crowd for known criminals and/or terrorists. But no miscreants were fingered and no evil-doers taken into custody. On the other hand, when they learned somewhat later that the technology had been used, irate citizens, concerned about privacy rights, complained loudly.

Local law enforcement officials, however, believed the time was ripe. Since 1997 the National Institutes of Justice had supported research into face-recognition software to the tune of $8 million, and several systems were said to be ready for public trial. One package in particular, the "FaceIt" system produced by Visionics, Inc., seemed mature. Visionics software converts a photo or a video image to a mathematical equation based on an analysis of 80 facial points between the nose, cheekbones, and eyes. The equation is then saved as a "faceprint." Using the Visionics system, a surveillance camera can scan a face in a crowd and within a minute or less compare it to thousands of faceprints found in a police database.

Visionics President Joseph Atick said his technology had already been proven in Britain. Atick claims that after it was adopted in 1998 for use on the streets in a dangerous area of Newham (a London borough), crime dropped more than 40 percent in the first year. (Of course, it's not clear whether crime dropped because cameras were visible or because criminals thought their faces could be computer ID'ed.)

A sign in Tampa's Ybor City district tells passersby that they are being monitored.

In any case, the police in Tampa were not dissuaded by the ruckus surrounding the use of face-recognition technology at the Super Bowl. In mid-summer they installed 36 surveillance cameras in Tampa's entertainment district, known as Ybor City, and settled back to wait for the faces they scanned on the streets to match up with faceprints in a database of 30,000 wanted felons and missing children.

Local citizens, the American Civil Liberties Union, and members of Congress 5 (including Texas Republican Dick Armey) called for shutting the cameras down, but project director Bill Todd, a Tampa detective, insisted that what some residents were calling a "virtual lineup" was not only constitutional, it was efficient. "This is no different than a police officer standing on a street corner with a handful of wanted pictures, except that it's more accurate and stops trouble faster," he told *U.S. News & World Report* (August 6, 2001).

As part of its publicity campaign, the police handed out a sample picture taken from one of the surveillance cameras. The picture ran in the June 30 [2001] *St. Petersburg Times* and was reprinted in *U.S. News,* along with the story quoted above.

Many visitors to Ybor City expressed their displeasure with the surveillance system by wearing Groucho glasses or making rude gestures in the direction of the cameras. Civil liberties specialists complained vociferously.

Given the hostile atmosphere surrounding their new crime-busting technology, Tampa police must have been overjoyed when the individual in their sample picture was identified almost immediately by a woman in Oklahoma who insisted the photo was that of a wanted man—namely, her deadbeat ex-husband.

Three Tampa police officers tracked down the man in the photo, Rob Milliron, at the construction site where he worked—pulling him aside to question him about the charges against him in Oklahoma for felony child neglect.

But the unlucky Milliron had not been identified by the exacting science of face-recognition software, only by a woman whose memory was apparently somewhat careless when it came to ex-husbands. As it turned out, Milliron was innocent—he had never been to Oklahoma, never married, and had no children.

Milliron was upset by his interrogation in front of a gawking crowd, and even more annoyed when he later discovered that the headline below his photo in the magazine had read, "You Can't Hide Those Lying Eyes in Tampa." "It made me out to be a criminal," he said (*St. Petersburg Times*, August 8, 2001).

Face-recognition technology got even more attention when it was demonstrated by British comedian John Cleese on a BBC television special, "The Human Face," which was shown on The Learning Channel on August 27 [2001]. Cleese, wearing a series of disguises, including one particularly lady-like getup, was immediately identified by the surveillance system. But his last disguise, which included a hat pulled low over his forehead and a large pair of dark glasses, foiled the system.

In real life, however, Ybor City's searching cameras had yet to uncover a wanted baddie. In fact, none of the face-recognition software seemed to be pulling in the bad guys. According to *Wired News* (August 15, 2001), the "Missing Child Locator Agent," a web crawler, had yet to make a match. Another technology, the "Identiface," which is intended to be used by cops to "identify suspects during mobile stakeouts," had so far made only one match its promoters described as successful. That match was of a photo of a dead man, matched to his driver's license photo. (His license photo was ranked only fourth, though, in a series of possible matches.)

The possibility that a database of driver's license pictures might be used to match faces in a crowd raises even more concerns about privacy. One city council member in Jacksonville, Florida, suggested that her community should outlaw the technology before it was misused. And the possibility of widespread abuse became apparent with the suggestion that databases might be sold or shared with third parties. According to police in Tampa, it is their practice to discard information on faces in the crowd that don't match anyone in their database. But there's no requirement that scans from the public streets be discarded, or that driver's license photos not be scanned.

Visionics's Atick knew that something had to be done to turn what appeared to be a negative tide against the company's face-recognition technology. In a preemptive strike on August 8 [2001]—at about the same time it was revealed that Visionics was selling the technology to that bastion of civil and privacy rights, China—Atick called on Congress to pass legislation to regulate its use. And according to Julia Scheeres's September 5 [2001] report for *Wired News*, the "biometrics" industry, of which faceprinting is only a part, is now trying to find a few heart-warming "Good News Biometric Stories" to counteract opposition.

Exploring the Message

1. What is face-recognition technology and how does it work? Have you read or heard other references to this technique, especially since 9/11?
2. According to Rothstein, how successful has this faceprinting technology been? What examples does she use to make her point? Which did you find most convincing?
3. What privacy concerns have been raised about the use of photo databases (see paragraph 14, for example)?
4. Why did Rothstein conclude with the information about Visionics and the "biometrics" industry (paragraph 15)? How does this material further her purpose?

Investigating the Discourse Community

1. Why did the *Bulletin of Atomic Scientists* run this article? What audience were they trying to reach? Go to the Web site at www.thebulletin.org to find out more about this publication and its goals. Were you surprised by what you found? How does it change your view of the role of scientists?
2. Where else would you expect an article like this one to appear?
3. Did you feel you were a part of the intended audience? Why or why not?

Understanding the Genre

1. How can you tell this article was not written solely for scientists?
2. What do sentence length, attributed quotations, and paragraph frequency tell you about the genre and its intended audience?
3. Describe the tone of the article. How do the examples and the parenthetical comments contribute to this tone?

Writing Activities

1. What forms of electronic surveillance have you encountered? Do the stores where you shop have surveillance cameras? How about your bank or the ATM machine you use? Are there cameras on campus—in the

dorms or the library perhaps? Write a position paper expressing your views about this kind of technology.

2. What is the Global Positioning System (GPS)? Is your car equipped with it? Have you rented a car with GPS? Find out more about this technology and the ways it is used to track people. Write a report for your classmates explaining GPS, summarizing the privacy issues surrounding it, and linking those issues to the casebook readings.

Talk Show Telling versus Authentic Telling: The Effects of the Popular Media on Secrecy and Openness
Evan Imber-Black

Evan Imber-Black, Ph.D., directs the Center for Families and Health at the Ackerman Institute for the Family in New York City. She is also a professor in the Psychiatry Department at Albert Einstein College of Medicine and a past president of the American Family Therapy Academy. Her published works include Rituals of Our Times *(1992) and* Secrets in Families and Family Therapy *(1993). The following article is excerpted from of her book* The Secret Life of Families: Truth-Telling, Privacy, and Reconciliation in a Tell-All Society *(1998).*

Well, my guests today say that they can't bear to keep their secrets locked inside of them any longer. And they've invited their spouse or lover to come on national television to let them hear the secrets for the first time.

—Montel Williams

The young woman entered my therapy room slowly, with the usual hesitation of a new client. I settled her in a chair, expecting to begin the low-key question-and-answer conversation that usually takes the entire first session. Almost before she could pronounce my name, she began telling me a deeply personal and shameful secret. In an effort to slow her down and start to build a relationship that might be strong enough to hold her enormous pain, I gently asked her what made her think it was all right to tell me things so quickly. "I see people doing it on *Oprah* all the time," she replied.

Throughout history human beings have been fascinated by other people's secrets. In great literature, theater, and films we view how people create and inhabit secrets and cope with the consequences of planned or unplanned revelation. Life-changing secrets are central to such ancient dramas such as *Oedipus* or Shakespeare's *Macbeth* as well as to twentieth-century classics such as Ibsen's *A Doll's House*, Eugene O'Neill's *Long Day's Journey into Night*, Arthur Miller's *Death of a Salesman* and *All My Sons*, or Lorraine Hansberry's *A Raisin in the Sun*. Like me, you may remember the poignancy of the sweet secrets in the O. Henry tale "Gift of the Magi," where a wife secretly cuts and sells her hair to buy her husband a watch for Christmas, while he, unbeknownst to her, sells his watch in order to buy silver combs for her hair. Contemporary popular films, such as *Ordinary People, The Prince of Tides,* or *The Wedding Banquet,* also illustrate the complexity of secrets and their impact on every member of a family. Literary and dramatic portrayals of perplexing secrets and their often complicated and messy resolutions help us to remember that keeping and opening secrets is not simple. Perhaps most important, they help us appreciate our own deep human connection to the dilemmas of others.

Since the advent of television, however, we have begun to learn about other people's secrets and, by implication, how to think about our own secrets in a very different way. Exploiting our hunger for missing community, both afternoon talk shows and evening magazine shows have challenged all of our previously held notions about secrecy, privacy, and openness. While such shows have been around for nearly thirty years, in the 1980s something new began to appear: celebrities began to open the secrets in their lives on national television.[1] As we heard about Jane Fonda's bulimia, Elizabeth Taylor's drug addiction, or Dick Van Dyke's alcoholism—formerly shameful secrets spoken about with aplomb—centuries of stigma seemed to be lifting. Other revelations enabled us to see the pervasiveness of wife battering and incest. The unquestioned shame and secrecy formerly attached to cancer, adoption, homosexuality, mental illness, or out-of-wedlock birth began to fall away.

This atmosphere of greater openness brought with it many benefits. In my therapy practice I experienced an important shift as the people I worked with displayed a greater ease in raising what might never have been spoken about a decade earlier. Frightening secrets lost some of their power to perpetuate intimidation. Those who had been silenced began to find their voices and stake their claim as authorities on their own lives.

But as the arena of the unmentionable became smaller and smaller, a more 5
dangerous cultural shift was also taking place: the growth of the simplistic belief that telling a secret, regardless of context, is automatically beneficial. This belief, promulgated by television talk shows and media exposés, has ripped secrecy and openness away from their necessary moorings in connected and empathic relationships. Painful personal revelations have become public entertainment, used to sell dish soap and to manufacture celebrity.

If cultural norms once made shameful secrets out of too many happenings in human life, we are now struggling with the reverse assumption: that opening secrets—no matter how, when, or to whom—is morally superior and automatically healing. The daily spectacle of strangers opening secrets in our living rooms teaches us that no distinctions need be drawn, no care need be taken, no thought given to consequences.

Talk Show Telling

From a *Sally Jessy Raphael* show in 1994, we hear and see the following conversation:

Sally: Let's meet David and Kelly. They're newlyweds. They got married in December. . . . As newlyweds, what would happen if he cheated on you? What would you do?

Kelly: I don't know.

[Before David begins to speak, the print at the bottom of the screen reads, "Telling Kelly for the first time that he's cheating on her," thus informing the audience of the content of the secret before Kelly is told.]

David: I called Sally and told the producer of the show that I was living a double life. . . . I had a few affairs on her.

Sally (to Kelly): Did you know about that?

[Camera zooms in on Kelly's shocked and pained expression; she is speechless and in tears, and she shakes her head while members of the audience chuckle.]

Sally: Kelly, how do you feel? On the one hand, listen to how awful and bad this is. On the other hand, he could have just not ever told you. He loves you so much that he wanted to come and get this out. . . .

In the late 1960s the *Phil Donahue Show* began a new media format for sharing interesting information and airing issues. This shifted in the late 1970s and 1980s to celebrity confessions and the destruction of taboos. In the 1990s talk TV brings us the deliberate opening of secrets that one person in a couple or a family has never heard before. In a cynical grab for ratings and profits, the format of such shows has changed rapidly from one where guests were told ahead of time that they were going to hear a secret "for the first time on national television" to one where guests are invited to the show under some other ruse. These programs are referred to as "ambush" shows.

According to former talk show host Jane Whitney, "Practically anyone willing to 'confront' someone—her husband's mistress, his wife's lover, their promiscuous best friend—in a televised emotional ambush could snare a free ticket to national notoriety. *Those who promised to reveal some intimate secret to an unsuspecting loved one got star treatment*" (italics added).[2] Presently there are over thirty talk shows on every weekday. Forty million Americans watch these shows, and they are syndicated in many other countries.[3] Even if you have never watched a talk show, you live in an environment where assumptions about secrets have been affected by talk show telling.

Opening painful secrets on talk TV shows promotes a distorted sense of values and beliefs about secrecy and openness. While viewers are drawn into the sensational content of whatever secret is being revealed, the impact on relationships after the talk show is over is ignored. Indeed, when there has been severe relationship fallout, or even tragedy following the opening of a secret, talk show hosts and producers claim they have no responsibility, intensifying the belief that secrets can be recklessly opened without any obligation to be concerned about the aftermath. Consider the following:

- In one notorious incident in 1995, a young man named Jonathon Schmitz murdered an acquaintance, Scott Amedure, following an unwelcome revelation on the *Jenny Jones* show.[4] Schmitz had been told that he was coming on the show to meet a "secret admirer." He was not told that the show was about "men who have secret crushes on men."[5] When his shock and humiliation resulted in Amedure's murder, the host and producers insisted they had no responsibility.
- On the *Montel Williams* show, a woman heard for the first time that her sister had been sleeping with her boyfriend for several years. She came on the show after being told it was a show about "old boyfriends."
- Former talk show host Jane Whitney describes a show she did called "Revealing Your Double Life." A mother was invited on who had no idea why her son had cut himself off from her for two years. Whitney, of course, knew that the son was about to reveal his pending sexual reassignment surgery. When she met the mother just before the show, the woman implored her, "Do you know what's wrong? We were always so close. I don't know what's happened. Is he sick? Does he have AIDS?" Assuring the mother that "everything would be all right," Whitney lied and kept the secret in order to maximize its revelation on the show.[6]
- Ricki Lake invited on a man who had been keeping his homosexuality a secret from his family. His roommate announced that he had taken it upon himself to tell the man's family this secret.[7]

When such actions occur over and over again on talk TV, we lose our capacity to ask a critical question—namely, under what circumstances do we have the right to open another person's secret?

On talk television, husbands hear for the first time that their wives want a divorce; mothers are told the secret of their daughters' sexual abuse; wives discover that their husbands tell friends about their sexual relationship. And all of this occurs in a context in which the host disingenuously denies any responsibility for what is set in motion in the complex ecology of family relationships.

Talk show telling ignores the importance of committed relationships. Telling can be anonymous and disguised. A studio audience and a viewing audience consisting of strangers hear the previously hidden details of our lives. Commercial breaks cavalierly interrupt the opening and hearing of a painful secret. Eavesdropping stands in for sincere listening. Voyeurism substitutes for witnessing. The host's pseudo-intimate hugs and caresses replace genuine healing.

When secrets are opened on television, several peculiar triangles are created. The relationship between the person telling the secret and the person hearing the secret is immediately invaded by the audience, the host, and the "expert," each with a calculated and repetitious role. These roles are imbued with arrogance: the belief that one knows what is best for other people to do about the secrets in their lives. Talk show telling involves opening secrets to a huge group of uninvolved, faultfinding listeners who have no responsibility for the relationship after the talk show ends.

When a secret is about to be revealed, captions are placed below the image of the person who has not yet heard it. The audience sees such words as "About to hear that his wife just had an abortion" or "Jim is not Ellen's biological father." Thus the audience knows the content of the secret before the person whose life the secret affects. A context of humiliation is constructed. Often the audience laughs or gasps while the camera catches a close-up of the perplexed face of the listener. The recipient of the secret is, in fact, the last to know. This structure reduces empathy and enables the audience to feel separate from and superior to the ambushed guest.

The audience encourages further revelations through applause.[8] As viewers, we get the message over and over that opening a secret, regardless of consequences, gains attention and approval. Loudly applauded, cheered, jeered, and fought over, secrets are in fact trivialized. On talk shows, a secret of sexual abuse equals a secret about family finances equals a secret about being a Nazi equals a secret of paternity.

Once a secret is revealed, both the teller and the recipient are immediately vulnerable to the judgmental advice and criticism of strangers. Blaming and taking sides abound. Not a moment elapses for reflection on the magnitude and gravity of what has occurred. Every secret is instantly reduced to a one-dimensional problem that will yield to simplistic solutions.

Soon after a secret is opened, the host goes into high gear with some variation of the message that opening the secret can have only good results. Sally Jessy Raphael tells the young wife who has just discovered the secret of her husband's affairs in front of millions of unasked-for snoopers, "He loves you so much that he wanted to come and get this out." The message to all is that telling a secret, in and of itself, is curative. There is no place for ambivalence or confusion. Indeed, guests are often scolded for expressing doubt or hesitation about the wisdom of national disclosure of the intimate aspects of their lives.

The host's position as a celebrity can frame the content of a given secret and the process of telling as either normal or abnormal, good or bad. When Oprah Winfrey joins guests who are exposing secrets of sexual abuse or cocaine addiction with revelations of her own, the telling becomes hallowed. No distinctions are drawn between what a famous person with a lot of money and power might be able to speak about without consequences and what an ordinary person who is returning to their family, job, and community after the talk show might be able to express. Conversely, some hosts display initial shock, dismay, and negativity toward a particular secret, its teller, or its recipient. When a guest on the *Jerry Springer Show* who has just discovered that a woman he had a relationship with is a transsexual hides in embarrassment and asks the host what he would do, Springer responds, "Well, I certainly wouldn't be talking about it on national

TV!" A context of disgrace is created, only to be transformed at the next commercial break into a context of understanding and forgiveness.

Toward the end of any talk show on which secrets have been revealed, a men- 20
tal health therapist enters. A pseudo-therapeutic context is created. The real and difficult work that is required after a secret opens disappears in the smoke and mirrors of a fleeting and unaccountable relationship with an "expert" who adopts a position of superiority and assumed knowledge about the lives of people he or she has just met.[9] While we are asked to believe that there are no loose ends when the talk show is over, the duplicitousness of this claim is evident in the fact that many shows now offer "aftercare," or real therapy, to deal with the impact of disclosing a secret on television.[10]

The time needed even to begin to deal adequately with any secret is powerfully misrepresented on talk television. In just under forty minutes on a single *Montel Williams* show, a man told his wife he was in a homosexual relationship; a woman told her husband she was having an affair with his boss; another woman told her boyfriend that she was a transsexual; a wife revealed to her husband that they were $20,000 in debt; and a woman told her boyfriend that she had just aborted their pregnancy. An ethos of "just blurt it out" underpins these shows.

Talk show telling also erases age-appropriate boundaries between parents and children. Children are often in the audience hearing their parents' secrets for the first time. On one show an eight-year-old boy heard his aunt reveal that he had been abandoned by his mother because she "didn't want" him. Children may also be on-stage revealing a secret to one parent about the other parent, without a thought given to the guilt children experience when they are disloyal to a parent.[11] The impact on these children, their sense of shame and embarrassment, and what they might encounter when they return to school the next day is never considered.

Ultimately, talk show telling transforms our most private and intimate truths into a commodity. Shows conclude with announcements: "Do you have a secret that you've never told anyone? Call and tell us"; "Have you videotaped someone doing something they shouldn't do? Send us the tape." A juicy secret may get you a free airplane trip, a limousine ride, an overnight stay in a fancy hotel. While no one forces anyone to go on a talk show, the fact that most guests are working-class people who lack the means for such travel makes talk show telling a deal with the devil.

Notes

1. For a complete discussion of the history of talk television and the wider context in which it is embedded, see J. A. Heaton and N. L. Wilson, *Tuning In Trouble: Talk TV's Destructive Impact on Mental Health* (San Francisco: Jossey-Bass, 1995).

2. J. Whitney, "Why I Simply Had to Shut Up," *New York Daily News*, June 11, 1995, p. 6.

3. Talk television is extremely profitable. A typical show costs about $200,000 a week to produce, compared to an average $1 million a week for a

drama. In 1992, for instance, Oprah Winfrey's show earned $157 million, Phil Donahue's show $90 million, and Sally Jessy Raphael's show $60 million (Heaton and Wilson, *Tuning In Trouble*).

4. *Newsweek,* March 20, 1995, p. 30; *The New York Times,* March 12, 1995, p. A22, and March 14, 1995, pp. Al, Al0.

5. The tragedy attached to this particular show distracts our attention from an important dimension of many of these programs, which is that they commonly pander to feelings of homophobia, racism, and sexism. See Heaton and Wilson, *Tuning In Trouble,* for a full discussion of this issue.

6. Whitney, "Why I Simply Had to Shut Up."

7. J. A. Heaton, and N. L. Wilson, "Tuning In to Trouble," *MS. Magazine,* September/October 1995, V. 6, #2, pp. 45–48.

8. See R. Cialdini, *Influence: How and Why People Agree to Things* (New York: William Morrow, 1984), for a discussion regarding studies on compliance showing that once people agree to participate in something, they often go along with much more than they originally intended.

9. See L. Armstrong, *Rocking the Cradle of Sexual Politics* (New York: Addison-Wesley, 1994), for a thoughtful discussion of the impact of such "experts" on talk television when the topic is incest. According to Armstrong, such a structure diminishes the issue, reducing it from one with crucial political implications to simply a matter of personal opinion.

10. Jamie Diamond, "Life After Oprah," *Self,* August 1994, pp. 122–25, 162; also see Heaton and Wilson, *Tuning In Trouble,* for a thoughtful critique of the questionable quality of such "aftercare."

11. *Sally Jessy Raphael Show,* November 29, 1994, "We Want Mom to Leave Her Cheating Husband"; transcript by Journal Graphics.

Exploring the Message

1. What are the benefits of the "greater openness" that television talk shows encourage?

2. The author claims that talk show telling "promotes a distorted sense of values and beliefs about secrecy and openness." What are some of these distortions and why are they harmful?

3. According to Dr. Imber-Black, TV talk shows construct "a context of humiliation," create "a context of disgrace," and establish "a pseudo-therapeutic context." Explain what she means by each of these charges. Do you agree with her conclusions?

4. Why are people willing to reveal their secrets on television? What part does social and economic class play in their decision? What other motives might people have for giving up their privacy?

5. What technologies besides television make people vulnerable to public scrutiny? How do Imber-Black's insights and observations relate to the privacy issues raised by other readings in this casebook?

Investigating the Discourse Community

1. How does Imber-Black establish her professional credentials? How does this knowledge shape your response to her criticism of TV talk shows?
2. Do you expect a professor and therapist to write about television? Why or why not?
3. What do the author's comments about literature and films in paragraph 2 reveal about her educational background? What is she assuming about her intended audience?
4. In paragraph 1, when she discusses the ideal therapy environment, Imber-Black is operating out of a core set of assumptions common to professionals within her discourse community. What similar assumptions can you identify in the article?

Understanding the Genre

1. How do you know Imber-Black is not writing primarily for other therapists? What audience is she writing for? What features of her style would be different if she were writing to fellow professionals?
2. The author uses first-person plural pronouns—*we, us, our*—throughout her discussion. What persona and tone does this usage create?
3. This reading is an excerpt from a book. In what section of a bookstore would you expect to find the book? Where would you expect to see this book reviewed?

Writing Activity

Do you think talk show telling should be controlled or regulated in any way? If so, to what extent and by whom? Write a brief position paper in which you lay out your views on these questions.

Writer's Workshop

1. How have the readings in this section changed your views of privacy in the information age as you outlined them in the "Writer's Notebook" at the beginning of the casebook? Identify an appropriate writing situation, and write about some part or version of those views to a specific audience for a useful purpose. Any of the selections might serve as a model genre for your project.

2. Choose one of the selections from this casebook and write an update on one or two of the major issues raised or argued in the selection. For example, the ANA report was written in 1999. What progress has been made toward the organization's goals for legislative reform in health-related privacy and technology practices? The ANA Web site at www.nursingworld.org is a good place to begin, but you'll find a significant amount of additional material through library and Internet searches on the topic of health care reform.

3. You have read and written about a variety of issues in this casebook. Identify one that you would like to consider more fully, perhaps in the context of the profession you hope to enter: Legal remedies for piracy of writers' electronic publications? Protecting file privacy for clients in an accounting firm? Internal techniques for securing appropriate computer use in the classroom? Once you have decided on a topic, define a writing situation and genre that suit your purpose.

4. Working with a group of classmates, draw up a proposal for ensuring privacy in your school's dormitories. Decide on your audience (the Director of Housing? the Student Senate? the Dorm Council?), and determine your genre and format. You might choose to write an "action report," like the ANA report in this chapter, that includes recommendations, background, and discussion of the issues.

Casebook of Readings:
Weight, Body Image, and Identity

Writer's Notebook

"Weight and body image" is a personal, social, and professional issue. Write about your current attitudes toward the issue and the experiences or influences that have shaped your views. Reflect, too, on how the topic might intersect with your future professional life. Can you, for example, see yourself doing any on-the-job writing because of or on the topic?

Eating Disorders Information Sheets
from the BodyWise Handbook:
"Classroom Teachers" and "At Risk:
All Ethnic and Cultural Groups"
The National Women's Health Information Center

BodyWise, *published by the National Women's Health Information Center, is sponsored by the U.S. Department of Health and Human Services' Office of Women's Health (OWH). Staff members for this program have backgrounds in medicine, public health, education, management, administration, law, library science, social psychology, and women's studies. Their varied skills help them to fulfill the OWH goal of redressing "the inequalities in research, health services and education that have placed the health of women at risk."*

BodyWise, first published in 1999 and revised in 2000, targets middle school educators and other school personnel. Research shows that health and body image problems can begin as early as the age of eight. OWH hopes to educate adults who interact with these children and to encourage intervention in the development of various health problems that accelerate after this age. The project consists of an extensive handbook and a variety of informational packets that guide schools and related agencies in developing policies and programs of their own. "Classroom Teachers" and "At Risk: All Ethnic and Cultural Groups" are fact sheets taken from the BodyWise Information Packet.

Eating Disorders Information Sheet

Classroom Teachers

Teachers have a unique opportunity to help create an environment that enhances students' health and their capacity to learn. This information sheet is designed to provide basic information on eating disorders, how to help promote their early detection, and how to discourage disordered eating.

"Some fourth and fifth grade girls and even some third graders at school seem to be preoccupied with their weight and dieting. This past week, one fifth grade girl was diagnosed with anorexia. Fortunately, the girl's teachers noticed the early warning signs and alerted our Student Assistance Team and the girl's parents."

—School nurse, K-5 elementary school, Connecticut

Why should teachers be concerned?

Disordered eating affects learning outcomes. The irritability, decreased concentration, nausea, headaches, and malaise which often accompany disordered eating have a negative effect on students' learning. They lose the ability to concentrate in class and complete assignments. As preoccupation with food takes over, a student may retreat from social activities; lose interest in school work, family, and friends; and feel lonely, alienated, and disconnected from society.

Younger children are developing eating disorders. Children ages 7 to 13 years are being referred to eating disorder clinics in greater numbers, particularly in the last five years.[1] This increase is due both to the heightened awareness of the signs and symptoms of eating disorders and to their increasing incidence.

Students of all ethnic and cultural groups are vulnerable to developing eating disorders. Although rates of anorexia are higher among Caucasian girls, eating disorders occur among girls of all ethnic and

cultural groups. In addition, hundreds of thousands of boys and men are also experiencing this problem. Other information sheets in this packet address how eating disorders affect boys as well as different ethnic and cultural groups.

Become familiar with the signs and symptoms of possible eating disorders

The early detection of an eating disorder is important to increase the likelihood of successful treatment and recovery. In your interactions with students, you may notice one or more of the physical, behavioral, and emotional signs and symptoms of eating disorders.

Physical

- ◆ Weight loss or fluctuation in short period of time.
- ◆ Abdominal pain.
- ◆ Feeling full or "bloated."
- ◆ Feeling faint or feeling cold.
- ◆ Dry hair or skin, dehydration, blue hands/feet.
- ◆ Lanugo hair (fine body hair).

Behavioral

- ◆ Dieting or chaotic food intake.
- ◆ Pretending to eat, throwing away food.
- ◆ Exercising for long periods of time.
- ◆ Constantly talking about food.
- ◆ Wearing baggy clothes to hide a very thin body.
- ◆ Frequent trips to the bathroom.

Emotional

- ◆ Complaints about appearance, particularly about being or feeling fat.
- ◆ Sadness or comments about feeling worthless.
- ◆ Perfectionist attitude.

Office on Women's Health

Girl Power!

Serve as a role model to your students by being well nourished and feeling comfortable with your body

A teacher who models good health habits provides a more valuable health lesson than any textbook. Teachers may want to assess their own attitudes and behaviors about weight to ensure that they do not inadvertently model body dissatisfaction or promote size discrimination. For example, if students hear teachers discuss their diets, weight loss efforts may be perceived as desirable behaviors. A seemingly innocent conversation that starts with "You look good, have you lost some weight?" may indicate to students that a person's weight is the most important aspect of her or his physical appearance.

Questions to ponder include:

◆ Do I inadvertently promote fear of fat in students by my words and actions?

◆ Am I dissatisfied with my body size and shape?

◆ Am I always on a diet or going on a diet?

◆ Do I feel guilty when I eat certain foods, or do I refuse to eat certain foods while commenting that I am dieting to lose weight?

◆ Do I make negative comments about other people's sizes and shapes?

◆ Am I prejudiced against overweight children and adults? Has a family member ever complained that I was treating an overweight child unfairly?[2]

Integrate topics related to eating disorders into your health and science curricula

The following topics are compatible with national school health and science standards:

◆ Acceptance of diverse body shapes.

◆ Proper nutrition.

◆ Negative effects of dieting.

◆ Positive effects of moderate exercise and negative effects of excessive exercise.

◆ Elimination of harassment and teasing.

◆ Strategies to resist media and cultural pressures.

In grades one through five, focus on good nutrition, positive eating habits, and body acceptance, rather than eating disorders. As beliefs about the importance of thinness have not yet crystallized at this age, both girls and boys are open to positive messages about body image and self-esteem. Although obesity concerns are legitimate, it is not appropriate to present fat in food as "bad." Children at this age are very literal, and those susceptible to developing an eating disorder may become afraid of fat in their food and fat on their bodies.

Begin to discuss eating disorders between fourth and sixth grades. Although it is appropriate to define eating disorders, experts do not recommend providing detailed information to preadolescents about specific behaviors, such as inducing vomiting or taking laxatives. Providing these details may unintentionally encourage experimentation, particularly among students already engaged in weight loss behaviors.

In middle school, emphasize that eating disorders can be caused by multiple factors. Developing a scientific understanding of health is the focus of one of the national standards for middle school science education. The topic of eating disorders provides an excellent example of the bio-psycho-social nature of an illness students hear about in the media.

"When a boy attains puberty, he gets muscles. Boys think, 'I'm getting strong,' and they may start excessive exercise or bodybuilding. When a girl reaches puberty, she thinks, 'I'm getting fat.' I have an 11-year-old patient who won't eat because she's terrified of developing hips."

—Therapist, Washington, DC

Address issues related to eating disorders when teaching media literacy

One of the most important things you can do is to discuss the influence of the media on cultural attitudes toward body shape. A recent study in *Pediatrics* found that dissatisfaction with weight and shapes was very common among preadolescent and adolescent girls.[3]

The frequency of reading fashion magazines was positively and independently associated with dieting and exercising to achieve the perfect body.

When conducting media literacy lessons, include activities that help students differentiate reality from image and become savvy consumers. Students can be encouraged to:

- Evaluate and combat media stereotypes.
- Challenge unhealthy media messages that equate beauty and thinness with self-worth.
- Support products and messages that advocate healthy lifestyles.

Talk to students about growth and development during puberty

Reassure students of the normal diversity of body sizes and shapes that exists among students their age. Pre-adolescents experience significant physical changes during puberty. In fact, the only constant about puberty is "change." Growing up involves sexual maturation, height increases, and variable weight gains.

These changes begin as early as 8 years of age in girls and as late as 14 years of age in boys. Height and weight changes do not necessarily coincide. A girl who begins puberty at age 8 might put on weight before experiencing a growth spurt, or a boy who begins puberty at age 14 might grow taller but not heavier. Eventually, height and weight changes stabilize and students acquire their individual adult shapes.

Promote a safe school environment

Refuse to allow size and sexual discrimination, harassment, teasing, and name calling. Size prejudice hurts all students. Overweight students often experience psychological stress, discrimination, poor body image, and low self-esteem that may last a lifetime. Size prejudice leads students to strive to be thin for fear of ridicule and rejection. Those who are naturally thin may feel that they are valued mainly for their appearance.

In a school environment where comments about body size and weight do not exist, all students will feel safe and free to direct their energies into learning. Schools that promote respect for all cultures and highlight the contributions of women and minorities will enhance students' self-esteem and help them to excel.

Take immediate action when there is concern about a student

Recognize that you do not have the skills to deal with the underlying emotional turmoil that often accompanies eating and exercise problems.

Share information with your school's eating disorders resource person, school nurse, and other teachers or staff members who know the student. Find out if they have noticed similar signs and are concerned.

Decide together the best course of action and who should talk to the student and family members. For more information on how to talk to students and family members, see the information sheet on "**How To Help a Student.**"

Your goal is to communicate to the student that you care and refer her or him to a health care provider who is knowledgeable about eating disorders.

A student may tell you about a friend before you notice any signs yourself.

- Ask the students to describe what they have seen or heard their friend say.
- Tell them that you will follow through and talk with their friend.
- Discuss whether they want the conversation to be confidential or whether you may use their name(s) when you talk with their friend.
- Reassure them that talking with you was the right thing to do. Let them read the fact sheet "How To Help a Friend."
- Ask students if they are worried about having an eating disorder themselves.
- Consider whether they need to talk with a counselor about their concern for their friend.

Resources for Classroom Teachers

The BodyWise Information Packet includes a list of eating disorders resources selected specifically for middle school personnel, including curricular support materials and reading lists for students.

Eating Disorders Catalogue

A free *Eating Disorders Resource Catalogue*, featuring a complete listing of current and classic books, is available by contacting:

Gurze Books
P.O. Box 2238
Carlsbad, CA 92018
Tel: (800) 756-7553
Web site: www.gurze.com.

Educational Organizations

The National Women's Health Information Center
Tel: (800) 994-9662
Web site: www.4woman.gov

Girl Power!
Tel: (800) 729-6686
Web site: www.health.org/gpower

American Anorexia/Bulimia Association
Tel: (212) 575-6200
Web site: www.aabainc.org

National Association of Anorexia Nervosa and Associated Disorders
Tel: (847) 831-3438
Web site: www.anad.org

Eating Disorders Awareness and Prevention, Inc.
Tel: (206) 382-3587
Referral Hotline: (800) 931-2237
Web site: www.edap.org

Harvard Eating Disorders Center
Tel: (617) 236-7766; Web site: www.hedc.org

Massachusetts Eating Disorder Association, Inc.
Tel: (617) 558-1881
Web site: www.medainc.org

Pennsylvania Educational Network for Eating Disorders
Tel: (412) 366-9966
E-mail: PENED1@aol.com

Center for Media Literacy
Tel: (800) 226-9494
Web site: www.medialit.org

Definitions

Anorexia nervosa is self-starvation. People with this disorder eat very little even though they are thin. They have an intense and overpowering fear of body fat and weight gain.

Bulimia nervosa is characterized by cycles of binge eating and purging, either by vomiting or taking laxatives or diuretics (water pills). People with bulimia have a fear of body fat even though their size and weight may be normal.

Overexercising is exercising compulsively for long periods of time as a way to burn calories from food that has just been eaten. People with anorexia or bulimia may overexercise.

Binge eating disorder means eating large amounts of food in a short period of time, usually alone, without being able to stop when full. The overeating or bingeing is often accompanied by feeling out of control and followed by feelings of depression, guilt, or disgust.

Disordered eating refers to troublesome eating behaviors, such as restrictive dieting, bingeing, or purging, which occur less frequently or are less severe than those required to meet the full criteria for the diagnosis of an eating disorder.

End Notes

[1] Brownell, Kelly D., and Christopher G. Fairburn. *Eating Disorders and Obesity*. New York: Guilford Press, 1995.

[2] Adapted from Ikeda, Joanne, and Priscilla Naworski. *Am I Fat? Helping Young Children Accept Differences in Body Size*. Santa Cruz, CA: ETR Associates, 1992.

[3] Fields, Allison E., et al. "Exposure to the Mass Media and Weight Control Concerns Among Girls." *Pediatrics*, 103 (3) 1999, p. e36.

Eating Disorders Information Sheet

At Risk: All Ethnic and Cultural Groups

This information sheet is designed to raise awareness that disordered eating behaviors can occur among all ethnic groups. It highlights findings from recent studies and provides suggestions on how to discourage disordered eating and promote the early detection of eating disorders among all students.

Women and girls of all ethnic groups are susceptible to eating disorders

Many people believe that eating disorders commonly occur among affluent white females. Although the prevalence of these disorders elsewhere in the population is much lower, increasing numbers of cases are being seen in males and minorities.[1]

Girls and women from all ethnic and racial groups may suffer from eating disorders and disordered eating. The specific nature of the most common eating problems, as well as risk and protective factors, may vary from group to group, but no population is exempt.[2] Research findings regarding prevalence rates and specific types of problems among particular groups are limited, but it is evident that disturbed eating behaviors and attitudes occur across all cultures.[3]

Large percentages of African American, American Indian, and Hispanic females are overweight. Being overweight is a risk factor for engaging in disordered eating behaviors. Risk factors and incidence rates for eating disorders can vary dramatically among subgroups of a specific population.

Group identity may play a role in eating disordered development

Strong identification with a group culture can increase self-esteem and provide community support that helps protect young people from developing many health risks, including disordered eating and eating disorders. Young people may reject their group values and be more

susceptible to peer pressure and media messages regarding beauty.[4]

Latina women were almost expected to be more overweight. Latina women living in Puerto Rico were not uncomfortable with extra weight. To them, it wasn't extra. It wasn't an issue.[5]

—Laura, Puerto Rican native who had bulimia as a teenager

Eating disorders among ethnically and culturally diverse girls may be underreported and undetected

Eating disorders among ethnically and culturally diverse girls may be underreported due to the lack of population-based studies that include representatives from these groups. The perception that non-white females are at decreased risk may also contribute to the lack of detection. Stereotyped body images of

Office on Women's Health

ethnically diverse women (e.g., petite Asian American, heavier African American) can also deter detection. In addition, for some ethnic and cultural groups, seeking professional help for emotional problems is not a common practice.

Girls of different ethnic and cultural groups often receive treatment for the accompanying symptoms of an eating disorder, such as depression or malnutrition, rather than for the eating disorder itself. When these girls are finally diagnosed as having an eating disorder, the disorder (especially anorexia), tends to be more severe. This problem is exacerbated by the difficulty they may have in locating culturally sensitive treatment centers.

To deal with my eating disorder, I had to face my loneliness and insecurity. I had to shift my perspective and my lifestyle before I could let go of the excess weight and work on becoming strong and healthy. Now I realize that my experience is shared by many Black women.[6]
—Victoria Johnson, African American fitness expert

School personnel can help

Here are some ideas:

◆ Provide students with diverse role models, of all shapes and sizes, who are praised for their accomplishments, not their appearance.

◆ Invite community representatives to speak about specific cultural attitudes toward food preferences, dietary practices, and body image.

◆ Provide students with information on the relationship between nutrition and overall health.

◆ Gather and disseminate culturally sensitive materials on eating disorders, puberty, and other adolescent health issues.

◆ Conduct media literacy activities that allow students to examine critically how magazines, television, and other media—including those targeting specific cultural groups—present the concept of beauty.

◆ Encourage children and adolescents of all ethnic and cultural groups to exercise and participate in sports and other athletic activities.

◆ Advocate for a safe and respectful school environment that prohibits gender, culture, and racial stereotyping as well as sexual harassment, teasing, and bullying.

Definitions

Anorexia nervosa is self-starvation. People with this disorder eat very little even though they are thin. They have an intense and overpowering fear of body fat and weight gain.

Bulimia nervosa is characterized by cycles of binge eating and purging, either by vomiting or taking laxatives or diuretics (water pills). People with bulimia have a fear of body fat even though their size and weight may be normal.

Overexercising is exercising compulsively for long periods of time as a way to burn calories from food that has just been eaten. People with anorexia or bulimia may overexercise.

Binge eating disorder means eating large amounts of food in a short period of time, usually alone, without being able to stop when full. The overeating or bingeing is often accompanied by feeling out of control and followed by feelings of depression, guilt, or disgust.

Disordered eating refers to troublesome eating behaviors, such as restrictive dieting, bingeing, or purging, which occur less frequently or are less severe than those required to meet the full criteria for the diagnosis of an eating disorder.

End Notes

[1] "Practice Guidelines for Eating Disorders." *American Psychiatric Association Practice Guidelines.* Washington, DC: American Psychiatric Press, 1993.

[2] Striegel-Moore, R.H. & Smolak, L. "The Influence of Ethnicity on Eating Disorders in Women." In RM Eisler, M Hersen (eds), *Handbook of Gender, Culture, and Health.* Mawhaw, NJ: Lawrence Erlbaum, in press.

[3] Dounchis, J.Z., Hayden H., Wifley D.E. "Obesity, Eating Disorders, and Body Image in Ethnically Diverse Children and Adolescents." In J.K. Thompson, L. Smolak (eds), *Body Image, Eating Disorders, and Obesity in Children and Adolescents: Theory, Assessment, Treatment, and Prevention.* Washington, DC: American Psychological Association, 2000.

[4] Root, M.P.P. "Disordered Eating in Women of Color." *Sex Roles,* 22 (7/8), 525-536, 1990.

[5] Thompson, B.W. *A Hunger So Wide and So Deep.* Minneapolis, MN: University of Minnesota Press, 1994, p. 29.

[6] Crute, S. (ed.) *Health and Healing for African-Americans.* Emmaus, PA: Rodale Press, Inc., 1997, p. 92.

Exploring the Message

1. What signs and symptoms are most common in the early stages of an eating disorder? What do students' ethnic or cultural backgrounds have to do with their developing problems and with a teacher's ability to recognize and intervene?

2. What explicit and implied relationships between eating disorders and teaching are revealed in these Fact Sheets? For example, what does it mean for a teacher to be a good role model on the topic? Do OWH's assumptions seem well founded, appropriate, and fair to you?

3. Write a paragraph describing the approach a teacher should take with a student who reveals a friend's possible eating disorder. Are there other adolescent problem-related situations where this approach would be helpful?

4. What is "media literacy" in the context of eating disorders? Can you think of examples that would be appropriate for teaching at the middle school level?

Investigating the Discourse Community

1. What do these readings assume about the scope of a teacher's responsibilities? What distinct assumptions are raised in each reading?

2. In what ways do the Fact Sheets specifically target middle school rather than high school educators? What other school personnel would benefit from the advice offered? Give specific examples to support your answers.

3. How would you compare the voices in the two Fact Sheets? Do their uses of research contribute to any differences you see? Does one or the other style seem more appropriate for the intended audience? On what experiences and beliefs do you base your analysis?

Understanding the Genre

1. Each of the selections begins with a brief overview of upcoming content. What other organization and design elements do the Fact Sheets share? Are the designers' choices effective for the intended audience and purpose? What accounts for differences between them?

2. How do the Fact Sheets use graphics to communicate content and reveal values? Select at least two examples to describe in detail. Would you include more or fewer visuals if you were to revise the documents?

3. The *BodyWise* Handbook and Fact Sheets are available in identical versions in print and on the Web. The Web version does not make use of *hypertext* (see Appendix A, p. 279). Where might this linking technique have

been used, and would it be a useful or appropriate medium change to suggest to OWH?

4. Who, finally, should be responsible for actually treating specific eating disorders? Does this account for anything in the organization of these Fact Sheets?

Writing Activity

Using the two readings as models, create a brief one- or two-page fact sheet on a topic of importance to students in your major or to members of a group to which you belong. Select an appropriately narrow focus to allow you to approach the topic from multiple perspectives. For example, "Classroom Teachers" tells teachers the why, what, and how of an effective educator's response to eating disorders. Include images and other design elements in your layout.

Fat World/Thin World: "Fat Busters," "Equivocators," "Fat Boosters," and the Social Construction of Obesity
Karen Honeycutt

Karen Honeycutt is an Assistant Professor of Sociology at Keene State College in New Hampshire. Her research interests include mass media, popular culture, and social inequalities based on race, class, gender, and sexuality. Dr. Honeycutt's extensive research on obesity was completed while writing a dissertation at the University of Michigan. This article on the topic appears in a collection of essays entitled Interpreting Weight: Social Fatness and Thinness *edited by Jeffrey Sobal and Donna Maurer.*

Do I feel more attractive [since losing weight]? God, yes. I look at myself in the mirror more—I catch myself glancing into one every time I pass it. And I used to avoid looking into big plate-glass windows in the past, because I didn't like my reflection, or was too scared to see what I really looked like. I don't mind seeing myself any more. (Jessica)

I went to Jenny Craig for several months. When I first started, I went to one of their group meetings, and the counselor asked if anyone had gone off the program that week. I looked around and no one was raising their hands, but I decided to be honest and raise mine. So I did and everyone turned and stared at me and started saying, "Was it worth it? Was it worth it?" They were all so mad at me for going off. But I know there were other women there who had too. I was just the only one brave enough to admit it. But I never did again. [laughs] (Laura)

Fat bodies are beautiful. I think all of you are just gorgeous. I saw you out in the pool yesterday, and the fat was billowing out around you, and I thought it was just wonderful. You've made me believe that I'm beautiful too. (Leslie)

While Jessica, Laura, and Leslie were or are all considered "overweight"[1] by American standards, they dealt with this "problem" very differently. Jessica dieted and lost sixty-three pounds (she is a "Fat Buster," in the terms I am using in this chapter). Laura decided to try to stop dieting altogether and accept herself as she was, but did so on her own (she is an "Equivocator"). Leslie joined a national fat activist organization (and thus she is a "Fat Booster" in my classification scheme).

The experiences and outlooks of these three women seem to be three different responses to the same "master narrative" about weight in the United States. In this chapter I argue that the "alternative realities" that the women appear to be constructing for themselves are, in many ways, simply different surface-level responses to the same dominant notions of attractiveness.

Theoretical Framework

Throughout this chapter I blend social constructionist theory, an interactionist perspective, and a cultural studies approach with an emphasis on ideology and audience reception.

Social Constructionist Theory

Is "obesity," presumably objectively defined, a problem in and of itself? A social constructionist perspective would argue that it is more fruitful and interesting to look at the *process* by which obesity has become regarded as a problem (Spector and Kitsuse 1977). In this chapter I do not begin with the assumption that obesity, or being fat, is a problem; rather, consistent with a social constructionist approach, I briefly examine the literature on obesity that demonstrates how it has been *defined* as such, and then I look at how different groups of women have responded to the definition and the process by which their positions are socially reinforced.

Interactionist Perspective

In this chapter I use a modified framework of symbolic interactionism. As enumerated by Ritzer (1992:348), a symbolic interactionist approach emphasizes that human thought is shaped by social interaction, that interaction is made possible by the meanings and symbols that people develop, and that people may change those meanings and symbols. Meanings are critically important to interactionists; as Herbert Blumer wrote, "The nature of an object . . . consists of the meaning that it has for the person for whom it is an object" (1969:11).

Two of the three groups of women that I studied participate in official organizations that reinforce the women's position (e.g., losing weight as being good or bad). In this chapter I show that for the women in those organizations, the meanings created as part of their membership were critical in their construction of fatness as a problem (or not a problem).

Cultural Studies Approach with an Emphasis on Ideology and Audience Reception

Since I am interested in looking at weight—and especially the definition of overweight—as a cultural phenomenon, a cultural studies approach is fruitful. Douglas Kellner (1995:8–9) suggests a three-pronged approach to critical cultural studies: an analysis of the political economy of the production of culture; an analysis of texts, including the importance of ideology (hegemony theory); and an analysis of audience reception of those texts. For example, a cultural studies approach that focuses on political economy would emphasize that to understand a cultural product or outcome—like women's responses to certain constructions of beauty—it is necessary to understand the socioeconomic context in which it is created. Naomi Wolf's (1991:17) work on the diet industry would be included in this category. On the other hand, those writers who focus on ideology—"the terrain of ideas so centrally constitutive of our worldview that we fail to notice what they are" (Press 1991:15)—tend to conduct analyses of particular texts, showing how those texts contribute to (or less often, go against) the dominant ideology. These studies often use Antonio Gramsci's (1971) notion of hegemony theory, which explains how and why dominated people consent to rule by a few even when such rule is demonstrably against their own interests; in short, he focused on ideology (as opposed, for example, to coercion) to explain this consent. Jean Kilbourne's (1994) analysis of advertising falls into this category. Finally, theorists who look at audience reception argue that not all groups respond to dominant ideologies in the same way; for example, some groups attempt to construct counterhegemonic notions of fatness. Marcia Millman's (1980) study of fat people falls in this category.

Of course, these three approaches can be combined. In this chapter I begin with the contention that almost all the research and popular literature on obesity demonstrates an "ideology in action," and clearly the ideology in this case is that women can never be quite thin enough. Several authors (e.g., Chapkis 1986; Hesse-Biber 1996; Orbach 1978) have argued that the intense focus on thinness, particularly *women's* thinness, is extremely damaging to women. I examine why women in three different groups appear to react so differently to the same societal "messages"; in other words, why some women seem to "buy into" hegemonic notions of attractiveness more than others. Specifically, I analyze how many women construct their body size as problematic (or not) within a culture that has very narrowly defined boundaries of acceptance. Most interesting as a test of hegemony theory are those women for whom hegemonic notions appear to *fail*.

Methods

Most of the data for this chapter come from in-depth qualitative interviews conducted between 1992 and 1998 with women in three groups: forty-six in the weight-loss group (the Fat Busters), nineteen in the nondieting, nonactivist group (the Equivocators), and twenty-one in the nondieting, activist group (the Fat Boosters). The interview data are supplemented by participant-observation at weight-loss meetings and fat-activist functions. Further, when appropriate I discuss documents the groups use to bolster their arguments.

The Master Narrative and Three Responses

Study after study confirms that the "master narrative" about weight in the United States is overwhelmingly negative. The literature certainly shows a revulsion toward obesity and obese people that appears to run very deep. For example, English (1991) asserted that fat people are subjected to a unique and more intense form of stigmatization than other deviant groups because of the highly visible obese condition and the societal tendency to attribute personal responsibility to fat people for their condition. Garner and Wooley noted that the social stigma against the obese "is extraordinary in its magnitude and pervasiveness" (1991:729). Other studies have consistently found that overweight and obese individuals are considered unattractive, unpleasant, sexless, lazy, and poor workers (e.g., Clayson and Klassen 1989; Harris, Walters, and Waschull 1991; Hiller 1981, 1982; Rothblum, Miller, and Garbutt 1988). Studies have also found that even women who are not "overweight" by medical standards still consider themselves so and are obsessed with losing weight (e.g., Hesse-Biber 1991; Ogaitis, Chen, and Steelman 1988; Wadden, Stunkard, and Liebschutz 1988).

Given that the master narrative is so negative, how do women respond? This was the question I began with when I interviewed women in three different groups (see Table 1): those who dieted and lost weight (the Fat Busters); those who, while they were considered overweight, said they were "trying to accept themselves as they were" but were doing so on their own (the Equivocators); and those who joined a national fat activist organization, NAAFA, the National Association to Advance Fat Acceptance (the Fat Boosters).

This typology describes the three groups of women in terms of whether or not they accept the mainstream societal definition of beauty as being possible (i.e., whether or not they believe they *can* be thin) and whether or not they seem to take a "passive" or "active" stand. It highlights the importance of social interaction for taking an active stand; I will discuss this more later in this chapter.

The Equivocators are passive because, while they are unhappy about being fat, their most common *reaction* was simply to feel bad about themselves because

Table 1   Typology of Reactions of Overweight Women to Societal Discourse

	Passive	Active
Accept societal definition of beauty as being possible.	Feel bad about oneself: "Thin is beautiful; I'm not working hard enough to lose weight; I have no will power; I am a failure; I am ugly." (nondieting, nonactivist group: the Equivocators)	Diet, lose weight: "Thin is beautiful and I can make myself thin" (weight-loss group: Fat Busters)
Reject societal definition of beauty as being possible.	Feel bad about oneself: "I can't be thin, but how can I be happy with myself when everyone and every-thing around me tells me I'm ugly?" (nondieting, nonactivist group: the Equivocators)	Refuse to diet: "Fat is just a word; fat is not ugly." (nondieting, activist group: Fat Boosters)

of it. They were not currently dieting (so they were not actively trying to lose weight, which presumably would have made them feel better), nor did they join an organization like NAAFA that would have given them social support in their decision not to diet. Therefore, their decision was, by my terms, more passive than that of those in the weight-loss and fat-activist groups.

The Equivocators also were unusual in that they expressed both belief and disbelief that meeting a societal construction of beauty—that is, losing weight and becoming thin—was even possible. While the Fat Busters overwhelmingly believed that becoming thin *was* possible—after all, they had done it themselves— and the Fat Boosters overwhelmingly expressed a belief that becoming thin was *not* possible, usually because their own dieting experiences had (they argued) ul-timately made them even fatter, the Equivocators were ambivalent. Some women in this category stated sadly that while they could *lose* weight, they could never keep it off; thus they seemed to believe what Fat Boosters believed. Other Equivo-cators expressed the belief that since they had lost weight in the past, they could again if only they tried harder—that is, they sounded very much like Fat Busters—but they were not up to dieting at this time. Interestingly, many Equivo-cators expressed *both* sentiments; that is, at times during the interview they would speak wistfully of thin women but argue that thinness did not seem to be a realistic goal for themselves, while later in the interview they would admit that they had not given up entirely on being thin, they just weren't ready to diet *right now*. This ambivalence should not be surprising given the Equivocators' lack of social support. In comparison to Equivocators, some of the Fat Boosters may have been larger, but their group's antidiet stand sustained them in their decision not to change their body size.

Weight-Loss Group: Fat Busters

Between 1992 and 1997 I conducted interviews with forty-six women whom I call "Fat Busters." Thirty-two were white, while fourteen were women of color, mostly African-American. They ranged in age from nineteen to sixty-one. These women had lost from thirty to eighty pounds, mostly through conventional methods such as calorie-cutting and increasing exercise on one's own or through commercial programs like Jenny Craig, Nutri-System, or Weight Watchers. At the time of the interview they had kept the weight off for anywhere from six months to several years.

Before being interviewed, Fat Busters completed a four-page survey to elicit information about three areas. First was how their feelings about various things had changed (if at all) since they lost weight (e.g., "Since I lost weight . . . men pay more attention to me," ". . . I am more attractive," ". . . I pay more attention to my appearance"). Second was how they felt about their own attractiveness both before and after losing weight (e.g., "I used to secretly wonder what my significant other saw in me because I was heavy," "In the past, I have avoided going to reunions or to visit old friends because I was embarrassed about my weight"). Third was how they felt about other overweight people once they were thin (e.g., "I look at overweight people now and feel sorry for them," "If I can lose weight, anyone can," "Our society puts too much emphasis on weight"). The survey included both closed-ended items such as those just described, which were rated on a five-point Likert scale of "strongly disagree" to "strongly agree," and open-ended questions that asked respondents to discuss their weight-loss experience in more detail. In addition to data from the interviews and surveys, this section includes some discussion of weight-loss literature (e.g., handouts from weight-loss group meetings) and weight-loss meetings.

Several themes emerged from my interviews with Fat Busters. First, when they were fat, these women were acutely aware of themselves as *being* fat. During the interviews, I asked when the women felt their "fatness" most strongly. While some were able to pinpoint times when they felt particularly aware of being overweight (and particularly vulnerable to being *noticed by* others as being overweight)—times such as walking down the street eating an ice cream cone, or waiting to buy high-calorie foods in the checkout line at the supermarket—for many women awareness of their overweight status seemed to be constant. Mindy and Carol were typical in this respect:

> It's hard to pinpoint times when I felt it more. I mean, it was just always *there*. I was always aware, no matter what I was doing, that I was really heavy. (Mindy)

> When was I aware of myself as being overweight? [laughs] When was I *not*? Even if I wasn't doing something connected with my weight, like even if I wasn't on a diet or trying on clothes, I was still always very conscious of being this humongous person. (Carol)

A second theme was a strong belief in their own power to control their weight—and, by extension, a strong belief in *others'* power to control *their* weight.

Many Fat Busters voiced some disapproval of other people—usually women—who were overweight. The vast majority indicated either agreement or strong agreement with the statement on the survey, "If I can lose weight, anyone can." While medical research indicates a strong genetic component to obesity, those studies are not consistent with the recent weight-loss experiences of the women in my study. That is, the women I interviewed seemed to be "success stories" that the medical studies imply are rarities. Thus, relying on their own recent experiences, many tended to judge others rather harshly:

> It's not easy [to lose weight], I'm not saying that. I'm just saying that even if there *is* some genetic factors involved, you can overcome them. *I* did. Just eat less and exercise more. (Mindy)

> I think there may be some genetic component to obesity. But all I'm saying is that if anyone did what I did, they would lose weight too. It was hard, but I did it. (Dana)

This belief in their own control was also constantly socially reinforced through interactions with others at meetings at weight-loss centers. For example, women who lost weight were awarded with applause and with ribbons for achieving certain milestones. In addition, women that I interviewed from one particular weight-loss center always used the phrase "When I lost *my* weight" rather than the more common usage, "When I lost weight." They did not seem to even be aware of this until I pointed it out and asked them about it. The literature available at meetings also reinforced their sense of control. For example, the fact that weight-loss "success stories" are prominently featured in such literature implicitly argues that *these* women, too, can lose weight if only they try hard enough.

A third theme was that weight loss was consistently equated with improved 20
appearance—and more specifically, *feminine* appearance and attractiveness to men. In this way, weight loss can be seen as an accommodation of gender norms. Although many respondents mentioned health concerns as a reason for wanting to lose weight, when they spoke in more detail what they said more often than not equated weight loss with improved *appearance*. Thus notions of femininity, of being the "correct" weight to be attractive to the opposite sex, were very much a part of many women's weight-loss narratives. More specifically, very few mentioned "feeling healthier" once they lost weight; rather, they were much more likely to say they "felt prettier."

Fourth, the women in my study saw their lives as having been significantly transformed with the weight loss. Specifically, they generally indicated on their surveys that they considered themselves more attractive, more assertive, more outgoing, happier, emotionally stronger, and sexier since losing weight. *All* the women interviewed mentioned in some form or another how their lives had changed for the better since they lost weight (although some emphasized more changes than others):

> I definitely feel more attractive, but it's a weird feeling. I was sitting in a bar with a girlfriend recently, and this man was staring at me, and all I could think was, do

I look that awful? Is my lipstick on my teeth or something? Then I realized he was looking at me because he found me attractive. It was like, revelation! (Lynn)

Nondieting, Nonactivist Group: The Equivocators

In 1992 and 1993 I interviewed nineteen women who were not currently dieting and who in fact had responded to an ad for "women who are comfortable with their bodies despite being 'overweight' by conventional standards." I had intended that this group be a counterpoint to the women in the weight-loss group, but it did not work out this way. Most striking in the interviews was the fact that although these women had identified themselves as being "happy with themselves despite their weight," during the interviews most expressed strong dissatisfaction with their bodies. They tended to be ambivalent about the process of losing weight, equivocating on whether or not they even believed it was possible for them to do so. They thus became the nondieting, nonactivist group: the Equivocators. Sixteen were white, while two were African-American, and one was Hispanic. They ranged in age from twenty-one to forty-five.

Several themes emerged from my interviews with the Equivocators. First, many had been fat since childhood, and the feelings they expressed during interviews showed many common bonds:

> It was awful being fat as a child. If I think I have it bad now, I just think back to then and realize how much better off I am. Kids would call me fatso all the time. They'd laugh when I got on the school bus because I couldn't walk down the aisle without touching the sides. (Marie)

> It's hard being different in childhood. Sometimes I would look in the mirror and think, you're not that fat. Then I would look again and be repulsed. But I'm not sure if I really hated myself that much—I mean I always felt like I was a good person inside. Maybe I was just responding to other kids' views of me. (Donna)

Second, the Equivocators were ambivalent about their own ability to lose weight. All had attempted to lose weight many times. Sometimes they did, but they always gained it back. Even so, some still believed they could lose weight if they tried hard enough:

> I *could* lose weight if I wanted to. I've done it enough in the past. I mean, I can't blame people for being disgusted [at my weight]. I'm disgusted with myself sometimes. (Donna)

Third, all of the Equivocators mentioned things they had given up because of their weight. The following are typical:

> Sometimes I think about all the things I've given up and I just can't believe it. My tenth-year high-school reunion was last year and I would have loved to go, but there was no way I was going to let them see me this way. (Melissa)

In the past, I have avoided so many things. It's just crazy. It's like I think I don't deserve to do fun things, just because of my weight. But when I go on a diet and lose a few pounds, suddenly I deserve them. I deserve to be treated better when I'm thinner. I'm really trying to get over this. (Susan)

Overall, as I indicated in the typology of reactions earlier, the Equivocators seemed to have a passive response to societal constructions of beauty; that is, they often simply felt miserable about their size but did not get involved in a group that would help them either change their size or the way they feel about their size.

Nondieting, Activist Group: The Fat Boosters

Between 1996 and 1998 I interviewed twenty-one members of NAAFA, the national fat activist organization. All of those interviewed were fat (although not all members of the organization are). Thirteen respondents were white and eight were women of color, seven of whom were African-Americans. They ranged in age from twenty-one to sixty. I also conducted participant-observation at regional NAAFA functions and at the national convention in July/August 1997, and analyzed documents produced by the organization.

Probably the most important theme that emerged in the interviews with Fat Boosters can be summed up by the statement of one: "My weight is my weight and I have to learn to live with it." The official NAAFA policy is that fatness is largely genetically determined and thus beyond individuals' control; this is in stark contrast with the Fat Busters' belief that they can reshape their bodies through dieting. For the Fat Boosters, joining NAAFA meant constantly hearing that "diets don't work." This message is reinforced in a number of ways: through members wearing buttons with a red line through the word DIET, through the group's championing of National No-Diet Day, and through members' interactions with each other. An example of the latter occurred during a dinner at the 1997 national convention. When one woman remarked how good the (high-fat and high-calorie) food tasted and how much she loved to eat, another woman angrily retorted, "We're trying to get across the idea that we're not fat because we love to eat, and you're not helping."

A second theme that became clear in my interviews, observations, and document analysis of this group was that they were attempting to change their own— and sometimes society's—definition of "fatness." For example, this became clear during the welcoming breakfast at the 1997 NAAFA convention, when the speaker, Glenn Gaesser, author of *Big Fat Lies: The Truth about Your Weight and Your Health* (1996), argued—to wild applause—that "moderate obesity" could actually be *good* for a person.

Third, it was obvious that members gained a sense of empowerment through 30 NAAFA, in particular through their interactions with other NAAFA members. For example, during a workshop at the 1997 convention, participants were encouraged to change their attributions about why people sometimes react negatively to them: "Don't automatically assume it's because of your weight," the group leader said; "maybe the person is just having a bad day" Leslie, who was quoted in the opening of this chapter, is another example who spoke of gaining more self-confidence as she spent time at the convention. The organization itself recognizes that interactions with other members is critical in maintaining self-confidence; and a popular workshop at the 1997 meeting was one that discussed strategies for "taking these good thoughts home with you."

The More Things Change, the More They Stay the Same . . .

My original intention was to examine *different* responses that women have to societal constructions of obesity. The more I worked on this project, however, the more problematic I found my original assumptions. While on the surface the women in this study appear to be reacting in ways vastly at odds with each other, on a deeper level the reactions seem more similar than I originally imagined.

First, the Fat Busters, the Equivocators, *and* the Fat Boosters in some ways define their identities *reactively*—i.e., in reaction to societal constructions that, I would argue, they are themselves perpetuating. The Fat Busters define themselves as "not-fat-any-more"; the weight-loss groups of which they were or are members are based on accommodating conventional notions about fatness. The Equivocators, with their expressed dissatisfaction with their bodies and their admission of how different they think their lives would be if they were thin, are similarly accepting of societal prejudices about obesity.

However, what might be less obvious is that the Fat Boosters also define their identities reactively: Their group *exists* because of the weight issue; it is salient in everything the group does and thus perpetuates a kind of us-versus-them (fat-versus-thin) mentality. For example, in a recent national NAAFA newsletter the editor expressed disdain at news and journal stories about people who had lost weight and kept it off. Other newsletter articles suggested that food restriction of any kind (other than that required for certain diseases like diabetes) is a "sellout." Similarly, a book reviewer expressed anger that the author had suggested that there was a correlation between what people eat and their size. In short, the intense, self-conscious, and *defensive* focus on weight is inescapable.

My second point, which is closely related to the first, is that all three groups in many ways do not *challenge* the "fat-is-ugly" bias. It is clear that the Fat Busters perpetuated conventional constructions. The very groups they joined are committed to helping women "get over" being fat. In interviews, their own antifat biases, which were in many cases socially reinforced by their participation in weight-loss groups, also came through clearly:

> I really feel sorry for them [overweight people], but on the other hand, I lost weight so I know they can too. . . . Did you ever notice who drinks diet sodas and eats diet food? Diet jello, diet lunches, diet everything. Fat people do. Thin people eat normal stuff. I look at fat people sometimes and think, why are you drinking a Diet Coke, who are you trying to kid? I know they stuff themselves later, because I used to myself. (Lisa)

Sometimes when I see fat people I think, that's what I used to look like, and it really repulses me. (Mindy)

I remember years ago when I was heavy, I saw a talk show on TV that had some overweight women on it saying they liked themselves heavy. One of them said when she goes to bars with her make-up on and her clothes perfect, all the men are looking at her, not at the size-10 woman next to her. I remember thinking, no way. I just knew that wasn't true. (Andrea)

Similarly, the Equivocators perpetuated societal constructions when they expressed dissatisfaction with their bodies and antifat attitudes of their own. For example:

I can understand it when I'm sitting on BART [the subway system in the Bay Area] and no one wants to sit next to me because I spill over, I take more than my share of space. Anyone who sat next to me would have to really squeeze. (Diane)

Again, however, what isn't obvious is that the Fat Boosters also express conventional antifat biases. While they are ostensibly fighting *against* hegemonic constructions of attractiveness, they don't necessarily question the idea that "thin is beautiful"; rather, they argue that it's "not their fault" that they are fat and that they shouldn't be "blamed" for it. Admittedly, some—like Leslie, who was quoted in the opening to this chapter—truly do believe that "fat is beautiful too"; however, many others admit that if they had a choice, they would prefer to be thin themselves. While in some cases this may simply reflect a recognition that their lives would be easier (that is, they would be accepted more easily by members of society) if they were thin, in other cases I believe it reflects the same kind of "fat-is-ugly" belief that pervades mainstream society.

This underlying "there's-something-wrong-with-fat" view also comes out in one of the major items on NAAFA's platform: disseminating the view that whether or not one is fat is largely genetically determined, so fat people are not making a choice and, again, should not be "blamed" for their size. Rather than arguing, "I've chosen to be fat and so what? Fat is beautiful too"—which would obviously be quite a radical stand—the organization argues that their members' being fat is beyond their control, a substantially different argument, which implies a recognition that there is something inherently *wrong* with being fat. And since the organization also argues that fatness is not the huge health risk that the mainstream medical profession says it is, then what's wrong with being fat must be that it's ugly, unattractive, and deviant.[2]

Weight has an enormous impact on the everyday lives of women in all three groups. They are very aware of themselves as being "of a certain size," whether "average" or "fat," and this appears to be a large part of their identity. For example, the Fat Busters consistently indicated an intense fear of regaining their lost weight:

If I started gaining the weight back—it's really hard to even think about. When I was dieting all the time, going up and down, I felt totally out of control. I think if I started to get heavy again I would just feel out of control again. (Lisa)

There's no way I'll ever gain the weight back. No way. [shaking her head violently] It was just too painful to be overweight. I don't know what I would do if I got that way again. (Cheryl)

Fat Busters also indicated that they were "careful" about what they ate, that they "watched" their diets, that they had "good" days (when they did not eat "bad" foods such as chocolate or ice cream) and "bad" days (when they strayed from what they thought were "good" eating habits). Again, Cheryl is a good example:

Sometimes I think I should just be more relaxed about it, but then I remember what it was like to be fat and I can't [be more relaxed]. So I just read labels like crazy, and try to do extra exercise whenever I eat bad stuff. I just watch out all the time. [KH: Is this kind of vigilance tiring?] Yes. Yes. But I just figure it's the price I have to pay to stay skinny. (Cheryl)

Weight also had a large impact on the everyday lives of the Equivocators. As I mentioned earlier, several spoke sadly about things they had given up because of their weight, such as participating in activities they had enjoyed before they gained weight or seeing people who knew them when they were thinner. They clearly saw themselves differently at different weights, and recognized that other people saw them differently as well. Similarly, the Fat Boosters admitted that despite NAAFA's championing of the idea that "fat people should be able to do anything thin people do," some things they did at NAAFA functions—like wearing shorts or eating an ice cream cone in public—they simply would not do at home. (A few even mentioned that even though they did go swimming with other NAAFA members, they were still very aware of themselves as being "fat people" and very aware of others' reactions to them.) In other words, their group's call for the "normalization" of fatness has not had as large an impact on the women as they (or the group) would probably like.

Finally, women in the two groups who had formal ties to organizations (the weight-loss group and the fat-activist group) seemed to be very aware not only of their own weight, but also that of other women. For example, for many Fat Busters the fear of regaining weight manifested itself in constant surveillance of both themselves and other women. Dana is a prime example:

I'm very aware of my size now, maybe more now than when I was overweight. I look at other women on the street and I think, I'm thinner than her, I'm a little bigger than her but she's got small bones, I'm about her size and she looks good so I must be OK too. And then I'll go eat my yogurt. (Dana [lost 30 pounds])

Even the Fat Boosters showed the same kind of surveillance. For example, in NAAFA a distinction is made between two weight categories: "mid-size" and "supersize," for which the dividing line is size 48. Within the organization debates have raged over which group has more problems. Some supersize women say that midsize women, being closer to "average," don't understand how difficult it is to be supersize. Some midsize women have expressed jealousy because at some NAAFA social functions (such as dances), the supersize women seem to get the most attention from men. In addition, one NAAFA member told me, rather sheepishly, that she was able to go swimming at the national convention because she wasn't "the fattest woman here." While this might seem extreme, many of the women I spoke with did seem to be very aware of their size in comparison to that of other members.

Conclusion: Hegemony Theory Revisited

Defining their identities reactively; expressing antifat attitudes; the enormous impact that weight continues to have on their lives; and the surveillance of other women's bodies—what can be concluded from all of these? I argue that the intense preoccupation with weight—and negative judgments of perceived overweight—that the literature shows most American women have, regardless of size, is perhaps even more pronounced with women who either were or are overweight themselves. While this might not be surprising for Fat Busters and Equivocators, I did find it surprising for the Fat Boosters.

Early cultural studies work on "audience reception" tended to portray people as passive receptors who were indoctrinated into dominant ways of thinking through cultural products, e.g., the mass media. More recent work on audience reception, though, has reminded us that hegemony is never total; rather, individuals and groups can potentially make sense of dominant ideas in different ways (Croteau and Hoynes 1997). I originally embraced this "active audience" view, expecting to argue that in the case of fat women, not all of them simply passively accept mainstream society's view of them as being ugly and morally deviant. Rather, I expected to argue, many actively reject constructions and norms of beauty that devalue and exclude them. Certainly I have collected a great deal of data on Fat Boosters that would support this contention; NAAFA newsletters, in particular, consistently support a view of the world that includes "fat" in its definition of beauty.

However, as I detailed in the previous section, the women participating in this project seemed to accept, on many levels, the larger society's prejudice about their body size. Thus my original suppositions about the inherent distinctiveness of the women's reactions in the three groups were not supported. Instead, in this chapter I have shown that in many ways the Fat Busters, Equivocators, and Fat Boosters do not challenge conventional definitions of beauty, but bolster them, colluding in constructions that exclude large numbers of women. 45

Notes

1. I put the word "overweight" in quotation marks to indicate that it is a social construction. In fact, there is no clear definition of words like "overweight" or "obese" in most of the literature; the words are often used as

though their definition were obvious. This is not only imprecise but it also obscures the fact that weight status is culturally contingent (i.e., what is considered "overweight" in the United States might very well not be considered so in the Caribbean) and ahistorical (i.e., standards of "ideal" weight have changed over time).

Members of NAAFA prefer the word "fat"—despite, or maybe because of, the fact that it is so emotionally "loaded"—and argue that "overweight" has hidden implications: "Over whose weight?" they ask. I have tried to use the word *fat* simply as an adjective, especially when referring to respondents who are NAAFA members. (This was a bit jarring at first, given that it has such negative connotations in the United States.)

2. Note the parallel here between the size acceptance movement, of which NAAFA is a main proponent, and the gay rights movement. Of course, I understand that from a social movement perspective, to argue that something is not a "choice"—that one is born a certain way—makes political sense in that people are (presumably) less likely to blame someone for being gay or fat if it is not their "choice." However, my point here is that simply asking the question "Is it a choice?" implies at least two things: first, that there is a "hierarchy of sexual orientations" or a "hierarchy of body sizes" and that being straight or being thin is *inherently better* than being gay or being fat; and second, that given the choice, gay or fat people would prefer to be straight or thin. So while it may seem quite progressive and tolerant to say "Those poor people were born that way so we'll give them the same things (e.g., political rights, antidiscrimination protection) that everyone else gets," it doesn't necessarily mean that homosexuality or fatness is considered to be as "good" an "option" of sexual orientation or body size as heterosexuality or thinness. To me, a more interesting (and certainly more provocative) way to answer the question "Is it a choice?" is to say, "Well, maybe it is, but so what?"

References

Blumer, H. 1969. *Symbolic Interactionism: Perspective and Method.* Englewood Cliffs, NJ: Prentice-Hall.

Chapkis, W. 1986. *Beauty Secrets: Women and the Politics of Appearance.* Boston: South End.

Clayson, D. E., and M. L. Klassen. 1989. "Perception of Attractiveness by Obesity and Hair Color." *Perceptual and Motor Skills* 68:199–202.

Croteau, D., and W. Hoynes. 1997. *Media/Society: Industries, Images, and Audiences.* Thousand Oaks, CA: Pine Forge.

English, C. 1991. "Food Is My Best Friend: Self-Justifications and Weight Loss Efforts." *Research in the Sociology of Health Care* 9:335–45.

Gaesser, G. A. 1996. *Big Fat Lies: The Truth about Your Weight and Your Health.* New York: Fawcett.

Garner, D. M., and S. C. Wooley. 1991. "Confronting the Failure of Behavioral and Dietary Treatments for Obesity." *Clinical Psychology Review* 11:729–80.

Gramsci, A. 1971. *Selections from the Prison Notebooks of Antonio Gramsci,* edited by G. Nowell-Smith and Q. Hoare. London: Lawrence and Wishart.

Harris, M. B., L. C. Walters, and S. Waschull. 1991. "Gender and Ethnic Differences in Obesity-Related Behaviors and Attitudes in a College Sample." *Journal of Applied Social Psychology* 21:1545–66.

Hesse-Biber, S. 1991. "Women, Weight, and Eating Disorders: A Socio-cultural and Political-economic Analysis." *Women's Studies International Forum* 14(3): 173–91.

———. 1996. *Am I Thin Enough Yet? The Cult of Thinness and the Commercialization of Identity.* New York: Oxford University Press.

Hiller, D. V. 1981. "The Salience of Overweight in Personality Characterization." *Journal of Psychology* 108(2):233–40.

———. 1982. "Overweight as Master Status: A Replication." *Journal of Psychology* 110(1):107–13.

Kellner, D. 1995. "Cultural Studies, Multiculturalism, and Media Culture." Pp. 5–17 in *Gender, Race, and Class in Media,* edited by Gail Dines and Jean M. Humez. Thousand Oaks, CA: Sage.

Kilbourne, J. 1994. "Still Killing Us Softly: Advertising and the Obsession with Thinness." Pp. 395–418 in *Feminist Perspectives on Eating Disorders,* edited by P. Fallon, M. A. Katzman, and S. C. Wooley. New York: Guilford.

Millman, M. 1980. *Such a Pretty Face: Being Fat in America.* New York: Berkley.

Ogaitis, S., T. T. L. Chen, and L. C. Steelman. 1986. "Social Location, Significant Others and Body Image among Adolescents." *Social Psychology Quarterly* 49(4):330–37.

Orbach, S. 1978. *Fat Is a Feminist Issue.* New York: Berkley.

Press, A. 1991. *Women Watching Television: Gender, Class, and Generation in the American Television Experience.* Philadelphia: University of Pennsylvania Press.

Ritzer, G. 1992. *Sociological Theory,* 3rd edition. New York: McGraw-Hill.

Rothblum, E. D., C. T. Miller, and B. Garbutt. 1988. "Stereotypes of Obese Female Job Applicants." *International Journal of Eating Disorders* 7:277–83.

Spector, M., and J. I. Kitsuse. 1977. *Constructing Social Problems.* Menlo Park, CA: Cummings.

Wadden, T. A., A. J. Stunkard, and J. Liebschutz. 1988. "Three-year Follow-up of the Treatment of Obesity by Very Low Calorie Diet, Behavior Therapy, and Their Combination." *Journal of Consulting and Clinical Psychology* 56:925–28.

Wolf, N. 1991. *The Beauty Myth: How Images of Beauty Are Used Against Women.* New York: Morrow.

Exploring the Message

1. Briefly define "Fat Buster," "Equivocator," and "Fat Booster." Do these categories fit the people you know who deal with similar weight issues?

2. What is social constructivist theory? What role does it play in Honeycutt's approach to her topic?

3. Compare Honeycutt's initial hypothesis about the social construction of obesity with the major conclusions she reached after completing her research.

4. Describe the demographic diversity of the women Honeycutt interviewed and surveyed. How important is this variation to her conclusions?

Investigating the Discourse Community

1. Honeycutt asks, "Is 'obesity,' presumably objectively defined, a problem in and of itself?" What discourse communities would be most likely to define obesity as a problem and to see that definition as an objective one? What does the word "presumably" tell you about a sociologist's perspective on the topic?

2. In the description of her Sociology 101 course, Honeycutt says, "This course will introduce the 'sociological perspective' as a tool for understanding the connections between the individual's everyday life and larger-scale processes and structures within society." How is this perspective evident in "Fat World/Thin World"?

3. What types of readers does Honeycutt expect to read her essay? What clues lead to your conclusions?

4. Describe and analyze Honeycutt's primary research techniques. For example, how did she find and select people to interview for each of the major categories and were her selection strategies appropriate for her goals? What types of questions did she formulate and why?

Understanding the Genre

1. Define the role of each major section of the article. For example, what is covered in the "Theoretical Framework" section? Why is it included so early in the essay?

2. How would you define Honeycutt's persona? Did anything about her style surprise you in an article of this genre?

3. What strategies did Honeycutt use for synthesizing her extensive primary research and integrating it into the text of this brief article? Were her choices effective?

4. How beneficial was Table 1 to your understanding of the three major categories?

Writing Activity

Imagine you are Karen Honeycutt and have been asked to reframe this research for an article in a popular magazine, such as *Time* or *Vogue*. Select a magazine; analyze the persona that you would create, as well as the audience that you would expect to reach; and write an introduction and conclusion for the article.

Shallow Hal
Movie review by Roger Ebert

Roger Ebert has been the film critic for the Chicago Sun Times *since 1967. He is most widely recognized, however, as the co-host of the series "Siskel & Ebert," a name now synonymous with the television movie-review genre. Since Siskel's death in 1999, Ebert has hosted the show (now called "Ebert & Roeper at the Movies") with critic Richard Roeper. In 1975, Ebert became the first film reviewer to receive the Pulitzer Prize for criticism. His publications include screenplays, such as* Beyond the Valley of the Dolls *(1970); essay collections, such as* I Hated, Hated This Movie *(2000) and* The Greatest Movies *(2002); and an annual* Roger Ebert's Movie Yearbook.

*** (PG-13)

Rosemary: Gwyneth Paltrow   Hal: Jack Black

Mauricio: Jason Alexander   Walt: Rene Kirby

Tony Robbins: Himself

Twentieth Century Fox presents a film directed by Bobby Farrelly and Peter Farrelly.
Written by Sean Moynihan and the Farrellys. Running time: 113 minutes.
Rated PG-13 (for language and sexual content).

"Shallow Hal" is given words of wisdom at the deathbed of his father, who under the influence of pain-killers is speaking from the deepest recesses of his being. "Hot young tail," his father says. "That's what it's all about." He makes Hal promise to date only beautiful women, and to beware of falling in love—"that was the tragic mistake I made with your mother."

Hal (Jack Black) grows up to follow this counsel. He has no meaningful relationships with women because meaningful is not what he's looking for. With his running-mate Mauricio (Jason Alexander from "Seinfeld"), whose spray-on hair looks like a felt hat, he prowls the bars. His life is a series of brief encounters, until one day he is trapped on an elevator with Tony Robbins, the self-help guru, who hypnotizes him and tells him to look inside the women who he meets, for their inner beauty. Soon after, Shallow Hal begins to have extraordinary success with women—not least with a nurse and ex-Peace Corps volunteer named Rosemary, who looks exactly like Gwyneth Paltrow because that's the way Hal's mind is working these days. The movie plays with point-of-view shots to show us that Rosemary actually weighs about 300 pounds, but to Hal, she's slender and—well, Gwyneth Paltrow.

At first Rosemary thinks his compliments are ironic insults, and is wounded. Then she realizes he's sincere, and really does think she's beautiful. This has never happened to her before. They begin an enchanted romance, to the consternation of Hal's friends, who can't understand why he's dating this fatso. Of course, if the Tony Robbins hypnosis ever wears off . . .

"Shallow Hal," written with Sean Moynihan, is the new movie by the Farrelly brothers, Bobby and Peter. They specialize in skirmishes on the thin line between comedy and cruelty. "There's Something About Mary" had its paraplegic suitor; "Dumb and Dumber" had the little blind boy; "Me, Myself and Irene" was about a man with a Jekyll-and-Hyde personality, and so on. Whether we laugh or are offended depends on whether our lower or higher sensibilities are in command at the time. The Farrellys have a way of tickling the lower regions while sending the higher centers off on errands. Reader, I confess I have laughed.

"Shallow Hal" is often very funny, but it is also surprisingly moving at times. It contains characters to test us, especially Walt (Rene Kirby), who has spina bifida and an essentially immobile lower body. Kirby doesn't use a chair or braces, but lopes around on all fours, and is an expert skier, horseman, bicyclist and acrobat. Because he is clearly handicapped, we think at first his scenes are in "bad taste"—but he doesn't think so; his zest for life allows us to see his inner beauty, and his sense of humor, too, as in a scene where he explains why he's putting on rubber gloves.

There's something about the Farrellys that isn't widely publicized—they're both sincerely involved in work with the mentally retarded. There is a sense that they're not simply laughing at their targets, but sometimes with them, or in sympathy with them. "Shallow Hal" has what look like fat jokes, as when a chair collapses under Rosemary, but the punchline is tilted toward empathy.

Now here's a heartfelt message from Valerie Hawkins of Homewood, Ill., who writes: "Um, what am I missing, regarding 'Shallow Hal?' The trailer prattles on about how Hal now sees only the inner beauty of a woman. No, he doesn't. When he looks at an overweight woman and instead sees her as a thin woman, that's not inner beauty. What he's seeing is a typical tall, thin professional model type—which in some ways is more insulting than if he saw her as she really is and instantly rejected her."

This is persuasive. Hal sees Paltrow, who doesn't spend a lot of time wearing the "fat suit" you've read about in the celeb columns. What if she wore the fat suit in every scene, and he thought she was beautiful because of the Robbins training? This would also be funny; *we* could see her as fat but *he* couldn't. At the same time, screams of rage would come from the producers, who didn't pay Paltrow untold millions to wear a fat suit.

Hawkins has a good argument from our point of view and hers, but not from Hal's, because he *does* literally see an idealized beauty. To be sure, it is exterior beauty, not interior, but how else to express his experience visually?

I think we understand to accept the Farrellys' premise as filtered through the   10 realities of the marketplace, in which you do not put Gwyneth Paltrow into a movie where she doesn't look like Gwyneth Paltrow. (John Travolta played an Abominable Snowman from space in "Battleship Earth," and look how that went over.) By showing the idealized Paltrow, the Farrellys set up the third act, in which Shallow Hal does indeed see Paltrow as fat, and has to deal with how he feels about that. If she had been fat all along in the movie's eye, how could his test be made clear visually? Early and late, we see Paltrow as Hal sees her, which is not an evasion but maybe the point.

Whether or not you accept the fat-thin argument, the movie offers a good time. It's very funny across the usual range of Farrelly gags, from the spray-on toupee to a woman with a long second toe to a man with a tail. Paltrow is truly touching. And Black, in his first big-time starring role, struts through with the blissful confidence of a man who knows he was born for stardom, even though he doesn't look like your typical Gwyneth Paltrow boyfriend. He's not so thin, either.

Note: Only the most attentive audience members will catch the Farrellys' subtle reference to a famous poem by Emily Dickinson.

___

Exploring the Message

1. Write your own brief plot summary of the film based on information provided in the review. If you have seen the movie, add any significant events that you think Ebert should have included.
2. What are the major themes of "Shallow Hall"? What are Ebert's attitudes toward the filmmakers' handling of these themes?
3. What point is Ebert trying to argue in his discussion of the character Walt? Does he succeed in persuading you of his point of view?
4. What is Valerie Hawkins's criticism of the film? What position does Ebert take in response to her argument? What are your reactions to each point of view?

Investigating the Discourse Community

1. How would you describe Ebert's persona?
2. As you may already know, Ebert has dealt with weight issues in his own life. Does this insight affect your responses to his views of "Shallow Hal"?
3. What assumptions about the nature of Hollywood and the movie industry drive Ebert's arguments about the way the filmmakers handle Hal's

definition of beauty? Where else in the review does Ebert use his understanding of films and filmmaking to strengthen his points?

4. Why does Ebert include the responses of Valerie Hawkins in his review? Suggest several effects that their inclusion could have on his readers?

Understanding the Genre

1. How does Ebert integrate plot into his evaluation of the film? Analyze several examples.

2. What would you say is the central purpose of this review? How does this purpose determine the details and examples that Ebert includes and excludes?

3. To what extent does this review conform to your expectations of a film review? For example, what elements are common to reviews and which seem unique?

4. Why does Ebert write that Mauricio's "spray-on hair looks like a felt hat"?

5. Ebert has said, "If I value television because it allows me to exchange views with a colleague I respect, I value print because it allows me to be uninterrupted." Respond to this insight into how the same medium, a review, is shaped into distinct genres.

Writing Activity

Select a film whose major theme—or, as in the case of "Shallow Hal," whose handling of a major theme—is socially or politically controversial. Write a review similar to Ebert's, aimed at a general audience, or identify a publication whose reviews you read regularly and write a review appropriate for its readers.

Let Us Refer You. Today.
American Society of Plastic Surgeons

The American Society of Plastic Surgeons (ASPS) is a professional society first organized in 1931 by board-certified surgeons who perform cosmetic and reconstructive surgery. A visit to the group's Web site, as suggested in the 2003 advertisement shown here, offers prospective patients photographs and information about the kinds of surgeries performed, including liposuction, and a guide to finding a qualified physician. Physicians also use the site to learn about ASPS membership and to conduct professional discussions in a private forum.

Exploring the Message

1. What major points about plastic surgery are made in the text of the ad? What are your reactions to these points?
2. What points are made through the graphics, both the photograph and the logo? For example, why might ASPS have selected this particular man for its ad?

3. On its Web site, ASPS issues this warning: "To be a good candidate for liposuction, you must have realistic expectations about what the procedure can do for you. It's important to understand that liposuction can enhance your appearance and self confidence, but it won't necessarily change your looks to match your ideal or cause other people to treat you differently." Is this statement consistent with the message conveyed by the ad? What might explain any differences?

4. How do the messages in the ad compare to other print and television ads you have seen on this topic?

Investigating the Discourse Community

1. List the ASPS's underlying assumptions about people's attitudes toward plastic surgery.

2. Are men the only projected audience for this ad?

3. What image of the organization is the ASPS trying to project? Does it succeed? Surf its Web site to see if that image is conveyed consistently: www.plasticsurgery.org.

Understanding the Genre

1. How would you describe the balance of text, open space, and image in the ad? What does the arrangement reveal about the designer's motives regarding the appearance and tone of the ad?

2. Comment on other elements of the ad layout. How does it focus viewer attention?

3. Why does the ad include the caption "Actual ASPS patient"? Why is it not displayed more prominently?

4. How do the strategies used in this ad by a professional organization on the general topic of plastic surgery compare to tactics used in ads you have seen for other kinds of self-improvement?

Writing Activity

Create your own commercial or public service ad for a group, a product, or an idea. You might stay with the self-improvement topic or focus on a related theme, such as women's or men's health. Next, decide on the magazine where you would place the ad, for example *O, The Oprah Magazine* or *Men's Health*. Based on your analysis of the audience for the magazine, find a photograph or other visual image, create text, and design your layout.

Buff Enough?
Book review by Jonathan Rauch

Journalist Jonathan Rauch was born in Phoenix, Arizona, in 1960 and educated at Yale University. He has been a correspondent for The Economist *and* The Atlantic, *a columnist for the* National Journal, *and a guest scholar at the Brookings Institution. An openly gay author, Rauch writes on a range of public policy and social issues, including affirmative action, immigration, gay marriage, and hate-crime legislation. His thinking on what he believes is a crisis in American democracy can be traced through the books* Kindly Inquisitors *(1993),* Demosclerosis *(1994), and* Government's End: Why Washington Stopped Working *(1999). "Buff Enough?" was published in November 2000 in* Reason, *a monthly nonpartisan magazine on politics and culture.*

By the time I graduated from high school, I had reached my full height—not quite five feet, eight inches—and I weighed 105 pounds. Much earlier, when I was about 9 or 10, I had begun to notice that I was preoccupied with certain aspects of my appearance. After one of my father's friends made a good-natured jibe about my "nice little potbelly," I worried for months about my stomach and tried to keep it covered all the time. I would also spend long sessions in front of the mirror, using water and gel and combs and brushes to smooth out what I thought were imperfections in my hair. None of that, though, prepared me for what was to happen when I reached high school.

Today when I look at pictures of my teenaged self I see a strikingly thin but hardly hideous boy. What I saw then, however, was a monster. I was grotesquely thin. As if that were not enough, I also had bandy legs, pimples, and a mild back deformity called kyphosis that made me look slightly hunched no matter how straight my posture. I felt that my body was weird, monstrous, and also alien, something I was cursed with and trapped in. Sometimes I would fantasize about chopping off my arms and legs and throwing them into the sea, just to be rid of them.

I made sure that no one had any idea how I felt. I had no use for obtuse reassurances ("There, there, you look just fine") and no appetite to be packed off to a shrink. The isolation and secrecy were harder to bear than the malady itself. My best hope, as I saw it, was to grow up and either fill out or stop obsessing. To an extent, both happened; but by the time I graduated from college I still weighed less than 120 lbs., and although my self-loathing had ebbed quite a bit, it had not gone away. I felt freakish not only physically but emotionally, because it never occurred to me that anyone else had experienced anything like what I was going through.

What a difference it might have made if, by some time-twisting miracle, I could have been handed a copy of *The Adonis Complex: The Secret Crisis of Male Body Obsession,* by Harrison G. Pope Jr., Katharine A. Phillips, and Roberto Olivardia. I first heard of the book from a 22-year-old gay acquaintance who had somehow gotten hold of the bound galleys and was carrying them around like a Bible. His hatred of his own appearance had driven him to a compulsive and often dangerous promiscuity (if he was having sex, he couldn't be all that ugly). The Adonis Complex was a revelation to him, as it would have been to me, had it existed when I was his age.

So the first and most important thing to say about *The Adonis Complex* is: Hooray! For years, the scientific and popular literature has been full of hand wringing about eating disorders and body obsessions in women; but about men, next to nothing. The authors originally focused their own clinical work—in psychiatry and psychology at the Harvard and Brown medical schools—on women. Only gradually did they realize that "body dysmorphic disorders," as body obsessions are officially called, are also common in men, who almost never reveal or discuss them. "We want to tell these men and the people who love them," Pope and his colleagues write, "that they no longer need to suffer alone, that the Adonis Complex—this secret crisis of male body obsession—afflicts millions in our society and around the world."

They have compiled many cases. Kevin, an enormous bodybuilder, is convinced his arms look like "sticks" and sometimes won't go outside all day "because I'm afraid people will think I look too small." Scott works out compulsively, loses his girlfriend, and refuses to go to the beach for fear of being thought too small. Joe counts every hair that falls into the sink and is so mortified by his hair loss that he drives recklessly, hoping to die: "If I have to go through life looking like this, I don't want to live." Barry becomes obsessed with his weight and starves himself down to 85 pounds. Ben, also weight-obsessed, binges and purges twice a week, wolfing down four Big Macs, three Whoppers, six pieces of chicken, four large containers of french fries, and two milk shakes, and then forcing himself to vomit it all back up. The authors have learned a great deal about what ails these men and how to help them. Their writing is clear, personable, and unfailingly reasonable. They provide tests you can take to spot body obsessions in yourself and others. Anyone who struggles with a body obsession, or knows a man who might, could use this book.

You are right, though, to sense a "but" coming. Mental health professionals can rarely resist the temptation to put society on the couch. *The Adonis Complex*, in the authors' reckoning, is really two quite different sorts of pathology. One afflicts individuals, men like Kevin and Joe and Ben. The other is a social disease.

In 1964, G.I. Joe sported a respectable but unremarkable physique; if he were five feet, 10 inches, he would have had a 32-inch waist, a 44-inch chest, and thin 12-inch arms. By 1991, G.I. Joe's waist had shrunk to 29 inches, and his arms had grown to 16. He had, in other words, become a bodybuilder. Star Wars action figures—Luke Skywalker and Han Solo—were ordinarily athletic in 1978, but by 1995 they were on steroids.

Then there are the ads, and the models, and the magazines. One of the book's most interesting charts shows the percentage of male models appearing shirtless or otherwise "undressed" in *Glamour* and *Cosmopolitan*. In both magazines, the proportion stays under 10 percent in the 1960s and 1970s, but then in the 1980s it takes off, almost tripling. And the undressed men become much more muscular.

The authors compile more evidence in this vein, but you don't need to examine it to know that something happened in the last 15 or 20 years. Call it the Buff Revolution. Suddenly there were half a dozen physique magazines on every 7-Eleven newsstand. Suddenly buses prowled through the cities bearing ads in which, for no discernible reason, a barechested young man with a chiseled and tanned and shaved-down torso displayed a microwave oven (a microwave oven?). Suddenly there was the Soloflex man, and Calvin Klein underwear ads, and WWF wrestlers on steroids, and Arnold Schwarzenegger, and *GQ*, and a gym on every corner. You could hardly walk 100 feet in any direction without encountering a muscle shrine.

To the authors, what all this suggests is that men are increasingly being manipulated by opportunistic advertisers and marketers and merchants. They write, "These 'male body image industries'—purveyors of food supplements, diet aids, fitness programs, hair-growth remedies, and countless other products—now prey increasingly on men's worries, just as analogous industries have preyed for decades on the appearance-related insecurities of women." Men therefore are "victims" of "what our society is doing to contemporary men's views about their bodies." They are "indoctrinated" by exposure to more supermuscular images than any previous generation has ever encountered.

As a result, the cases of full-blown body dysmorphic disorder, cases like Kevin's and Scott's and Joe's and Ben's, are only the tip of the iceberg. "For every severe or dangerous case," the authors write, "there are dozens of less severe cases—men who cope quietly with emotional pain about some aspect of how they look." The body image concerns of boys and men "range from minor annoyances to devastating and sometimes even life-threatening obsessions—from manageable dissatisfaction to full-blown psychiatric body image disorders." Even minor discontents, apparently, are evidence of society's Adonis Complex.

In at least five passages, the authors go out of their way to say that body image concerns are not pathological unless they cause distress or impairment. There's nothing wrong, they say, with working out or dieting to look good. Yet the authors do not seem to believe themselves. They note, with italics and exclamation point, a study in which *"95 percent of college-age men expressed dissatisfaction with some part of their bodies!"* (Of course they did; and the other 5 percent were lying.) The authors further note that, according to one estimate, in 1997 American men "spent a shocking $3.5 billion on men's toiletries (hair color, skin moisturizers, tooth whiteners, etc.)." (That would be about $36 per year for every adult male.) They note, not approvingly, that gyms are full of college students who pay "$400 per year out of their own pockets" to work out, even though "most could use their own college gyms for free if they wanted." All of this they see as signs that Americans are excessively preoccupied with their appearance.

The treatment for the serious cases of Adonis Complex is therapy and antidepressants. The treatment for the milder ones is consciousness raising: "It's time for men to liberate themselves from the artificial and unattainable standards that Western society and the media have imposed upon them in the last 20 or 30 years." The authors speak more than once of "liberation" in describing their social prescription, and they are well aware of the feminist themes their book echoes. Just as *Penthouse* and "Charlie's Angels" have insidiously stereotyped and exploited women, so the buff culture insidiously stereotypes and exploits men.

Fair enough, up to a point. Muscle marketing does indeed distort many men's and boys' image of the healthy male physique. Men should be more widely aware, as the authors suggest, that those big, "healthy" muscles they see in the sports nutrition ads are often unattainable without drugs. The makers of action figures and Saturday morning cartoons would do everybody a favor by taking their characters off steroids. Still, one suspects that there is a baby somewhere in the bathwater that *The Adonis Complex* throws out in its rush to emancipate men from hard stomachs and pendulous pecs. One wonders: Is there only something wrong with the buff culture? Or is there also something gloriously right about it?

The muscular male physique is spectacularly beautiful, and not just to women and gay men. The appeal of big muscles to men is probably innate and universal, for reasons that an evolutionary psychologist would have no trouble explaining. Has any society anywhere exalted soft, shapeless men? Has any schoolboy, ever, wanted smaller muscles? But for many years, probably since the first colonists landed, American men repressed the explicit pursuit or adulation of male beauty. . . . A man could be beautiful only if he wasn't trying and didn't care; he could be "naturally athletic," or "well toned," but working on his body for its own sake was vain or eccentric or something even worse, something unmentionable. Men pretended not to notice other men's biceps (someone might get the wrong idea!). Male models looked fit but safely shy of hunky. Ronald Reagan passed for beefcake, partly because his physique was so bland and sexless. The notion of pumping a man up, shaving him down, and displaying his naked torso on the side of a bus would have seemed altogether too—well, you know, too Greek.

In the 1970s, as the cultural climate grew more hospitable to overt eroticism and as homosexuality came to seem less dangerous and more titillating, it became increasingly possible for a man to express admiration or envy of male beauty, even if in guarded terms. Meanwhile steroids, dietary supplements, and plain old sweat made muscles bloom as never before. In the early 1980s, the dam finally broke. Male hunkiness ceased to be taboo. Advertisers and marketers took full advantage of the change, and so pushed it along. I doubt, however, that they caused it. In any case, I think the great majority of men—the ones who do not have body dysmorphic disorder—should welcome the new climate.

Being mental health professionals, the authors of *The Adonis Complex* tend to regard the pursuit of beauty for its own sake as frivolous, and the pursuit of beauty at the expense of health as irrational, even crazy. They cite a survey that asked men, "How many years of your life would you trade to achieve your weight goals?" The answer so shocks them that they italicize it: "*17 percent of men said they would give up more than three years of their lives. Eleven percent would sacrifice five years.*" Why is that terrible, or even surprising? Ambition of any sort is a kind of neurotic itch, given that we all wind up dead anyway. Celebrity and power will shorten your life, on average, but it is human nature to want to be famous and powerful—and beautiful. When I was 16 and skinny and pimply and weak, if you had told me I could instead be muscular and handsome and strong at the cost of living to be 73 instead of 77, would I have been crazy to take the deal? Or crazy not to take it?

At last men are free to pursue beauty for its own sake, and if the pursuit is sometimes maddening it can also be (yes) liberating. American men, always intent on remaking something, are turning their restless creativity on their own bodies. This is healthier, I think, than the authors of *The Adonis Complex* allow. For millions of men, the gym is itself a form of therapy. When I was in my 20s, I began working out religiously. For a while the gym became my second home. Was I driven, even a shade compulsive? Maybe. But little by little my body changed, and I changed inside of it. I came to feel I belonged in a gym, sweating and flexing, and then later, more slowly, I came to feel that I belonged in my body.

I am not suggesting that my obsessive self-loathing was good for me because   20
I overcame it. I am saying that self-loathing is one thing and the male pursuit of beauty is another, and it is important to distinguish between the two. That the one is unhealthy does not make the other so, any more than driving is unhealthy because some people die in accidents. The Buff Revolution was liberating rather than oppressive, even if, like all liberations, it enticed some people to excess or illness. Gradually, I suspect, many of the excesses will subside. America is only just learning to cope with the intoxicant of male beauty. With time, and with the help of books like *The Adonis Complex*, more and more men will learn to be buff without being crazy.

Exploring the Message

1. What is the thesis of *The Adonis Complex?* What major points do the authors raise in support of their position?
2. What is Rauch's thesis? Which of Pope, Phillips, and Olivardia's points does Rauch accept and which does he challenge?
3. Whose thesis do you find most convincing? Which of the authors' examples or arguments and what personal experiences support your position?
4. Describe Rauch's childhood battle with weight. Do you recognize his experiences either in your own or others' childhood experiences?
5. What views of gender differences and feminism emerge in the review?

Investigating the Discourse Community

1. How do Rauch's personal experiences with weight and body image affect his response to *The Adonis Complex?* Given his experiences, were you surprised by the conclusions he came to? Does the fact that he is gay seem relevant to his argument?
2. How does Rauch compare to Pope, Phillips, and Olivardia in his views on the nature vs. nurture debate? If this idea is unfamiliar to you, use an Internet search engine to learn more.

3. Visit the *Reason* Web site (http://reason.com/) and speculate on the interests and social views of the readers of the magazine. Does Rauch effectively target this group?

4. Why do Rauch and the authors of the book use so many popular culture examples? What other kinds of examples are used and with what degree of success?

Understanding the Genre

1. Name the mediums and genre of this selection. Where else might you look for similar models of this genre?

2. How would you describe Rauch's writing style? Begin with a close reading of paragraphs 3 and 15.

3. Describe and analyze Rauch's organization. Consider, for example, where Rauch places his objective description of the book's content and his use of sentences such as "You are right, though, to sense a 'but' coming" (par. 7).

4. Has Rauch chosen an effective title? Why or why not?

Writing Activity

Write a review of a book or article written on a topic of interest to students in your major or with your probable professional goals. It might be a textbook you read for a class or an essay you discover in a special interest magazine. Use Rauch as a model for combining personal reflection and experience with professional critique.

Writer's Profile Two:
Where Am I Going as a Professional Writer?

Chapters 3 and 4 introduced a variety of concepts and skills necessary to becoming a successful writer in a professional setting. As you practiced the related primary research techniques and investigated your major or an area of interest, you have been laying the groundwork for "Writer's Profile Two." This research report requires you to (1) identify a probable career path, (2) conduct additional research into the qualities of a successful writer in that discourse community, and (3) analyze your preparation for becoming that writer. Your audience will be students with similar career plans or interests. Read the entire assignment before you begin your research.

Step 1:　Plan to use a Project Notebook to complete the research for this profile and to develop your thesis and plan. Review the model notebook on pp. 58–60.

Step 2:　Reread your "Writer's Notebook," "Writing Activities," and "Writer's Workshops" to bring together your current insights into your chosen discipline's *who, what, when, where, how,* and *why*. Although your general topic is assigned for this project, you can begin to shape and narrow its focus by writing a narrative presentation based on your earlier research into your major and on any personal experiences with the profession you have selected.

Step 3:　In your notebook, outline four or five specific goals for your research and the final profile. Consider topics you have special interest in, questions about, or insufficient information on. Use the question format suggested in the model notebook (p. 60).

Step 4:　Consider and select from the following research options to identify a coherent strategy for gathering the information you will need to achieve your writing goals.

- *Interviews* with practicing professionals, preferably from outside the university (If you are unable to find someone available for an in-person interview, consider setting up an e-mail or synchronous chat interview if this technology is available to you.)
- *Observations* of the workplace
- *Participation* in a professional listserve
- *Analysis* of documents typical of the profession, such as brochures, reports, Web sites, lesson plans, and proposals

Your goal is to significantly expand your knowledge of the writing practices and other core traits of the discourse community you have selected. Your professors, local professional societies or organizations, and the Internet are good resources for identifying people, places, texts, and listserves.

Step 5:　Before you actually arrange times or begin your research, prepare a brief proposal in your Notebook that outlines your research plans. Include choices of techniques, a time frame, and specific names and places. Meet with your peers and instructor to review your goals and research plans.

Step 6:　Using the suggestions in Chapter 3 (pp. 62–63), prepare questions and arrange all appointments.

Step 7:　As you undertake your research, complete double-sided notebook entries for all activities, with your reflections on the experiences. Make note of how the information gathered compares with your expectations and how it compares with the results of your interview with the two professors that you conducted in Chapter 3 (p. 63). Include, too, discoveries about the overlap and contrast between yourself and the professionals you meet.

For example, at the start of his project notebook, Eastern Illinois University student Scott Josephus wrote:

> The career I hope to pursue is an unusual one: game design. For as long as I can remember, I have loved playing games and reading, so this feels like a natural fit for me. The games that I particularly like either have a strategic or storytelling side to them, and because of this I chose to major in English. For any game from chess to Yahtzee you have to be able to explain the rules clearly and concisely. For a game that involves storytelling, not only do you have to be able to design the rules and explain them, you also have to design the world in which the story takes place and imagine the stories that will happen there.

Scott's research confirmed the role of creativity in game design, but in speaking with professional designers, he learned about the importance of attention to detail and empathy for users who don't yet share the creator's technical savvy. He concluded at the end of his notebook that "The game designer must be a creator, a writer, an editor, a numbers cruncher, a system designer, an artist, and a salesman. But, above all, and in support of everything else, he must be someone who loves games."

Melissa Petrucci, a Physical Education major who planned to be a Cardiac Rehabilitation therapist, discovered that "[m]uch to my disappointment, there is little need for creativity at the writing stage of scientific writing." But as she thought more about her observations and interviews, she decided that, although "this equates to boring for many people, this does not have to be the case. In scientific writing there is a lot of information to be learned and communicated, and thus science writers have to have many qualities to successfully relate that information to an audience." Those qualities included being a patient, observant researcher and making concise, descriptive interpretations of the results. For Melissa, this promised personal and professional satisfaction.

Be sure to review "Writing Profile One" and to consider the full range of *who, what, when, where, how,* and *why* characteristics as you begin to draw your own conclusions and comparisons.

Step 8:   In class, meet in small groups, if possible with students who have similar career plans, to compare notebooks and brainstorm ways to focus and design your profiles.

Step 9:   Write a draft of your profile and gather peer feedback before preparing a final version.

Chapter 5
Learning from Public Writing

Chapter Preview

Public writing occurs within a wide range of community settings and employs a variety of forms. As an irate consumer, a concerned citizen, a frequent volunteer, or an active member of a special interest organization, you might be called on to write a letter to the editor, an op-ed piece, or complaint letter; to issue a press release; to create a newsletter or pamphlet; to generate a proposal, an annual report, or an agenda; to post a Web site; or to put together a flyer, guidelines, instructions, a catalogue, or a manual. This chapter provides two thematic casebooks of readings in various genres for you to examine and respond to.

Opportunities for civic writing may overlap with your professional life. Employees of corporations and small companies often cooperate with local agencies by volunteering their time and talents. Cargill, a large international and multi-faceted agricultural and industrial products group, asks its employees to form volunteer councils for community projects such as literacy programs, and Sun Microsystems sees its "Community Action Volunteer Program" as an opportunity "to help employees share their time and talents with communities" by "matching people with complementary interests, skills and expertise to appropriate community projects."

Finding a Public Voice: Problem-Solving Strategies

An often used term for service-oriented public action is "Community Engagement Writing." In interviews held after he received the Nobel Prize in 2002, former President Carter told reporters that the most meaningful period of his life was not the four years of his presidency, as most would expect, but his time since as citizen Jimmy Carter. Because of his work with Habitat for Humanity and the Carter Center, he may, in fact, be the most visible American volunteer, committing his time and talents to working with others to make the world a better place. Among his contributions are frequent opinion editorials written for national newspapers and magazines. Undertaking such public writing projects is an especially effective means of participating in your community.

Solving Problems with Others: Analyzing the Writing Situation

In any public document you create, your handling of audience, purpose, persona, and message is strengthened by conscious rhetorical analysis. Because your actions are voluntary, rather than paid, and take place in an unstructured setting, you may be tempted to approach these situations informally and with less focus. Like effective professional writing, however, successful public writing requires close attention to and respect for the discourse communities that generate and receive it. When you volunteer, you are not just doing something for but are also acting with a group of fellow citizens, advocates, or recipients, usually to find a meaningful solution to a problem. These groups will appreciate your good intentions, new energy, and fresh ideas, but they will also benefit from your thoughtful study of their existing values and usual practices. For example, does the newsletter group operate on a leadership or collaborative model? Are annual reports written in a formal or informal voice? Are changes to the Web site made spontaneously by individuals or at predetermined times by an assigned Webmaster? This does not preclude negotiating changes in an organization; it only suggests a need to be fully considerate of all of the competing values, norms, and goals that might be involved when undertaking a writing project.

In addition to the usual strategies of primary and secondary research, actually participating in a collaborative activity is an especially good way to gain preliminary insights into a group's habits. Before writing a position paper suggesting your pet project for the local YWCA, for example, you might volunteer to join the small group responsible for the monthly newsletter. As a part of the team, you gain an understanding of the situation's *who, what, why, when, where,* and *how* (p. 43), and you gain credibility with the group.

Solving Problems Alone: Analyzing the Writing Situation

When you write as an individual, the communities to be considered can become more difficult to define and study, either because they are more general or at a distance. Approach it in the way you have other such audiences in your academic and personal writings. For example, when you write a letter to the editor criticizing the new transportation system being proposed for your community, your argument will be strengthened by your familiarity with previously published letters on the topic and your knowledge of the relevant facts.

Writer's Notebook

Add an entry to your notebook that re-creates a situation that inspired you to do some form of public writing—a letter of inquiry about a problem with a car purchase, an op-ed piece on a local politician for your school paper, a profile of your favorite dance teacher for the Arts Center newsletter, or an advice booklet for new members of your church, for example. What challenges did you face in deciding the who, what, when, where, how, and why of the task? What was your greatest accomplishment in the process? Looking back, what might you have changed?

Putting Your Discourse Analysis Skills into Service

The following thematically clustered casebooks provide examples of varied yet complementary approaches to public problem solving. In each case, the writer or writers have immersed themselves in the affected communities and shaped their chosen medium into a genre that serves their own and their readers' purposes.

As in Chapter 4, you should utilize the investigative skills you learned and practiced in Chapters 1, 2, and 3 to guide your reading and analysis and consult the checklists and guides on pages 12 (Chapter 1 checklist), 34 (Chapter 2 checklist), 43 (journalist questions), and 51 (style checklist). Keep the following questions in mind as you read:

- How has the author handled the rhetorical issues of audience, message, purpose, and persona?
- What insights into the author's writing practices are evident in the finished product?
- What does the selection reveal about the *who, what, where, why, when,* and *how* of the discourse community? For example,
  - What kinds of previous knowledge and experience does the author assume?
  - If research is involved, is it quantitative or qualitative?
  - How, exactly, does the piece define the problem and suggest solving it?
  - Does the author consider conflicting approaches from within the community?
- To what genre does the selection belong? What are the writing situation and the medium?
- What particular features of style and design are illustrated?

Also consider adding entries to your Writer's Notebook if the readings inspire future volunteer or writing projects.

Casebook of Readings: Targeting Discrimination

Writer's Notebook

Before reading the casebook on discrimination, take a few minutes to write about your opinions on and past experiences with the topic. How do you define the term discrimination? To what extent have you been aware of it in your everyday life? For example, have you encountered age, gender, or racial stereotyping that affected your actions or the actions of those around you? Have you written anything about the topic either as a citizen or a student? Were your efforts to communicate or initiate action successful?

Take Action: Children's Rights Are Human Rights
Marc Kielburger and Craig Kielburger

At age 12, Canadian Craig Kielburger happened to see a newspaper article about the murder of a young man who had been battling the abuses of child labor. Rather than sit back and let someone else solve the problem—or accept the received wisdom that adults were better suited to the task—Craig began a campaign that has become the 100,000-strong international Free the Children organization. His brother Marc, a Harvard graduate and Rhodes Scholar, is also an activist and helped to found the group Leaders Today. Together they composed the book Take Action! A Guide to Active Citizenship, *which has been featured on the Oprah Winfrey show. Their book reflects their belief that ordinary citizens can act to solve the world's problems if they have the right information and appropriate skills.*

*   *Take Action! *is a practical guide organized around "Seven Steps to Social Involvement," each of which is fully explained and then illustrated: Choose an Issue, Do Your Research, Build a Team, Call a Meeting, Make a Plan of Action, Take Action and Then Review, and Have Fun. "Children's Rights Are Human Rights" is taken from the section of the guide that applies the seven steps to specific social issues. It includes both instructions for action and an illustrative profile.*

Children's Rights Are Human Rights

It is important for young people to understand their rights. In 1989, world leaders gathered together to determine the rights of children. The result was the United Nations Convention on the Rights of the Child. This is an international agreement that establishes the rights of children and young people who are under the age of 18. Over 190 countries around the world have accepted and have promised to enforce this important agreement. No other international human rights treaty has been more widely adopted on an international level.

The convention can be divided into four categories of rights.

1. **Playing a part:** This section of the agreement says young people must be included in the decision-making process on important issues that affect them. The document also says that young people have the freedom to join with other young people to protect their rights and to express their opinions.

2. **Reaching their potential:** This section of the agreement protects important social rights of youth. Included in this list are the right to have access to education and the right to protect their culture and identity.

3. **Living well: The right to survival:** This section of the agreement says that there are certain basic things that all young people must have, such as adequate food and shelter, a reasonable standard of living, and access to health care.

4. **Being free from harm:** This section of the agreement says that all young people should be protected from abuse, neglect, economic exploitation (child labour), torture, abduction (kidnapping and trafficking), and prostitution.

So far, however, the rights that were agreed upon in this important convention have yet to be upheld in some places. Right now, as you read this, millions of children around the world are being exploited and abused, while some governments continue to break their promises to take "all appropriate measures" to defend the rights of these young people.

All children deserve the right to be a kid and have their rights protected. The United Nations Convention on the Rights of the Child was a big step, but it was not enough. The good news is that you can help.

One way you can help children is by raising money to promote education in the developing world. Primary schooling is guaranteed under the United Nations Convention on the Rights of the Child, yet millions of children around the world do not have the opportunity to go to school because there are no educational resources in their communities. Education is the key to breaking the cycle of poverty and ending the exploitation of children. You will find out how to raise money to help children go to school below.

Some other possibilities for action include the following:

✔ Join an organization concerned with children's rights. See Part 5 for contact information.

✔ Write to the government in the United States urging them to support the ratification of the United Nations Convention on the Rights of the Child. The United States is one of only two countries in the world that has not adopted this treaty. The other country is Somalia.

✔ Write letters and organize petitions to send to government officials to pressure them to make children's education a priority.

Thousands of candles can be lit from a single candle, and the life of the candle will not be shortened. Happiness is never decreased by being shared.

— Buddha
(c. 563–483 BCE)
Philosopher and teacher

How to Raise Money to Help Children Go to School

Choose an issue

One in five of the world's children between the ages of six and eleven do not attend school. Become enthusiastic about joining the campaign to help children go to school.

Do some research

Research topics such as education, child labour, and child poverty (refer to Step 2: Do Your Research beginning on page 4 in Part 1 for some helpful tips). You may also want to contact Kids Can Free the Children for help.

Build a team

Involve your friends or give a presentation in front of your class about how education can put an end to the exploitation of children. Ask for their help. A group of people can raise money much more easily than you can by yourself.

Call a meeting

Speak to your friends at school and in your community about participating in raising money to help children go to school. Ask them to become involved and meet with you to make a plan of action. You may also want to ask some adults for their support.

Make a plan of action

Here are a few costs you may want to keep in mind.

- $1500 pays the salary of a teacher for a year in a developing country.

- $1200 pays to put a concrete floor in a school.

- $300 buys a cow and feed or a small machine for a family as an alternative source of income so that children are freed from child labour and can go to school.

- $25 buys a desk for a child.

- $15 pays for a school kit for a child so he/she can have the tools to learn.

- With whom do you need to work to make your fundraiser successful?

- What materials will you need for your fundraiser? How many young people do you want to become involved in this campaign?

- Refer to the section 101 Fundraisers beginning on page 70 in Part 2 for fundraising suggestions.

- How will you advertise your fundraiser? Will you invite the media to your event?

You may even want to raise enough money to build a school in a developing country! Contact Kids Can Free the Children for detailed information.

Take action and then review

Make your fundraiser(s) a reality. Tell people about the event and why it is such a worthy cause. Make sure that people know how to contact you.

When your event is complete, send the money that you raised to Kids Can Free the Children, which will then send you information about the children and the community that you and your group helped. Share this information with all of the people who were involved in the fundraiser. Your supporters will then see the effect of their contribution and will be more likely to help in the future.

Soon after your event, bring your team together and discuss what aspects of the fundraiser were successful, as well as lessons the group learned that can be used to improve the next event.

Remember to thank everyone who participated in your event.

Have fun!

Have fun while organizing the event, and enjoy spending time with your friends while participating in a worthwhile cause.

Suggest a team activity to celebrate the hard work and dedication it took to contribute to the education of children in the developing world.

Profile: Chris Pettoni

Chris Pettoni is actively involved in Kids Can Free the Children's School Building Campaign, which promotes education for children in rural areas of developing countries. Chris was nine years old when he was first inspired to take action for children's rights. He attended a presentation given by Craig Kielburger on the exploitation of children around the world, and, very moved by what he learned, felt that he had to do something to help. By making presentations in his New Jersey school about Kids Can Free the Children and the issue of children's rights, Chris was able to motivate the students to establish a Free the Children committee and begin to fundraise for the School Building Campaign. By the end of the year, the team had raised over $3378 US, which was enough to build a school in Nicaragua, pay a teacher's salary for a year, and provide the new students with school supplies.

In October 1999, Chris was selected to represent his school on the Oprah Winfrey show, which was devoting an episode to children who were making a difference in the world. Chris was called out to present Craig Kielburger with a cheque for the money his school had raised. So impressed with the children's efforts, Oprah announced that she wanted to commit to building 50 schools in developing countries. "It was amazing to see our small school fundraiser reach out and touch so many people around the world," Chris said.

As Chris and his team continued to fundraise, they were able to pay for running water to be brought into a village in Nicaragua. The following year, Chris organized a school-supply drive to help several Kids Can Free the Children sponsored schools in South America that had been devastated by tropical storms. Now an active member of the Pompton Lakes, New Jersey chapter of Kids Can Free the Children, Chris continues his work to promote and protect children's rights by speaking out and fundraising to help children go to school.

Exploring the Message

1. What four rights are guaranteed to children under the United Nations agreement? Can you provide personal, local, national, or international examples that illustrate the need to discuss and work toward each of these rights?
2. Name the specific actions recommended by the Kielburgers. Could most readers realistically accomplish them?
3. What central point is being made in the Buddha quotation?
4. What civic and personal habits does the "Take action and then review" section nurture?
5. What words would you use to describe the evolution of Chris Pettoni's involvement in Kids Can Free the Children?

Investigating the Discourse Community

1. Find clues throughout the selection that reveal both the authors' credentials and their familiarity with their readers' attitudes and experiences. Do the Kielburgers effectively use their knowledge to achieve their purposes? For example, what would you say about the voice in the sentence "All children deserve the right to be a kid and have their rights protected"?
2. Can you identify the authors' underlying social attitudes or beliefs in their explanations of the steps? Provide two or three specific examples.
3. Analyze the strategy of opening "Children's Rights Are Human Rights" with an explanation of the United Nations' position.
4. How effective are both the details and their order in the bulleted "Make a plan of action" section?
5. List the specific facts or qualities that make Chris Pettoni a good choice for a profile.

Understanding the Genre

1. Describe and analyze the overall design of this example of the "guide" medium. Consider print size and styles, page layout, and graphics.
2. Discuss the organization and style of the presentation of the United Nations' four categories of rights. Why, for example, is the phrase "This section of the agreement" repeated in each point? What is the benefit of the parallelism in the second sentence in point 1?
3. Why do so many of the sentences in the selection begin with a verb?
4. How well would this selection work as a stand-alone document? How necessary are the cross-references under "Do some research"? Would additional references be useful elsewhere in the selection?

5. Describe the organization and style of the profile. How does it differ from the instruction segment of "Children's Rights Are Human Rights"? What qualities link the profile to the instructions?

Writing Activity

Take Action! is written for an audience of young people. Select any section—the review of the United Nations Convention on the Rights of the Child, the call to act, the "How to Raise Money to Help Children Go to School," or the profile—and rewrite and, if necessary, redesign it for a different audience. Use the library or Internet to gather any additional information that would help accomplish your goals.

Make Age Irrelevant by Beating Negative Attitudes
AARP Interview with Sally James

AARP is a nonprofit advocacy group of 35 million people who are 50 years and older. The vast majority of the group's work is accomplished by volunteers, from the Board of Directors to local chapter leaders. Once named the American Association of Retired Persons, the organization officially changed to AARP in an effort to attract youth-oriented Baby Boomers as they began to turn 50. The name change also reflects the fact that an increasing number of members, around half, continue to work either full or part time. Despite the group's changing self-image and goals, it continues to face externally imposed limits in the form of age discrimination—from job loss to media stereotyping.

Operating on the local, state, and national levels, AARP communicates with its members in many different print, radio, and electronic formats. It provides up-to-date resources and information through feature articles, question and answer sheets, fact sheets, interviews, and profiles. The following selection was taken from the "Discrimination" link on the AARP Web site in March 2003.

Sally James knows about the barriers older adults face in making career transitions. She is the Executive Director of Career Encores, a non-profit corporation that links employers with job seekers 50 years and older in Southern California. Over the past 13 years, she has helped thousands of older adults find meaningful employment. In a recent interview with AARP, Sally talked about how attitudes can hinder a job search. What job seekers think about themselves and what many employers think about older workers can create formidable obstacles. We asked her to address some of these attitudes.

Typical Older Workers' Attitudes

"As an older worker, I am not welcomed in the workplace." Ms. James comments: "Many times, older job seekers build their own barriers. They have convinced themselves that due to their age they are not welcomed in the workplace. This kind of thinking is society driven. Our society keeps telling that to us." Turn this thinking around by showing that you have something to offer. Join a job or career support group or workshop to learn from others who are managing their career transition. These groups can also help you identify your skills and set your career goals.

Sally tells older adults to stay in touch with the new flexible work world and to keep their skills current. In a job interview, "you want to sell something that is used in the year 2000 and not in 1980."

To fit in better, many older adults think they must look younger. Sally James believes that this is not necessary. "We have to accept aging as a part of life and we have to be comfortable about it." However, attention to one's appearance is still important. Before the interview, learn about the company's dress code. Find out what is acceptable and what is not acceptable. Go to the lobby and look around. In some cases you might want to dress a little more formally; in other cases, you might need to dress more informally. Sally said, "If you are wearing your famous blue suit and they are all wearing blue jeans, your wardrobe selection might make you look older."

"I'm too old to start a new career." Sally hears this kind of thinking all the 5 time. Many of her clients cannot imagine themselves doing anything new or different because they have been in one field for their entire work life. "I've been an engineer all my life; that is all I know and can do." They define themselves by their previous job titles and not by what they can do. After doing a job for over 20 years, they lose sight of what they actually did in their job. Look at the skills acquired in a career and do not focus on the job title.

In Career Encores' workshops, participants are asked to write down specifically what they did in their jobs and life roles, highlighting their accomplishments. Participants are amazed to see how their lists of skills become longer and longer. They realize that skills acquired from past work can be transferred to many new options that they never considered before.

"I sure know more than this young person who is interviewing me or supervising me." Since many older adults have a great deal of experience, they have a tendency to think that they could do the job better. However, Sally warns the older worker to be careful in the interview. After getting the job, you should "sort through the company's culture before you start giving advice." One client told Sally, "I think that I blew the interview because I told the interviewer how to run his shop." Be open and show a willingness to learn new ideas and skills. By accepting the fact that you can learn from a younger person, age becomes irrelevant both in the hiring process and on the actual job.

Typical Employers' Attitudes

"I want to hire mature people, but don't send anyone over 60." This statement is blatantly discriminatory but Sally has heard it a few times. Most employers will not say this directly, but many hiring managers harbor such attitudes. The job interview is critical, but to get that important interview, an applicant's resume must clearly relate abilities to a specific job. Omit many of the earlier dates on the resume. Of course, Sally knows that older applicants cannot hide their age once they walk into the interview. But the mature job applicant can demonstrate a high level of energy and how he/she can be responsive to the company's needs. Career Encores' staff tells their clients, "You are not talking about when you were in high school and not talking about your grandkids, you are talking about the company's needs and how you can fill those needs."

"This person seems overqualified." If an employer says this directly or even thinks this, Sally believes that the applicant has not marketed himself or herself correctly. Many times experienced adults will scare off a potential employer by listing all their qualifications. If you are an older adult trying to return to the workforce or seeking part-time work, share the skills and experience that match the job qualifications.

"I want to hire older people because they are cheaper. They are retired and are receiving Social Security and don't need a lot of money." Sally stresses, "Remember, you have valuable skills and experiences." You should be treated as an individual and compensated equally. Age should never play a role in salary determination.

"This person may retire soon—so why should I hire him?" Get the employer to stop thinking about age. Before the interview, do your homework. Research the company and the position. Be able to describe your skills and experience in terms of the organization's needs and requirements. Communicate your enthusiasm for another professional development opportunity. "And all of a sudden, they stop seeing your age. They start thinking that you fill a need."

Making Age Irrelevant Is Critical

Making age irrelevant is critical for the older job seeker, but Sally James talked about one employer who likes hiring the older worker. This employer said, "I like to hire your people because they come in on Monday and they have not been surfing all weekend. Surfers never come in on Monday." This kind of thinking, however, might be changing. According to Sally, "We have an increasing number of older surfers in Southern California."

Career Encores links employers with job seekers who are 50 years and older in Southern California. To learn more about this organization, visit the Web site listed below:

URL: http://www.careerencores.org

Exploring the Message

1. Name the three typical attitudes older workers have toward the job search. What makes each problematic and how can the applicants revise their approach?

2. What are the four typical employer attitudes toward older job applicants? How can would-be workers mediate those attitudes?

3. What makes "I want to hire older people because they are cheaper" different from the other three employer comments?

4. Can you identify any overlap or interesting contrasts between the problems older workers face and those encountered by younger workers who are female, black, Asian American, Hispanic, or immigrants?

Investigating the Discourse Community

1. Describe Sally James's overall attitude toward the older worker's job search. How does she reveal her credentials for offering advice? Did you find her convincing or helpful?

2. In several places in the article, James offers strategies similar to ones you have been learning for analyzing a group or organization. Identify a few examples and try to add additional advice based on your experience with discourse community analysis.

3. The line "As an older worker, I am not welcomed in the workplace" is typical of the way each subsection of the two major body sections of the article begin. Whose voice is represented? What makes this an effective strategy?

4. What purpose is served by ending the article with a new and illustrative voice?

Understanding the Genre

1. How would you label the genre of this selection? What mediums are involved? Does the selection make good use of those mediums? Is the genre an effective choice for the purposes it serves and for the Web environment?

2. Analyze the approach to quotation taken throughout the article. How many different voices are incorporated into the piece? The section under "Typical Older Workers' Attitudes" is a good place to start your analysis.

3. Outline and analyze the organization of the article. Can you suggest an alternative arrangement?

Writing Activity

Write a concise but detailed document that offers advice to a group that you are part of or know well. Make use of an appropriate medium—for example, a question and answer sheet or a fact sheet—or create a hybrid genre like the one used in "Making Age Irrelevant." Your topic might be job searches for people in a different demographic group or perhaps finding the right fit as a volunteer.

Just Walk On By: A Black Man Ponders His Power to Alter Public Space
Brent Staples

Brent Staples earned a Ph.D. in psychology from the University of Chicago in 1982. By 1985, however, he had shifted to a career in journalism and landed a job with the prestigious New York Times, *where he remains as a reporter and member of the editorial board. A long-time journal keeper, Staples often uses the personal essay and memoir for the dual purposes of self-reflection and public expression. His memoir,* Parallel Time: Growing Up in Black and White *(1994), describes his coming of age during the 1950s and 1960s in a poor and troubled family. He also traces his subsequent alienation from that family as he moved away from Chester, Pennsylvania, where his siblings later fell victim to drugs and violence. A selection from "Just Walk On By" eventually became a part of this memoir; the following essay version, however, was written much earlier for a special 1986 issue of* Ms. *magazine, where a number of men were asked to write in response to the question "Can Men Have It All?"*

My first victim was a woman—white, well dressed, probably in her early twenties. I came upon her late one evening on a deserted street in Hyde Park, a relatively affluent neighborhood in an otherwise mean, impoverished section of Chicago. As I swung onto the avenue behind her, there seemed to be a discreet, uninflammatory distance between us. Not so. She cast back a worried glance. To her, the youngish black man—a broad six feet two inches with a beard and billowing hair, both hands shoved into the pockets of a bulky military jacket— seemed menacingly close. After a few more quick glimpses, she picked up her pace and was soon running in earnest. Within seconds she disappeared into a cross street.

That was more than a decade ago. I was 22 years old, a graduate student newly arrived at the University of Chicago. It was in the echo of that terrified woman's footfalls that I first began to know the unwieldy inheritance I'd come into—the ability to alter public space in ugly ways. It was clear that she thought herself the quarry of a mugger, rapist, or worse. Suffering a bout of insomnia, however, I was stalking sleep, not defenseless wayfarers. As a softy who is scarcely able to take a knife to a raw chicken—let alone hold it to a person's throat—I was surprised, embarrassed, and dismayed all at once. Her flight made me feel like an accomplice in tyranny. It also made it clear that I was indistinguishable from the muggers who occasionally seeped into the area from the surrounding ghetto. That first encounter, and those that followed, signified that a vast, unnerving gulf lay between nighttime pedestrians—particularly women— and me. And I soon gathered that being perceived as dangerous is a hazard in itself. I only needed to turn a corner into a dicey situation or crowd some frightened, armed person in a foyer somewhere, or make an errant move after being pulled over by a policeman. Where fear and weapons meet—and they often do in urban America—there is always the possibility of death.

In that first year, my first away from my hometown, I was to become thoroughly familiar with the language of fear. At dark, shadowy intersections in Chicago, I could cross in front of a car stopped at a traffic light and elicit the *thunk, thunk, thunk, thunk* of the driver—black, white, male or female—hammering down the door locks. On less traveled streets after dark, I grew accustomed to but never comfortable with people who crossed to the other side of the street rather than pass me. Then there were the standard unpleasantries with police, doormen, bouncers, cab drivers, and others whose business it is to screen out troublesome individuals *before* there is any nastiness.

I moved to New York nearly two years ago and I have remained an avid night walker. In central Manhattan, the near-constant crowd cover minimizes tense one-on-one street encounters. Elsewhere—visiting friends in SoHo, where sidewalks are narrow and tightly spaced buildings shut out the sky—things can get very taut indeed.

Black men have a firm place in New York mugging literature. Norman Podhoretz in his famed (or infamous) 1963 essay, "My Negro Problem—and Ours," recalls growing up in terror of black males; they "were tougher than we were, more ruthless," he writes—and as an adult on the Upper West Side of Manhattan, he continues, he cannot constrain his nervousness when he meets black men on certain streets. Similarly, a decade later, the essayist and novelist Edward Hoagland extols a New York where once "Negro bitterness bore down mainly on other Negroes." Where some see mere panhandlers, Hoagland sees "a mugger who is clearly screwing up his nerve to do more than just *ask* for money." But Hoagland has "the New Yorker's quick-hunch posture for broken-field maneuvering," and the bad guy swerves away.

I often witness that "hunch posture," from women after dark on the warren-like streets of Brooklyn where I live. They seem to set their faces on neutral and, with their purse straps strung across their chests bandolier style, they forge ahead as though bracing themselves against being tackled. I understand, of course, that the danger they perceive is not a hallucination. Women are particularly vulnerable to street violence, and young black males are drastically overrepresented among the perpetrators of that violence. Yet these truths are no solace against the

5

kind of alienation that comes of being ever the suspect, against being set apart, a fearsome entity with whom pedestrians avoid making eye contact.

It is not altogether clear to me how I reached the ripe old age of 22 without being conscious of the lethality nighttime pedestrians attributed to me. Perhaps it was because in Chester, Pennsylvania, the small, angry industrial town where I came of age in the 1960s, I was scarcely noticeable against a backdrop of gang warfare, street knifings, and murders. I grew up one of the good boys, had perhaps a half-dozen fist fights. In retrospect, my shyness of combat has clear sources.

Many things go into the making of a young thug. One of those things is the consummation of the male romance with the power to intimidate. An infant discovers that random flailings send the baby bottle flying out of the crib and crashing to the floor. Delighted, the joyful babe repeats those motions again and again, seeking to duplicate the feat. Just so, I recall the points at which some of my boyhood friends were finally seduced by the perception of themselves as tough guys. When a mark cowered and surrendered his money without resistance, myth and reality merged—and paid off. It is, after all, only manly to embrace the power to frighten and intimidate. We, as men, are not supposed to give an inch of our lane on the highway; we are to seize the fighter's edge in work and in play and even in love; we are to be valiant in the face of hostile forces.

Unfortunately, poor and powerless young men seem to take all this nonsense literally. As a boy, I saw countless tough guys locked away; I have since buried several, too. They were babies, really—a teenage cousin, a brother of 22, a childhood friend in his mid-twenties—all gone down in episodes of bravado played out in the streets. I came to doubt the virtues of intimidation early on. I chose, perhaps even unconsciously, to remain a shadow—timid, but a survivor.

The fearsomeness mistakenly attributed to me in public places often has a perilous flavor. The most frightening of these confusions occurred in the late 1970s and early 1980s when I worked as a journalist in Chicago. One day, rushing into the office of a magazine I was writing for with a deadline story in hand, I was mistaken for a burglar. The office manager called security and, with an ad hoc posse, pursued me through the labyrinthine halls, nearly to my editor's door. I had no way of proving who I was. I could only move briskly toward the company of someone who knew me.

Another time I was on assignment for a local paper and killing time before an interview. I entered a jewelry store on the city's affluent Near North Side. The proprietor excused herself and returned with an enormous red Doberman pinscher straining at the end of a leash. She stood, the dog extended toward me, silent to my questions, her eyes bulging nearly out of her head. I took a cursory look around, nodded, and bade her good night. Relatively speaking, however, I never fared as badly as another black male journalist. He went to nearby Waukegan, Illinois, a couple of summers ago to work on a story about a murderer who was born there. Mistaking the reporter for the killer, police hauled him from his car at gunpoint and but for his press credentials would probably have tried to book him. Such episodes are not uncommon. Black men trade tales like this all the time.

In "My Negro Problem—and Ours," Podhoretz writes that the hatred he feels for blacks makes itself known to him through a variety of avenues—one being his discomfort with that "special brand of paranoid touchiness" to which he says blacks are prone. No doubt he is speaking here of black men. In time, I learned to smother the rage I felt at so often being taken for a criminal. Not to do so would surely have led to madness—via that special "paranoid touchiness" that so annoyed Podhoretz at the time he wrote the essay.

I began to take precautions to make myself less threatening. I move about with care, particularly late in the evening. I give a wide berth to nervous people on subway platforms during the wee hours, particularly when I have exchanged business clothes for jeans. If I happen to be entering a building behind some people who appear skittish, I may walk by, letting them clear the lobby before I return, so as not to seem to be following them. I have been calm and extremely congenial on those rare occasions when I've been pulled over by the police.

And on late-evening constitutionals along streets less traveled by, I employ what has proved to be an excellent tension-reducing measure: I whistle melodies from Beethoven and Vivaldi and the more popular classical composers. Even steely New Yorkers hunching toward nighttime destinations seem to relax, and occasionally they even join in the tune. Virtually everybody seems to sense that a mugger wouldn't be warbling bright, sunny selections from Vivaldi's *Four Seasons*. It is my equivalent of the cowbell that hikers wear when they know they are in bear country.

Exploring the Message

1. What has Staples learned about the relationship between black and white Americans when they inhabit the same public spaces? Do his views coincide or conflict with your own experiences in similar circumstances?

2. How does Staples feel about the people who lock their doors, run away, or otherwise falsely accuse him of wanting to harm them? Are all of his responses what you expect them to be? Does he presume that they will be?

3. Describe the evolution of Staples's strategies for coping with the discrimination he faces. What does he learn about himself in the process?

4. How would you describe the attitudes of Norman Podhoretz and Edward Hoagland?

5. What is Staples's theory of "the making of a young thug"? How does he feel about the young men who become thugs?

Investigating the Discourse Community

1. What internal evidence marks this essay as having been written for *Ms.* magazine? Consider gender but also other demographic traits of the targeted reader.

2. How would you describe the general manner in which Staples approaches this personally but also socially significant problem? Is there evidence of his training as a psychologist? As a journalist? Consider the concluding paragraph, for example.

3. What range of characteristics does Staples's use of the Podhoretz and Hoagland examples reveal about him? About his assumed reader?

4. Why does Staples include so many different experiences in his essay, including those of other black men?

5. How do the experiences of the past few decades change the way today's readers might respond to Staples's claims about the scope of the discrimination faced by black men? Consider both specific events and general social attitudes.

Understanding the Genre

1. Outline and analyze the essay's organization. For example, why does Staples return to Podhoretz late in the essay?

2. What tone is Staples hoping to establish by opening the essay as he does? In writing *Parallel Time,* Staples edited the essay to include it in a chapter near the end of the book when he has moved to Chicago to attend graduate school. Here's the way he adapted the opening of the Hyde Park scene to suit the anecdote's new context and the book's genre:

> At night, I walked to the lakefront whenever the weather permitted. I was headed home from the lake when I took my first victim. It was late fall, and the wind was cutting. I was wearing my navy pea jacket, the collar turned up, my hands snug in the pockets. Dead leaves scuttled in shoals along the streets. I turned out of Blackstone Avenue and headed west on 57th Street, and there she was, a few yards ahead of me, dressed in business clothes and carrying a briefcase. She looked back at me once, then again, and picked up her pace. She looked back again and started to run.

Discuss the differences between the two versions, especially what they reveal about the two genres (personal essay and book-length memoir) they represent. Consider, too, that the Rodney King incident happened between the time the essay was published and the memoir was written.

Writing Activity

Identify a personal experience or series of events that taught you something significant about your place in society. Age, race, gender, sexual preference, and class are useful categories to explore through brainstorming or freewriting. When you've decided on a topic, identify an audience that might learn something from seeing the experience from your point of view, as Staples assumed middle class white women would learn from—and perhaps be changed by—understanding his feelings about their fears. Write either a portion of a memoir or a personal essay on your topic.

Reality Bites
Lisa Bennett

Lisa Bennett wrote this op-ed commentary in March of 2003 as a news release for the civil rights organization Human Rights Campaign. HRC works to change legal, political, and social practices that discriminate against lesbian, gay, bisexual, and transgendered Americans. Bennett, a former Harvard University Fellow, is Director of FamilyNet, one of the HRC Foundation's many ongoing national projects. Visit www.hrc.org/familynet to see the kinds of services and resources the organization offers, from help with adoption to advice on family law.

I have an idea for a new reality show. Call it "Not Married by America" and watch what happens when same-sex couples face everyday family challenges, like, say, birth, accidents and death. It may not be quite as funny as Fox's new "Married by America," where Americans get to vote on who should marry whom. But it might be refreshing to see a reality show about something . . . well, real.

Here's episode one. Susan and Mary, a happy couple in their 20s, are entertaining their parents at their home in Florida. As they sit down to dinner, Susan announces, "I'm pregnant!" Smiles and tears appear on every face. Then Mary drops the bombshell. "But we have to move to Pennsylvania." Cut to commercial. Pennsylvania, the women later explain, is the nearest state that will guarantee same-sex couples access to second-parent adoption, or the right of both to be legal parents of the child they will raise together.

Episode two. Joe and Brandon, a 40-something couple, are driving to the supermarket one morning when they pull over to help a stranded motorist on the side of the highway. A passing car hits Joe and he's rushed to the hospital. Although Joe and Brandon have been together for 14 years, the hospital won't let

Brandon visit Joe, let alone make medical decisions on his behalf. Hospital officials say he is not considered "family." Instead, they telephone Joe's parents, to whom he hasn't spoken in years.

Laughing yet? Wait. Here comes episode three. It's morning and Jonathan, age 5, is in his pajamas playing with his mother, Kathy. After a few minutes, she kisses him and says it's time for her to go to work. "Have fun with Mommy, sweetie," she says, nodding toward her partner, Sharon, who enters the room. "I'll see you tonight." Foreboding music. Later that afternoon, Kathy, who was born with a hole in her heart, has a fatal heart attack. Her son and his stay-at-home mom are left to fend for themselves, without even the cushion of Social Security survivor benefits because Kathy was denied the right to become Jonathan's legal parent.

OK. Now here comes the fun part. At the end of each episode, the American public can dial in to vote on what might have been a more fair ending, which might be something really surprising like equal rights under law. Polls have shown, after all, that 71 percent of Americans support hospital visitation rights for same-sex couples; 70 percent support employer-sponsored health insurance; 68 percent support Social Security coverage; and (note to network execs) 68 percent of high school seniors support adoption rights.

Or we could avoid putting the country through this whole saga and do something really radical and simply grant all families equal rights under law—by ridding discrimination based on sexual orientation and gender identity from marriage and adoption laws, and bringing equity to retirement, Social Security and tax laws.

Until this day becomes a reality, gay, lesbian, bisexual and transgender people can take steps to protect themselves with some important legal documents, such as domestic partner agreements, durable powers of attorney, hospital visitation authorizations, last wills and testaments, living wills, and, if appropriate, co-parenting agreements.

None of these documents will provide them with the same rights and responsibilities that the strangers united on "Married by America" will receive when they say, "I do." But it could help keep their stories from appearing on "Not Married by America."

Exploring the Message

1. Name the different aspects of discrimination against gay, lesbian, bisexual, and transgendered people that are covered in "Reality Bites." Is Bennett accurate in her expectation that many of these issues will be new or surprising to you?

2. Is Bennett's thesis implied or directly stated? Why does she make this rhetorical choice?

3. What overall conclusions can be drawn from the statistics offered in paragraph 5? Why include them?

Investigating the Discourse Community

1. How narrow or broad is Bennett's intended audience? Does she have a good grasp of her readers' views, knowledge, and needs? Find specific evidence to support your views.

2. Describe the selection's predominant tone. How soon was it clear to you? Does it suit the specific focus and audience?

3. As an organization, The Human Rights Campaign Foundation believes that "there are many different types of families—some with children and some without. Some are families of origin and some are the families we choose." How do these assumptions operate in Bennett's op-ed piece? Can you identify other HRC or FamilyNet assumptions at work in the editorial?

Understanding the Genre

1. What purposes motivate Bennett to write this piece? Identify and critique the techniques she uses and choices she makes to accomplish her goals.

2. How does the title of the editorial function in relation to the author's organizing strategy?

3. Analyze Bennett's use of the current popularity of reality television shows. Why start with the three mock episodes, for example? Must the reader watch such shows to understand Bennett's point?

4. What are readers expecting when they read "Then Mary drops the bombshell" in paragraph 2?

5. Does "Reality Bites" meet your expectations for a successful op-ed piece? What would you add or change?

Writing Activity

Using Bennett's format, write an op-ed news release on a topic of importance to you. You might use her mock episode idea or find a similar strategy (perhaps based on music or film) for organizing your ideas and accomplishing your purpose. If a topic doesn't immediately occur to you, try brainstorming from the many forms of discrimination covered in this casebook. Identify two appropriate and specific publication sites (newspapers, newsletters, magazines, Web sites), at least one of which is on the Internet. Create two different versions of the piece for these contrasting mediums. For example, provide accompanying graphics and layout ideas for Web publication.

I Spy Sexism: A Public Education Campaign

Third Wave Foundation

The Third Wave Foundation, a New York–based activist organization, assists women between the ages of 15 and 30 and encourages them to become leaders in their communities. The group provides grants, scholarships, and training. Though brought together by gender, the group's issues range from reproductive rights to the environment to social justice. Among the Foundation's many ongoing activities are ROAMS (Reaching Out Across Movements), a networking tour for young activists, and the Web-based "I Spy Sexism." The "I Spy" pages reproduced here are linked to the Third Wave Foundation Homepage: www.thirdwavefoundation.org.

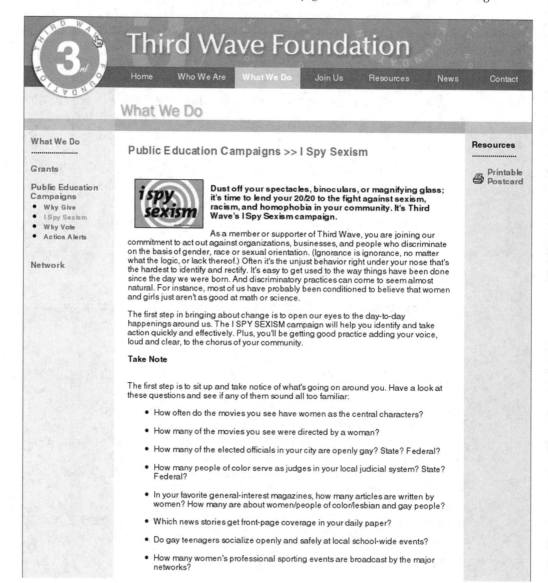

Third Wave Foundation

Home   Who We Are   **What We Do**   Join Us   Resources   News   Contact

What We Do

What We Do

Grants

Public Education Campaigns
- Why Give
- I Spy Sexism
- Why Vote
- Action Alerts

Network

Public Education Campaigns >> I Spy Sexism

Resources

🖶 Printable
   Postcard

Dust off your spectacles, binoculars, or magnifying glass; it's time to lend your 20/20 to the fight against sexism, racism, and homophobia in your community. It's Third Wave's I Spy Sexism campaign.

As a member or supporter of Third Wave, you are joining our commitment to act out against organizations, businesses, and people who discriminate on the basis of gender, race or sexual orientation. (Ignorance is ignorance, no matter what the logic, or lack thereof.) Often it's the unjust behavior right under your nose that's the hardest to identify and rectify. It's easy to get used to the way things have been done since the day we were born. And discriminatory practices can come to seem almost natural. For instance, most of us have probably been conditioned to believe that women and girls just aren't as good at math or science.

The first step in bringing about change is to open our eyes to the day-to-day happenings around us. The I SPY SEXISM campaign will help you identify and take action quickly and effectively. Plus, you'll be getting good practice adding your voice, loud and clear, to the chorus of your community.

Take Note

The first step is to sit up and take notice of what's going on around you. Have a look at these questions and see if any of them sound all too familiar:

- How often do the movies you see have women as the central characters?

- How many of the movies you see were directed by a woman?

- How many of the elected officials in your city are openly gay? State? Federal?

- How many people of color serve as judges in your local judicial system? State? Federal?

- In your favorite general-interest magazines, how many articles are written by women? How many are about women/people of color/lesbian and gay people?

- Which news stories get front-page coverage in your daily paper?

- Do gay teenagers socialize openly and safely at local school-wide events?

- How many women's professional sporting events are broadcast by the major networks?

- As a woman, can you walk home alone at night in your neighborhood without being nervous?

- Does your local newsstand carry lesbian and gay magazines?

- How many average-size or heavy women appear on your favorite sit-coms? Are they ever the central characters?

- How many women artists are covered in your art history classes?

- How much street crime is reported on your local news? By comparison, how much corporate/white collar crime is reported on your local news?

- How many local school principals (or chancellors or presidents) are women? How many are men? Compare that to the teacher female/male ratio?

These are just a few of the ways that sexism, racism, and homophobia are built into the culture we live in. No doubt, you can think of dozens more. In order to make change, we have to identify these practices and let it be known that we think it's lousy. So keep your eyes peeled. Carry a notebook and jot down incidents that strike you as unfair. Ask the people involved for their names, so they know you are watching. Talk to your friends. Ask them if they've ever witnessed similar behavior. Ask your teachers what they think of it? Let them know what you think.

Sound Off

Once you recognize unfair behavior for what it is, the next step is to let your feelings be known. You can download postcards that will help you get the word out.

1. First and most important, send a card to the wrongdoer. Let him or her or it know that you are watching and that you will continue to watch until the situation changes.

2. Send a card to a member of the media (newspapers, TV news programs, magazines, web sites). These are open channels you can use to get your message to people who share your views and want to help you make change.

3. Send a card to your elected officials (your Senator, the President of the United States or of the school board, or your Mayor). Their job is to listen to your concerns and act on them. If they don't respond to one postcard, get others to send more.

4. Send a card to Third Wave. We are a resource for you. We can put you in touch with others, near and far, who may be encountering the same situations. Third Wave will also document what you are doing and how you are working to change it.

5. And finally, send a card to a family member or friend. Although you may not talk much about it, you'll be amazed to find that people close to you often have the same concerns about unjust activities in your community. By sending them word of your own work in writing you will encourage and inspire them to take actions of their own.

That's it. It's that easy. And that's what we call MOVEMENT.

e-mail: info@thirdwavefoundation.org | tel: 212.675.0700 | fax: 212.255.6653 | mail: 511 W 25th St.. Ste 301, New York, NY 10001

I spied sexism/homophobia/racism!
(CIRCLE ALL THAT APPLY)

Dear _____ ,

I am writing to alert you that on _____
(DATE)

in _____ , I witnessed the following
(CITY AND STATE)

unacceptable behavior: _____

_____

_____

PLACE STAMP
HERE

I strongly object to your taking part in,
condoning, or ignoring such activity. I am
notifying members of the media, elected officials
and my family and friends that a problem exists.
I hope you will work to correct it.

_____

_____

_____

Thank you.

Sincerely, _____

I SPY SEXISM IS A PUBLIC EDUCATION PROJECT BROUGHT TO YOU BY THIRD WAVE FOUNDATION,
116 EAST 16TH STREET, 7TH FLOOR, NEW YORK, NEW YORK 10003. VOX (212) 388-1898;
FAX (212) 982-3321; E-MAIL THIRDWAVEF@AOL.COM; WWW.THIRDWAVEFOUNDATION.ORG

Exploring the Message

1. One of the Third Wave's slogans is "See it? Tell it. Change it!" How well does the "I Spy" site enact this philosophy of activism? Is it an approach you have tried or can see yourself using?

2. How many different kinds of social problems are identified in the "Take Note" section of the site? Does this undermine the "I Spy Sexism" title?

3. How would you describe the core message of the postcard? Are there secondary messages?

4. How many types of writing does the site encourage? Reread the sections that focus on writing and analyze the Foundation's faith in the power of writing. Do you agree with its assumptions?

Investigating the Discourse Community

1. What does the sentence "Often it's the unjust behavior right under your nose that's the hardest to identify and rectify" reveal about the site creator's view of potential visitors? How does the list of questions under "Take Note" expand on this view?

2. How would you describe the tone of the various pages in the "I Spy Sexism" section of the Third Wave Foundation Web site? Does it suit its intended audiences—both site visitors and those who will receive the postcards? Find several specific examples to support your views.

3. The site claims that if you participate in the campaign, you will "be getting good practice adding your voice, loud and clear, to the chorus of your community." How would you define "community" in this context?

4. Would you be likely to send one of the "I Spy" postcards? If so, under what circumstances and to whom? If not, why not?

Understanding the Genre

1. How effective is the step-by-step organization of this Web site? Review the guidelines for Web page layout in Appendix A (pp. 281–285) and suggest alternative arrangements for the campaign layout.

2. Does the site offer easy access to any additional information you might need before taking part in the campaign? Explain.

3. Evaluate the visual elements of the site. For example, what seems to be the thinking behind the design of the "I Spy" logo? Will it attract its intended audience?

4. Analyze the effectiveness of the fill-in-the-blanks postcard approach to encouraging activism. Do you normally use these preprinted forms of communication?

Writing Activity

Identify a problem that you believe needs public action and then create the text for a Web site campaign similar to "I Spy Sexism." Either use the step-by-step approach modeled by the Third Wave Foundation or come up with your own plan to motivate site visitors to act. Find or create an image to use as a unifying logo for your campaign. Finally, if appropriate, design a formatted postcard.

Stigma Watch: Being Alert to Mental Health Stereotyping
National Mental Health Association and Otto Wahl

According to its Web site, the National Mental Health Association is a "broad-based citizens voluntary movement" that has been working for more than a century to combat mental illness and the many social stigmas that accompany it. The association's national and community-level activities include advocacy, public education, research, and treatment services, with the goal of creating a more "just, humane, and healthy society." "Stigma Watch," a multigenre action packet, is one of NMHA's many ongoing educational projects. It calls on individuals not only to take responsibility for their behavior but to act as social advocates for others.

Dr. Wahl, who serves on the NMHA Public Affairs Committee, taught psychology at George Mason University. He has published two books with Rutgers University Press: Media Madness: Public Images of Mental Illness *(1995) and* Telling Is Risky Business: Mental Health Consumers Confront Stigma *(1999).*

Stigma Watch

As a society, we are bombarded with negative images of people with mental illnesses. The media and entertainment industries overwhelmingly present people with mental illnesses as dangerous, violent and unpredictable individuals. These inaccurate and unfair portrayals shape the public's perception of those who suffer from mental disorders as people to be feared and avoided.

This stigma has tragic consequences. Many people with mental health problems fail to seek treatment because of the shame associated with their illness. And most will experience some form of discrimination, whether in the workplace, health insurance plans or social settings.

The National Mental Health Association's Stigma Watch program tracks news and entertainment coverage of mental health issues for fairness and accuracy. Our goal is to correct and prevent stigmatizing advertising, television and radio programming, and print features.

NMHA regularly receives reports of stigmatizing incidents through our Stigma Watch line (1-800-969-NMHA) and the affiliate network. (NMHA responds to all stigmatizing incidents which are broadcast and/or distributed nationally. Local occurrences are referred to the affected affiliate area.)

Usually, NMHA responds to these events by contacting the offending organization or sponsors by phone and correspondence. Depending on the incident, NMHA will develop a more targeted strategy to seek the discontinuance of the ad or program. NMHA also works closely with the New York City–based National Stigma Clearinghouse to identify and respond to stigmatizing media depictions.

NMHA has successfully assisted several large corporations in avoiding inappropriate messages about mental illness in their entertainment programming and advertising campaigns. Sprint and Paramount Television Group are just a few of the organizations that have responded positively to our concerns.

Stigmatizing Media Images Affect Children
Otto Wahl, Ph.D.

The tragedies of Columbine and similar incidents have led to impassioned calls for increased mental health services for children and adolescents. While there is little doubt that increases are needed and long overdue, this focus alone overlooks an important fact. Even when services are available, children and their parents often fail to make use of them. Although research has revealed that nearly one in five adolescents experience a psychiatric problem, most, including those who acknowledge and express concern about those problems, do not seek professional help.

One factor that contributes to this troubling statistic is stigma. The negative attitudes about mental illnesses that pervade public thinking are hardly exclusive to the adult population. Children learn from a very early age that psychiatric problems are seen as failures of character and will and that those who admit to such problems or receive psychiatric treatment are likely to be avoided and looked down upon by their peers. Even second and third graders appear to have already assimilated the idea that people with mental illnesses are to be viewed less favorably than others.

From where do these negative views come? Certainly, they are influenced by the attitudes and behaviors of adults. Children are witness to disparaging references of those who are disliked or who have divergent opinions as "crazy," "nuts" or "insane." Children hear adults complain about people driving "like madmen" or behaving "like lunatics" when they are upset. Children are aware of the hushed and embarrassed tones used by adults when referring to relatives who have undergone psychiatric treatment. In other words, children learn easily that it is bad to be associated with labels that indicate a psychiatric problem.

Children are also indoctrinated to negative beliefs about mental illness through the entertainment media. Films for children often provide stigmatizing images and ideas. Take, for example, *Good Burger,* a recent film based on the popular Nickelodeon series, *Keenan and Kel.* Within this whimsical children's movie is a sequence at the Demented Hills Asylum, where the heroes encounter unkempt psychiatric patients in straitjackets who do things like disrupt a card game by eating the cards and growl menacingly at visitors. For somewhat older children, a recent chart-topping MTV video by the music group N'Sync (entitled "I Drive Myself Crazy") provided similar images of spaced-out psychiatric patients in straitjackets and padded cells, with the repetition of lyrics featuring the word "crazy." These stereotypes label people with mental illnesses as frightening, unattractive and undesirable. They are being established or perpetuated within impressionable young minds.

It is small wonder, then, that children and adolescents do not seek psychiatric help. They believe that to seek help would identify them as one of those unlikable persons they have seen or heard about and leave them vulnerable to ridicule and rejection. As Tipper Gore observed in a May 1999 *Time* magazine article: "If we are serious about stopping the violence and helping our children, adults need to erase the stigma that prevents our kids from getting the help they need for their mental health."

Fighting the stigma of mental illness—a task that includes changing the sometimes stigmatizing ways we ourselves refer to mental illness and challenging the media images that communicate negative stereotypes to our children and adolescents—is a fundamental task for helping to ensure that available mental health services will be used successfully by children and their families.

Stigma Watch Sample Letter

(DATE)

(NAME)

(TITLE)

(COMPANY NAME)

(STREET ADDRESS)

(CITY/STATE/ZIP)

Dear (Mr./Mrs./Ms._____)

I am writing to protest (NAME OF COMPANY)'s marketing campaign for (NAME OF PRODUCT). In addition to its disparaging theme, the campaign features (TELEVISION/

RADIO/INTERNET) advertisements which make a mockery of the seriousness of mental illnesses and stigmatize those who suffer from them.

I want you to know that mental illnesses are very real. Each year, 51 million American adults and children suffer from these disorders. Unfortunately, though, these individuals and their families suffer further because of misunderstanding and discrimination in our society. The stigma associated with mental illnesses, to which the (NAME OF CAMPAIGN) campaign contributes, keeps many people from seeking treatment and moving on to more fulfilling and productive lives.

I hope you will send out the message that mental illnesses are not a trivial matter and discontinue the (NAME OF CAMPAIGN) advertising campaign. (NAME OF YOUR OR-GANIZATION) would be happy to advise you on appropriate and sensitive portrayals of people with mental illnesses.

I look forward to hearing from you.

Sincerely,

(NAME)

Exploring the Message

1. What are the primary consequences of stigmatizing people with mental illness, according to NMHA and Dr. Wahl? Are there special circumstances when children are involved?

2. What stereotypes of mental illness are perpetuated by the media? Can you think of additional examples of television shows, movies, or advertising campaigns that support NMHA's claims?

3. What is *labeling* and what role does it play in perpetuating stereotypes? Were you familiar with this term?

4. What actions does "Stigma Watch" suggest be taken in response to negative news coverage, entertainment, and advertising?

Investigating the Discourse Community

1. NMHA believes that "every person . . . has the right and responsibilities of full participation in society." Visit the organization's Web site at www.nmha.org and identify other assumptions that underlie the "Stigma Watch" approach to social change. Identify specific connections between these assumptions and the language used or the points made in the selections.

2. Why did NMHA choose to include Dr. Wahl's article with the "Stigma Watch" materials? Consider the nature of the organization, as well as message, voice, and audience in your response. Why would a similar article have been less appropriate on the "I Spy Sexism" site?

3. What relationship does the sample letter first assume and then promote between the writer and the company receiving the complaint? What alternatives might you suggest to this approach?

Understanding the Genre

1. How would you describe the genre of Dr. Wahl's article? How does it differ in content, scope, style, or format from an article on the same topic that he might publish in a professional journal or even a popular magazine?

2. How well do the three components of the action packet complement one another? What changes or additional support would you add?

3. What in the individual writer's circumstances would require changes in the sample letter? Suggest a few sample revisions.

4. How would you compare the "I Spy Sexism" postcard and the "Stigma Watch" sample letter as advocacy campaign genres? Might the ages of the probable writers and readers have influenced the length, style, and design of the documents?

Writing Activity

If you completed the writing activity for "I Spy Sexism," (p. 180), add one of the genres employed by "Stigma Watch" to your project: a brief background essay or a full sample letter. If you did not undertake the "I Spy Sexism" project, select an advocacy project of interest to you and create text for an appropriate combination of genres to accomplish your goals: main page description, background essay, and/or sample postcard or letter.

Writer's Workshop

1. Did the readings in "Targeting Discrimination" remind you of any experiences with discrimination that you had forgotten? Did the readings change your opinions on the topic? Identify an appropriate public writing situation and write about a personal experience or explain some part or version of your current views to a specific audience for a useful purpose. Any of the genres modeled in the casebook would be possible vehicles for your project. You might, for example, write an op-ed piece (a personal commentary appearing opposite the editorial page) on what you now see as significant causes or effects of public acts of discrimination.

2. Identify a form of discrimination not covered in the casebook, including more subtle forms of stereotyping—those experienced by blonds, short people, and left-handed people, for example. Conduct either primary or secondary research to explore the topic more fully, and then find an appropriate writing situation and genre for conveying your results.

3. Identify a movie or book that makes some form of discrimination one of its central themes. Write an op-ed style movie or book review for your campus or local paper.

Casebook of Readings: Responding to Homelessness

Writer's Notebook

Use your notebook to record your past experiences with homelessness, including personal interactions, conversations, readings, and writing projects, for example. Also, reflect on your current attitudes toward homelessness, including its causes and possible solutions.

National Alliance to End Homelessness Web Site: Home Page and FAQ

NAEH is a highly regarded and influential coalition of nonprofit, public, and private organizations. In 2000, this Washington, D.C.–based group published the Ten Year Plan to End Homelessness. *As outlined on its Web site, this proposal is an aggressive and optimistic effort to redirect energies away from steps to simply manage homelessness toward steps to prevent and end it. Among the Alliance's first priorities is gaining governmental support for making more permanent housing available to those who are most vulnerable to falling into homelessness. Programs to provide housing for youth aging out of foster care and housing linked with services for homeless people with mental illness, for example, are targets for their efforts. This Home Page and FAQ are part of NAEH's extensive Web site:* www.endhomelessness.org/index.htm.

National Alliance to End Homelessness

The National Alliance to End Homelessness is a nonprofit organization whose mission is to mobilize the nonprofit, public and private sectors of society in an alliance to end homelessness. (more...)

The following resources can be found on this site:

The Ten Year Plan to End Homelessness- the plan that challenged America to change its thinking and pursue steps to go beyond managing homelessness to ending it in 10 years

Ten Essentials Toolkit- comprehensive resources to help communities prevent and end homelessness - features the ten essentials that every community needs to end homelessness

Leadership to End Homelessness Audio Conference Series / Best Practices - presenting the leading strategies among states, local jurisdictions, and nonprofit organizations to prevent and end homelessness

Housing First Network- resource hub for those interested or engaged in a housing first approach to shorten homeless-ness in their communities (best practices, FAQ, listserv...)

Ending Youth Homelessness - details on federal policy, best practices, and research in ending youth homelessness

Alliance Online News - the latest information on promising new practices, federal policy and program developments, grant opportunities, pertinent research, and upcoming events.

Homes for Homeless Families Initiative- a national campaign to increase Housing Choice Vouchers and other federal resources to end homelessness among families

Ending Long-term Homelessness Services Initiative (ELHSI) - an initiative to provide services in permanent supportive housing to help end chronic homelessness

Navigation menu

- Home Page
- About The Alliance
- Background and Statistics
- Policy and Legislation
- Best Practices & Profiles
- Publications/Resources
- Fact Sheets For Kids
- What You Can Do
- Links
- FAQ
- Contact Us

Search the Alliance Site

[Search]

Make a Donation

Conference on Ending Family Homelessness

Elections '04 Get Involved!

Employment Opportunities

Join the Alliance!

Email: [   ]
[Submit]

News and Highlights

House Committee Passes VA-HUD Appropriations for FY 2005

New Homelessness Bill Introduced

Fannie Mae and Alliance Kick Off Partnership

Analysis of Proposed McKinney-Vento Funding

Continuum of Care and Emergency Shelter Grants

Shelter Requests Increase in 2003, say U.S.Mayors

Housing Remains Out of Reach for Millions

States Plan to Prevent Homelessness Among Reentering Prisoners

President's Report on Mental Health System

Compact to End Long-Term Homelessness

Strategies for Philanthropy in Ending Homelessness

Upcoming Events

National Alliance to End Homelessness
1518 K Street NW, Suite 206
Washington, DC 20005
(202) 638-1526
naeh@naeh.org

Home ||Background and Statistics||Policy and Legislation
Best Practices and Profiles||What You Can Do||Publications/Resources
Discussion Forum||About The Alliance||Contact us ||Links ||Fact Sheets for Kids

National Alliance to End Homelessness

Home Page

About The Alliance

Background and Statistics

Policy and Legislation

Best Practices & Profiles

Publications/Resources

Fact Sheets For Kids

What You Can Do

Links

FAQ

Contact Us

Frequently Asked Questions

1. How can I get assistance if I am homeless or about to become homeless?
2. Where can I find information on funding for new or existing programs to address homelessness?
3. How many people are homeless in the U.S.?
4. How many people are homeless in my state?
5. Where can I find information on places to volunteer in my community?

How can I get assistance if I am homeless or about to become homeless?

As an advocacy organization focused on systemic reform of our nation's social safety nets, we do not have the capacity to directly aid or refer people who are in immediate need of assistance. However, we do know of some places that may be more helpful in this regard. Immediate sources of aid in your community can be found by consulting your local department of social services or your local branch of the Salvation Army or United Way (http://national.unitedway.org/help/). You may also find it helpful to consult the following directories of homeless service providers and advocacy groups:

- http://www.hud.gov/homeless/hmlsagen.cfm
- http://www.nationalhomeless.org/direct1.html

<return to top>

Where can I find information on funding for new or existing programs to address homelessness?

A comprehensive resource on relevant federal funding opportunities is available at http://www.whitehouse.gov/government/fbci/

Additional funding and fundraising resources may be found at http://www.idealist.org/tools/fundraising.html

Another resource we'd recommend is "Homelessness: Key Findings & Grantmaking Strategies" (http://www.SchwabFoundation.org/files/homeless/Homelessness.pdf), which reflects present priorities and strategies in preventing and ending homelessness from a philanthropy perspective.

<return to top>

How many people are homeless in the U.S.?

Due to the circumstances of homelessness, it is very difficult to come up with a reliable number of people who experience homelessness. The most recent national count was conducted in 1996. Based on this count, it was estimated that between 2.3 and 3.5 million people experienced homelessness over the course of that year. Data collected by various local jurisdictions since that time indicates that the number has risen and is continuing to rise each year. Further details on the 1996 study and others can be found in our Background and Statistics section.

<return to top>

How many people are homeless in my state/city/town?

There is currently no central place where information is collected specifically on the number of people who experience homelessness in each state, city or town. Various states and local jurisdictions may nevertheless have estimates that are based on local counts and information collected from homeless service providers. To connect with organizations in your area that may be able to help you find such estimates, go to http://www.nationalhomeless.org/direct1.html

Another useful resource would be state and local consolidated plans, known as "conplans." Conplans are required by the U.S. Department of Housing and Urban Development (HUD) for any locality that receives funding from a range of HUD programs. They are required to include some estimate about the extent of homelessness in that community. These estimates vary widely in terms of reliability, but they can be helpful, given that their limitations are taken into proper account. To find out if your area has a conplan that is available online, see http://www.hud.gov:80/offices/cpd/about/rulesandregs/conplan/local/

<return to top>

Where can I find information on places to volunteer in my community?

The following are two national directories that offer information on local homeless service providers:

- http://www.hud.gov/homeless/hm1sagen.cfm
- http://www.nationalhomeless.org/local/local.html

<return to top>

**National Alliance
to End Homelessness**
1518 K Street NW, Suite 206
Washington, DC 20005
(202) 638-1526
naeh@naeh.org

Home ||Background and Statistics||Policy and Legislation
Best Practices and Profiles||What You Can Do||Publications/Resources
Discussion Forum||About The Alliance||Contact us ||Links ||Fact Sheets for Kids

---

Exploring the Message

1. What did you learn from the Home and FAQ pages about the programs, services, and resources offered and not offered by the NAEH? Was there adequate explanation for the Alliance's choices?

2. To whom can the homeless turn for immediate assistance?

3. What can the average citizen do to help end homelessness?

4. According to the FAQ page, how extensive is America's homelessness problem? What makes this a difficult question to answer?

Investigating the Discourse Community

1. What do these Web pages reveal about the expertise and priorities of the Alliance? Find several examples to support your response.

2. What audiences do the Home Page and FAQ pages seem to target? Provide specific evidence for your answer.

3. What do the linked categories of resources, which are listed in the left-hand column, and the specific programs detailed in the center column tell you about the organization's values and mission?

4. How does the News and Highlights column serve the Alliance's purposes?

Understanding the Genre

1. Is the Home Page easy to read and navigate? What design features promote or impede readability? Are there changes you would suggest to the Webmaster?

2. Explain the varied technical approaches the site designer uses to help visitors find answers to questions and become active in the Alliance. Why are so many options provided?

3. Why are there no questions about the Alliance on the FAQ page? Did the FAQ page meet your expectations in other ways? Where did those expectations come from?

4. What might account for the lack of photographs or complex graphics on this site?

Writing Activity

Using one of the directory search engines suggested in Appendix A (p. 275), locate a Web site on a topic you already know a great deal about, a site that does not already offer an FAQ page. Study the site and create the text of an FAQ page that would help visitors find core information about the topic. Include links to relevant sections of the main site and to other Web resources.

Transitions: Newsletter of the Center for Women in Transition
Champaign County, Illinois CWT

In 1994, the Women's Emergency Shelter of Champaign County, Illinois, was reincorporated as the Center for Women in Transition (CWT). The change highlights the group's core mission: to help women and their children prepare for independent living. While most shelters limit residents to a month or two of temporary support, CWT allows a stay of up to two years, during which time women are provided with counseling and educational opportunities meant to overcome the circumstances that led to their homelessness—financial, physical, emotional, and family challenges. Founded and originally run by volunteers, the Center continues to depend on community contributions of time and money to meet the needs of its residents. Volunteer opportunities range from working with children to coordinating the shelter's recycling program. The following is the inaugural issue of Transitions, *the Center's newsletter, which was given this new title and format in the fall of 1996. It captures the range of challenges that must be met and talents that must be sought to maintain a complex community program for the homeless.*

Volume Number 1, Issue 1
Fall, 1996

TRANSITIONS
Newsletter of the Center for Women in Transition

508 East Church Street • Champaign, IL 61820 • 217/352-7151

Clara Forbes

BEAUTIFUL HOUSES, STRONG WOMEN

On June 1, 1996, the Center for Women in Transition held its first annual Porchlight Festival, an event to celebrate our achievements of the last year with our supporters and neighbors. Though rain poured down throughout the morning, at 1 p.m., the sun peaked through to allow us an afternoon of food, fun, music and the grand moment-the dedication of our two beautiful homes: the Deloris Evans House and the Clara Forbes House.

Deloris Evans is one of the founders of CWT. She is a dedicated and tireless advocate for women and children. She has worked on homeless issues as a member of the City of Champaign's Homeless Task Force and as a current board member for Homestead Corporation which is currently developing the SRO (Single Room Occupancy) apartment building for homeless single adults. Deloris has championed the rights of abused children and jobless teens, and actively promotes understanding and respect for racial and cultural diversity. Deloris will step down from our board this fall, but she'll never be far from our doorstep. Her bountiful heart and strength have left a sturdy legacy. In her honor, the house originally known as the Women's Emergency Shelter, will now be known as the Deloris Evans House.

Our second and recently completed shelter, the Forbes House, was a joint project with numerous community groups and individuals to restore this 1880s Italiannate structure, which was the home of Stephen and Clara Forbes from 1884 to 1914. Stephen Forbes was a renowned entomologist at the University of Illinois

and is considered the Father of Ecology. Clara Forbes was a founder of the Julia Burnham Hospital and a board member of the hospital for 20 years. She also was an organizer of the Unitarian Church, a charter member of the Champaign Social Science Club and active in the work of the Outlook Tuberculosis sanitarium. A friend remembered Clara Forbes as having a "firm grasp upon real values of life and generous treatment of those in difficulty and trouble. Her kindly, generous, constructive, buoyant way of meeting situations, her staunch and firm championship of right were well known." This early pioneer has left us a wonderful heritage for contemporary times. The Forbes House will officially be known as the Clara Forbes House.

Deloris Evans

We are proud and honored to have our beautiful homes named after two distinguished and strong women of our community.

2

Letter from the Executive Director

What a wonderful beginning to our 11th year as an agency: a second beautiful house, more staff, and time to concentrate on building programs, not moving and renovating housing.

Homelessness is not and does not have to be a way of life for women and their children. With strong community programs and resources, and a woman's own commitment to explore each opportunity presented, homelessness need only be a short passageway to a stronger place.

It is our mission to encourage women to take hold of opportunities and acquire the means, skills, and education to fulfill their dreams. We also help them create a new vision for themselves and to take positive charge of their families' lives. We are now able to offer residents stays of up to two years to accomplish our mission.

While I do not expect more than 5% of all residents to stay two years, I do expect to develop a greater sense of community within our houses and thereby encourage women to stay the amount of time that works for them. We have established groups for support, parenting, budgeting and nutrition. Additional activities are needed: job training, self-esteem building, creative writing and art are all necessary components to our program.

Thanks to your support we have taken an abandoned, neglected house and raised $220,000.00 (and a $30,000.00 mortgage) to make it a viable part of the Center. Last year we served 147 women and 90 children. This year these figures will double, but so might the numbers of homeless in the next two years with the implementation of Welfare Reform. Much hard work is still ahead.

Let's continue to work together. Building houses is good work, building stronger lives is great work.

Kathy Sims, Executive Director

Upon completion of the Forbes House in January, we realized that its gorgeous interior cast a shadow on the Evans House. After serving over 3,000 women in its eight years of service as an emergency/transitional shelter, it was looking a little tired. Fresh paint, new carpeting, refinishing and installation of hardwood floors and a top-to-bottom cleaning have rejuvenated its luster. Thanks to the following groups for restoring vitality to the Deloris Evans House:

Junior League of Champaign-Urbana
Mt. Olive Baptist Church
Altrusa Club
Americorps Service members
Hillel Foundation

Three bedrooms could still use some loving touches. If you would like to adopt-a-room, please contact Kathy Sims, 352-7151.

ADOPT-A-PLAYGROUND

Children need a place to play.

Ask us about our ideas for a children's playground in the spring. Call Kathy Sims, 352-7151.

ADOPT-A-ROOM PROJECT A HUGE SUCCESS

With an idea which Paul Adams, City of Champaign's Neighborhood Services Director, brought with him from Iowa, we placed all our rooms in the Forbes House up for adoption. This meant an organization or church group could assist the Center with some direct contributions by helping paint, wallpaper, contribute new and used furniture and essentially give

their chosen room a charming individuality. The project was a tremendous success.

We recognize and thank the following organizations for their adoption of rooms in the Clara Forbes House:

John L. Kelly Chapter Credit Unions
Telephone Pioneers
First Presbyterian Church of Urbana
First United Methodist Church of Urbana
Altrusa Club
Time-Warner Cable

Forbes House

— 3 —

THINK TRANSITIONAL, NOT EMERGENCY

Thanks to a three-year grant from the Housing and Urban Development folks (HUD), we now have the luxury of offering 32 women and their children an opportunity for extended stays of up to two years. This moves the Center into the category of transitional housing and away from emergency shelter.

This is important! We may serve fewer, but it is our intent to serve with stronger programs, more support services and greater opportunities for women and their families to acquire better skills, training and stability. With Welfare Reform imminent, women will need time, support services, and supportive people to make the difference.

These women must go back to school, secure jobs that pay more than minimum wage, retire old debts and begin to save money and set goals. (This year, after four months, we had one family pay off over $3,000 in debt, save another $1,000 and move into housing on more solid ground.) This takes time, patience, and a lot of hard work — exactly what the Center does best.

Although we are now transitional housing, we will keep up to five beds/couches for emergencies.

Volunteer Information

The Center for Women in Transition needs many volunteers to assist us with carrying out our programs and running our two houses at 506 and 508 East Church.

If you are a creative, caring, energetic individual who is interested in serving your community while also learning more about the issues that affect women and children in our society, please call Kimberly at 352-7151.

Positions available: house supervisor; maintenance assistants-recycling, painting, building; kitchen assistants; children's program assistants and more! House supervisors especially are needed.

Volunteer Orientations will be held on the following Saturdays from 10 a.m. - 1 p.m.

November 9 and December 14

All orientations are held at the Center for Women in Transition at 506 East Church.

Time commitment and schedules vary with each position. All volunteers interested in volunteering on a regular basis must attend one of the volunteer orientations. We also need groups of volunteers to help on a Saturday or Sunday with painting, cleaning, moving, organizing, etc.

Thank you for your support and I hope to see you at the Center!

Kimberly Bielefeld
Services Coordinator

C-U'S HOMELESS PROGRAMS TAKE HARD HIT ON STATE LEVEL

Center for Women in Transition lost $30,000 in state funding from the Department of Commerce and Community Affairs. Salvation Army lost $70,000 Men's Emergency Shelter lost $40,000 and closed its daytime drop-in center. Greater Champaign Aids Project lost $15,000.

Why were these programs cut? Less money on the federal level was designated to homeless programs. More programs seeking funds to meet growing homeless needs increased competition for funds. More money was concentrated in Chicago, and less for downstate.

This may be a sign of things to come which means that we have to rely on community support now more than ever in order to keep these vital and irreplaceable programs alive. Imagine what would happen to people if the above programs did not exist? Where would PEOPLE go who have no other place to go?

Important Fact from the Center for Women in Transition:
Last year, over 600 unduplicated women with over 700 children requested our services. CWT was able to serve 147 women and 90 children directly with shelter and support services. This year, with both houses open for a full year, we anticipate serving 250 women and 150 children.

Interesting Fact from the National Coalition for the Homeless:
Congress appropriated $11.2 billion more to defense spending than the Pentagon even asked for. The minimum level of funding needed to meet the needs of homeless persons for all the federal programs that address homelessness combined is $2.5 billion.

HOLIDAY ADOPT-A-FAMILY

A beautiful tradition at CWT each Christmas holiday has been the adoption of families and single women by families, businesses and church groups.

We will supply the names, ages, sizes and a small wish list of a family or single woman, and a holiday guide list to help you help us keep it simple.

We try not only to make the Christmas for our residents a festive one, but also for our former residents who work with our Aftercare Program.

If you would like to help us celebrate the spirit of Christmas by adopting a single woman or family, please call us and ask for a family or woman and our Holiday Guide.

---4---

The Center for Women in Transition is a United Way agency. Please pledge through your employer during this year's campaign. The United Way does make a difference.

**GIVE
CHAMPAIGN COUNTY
A HAND!**

United Way

BOARD OF DIRECTORS
Board President, *Jack Cramer-Heuerman*
Vice President, *Christina Collins*
Secretary, *Amy Bryant*
Treasurer, *Andrea Ballinger*
Denise Fenske
Terri Giesing
Kandi Hart
Martha Harter
Diane Nesbitt
Jan Simon
Doug West, past President

**Special Thanks to Outgoing Board Members
for their 9 years of Dedicated Service:**
Deloris Evans
Sylvia Herzog
Pat Phillips
Pat Schutt

**CENTER FOR WOMEN IN
TRANSITION PROGRAM STAFF**
Executive Director, *Kathy Sims*
Services Coordinator, *Kimberly Bielefeld*
Client Advocate, *Barbara Walker-Jelks*
Client Advocate, *Deloris Akins*
Children's Program Coordinator,
    Audrey Peppers
Aftercare Program, *Antwanette Newton*
Outreach (Americorps Member),
    Megan Miller
Cook/Nutrition Education,
    Angella Dixon-Shannon
Maintenance Coordinator, *John Barclay*

WISH LIST

Laundry Hampers
Socks and Underwear
Tampons
Folding Office Tables
Hats & Mittens (Adults Only)
Towels
Baby Care Items
Alarm Clocks
Cough & Cold Medicine
Sheets
Display Board
Deodorant
Blankets
Chapstick
IBM 386 or 486 (3)
Educational & Family Videos
Food
Office Supplies
Adding Machines
Blackboards
Dry Erase Boards
Sewing Machines (2)

CENTER FOR WOMEN
IN TRANSITION
508 E. Church St.
Champaign, IL 61820

Nonprofit Organization
U.S. Postage
P A I D
Champaign, IL
Permit No. 178

Exploring the Message

1. Why did the Center call its dedication party a "Porchlight Festival"? Who was invited and why?

2. What do the two women for whom the CWT houses are named have in common?

3. Another CWT publication, its volunteer flyer, says there is something for everyone who wants to volunteer. Does the newsletter convey this message, too? Name the actions that the newsletter invites readers to take.

4. In March of 2004, the Center broke ground for a third Center house. It adds five additional bedrooms. There are, however, annual requests for assistance from over 400 women and 400 children per year. How does the Center explain, then, its decision to act as a transitional housing agency rather than an emergency shelter?

Investigating the Discourse Community

1. Who is likely to read *Transitions?* What in the newsletter supports your answer?
2. How would you describe the voice of the newsletter articles? What messages does the tone convey about the Center?
3. Based on your reading of the newsletter, especially the "Letter from the Executive Director," write a brief description of the CWT's mission.
4. Why do you think the newsletter was given a new format and a new title at this point in the agency's history—several years after its founding and two years after the opening of the Center?
5. How extensive is the support the Center currently receives from its community? Why is this an important message to convey in the newsletter?

Understanding the Genre

1. Would you describe the newsletter as having a professional appearance? Does its look seem appropriate for an organization such as CWT?
2. How suitable and useful are the photographs and graphics in the newsletter?
3. Is the content of the newsletter easily accessed if a reader has a specific question or goal? Should it be in this genre?
4. Comment on the decision to include the Executive Director's comments as a "letter."

Writing Activity

Create a plan for an inaugural newsletter for a group to which you belong or an organization with which you are associated—your dorm, your softball team, the community center where you volunteer, for example. What content would you include? For example, what current events, future plans, topical information, and history would be interesting and useful to your likely readers? What mediums would best suit your content and purpose? How would you arrange the material, including graphics? Write drafts of one or two of the parts of the newsletter, illustrating the voice and scope you propose.

Let's Solve S.F.'s No. 1 Problem
Mike Sullivan and Plan C

Mike Sullivan is a San Francisco activist and member of a group that calls itself Plan C. This political action committee (PAC) was organized in 2001 to improve the city's quality of life through grassroots action. Its goal is to represent a view independent of what it sees as the two extremes—Plans A and B. Through citizen education, lobbying, candidate endorsement, and policy initiation, Plan C has forwarded an agenda that includes coping with the city's homeless problems as well as eradicating barriers to middle-class home ownership. Sullivan has been active in other citizen groups, including Friends of the Urban Forest; he is also a practicing lawyer, a certified arborist—and Webmaster of the Harold and Maude Home Page.*

The daily newspaper the San Francisco Examiner *prints a Plan C op-ed column each month. "Let's Solve S.F.'s No. 1 Problem" appeared in September of 2002.*

Homelessness has become public issue No. 1 in San Francisco. It's no secret why—our homeless policies have utterly failed, and the evidence is everywhere—with hundreds of homeless dying on our streets, our emergency rooms clogged with homeless-related health problems and our streets and parks overrun with behavior that shouldn't be tolerated in any civil society.

Regrettably, some of the very qualities that make San Francisco a wonderful place have also contributed to the plight of the homeless. A progressive and compassionate city, San Francisco has developed policies and programs over many years that were intended to help the homeless.

Now, with years of experience under our belts, it's time to acknowledge the fact that our good intentions often have failed to bring about positive results.

One good way to assess progress is to compare our situation with other cities, in California and across the nation. The comparison is unflattering. We have more deaths on the street and more palpable suffering than other cities, despite spending more on homeless services per capita.

The homeless aren't escaping homelessness, residents and tourists are frightened by behavior on our streets, the police are inundated and businesses are fed up. Clearly, the status quo isn't working.

By almost any measure, San Francisco spends more on homelessness, with less to show for it, than other cities nationwide.

Which takes us to the subject of leadership. We need some—badly. For too long, our city's leaders have tinkered around the edges of the status quo on homelessness, bowing to a homeless industry that advocates for that status quo. Perhaps some of our leaders concluded that this was the "safe" political path. If so, it's safe no longer—polls show that the problem has gotten so out of control that homelessness is now the No. 1 issue in voters' minds.

What can we do? We can start by looking at successful "best practices" that have worked in other cities. Our grass-roots organization, Plan C San Francisco (www.plancsf.org), supports the Care Not Cash (Proposition N) ballot initiative because it adopts a "best practice" used by the majority of cities nationwide that are successful in helping the homeless.

It replaces cash assistance checks with vouchers for food, shelter and other care. Homeless people get the services they need—not alcohol and drugs. And San Francisco stops being a magnet for other cities' substance abusers, who come here for the cash.

Opponents of Care Not Cash will tell you it's mean-spirited to take money   10
away from people who so badly need it. But isn't it even worse to provide cash to people who use it to kill themselves? Where does that weigh in their calculation?

And don't listen to the proponents of Exits from Homelessness (Proposition O). It's bad legislation, crafted at the eleventh hour with no public input. It will cost millions of dollars that aren't budgeted. Worse, it undermines key parts of Care Not Cash—although it is wrongly portrayed as companion legislation.

What else can we do? We need comprehensive solutions that draw on policies that have worked in other cities. The San Francisco Planning and Urban Research Association (SPUR) recently completed an excellent study of the homeless problem (www.spur.org/Homelessness.pdf).

A detailed description of that study is beyond the scope of this piece, but SPUR's recommendations include the following: providing vouchers for care and services instead of cash payments; increasing the supply of supportive housing (housing that includes on-site mental health and substance abuse services); enforcing standards of civil behavior and quality of life laws; improving shelter conditions; and increased funding for affordable housing, particularly residential hotels.

These aren't new ideas, but taken together they outline a three-pronged approach to homelessness: being compassionate enough to spend the money needed to address the problem, being smart enough to spend the money in ways that will help keep people off the streets, and being firm enough to insist that antisocial behavior in our public spaces has got to stop.

Compassion, smarts and firmness. So far, San Francisco is one for three.   15

Exploring the Message

1. What specific problems make San Franciscans rate homelessness their No. 1 public issue? How does the homeless situation in your community compare to theirs? What might account for any significant similarities or differences?

2. According to Sullivan, what groups of people are negatively affected by the city's current policies?

3. What explains the failures of leadership outlined by Sullivan? Do his accusations seem well grounded?

4. How, specifically, would "Care Not Cash" solve the homelessness problems? What additional solutions are suggested? Based on your reading of the other selections on homelessness, what response do you have to Plan C's positions?

Investigating the Discourse Community

1. Would the San Francisco Coalition on Homelessness, who devised the Vehicularly Housed Residential Community (pp. 199–206), define leadership in the same way that Sullivan has in this article? What other comparisons between the values and goals of Plan C and the Coalition emerge from a critical reading of the two selections?

2. Reread the first two paragraphs of the Sullivan selection. How would you describe the shift in tone—and the motives for the shift?

3. How has Plan C arrived at its proposed solutions? What does this reveal about the group's working habits and process?

4. After studying the op-ed more carefully, do you think Plan C accomplishes its goal to occupy a middle ground between extreme positions on homelessness? What would those two extremes be?

5. Why would the *San Francisco Examiner* allow Plan C to publish op-ed columns on a regular basis?

Understanding the Genre

1. Sullivan laments that he cannot provide a full explanation of the SPUR study on homelessness. Where else in the article are the space limitations of an op-ed column evident, and what strategies does Sullivan use to counteract this limitation?

2. Describe and evaluate the organization of this article. What cues does Sullivan employ to highlight the structure and thus assist readers in following his argument?

3. How effective is the "three-pronged approach to homelessness" slogan that shapes the final two paragraphs? Is it a strategy you've seen in other op-ed columns?

Writing Activity

Identify a recent national or local problem of public interest and use the library and Internet to locate at least two or three op-ed columns that propose solutions to the problem. After studying the design and execution of the selections, write an advice article for your classmates, outlining successful strategies for writing problem-solving op-ed columns. Use your selections as comparative examples.

Vehicularly Housed Residential Community:
Project Description

Vehicularly Housed Residential Association[1]
& the Coalition on Homelessness, San Francisco

The first collaborative writing project of the group that was to become the Coalition on Homelessness (COH) was a spontaneous plan for a nongovernmental organization of social service workers and the homeless. It was written on a napkin, on the spur of the moment, out of the frustrations that each of the groups had experienced when working alone. This spirit of outreach and cooperation continues to define the Coalition's mission and day-to-day working process. Since 1987, each of the group's many successful projects has passed from strategy-defining small workgroups to widespread community critique before being enacted. Coalition projects include 24-hour drop-in centers, programs for women with mental disabilities, and a 144-unit permanent housing center that, as proposed in the Vehicular Housing plan, employs its residents to build, maintain, and support the program. The proposal excerpted here typifies a cooperative approach to solving problems; it is the result of collaboration between the Coalition and a community organization created by people who were already living in their vehicles on the streets of San Francisco.

This project plans to convert presently unused land into a site upon which vehicularly housed people can park their vehicles in a stable, safe and clean environment, complete with basic amenities and services. The SF Vehicularly Housed Residential Community (VHRC) will provide an innovative new alternative to living on the streets by creating a thriving, stable, and diverse living option, free from the ongoing dangers of living on the streets. The cornerstone to the success of this project is the active role that tenants will play in its development and upkeep. A strong commitment to tenant economic development and training will further the goal of creating a self-sufficient, low-rent living option. This model combines community and self-determination with job creation and training to stabilize and improve the living conditions of its residents.

The key features of this project include:

- Conversion of a presently unused plot of land into rental spaces for approximately 60 vehicle dwellings;
- The provision of basic amenities, including showers, bathrooms, black water disposal, water, mail service, lighting, and garbage pickup;
- Creation of a thriving community space for events and services, including collaboration with local service providers to bring voluntary services on site (e.g. health care provided by the Health Care Clinic Consortium SOS program);
- Active partnership between residents, a nonprofit agency, service providers, and the City;

- Tenant employment and training in the improvement of the partially improved land, including clearing the property, grading, erection of non-permanent community buildings and landscaping;
- Management, operation and maintenance of the community primarily by tenants, initially in partnership with a nonprofit agency;
- The development of a Community Handbook of rules and regulations to facilitate an ordered and respectful living situation, including rules regarding eligibility, rent expectations, dispute resolutions, tenants rights and other guidelines;
- Creation of a self-supporting housing option that facilitates mutual support and empowerment, with the goal of stabilizing and improving the living conditions of its residents;
- Economic development opportunities, including job creation and training, in order to sustain the economic vitality of the lot and create employment opportunities;
- Potential for replication in other sites around the City.

This project is planned as a pilot project, with the goal of developing several such sites throughout the City.

Project Need:

There are currently hundreds of 'houseless' people who live in their vehicles throughout San Francisco. While these vehicularly housed people have found a way to stay off of the street, they continuously face displacement and potential loss of their homes due to enforcement of an assortment of laws, and through the dissatisfaction of nearby merchants and housed neighbors. The Vehicularly Housed Residential Community will create a healthy living environment for people presently residing in vehicles—benefiting not only those who will live there, but San Francisco as a whole. This plan has the support of vehicularly housed people throughout the City, local service providers and business people, and is constantly gaining support as the project develops.

The VHRC will not be a shelter, but a cooperative living alternative. More than a trailer park, the VHRC is a real community designed to provide jobs and training, as well as a centralized location for health care provision and other services. On-site showers, laundry facilities, and a community kitchen will provide VHRC residents with a far more healthy living environment, which will have positive physical and mental health benefits, while assisting in job readiness. By creating a more stable living situation, the VHRC will help many people move out of homelessness and into stable housing. The VHRC will also protect residents from the violent crimes that they are presently vulnerable to while parked on city streets.

The health risks of people living in vehicles on the street is continuously compromised due to ongoing relocation from one area to another. A site such as this plan proposes would act both to reduce the health risks resulting from such relocation, while at the same time allowing health care providers to offer ongoing health services to VHRC residents (see Appendix A, letter of support from San Francisco Community Clinic Consortium).

This is a pilot project that, if successful, can be replicated on other sites to further meet the needs of the many vehicularly housed residents of our City. The VHRC will strive to breed a greater understanding amongst different members of the community—both vehicularly and permanently housed. No one model can meet the needs of all vehicular residents, but the VHRC is the first steps towards creating an alternative site upon which people can live in their vehicles.

Project Design:

Site Criteria

The Vehicularly Housed Residential Association, with the support of its Advisory Board, is currently looking for appropriate sites for the VHRA project. The criteria being sought for the site include an area of approximately 100,000 square feet or greater in a nonresidential area. The land must be level and either paved or pavable. It is necessary that the site be free of environmental toxics. The site must be close to public transport, and preferably in nearby proximity to stores. The site must be amenable to adapting existing buildings to use for the amenities spelled out above, or be available for either permanent or temporary structures to be built for this purpose.

The property will most likely be leased by the City from the public or private owner at a nominal cost. The City will in turn sublet the property to a nonprofit agency selected through a Request for Qualification process described below. The Master Lease agreement between the City and the owners will be consistent with all legal requirements and restrictions.

The Residential Spaces. There will be two space sizes available for parking ve-   10 hicles. The larger size will accommodate large buses, while smaller spaces will be aimed at vehicles such as vans or small trailers. The large spaces will be approximately 40' × 18' (720 sq. ft.), and the medium-sized spaces will be approximately 30' × 18' (540 sq. ft.). An estimated 55–60 spaces will fit in this site in its present state. More vehicles can be accommodated if the property is graded. Vehicularly housed individuals are involved in a community design process with the assistance of architect John Patino. The ultimate distribution of space sizes will be determined after a survey has been done of interested tenants prior to the pre-leasing site preparation.

On-Site Amenities and Services. The initial, basic amenities will include showers, bathrooms, black water disposal, potable water, mail service, lighting, a community kitchen and garbage pickup. The costs of these amenities will be included in the operating expenses of the site and built into the rent structure. Electricity for personal use will be available to those who wish to pay for the service. A pre-determined number of sites will be equipped with hook-ups that can be turned on at the request of the vehicle tenant. This cost will be separate and above the cost of rent.

Additional amenities being considered include an on-site laundry facility, oil recover, pay phones, a community bulletin board, and others. Temporary structures such as office trailers or other buildings that are easily dismantled will be placed on the site.[2] The community buildings will hold showers, bathrooms, an office, and a community space. They will also allow room for classes, clinics, and other services. Some of the on-site services that have been suggested include GA clinics, vet services, computer and other classes, vocational training, and other services and activities the community wishes to initiate. The San Francisco Health Care Clinic Consortium of Health Care for the Homeless presently provides health care to many vehicularly housed residents around the city, and has expressed interest in weekly visits to the lot.

Tenant Eligibility. Tenants will be screened for eligibility. Once they have been admitted into the lot, residents will sign a lease upon entering the VHRC. Individuals can stay for as short a time as one week, and there will be no limits on how long an individual or family can stay on the lot. This will help establish continuity and stability.

Income. Tenancy in the VHRC is aimed at very low income individuals who are living in their vehicles. Income eligibility will be set at 35% or below HUD's Area Mean Income for San Francisco PMSA.[3] Individuals and families receiving public benefits will automatically qualify. A limited number of spaces will be designated for individuals who earn up to 50% PMSA and can show long term residency in a vehicle.

Vehicle eligibility. Vehicles housing mobile residents will qualify for the spaces. This includes buses, trucks, trailers, vans and cars. All vehicles will have to be registered in San Francisco. A non-operational registration is sufficient to meet this criteria. Vehicles will have to meet basic health and safety standards governing Vehicular Residential Parks pursuant to the California Housing Code Title 25, Ch.2.[4]

A voluntary program may be initiated to assist car dwellers in acquiring larger vehicles such as trailers. This may be done through the purchase and renovation of trailers on-site or nearby.

San Francisco residency. All VHRC tenants must be residents of San Francisco. Residency will be established upon being in San Francisco for 30 days.

Household composition. The majority of people presently living in vehicles are single adults and couples. The VHRC will also be open to families in order to provide a safer environment than living on the streets. All community facilities of the VHRC, including bathrooms, showers, and community spaces will be accessible to people with disabilities.

Pets will be permitted.

Non-discrimination policy. The VHRC will be open to people regardless of their race, gender, culture, ethnicity, sexual orientation, disability, nationality or immigration status.

Management and Decision Making

The VHRC will be managed through a collaborative partnership between a nonprofit organization ("Nonprofit Partner") and tenants of the VHRC. Management and operation of the VHRC will be transferred fully to a newly established tenant run nonprofit during the second stage of the project. An on-site resident manager, who will be selected by the Tenant Council and contracted by the Nonprofit Partner, will be hired from amongst potential or existing residents. This individual will receive a salary and a large vehicular space for his or her services.

Decisions regarding VHRC guidelines and day to day operations will be made by a council ("Council") made up of a majority of tenants, with representatives from the Nonprofit Partner, and other elected members. The Council will set up the rules and make decisions regarding the ongoing management of the VHRC. Selected decisions will also be made through input from all tenants at meetings of the whole.

Rules will be made based on *conduct, not status,* consistent with the concepts of respect and dignity inherent to the VHRC. The rules and expectations of the community will be determined through a joint planning group of the nonprofit managers, vehicular residents, and chosen advocates and/or service providers, and codified in the Community Handbook. The Handbook will act as the general guidelines for tenants, management, and others who are visiting the community. Policy changes implemented through the Council.

The community will attempt to resolve disputes through its Council, and an arbitration process will be established for this purpose. Violations of the rules and guidelines that are set out in the Community Handbook will be addressed in this fashion.

The Nonprofit Partner . . .

Office Staffing . . .

Shared Responsibilities Between Nonprofit and Tenants . . .

Tenant Fund . . .

Tenant Selection and Lease-up

The initial tenants will be selected using the criteria chosen during the planning process and clearly defined in the Community Handbook. Prospective tenants will be provided with a written statement of the basic rules and expectations of the community so that they can determine if the community is appropriate for their needs. . . .

Community Living—Everyone Works

Once the VHRC is up and running, every individual who lives on the property will be involved in the upkeep of the property as a part of their payment. While a set rent will be charged per space, every adult on the property will be responsible for doing his or her share of the work. Work activities will include security, maintenance, administration, participation in the income generating activities and other jobs. Work schedules and options will be flexible to facilitate employment schedule, disability, or other special circumstance.

A major goal is the demonstration of tenant managed and maintained housing. After the renovation, the day to day management, operation, and maintenance of the property will transition largely to tenants. After 18 months, a transition period will transfer management of the VHRC from the Nonprofit Partner to the Tenant Nonprofit. This will have both intrinsic and economic benefits. Empowerment and community are two of the main intrinsic benefits of tenant management. Creating a management structure in which tenants make all necessary decisions about where they live will facilitate the development of community and will facilitate the empowerment of tenants. At the same time, tenant management is the key to inexpensive day to day operation and maintenance necessary to make this project work.

A Sanitary and Safe Environment

Keeping the VHRC Clean . . .

Security . . .

Rent Structure . . .

Tenants' Rights[5] . . .

Community Economic Development: . . .

Preparing the Site for Occupancy:

Site Preparation

Most of the property is presently paved and in fair condition. In order to prepare the property for the commencement of the VHRC, the following improvements may be made:

- Re-pave some areas of site if necessary.
- Clear overgrown vegetation.
- Build two community structures: one for the showers and bathrooms, and one for the community space and office.
- Install any necessary electricity, water, sewer and plumbing.
- Install lighting where necessary.

Tenant Employment in Renovation and Start-up

All new employment opportunities connected with the VHRC will include job creation for tenants and potential tenants, through requirements built into the requisite public bidding process. Training and services will be provided for the work crew. This will remain consistent from the pre-leasing stage throughout the duration of the project. Individuals eligible for eventual tenancy will be selected by the Nonprofit Partner. The work crew will have the option of moving onto the property to assist in its renovation. Rent will be a part of the workers' compensation during this time, and wages will be paid as a part of startup costs.

Funding the Development Process

In order to make this project work, it is necessary to explore many creative financing options. A consistent goal must be to keep costs down so that rent can remain low, while ensuring that the basic amenities necessary for a healthy community are provided.

It is essential that the rent for the property be kept as low as possible. The Port may be persuaded, with the help of the City, to provide the land for a nominal fee for the duration of the project. In exchange, the value of the property will be improved through the development of the project. Donations of services and materials should be sought through a collaborative effort between the City and VHRC residents.

Funding for the development costs for the project will be sought through several avenues. Possible sources of funding that have been identified include the Homeless Facilities pool set aside from Community Development Block Grant funding. Remaining funds will be sought through the SF Redevelopment Agency, Habitat for Humanity and other private foundations, and State and Federal grants.

Conclusion:

This proposal lays out an innovative way to address the crises facing a portion of the homeless community of San Francisco. This model project will create a safe and healthy community that has built into it the common sense and inherent dignity that will make it work.

Footnotes:

1. The Vehicularly Housed Residential Association is a community organization made up of people who reside in vehicles, primarily in the area East of 3rd Street.
2. Temporary structures are being contemplated to comply with Port requirements for this use of their property.
3. 35% of area mean income for San Francisco under the HUD guidelines is $15,019 for a single adult, $17,164 for a family of two and $19,310 for a family of three.
4. California Housing Code, Title 25, Ch. 2. "Mobilehome Parks, Special Occupancy Trailer Parks."
5. California Civil Code §799.207 "Recreational Vehicle Occupancy Law."

Exploring the Message

1. List the core traits of the proposed project, including the services, obligations, and opportunities to be offered to residents. Were you surprised by any of the proposals? Are there ideas you might refine or add if you were part of the community reviewing this proposal?
2. What definition of the term *community* emerges in the "Project Need" section of the proposal? How does this image compare to your experience of living in a community?
3. In what ways does this group propose to benefit the San Francisco community as a whole? Are there other benefits you can foresee?
4. Based on your reading of the National Alliance to End Homelessness Home Page and FAQ (pp. 187–189), how would that group respond to this proposal?

Investigating the Discourse Community

1. The project description calls the residential community a partnership among its various participants. Who are these people and what elements have been put into place to ensure that the relationship remains a true partnership? How does this structure reconcile with the Coalition on Homelessness's core mission?
2. What current conditions and risks are used to persuade skeptical readers of the need for this project? Who might those readers be?
3. Identify ideas or expressions in the proposal that seem to reflect the collaborative nature of this writing project. Consider the experiences, assumptions, and goals of the various participants.

4. Several individuals and groups who do not belong to either the Coalition or the Association are referenced in the proposal. What purposes do these references serve in the document?

Understanding the Genre

1. What are the three major sections of this proposal? Define the goal of each section, explain the relationship among the sections, and analyze their order.
2. How would you describe the use of language in the project description? For example, the proposal is for a "vehicularly housed residential community" but each person is to live in a "home." What accounts for the variations in word choice? What are the effects of the changes in diction levels?
3. Select one of the major points in the "Project Design" section and analyze the effectiveness of the explanation provided.
4. Why is there no specific budget in this proposal?

Writing Activity

Write a preliminary proposal for a project to solve an ongoing problem in your home or campus community, such as illegal skateboarding on the streets of a residential area or graffiti on campus buildings. If possible, work with others to represent as many aspects of the problem as possible. If full collaboration is not possible, use primary research methods to gather a variety of points of view. Include the three sections modeled in the selection: project overview, background assessment, and detailed description.

"Can You Spare 20p for a Cup of Tea?" Campaign Poster

Thames Reach Bondway (TRB)/Imagination (GIC) Ltd.

Thames Reach Bondway, a leading London charity, helps over four thousand homeless people a year to move off the streets and into housing. After acting to keep these "rough sleepers" safe, the organization works to ensure the health, skills, and family connections necessary to long-term well-being. Innovative programs include a "Rapid Intervention Team" using taxis to roam the streets in search of those in need of most immediate help. The "Can You Spare 20p for a Cup of Tea?" poster was designed by one of London's leading design groups, Imagination (GIC) Ltd., as part of a campaign to curtail drug use among London's panhandlers. TRB's motive is to redirect individual acts of charity into more comprehensive social action. The premise is effectively captured in the slogan of one of their related public campaigns— "Your Kindness Could Kill."

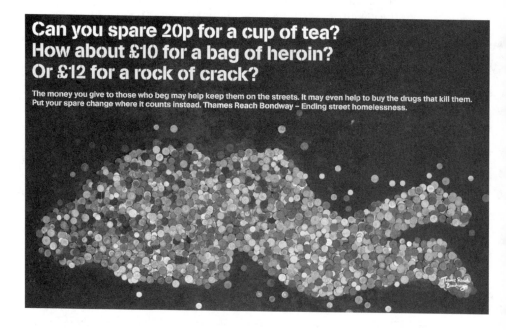

Exploring the Message

1. What messages are conveyed in this poster? What emotions and senses are evoked? What details stand out in your memory as you look away from the poster?

2. What action does TRB expect of the poster's viewers? Visit the Web site of Thames Reach Bondway to see what other activities the organization sup-

ports for those who wish to respond to homelessness and its related problems.

3. Compare the assumptions about homelessness and begging in this poster to student writer Nicole Stewart's in "These Are Our Neighbors" (pp. 210–213). Have you had experiences that help you to understand their positions? What responses have you had in similar situations?

Investigating the Discourse Community

1. What underlying values are conveyed in this poster?
2. How would the poster need to be revised to be used by a charity in your hometown? Explain.
3. The "Your Kindness Could Kill" campaign tells us that a majority of panhandlers on the streets of Camden, Westminster, and the West End of London are not, in fact, homeless, but are highly likely to have drug addictions. How does this information add to your motivation to respond as this poster encourages you to?

Understanding the Genre

1. Outline what you see as the poster's underlying design strategy.
2. Evaluate the success of the physical layout of text and image. For example, does the poster effectively direct the eye of the viewer? Are messages and details easily interpreted?
3. Does the poster convey the right tone for the campaign? How and why?

Writing Activity

Use this poster or another one that features a pivotal image or photograph and redesign it by proposing a different photograph or image, reworking the layout, and, if necessary, revising the text to suit the new graphic. Write a brief analysis of your choices and goals.

These Are Our Neighbors
Nicole Stewart

A student at Parkland Community College in Champaign-Urbana, Illinois, Nicole Stewart wrote this article as part of a community writing project for her Advanced Composition class. Targeting readers of the Lifestyle page of her local newspaper, the Champaign News Gazette, *the author combines personal observations with a review of the film* Dark Days, *which she had seen on the Sundance Channel.*

Have you ever been approached by a panhandler at the Clark station on Mattis or the County Market on Broadway? Have you seen the man that sits every summer on the Cunningham Avenue exit ramp of I-74 with a sign that says, "Homeless Will Work For Food"? Have you seen men and women pushing shopping carts down University Avenue or sleeping in the rain shelter at the bus stop on Colorado Street? Everyone knows that homelessness is a huge problem in America, but it's not limited to metropolitan areas like New York or Washington, D.C. It's here, right in our own backyard.

One man has become a recognized fixture in campus town. I don't know if anyone knows his real name, but he's been given the nickname "Spare Anything." These two words are the shortened version of his panhandling tag usually reserved for working a large crowd. It's not uncommon to hear this phrase when exiting a campus bar on a Saturday night. Occasionally I see him in other parts of town, and then he delivers a longer plea, something to the effect of "Excuse me, Miss. Can you spare anything to help out a homeless family today?"

I've heard people speculate about Spare Anything. Some claim they've seen him pull wads of cash out of his pocket or drive off in a fancy car after a day of begging for change. I must admit, I've been skeptical of his motives. For all I know, he could be duping people out of their hard-earned cash or using the money to buy drugs or alcohol. After all, I've never actually seen this family of his.

I've been approached by Spare Anything often enough to recognize him long before I hear his familiar words. He's fairly short with unkempt hair and an unshaven face; his clothes are usually dark, faded, and worn; he has a distinctive, shuffling gait that might be the result of an old injury, or might just be due to exhaustion.

My typical response is to look at the ground while I dig in my pocket for whatever loose change or dollar bills I might have, and then move quickly on. I've always offered him something, probably just enough to appease my own conscience, but I've never looked Spare Anything straight in the face.

There are many stereotypes about the homeless. They're all drug addicts, or alcoholics, or mental cases. They brought it on themselves. They could change if they really wanted to. They're too lazy or too doped up to find or hold a real job. They're just looking for a handout, taking advantage of honest, hard-working taxpayers. I'm sure that some do take advantage of other people's generosity, but is it fair to assume that every person asking for change is a con artist? No, but it's a lot easier to ignore someone by imagining him to be a bad person.

There's a lot of information out there about homeless people in America. It's not that we're uninformed; it's that most of what we see, hear, or read about the homeless serves to strengthen the stereotypes we already carry. I wasn't fully aware of the characteristics I automatically and unfairly attached to homeless people until I saw a documentary on the Sundance Channel that provided a rude awakening.

Dark Days, filmed, produced, and directed by Marc Singer, gives its viewers the opportunity to see with their own eyes what homelessness is really like. The film centers on eleven people living in the Penn Station Tunnel in New York City. In order to capture the true experience of tunnel life, Singer sold most of his belongings and moved out of his apartment to live alongside the people who appear on screen. He wanted to make this film personal and let his audience know these people as he did. In showing the tunnel dwellers as regular human beings living in irregular conditions, Singer felt he could undo some of the damage done by others who have documented the condition of homelessness.

In a 2000 interview with CNN, Singer said, "I'm not the first one to have gone down there and done something, but I'm the first one to put in any time. Every other film or project done on people living on the street, they're just so inaccurate. When you watch all these other projects, you always see the little guy, sitting in the corner, feeling sorry for himself and blaming the whole world. You don't see a normal person."

Singer's goal was to capture the everyday lives of the people in this community and present them to his viewers as real people. The "cast members" are referred to only by first names: Greg, Ralph, Tito, Tommy, Henry, Ronnie, Clarence, Dee, Julio, Lee, and Brian. Viewers are allowed into the homes of these people, to see each one through Marc's eyes. When the characters talk to the camera, they are speaking to Marc. They are speaking to a friend. 10

Watching *Dark Days* was at times amusing and entertaining; at other times, it was unsettling and disturbing. The film honestly captures both sides of life in this particular community. Scenes that show people performing such ordinary tasks as brushing their teeth, cooking dinner, watching TV, and playing with their dog reveal the everyday, personal side. These folks know each other, respect each other, hang out and talk, joke around, help each other when help is needed. There are times when the viewer could easily imagine any of these people being a neighbor; their lives seem that normal.

But whenever the picture begins to get comfortable, Singer abruptly shifts back into the darkness of tunnel life. We see people asleep on piles of dirt and garbage, gathered around burning barrels, and doing drugs. There are also scenes in which someone opens up to Marc on camera and reveals a story from the past. Some of these scenes, such as Ralph's honest discussion of how he became addicted to crack, or Dee's emotional telling of the deaths of her sons in a fire, are heartrending. However, those were not the scenes that disturbed me the most.

The scene that touched me the most was the one in which Ralph and Tito are collecting food from a garbage bag on the street. The act itself is disturbing, but what made it so much more poignant was their enthusiasm over their discovery. That bag full of donuts, carelessly tossed out at the end of the day, could have been full of fifty-dollar bills. The men smiled and laughed, congratulated and slapped each other on the back as they loaded up as many donuts as they could fit into their plastic bags, all the while stuffing the sweets into their mouths and swallowing them down in huge happy gulps.

Admittedly, some of the people portrayed in this film have tainted pasts and most of them speak candidly about their mistakes. Several talk about drugs and crimes they've committed; others recall details about abusive homes or the indifferent foster care system. After telling Marc about his decline into homelessness, Ralph says:

> I'm being punished for every goddam thing I ever did wrong and still got more punishment to come 'cuz I done so much shit wrong. Sometimes I feel like crying because I was so damn selfish with myself, with everybody around me. It was all about me. I didn't care what anybody thought.

Ralph has obviously come to terms with his mistakes. At the time of filming, he hadn't smoked crack in over three years.

Later, Marc visits Ralph in his new apartment, which he got with the help of the Coalition for Homelessness and a Section 8 Housing Program. Ralph is extremely happy to be out of the tunnel and tells Marc, "To me, it's like it never happened at all and it never will happen again; never, ever, ever, never, never happen. I'll never go homeless again. That was like a nightmare, ya' know, and I woked up out of it . . . and I'm stayin' awake!" The look on Ralph's face as he spoke these words gave me goose bumps. The man I'd watched pull donuts out of the trash is now working, living, and surviving as well as anyone else. His triumph is almost overwhelmingly moving.

Throughout the film it's clear that Singer knows and trusts and genuinely likes these people. It's evident in the way they look at him and the things they share with him, but it's especially obvious in the way Singer reveals the feelings of being homeless. He has captured the emotions of this community—their heartache, their happiness, their humanity. Singer didn't set out to save anyone, but just to be a friend. The idea for the movie actually came from one of the guys in the tunnel. Singer put homeless people to work as his sound and lighting crew and even gave some of them part ownership in the film. His hope was that it would gross enough to put everyone he had met in an apartment of their own. Unfortunately, though *Dark Days* has won several awards, it hasn't made very much money and has left Singer thousands of dollars in debt and all but homeless himself.

Of course, not everyone can put themselves into poverty in an effort to help others, and I'm not saying that we should; but there are ways for anyone to help. A good place to start is the National Coalition for the Homeless. They run a lot of great programs all over the country, and they always need volunteers. To find out how to get involved, one can visit their homepage at www.nationalhomeless.org.

The first thing we have to do, though, is change our perspective. We need to take every preconceived notion about the homeless and chuck them out the window. And the next time we see someone we'd rather ignore, make ourselves take another look.

I haven't seen Spare Anything since I started writing this article, but I know it won't be long. Someday I'll be walking out of Mobil or Murphy's, and I'll hear the words that immediately bring to mind the picture of a man shuffling through a crowd, palm extended. The next time I look at Spare Anything I won't see what he might be—a drug addict, an alcoholic, a con artist. I'll look straight into his eyes and see what he definitely is—a person.

Exploring the Message

1. At the beginning of her article, how does the author feel about the homeless in her community and her relationship to them? How does she make these feelings clear? In what ways does her view change? How credible is the change?

2. What role does Spare Anything play in getting Stewart's message across? How effective is her use of this person?

3. Which scene in the film did Stewart find most touching? Can you explain why it affected her so much?

4. What does Stewart want her readers to do about the homeless in their community? Are her expectations realistic? useful? significant?

Investigating the Discourse Community

1. How does the author make it clear that she is part of the community she's addressing? Why does she do so? How effective is she in this regard? Point to specific details and examples to support your opinions.

2. Before she began working on this article, Stewart identified her audience as "middle class men and women who live in Champaign-Urbana and Champaign county—all races, but mostly white, ages 20–50." What does she do to address this audience? Consider the language, tone, and style she uses.

3. Does Stewart assume her readers have seen the film? How does her assumption affect the way she writes about the film?

Understanding the Genre

1. What two genres does Stewart combine in this article? Does one genre dominate? If you split the article into two parts, would each one be able to stand alone? Why or why not?

2. How well does the author cover the film? Do you know enough about the film and its director to follow Stewart's main points? What else would you like to know?

3. Is the author a credible first-person narrator? How important is her presence in the article?

4. What risk does Stewart take by including the sometimes graphic dialogue from the film? Why does she choose to do so?

Writing Activity

If you were an editor and you wanted to print Stewart's article as a conventional movie review, what revisions would you ask for? Make a list of particular additions, deletions, and rearrangements you would want her to make. Briefly explain your reasons for requesting each of these changes. To help you with this activity, look up other reviews of *Dark Days* to see what they do and don't do when compared to Stewart's treatment of the film. You can find reviews listed in the Internet Movie Database (www.imdb.com/) and the Movie Review Query Engine (www.mrqe.com).

Writer's Workshop

1. How have the selections in this casebook changed your views of homelessness as you outlined them in the "Writer's Notebook" at the start of the casebook? Identify an appropriate writing situation and write about some part or version of your current views to a specific audience for a useful purpose. Any of the selections in this or the "Targeting Discrimination" casebook might serve as a model genre for your project.

2. Visit the National Coalition for the Homeless Web site at http://www.nationalhomeless.org/index.html. Study the site carefully and compare the group's mission to the one expressed on the National Alliance to End Homelessness site (http://www.naeh.org/). What differences are evident in the organizations' structures and projects? After completing your analysis, write a letter to your local paper suggesting the kind of mission that you now feel would be most appropriate for a coalition on homelessness in your community.

3. A number of housing solutions for homelessness have been proposed by the writers in this casebook—the Vehicular Community, the Center for Women in Transition, and Care Not Cash, for example. Based on these proposals, create a questionnaire on options for housing the homeless, one that could be used to canvas local homeless people, government officials, and service providers. Consult Chapter 3 (pp. 62–63) on how to construct your questions, including how to use peer review to evaluate your document. The results of the questionnaire would be used by these same groups to help create new proposals or make changes in existing programs.

Writer's Profile Three: What Might I Do as a Public Writer?

Because even our public lives are often very heavily scheduled and take place among people we may not know very well, community groups and organizations choose to use many of the same decision-making procedures we associate with professional discourse communities. When a new volunteer suggests a project, for example, the group may request a proposal. Time is valuable, resources are usually limited, and the volunteer's expertise and level of commitment are unknown. A proposal formalizes a spontaneous suggestion and immerses the volunteer in a fuller understanding of the organization and the plan.

"Writer's Profile Three" is an opportunity to (1) identify a local group or organization that you would like to be involved with—a special interest club such as the Audubon Society, a volunteer community action group such as Habitat for Humanity, an organization such as the Girl Scouts, or an ad hoc group such as "Save Our Children's Museum," for example; (2) use primary research tools to study and become involved with this discourse community; (3) identify a need or problem faced by the group that could be partially resolved through a written document—a newsletter, Web site, or brochure, for example; (4) write a proposal for implementing that document. As part of the proposal, you will use the insights you have gained in the first two Writer's Profiles to represent your qualifications for completing the project should the proposal be accepted.

Actually creating the document is not a formal part of this assignment, though you may well decide to follow through with the group and your proposal.

If approved by the instructor, this project may be undertaken by a small group of two or three students, with each student completing an individual project notebook and the group submitting a single proposal.

Step 1: Use the Project Notebook to brainstorm possible groups or organizations. Examine your goals and motives: What might each organization offer you and what can you offer the organization? The expectation here is to establish a reciprocal and equally rewarding relationship. If you are having trouble identifying a group, review the organizations represented in the casebook readings, check the volunteer section of your local paper or yellow pages, talk to your friends, teachers, and parents, or visit campus offices that coordinate programs with your community. Consult your instructor before you make a final selection.

Step 2: Contact the group or organization and arrange to meet with someone to discuss the possibilities for completing this study. Be sure you are fully prepared to discuss your preliminary goals and motives.

Step 3: Arrange interviews and observations. Because community groups are often less predictable and formally organized, this stage of the project may involve attending meetings, dropping in to project sites, joining a listserve, or making phone calls. In all cases, study existing group documentation (written, published, and electronic) for insights into the community and its typical genres and styles. Record your steps and responses in your Project Notebook as you did in "Writer's Profile Two."

Step 4: Identify a problem or need that can be resolved in part or wholly through a written document. Your idea might initiate a project or be part of a project that is already underway or initiate a project. Good examples of similar projects are the *I Spy Sexism* Web site and the *Transitions* newsletter, each of which reflects the mission of the group and enacts an important goal.

Step 5: Begin to draft your proposal. This medium is shaped into different genres by each discourse community. In all cases, it's important to exactly follow a designated specific format to help practiced readers to quickly find and use the sections they need. For this assignment plan to include these typical elements:

- **A cover letter:** Convey that you are submitting a proposal; very briefly explain your project and goals; suggest a reasonable time schedule for the group to respond to your proposal.
- **Title Page:** Include your project title, the name of the organization, your name and contact information. Be clear, direct, and specific.
- **Introduction:** A concise but purposeful summary of the problem or need you are addressing, your solution, and your goals. This section will likely repeat some of the information provided in the cover letter. Readers pay special attention to this section, so concentrate on any unique or innovative aspects of the proposal. The first section of the "Vehicularly Housed Residential Community" proposal is a helpful model.

- **Background:** Using your primary research, write a concise narrative that establishes relevant history and contexts. Has this been tried before? Will it replace an existing document? Here you are establishing your understanding of the group and its needs. Accuracy is essential and helps establish your credibility.
- **Description:**

Detailed overview of the project	Budget
Timeline	Method of evaluation

- **Conclusion:** This is your final chance to highlight your purpose and encourage the group to accept your proposal.
- **Bibliography or Works Cited:** Cite any references used in the proposal (see Appendix B, pp. 287–313).
- **Statement of Qualifications:** Include a brief narrative resume focusing on your credentials for proposing and carrying out the project; include the qualifications of any others you would like to involve in completing the project.
- **Appendices:** Include any supporting documentation (for example, a sample of the genre you are proposing), letters of support for the project, or letters of approval for any actions that will require them.

  Step 6: Use small group peer critique to generate responses to your draft.

  Step 7: Revise, paying special attention to creating a consistent and easily navigated format. A clear and concise style is essential, too. Submit your notebook and proposal to your instructor.

Chapter 6

Becoming a Practicing Writer

Chapter Preview

In this chapter you will learn to identify and use the specialized tools and resources for conducting secondary research in your field or profession. You will also critique a professional essay on a topic that will become the focus for your researched writing in the next chapter.

Most public and professional writing involves research of one kind or another. Whether you are writing for a class, an employer, a client, or a community group, you first have to determine what you already know and what you don't yet know about the topic. Then you have to seek out the ideas and information you need to complete the project. This search can be formal or casual, narrow or extensive—but it's a central part of creating an effective piece of writing.

The Secondary Research Process: Resources, Techniques, and Styles

As you have already learned, there are two major types of research writing. In one type, a writer generates new information and reports the findings. The writing is based on *primary* or *field research*—on the writer's own observations, interviews, surveys, or experiments. In the second type, a writer collects existing information and explains it to an audience that needs or wants it. The writing is based on *secondary* or *library research*—on what the writer has read, analyzed, evaluated, and synthesized. Of course, it's possible to combine both kinds of research in a single document: social scientists, for example, frequently review the findings of other researchers before reporting their own results.

You are probably most familiar with secondary research; it's the kind usually required for undergraduate research papers. The computer revolution has radically changed and greatly improved secondary research. Databases, search engines, online archives, and electronic retrieval systems have opened the door to a world of information that might otherwise be unavailable to you. But as you know, doing research on the Internet or with other computerized sources can produce an overwhelming amount of information, much of it questionable. The increased access to more materials has also increased the need to know as much as you can about where to look and how to evaluate what you find. The first part of this chapter will help you to conduct secondary research efficiently within a specific field of study or profession.

Selecting and Using Secondary Sources

The changes brought about by computer technology both aid and complicate the secondary research process. You can quickly gather a long list of sources, but you have to decide which ones are most appropriate for your project. Your search will be more efficient and more productive if you know what kinds of sources are available and how you can use them.

Library resources are constantly changing, but every field or discipline has a set of specialized reference sources that you can use to track down the specific information you need. Becoming familiar with the research tools in a particular area of study will allow you to focus your search and help you to bypass irrelevant materials. (Table 6.1 provides a list of guides that can help you to identify the major resources in various disciplines.)

The following brief discussions target four types of resources for you to investigate in your field of research. The accompanying writing activities will help you become acquainted with these valuable materials and prepare you to complete the research you will undertake in this and the following chapter. After you have finished each of these exercises, take the time to exchange discoveries with students in your class who share your major or career plans.

Specialized Reference Works

General encyclopedias are often a good place to start an undergraduate research project. But as you advance in your major and prepare to enter a profession, you'll want to become acquainted with the specialized encyclopedias, dictionaries, bibliographies, directories, yearbooks, and biographical reference works that are used in your field. If you're working in special education, for example, you probably should know about the *Directory for Exceptional Children,* the *Special Education Handbook,* and the *Encyclopedia of Special Education,* among other resources.

Table 6.1 Disciplinary Guides to Research

Anthropology	*Introduction to Library Research in Anthropology*, by John M. Weeks, 2nd edition, 1998.
Art	*Art Information and the Internet: How to Find and Use It*, by Lois Jones, 1999.
Business	*The Business Library and How to Use It*, by Ernest L. Maier, 1994.
Education	*Education: A Guide to Reference and Information Sources*, by Nancy Patricia O'Brien, 2nd edition, 2000.
Film	*Oxford Guide to Film Studies*, by John Hill and Pamela Gibson, 1998.
History	*A Student's Guide to History*, by Jules R. Benjamin, 8th edition, 2000.
Humanities	*The Humanities: A Selective Guide to Information Sources*, by Ron Blazek and Elizabeth S. Aversa, 5th edition, 2000.
Literature	*Literary Research Guide: An Annotated Listing of Reference Sources in English Literary Studies*, by James L. Harner, 4th edition, 2002.
Music	*Music Reference and Research Materials*, by Vincent Duckles and Ida Reed, 5th edition, 1997.
Philosophy	*Philosophy: A Guide to the Reference Literature*, by Hans. E. Bynagle, 2nd edition, 1997.
Political Science	*Information Sources of Political Sciences*, by Frederick L. Holler, 4th edition, 1986.
	A New Handbook of Political Science, by Hans-Dieter Klingermann and Robert Goodin, 1998.
Psychology	*Library Use: A Handbook for Psychology*, by Jeffrey L. Reed and Pam M. Baxter, 3rd edition, 2003.
Science	*Guide to Information Sources in the Physical Sciences*, by David Stern, 2000.
Social Sciences	*The Social Sciences: A Cross-Disciplinary Guide to Selected Sources*, by Nancy L. Herron, 3rd edition, 2002.
Sociology	*Sociology: A Guide to Reference and Information Sources*, by Stephen H. Aby, 2nd edition, 1997.
Women's Studies	*Reader's Guide to Women's Studies*, by Eleanor Amico, 1998.

Some of these guides are available online or in electronic format. The *Guide to Reference Books*, edited by Robert Balay (11th edition, 1996), will help you find disciplinary guides for subjects not listed.

Or if you're studying sports medicine, you might want to be familiar with the *Manual of Sports Medicine*, the *Oxford Handbook of Sports Medicine*, or the *Dictionary of Sports Injuries and Disorders*.

These specialized reference works will give an overview of the field and provide you with explanations of key issues, definitions of important terms, selective bibliographies of supplementary sources, and information about future careers and employers. Table 6.2 lists some of the specialized encyclopedias for the major academic disciplines.

Table 6.2   Specialized Encyclopedias and Dictionaries in Major Academic Disciplines

ANTHROPOLOGY	*Encyclopedia of Social and Cultural Anthropology.* 2002.
ARCHITECTURE	*Encyclopedia of Architecture: Design, Engineering, and Construction.* 1990.
ART	*Dictionary of Art.* 34 vols. 1996.
ASTRONOMY	*International Encyclopedia of Astronomy.* 2002.
BIOLOGY	*Encyclopedia of Human Biology.* 1997.
BUSINESS	*Encyclopedia of Management.* 2000.
CHEMISTRY	*Macmillan Encyclopedia of Chemistry.* 4vols. 1996.
COMPUTERS	*Encyclopedia of Computers and Computer History.* 2 vols. 2001.
ECONOMICS	*Oxford Dictionary of Economics.* 2001.
EDUCATION	*World Education Encyclopedia.* 3 vols. 2001.
ENVIRONMENT	*Encyclopedia of Ecology and Environmental Management.* 1997.
FILM	*The Film Encyclopedia.* 2001.
FOREIGN RELATIONS	*Encyclopedia of U.S. Foreign Relations.* 1997.
	Encyclopedia of the Third World. 1992.
GEOGRAPHY	*Companion Encyclopedia of Geography.* 1996.
HISTORY	*Encyclopedia of American History.* 1996.
	Encyclopedia of World History. 2001.
LAW	*Encyclopedia of Crime and Justice.* 4 vols. 2001.
LITERATURE	*Encyclopedia of World Literature in the 20th Century.* 5 vols. 1998.
	The Johns Hopkins Guide to Literary Theory and Criticism. 1994.
MATHEMATICS	*McGraw-Hill Dictionary of Mathematics.* 1997.
MUSIC	*New Grove Dictionary of Music and Musicians.* 29 vols. 2001.
MYTHOLOGY AND FOLKLORE	*The Facts on File Encyclopedia of World Mythology and Legend.* 2004.
PHILOSOPHY	*Encyclopedia of Philosophy.* 8 vols. 1973, 1996.
PHYSICS	*Encyclopedia of Physics.* 2004.
PSYCHOLOGY	*Encyclopedia of Psychology.* 8 vols. 2000.
RELIGION	*Encyclopedia of Religion.* 16 vols. 2004.
RECREATION AND SPORTS	*Encyclopedia of World Sport.* 3 vols. 1996.
	Sports: The Complete Visual References. 2000.
SCIENCE AND TECHNOLOGY	*The Cutting Edge: An Encyclopedia of Advanced Technologies.* 2000.
	McGraw-Hill Encyclopedia of Science and Technology. 20 vols. 2002.
SOCIAL SCIENCES	*International Encyclopedia of the Social and Behavioral Sciences.* 2001.
WOMEN'S STUDIES	*Women's Studies Encyclopedia.* 3 vols. 1989–1991.

Writing Activity

Visit the reference section of your college library and make a list of at least ten specialized reference books in your major field of study, your future profession, or a current area of primary interest. Finding these sources can be as easy as using your library's online catalog to do keyword title or subject searches. Once you are in the right area of the reference room, browse to find what seem to be the most useful and up-to-date resources. Include authors/editors, titles, dates, call numbers, and cities of publication in your descriptive entries. Cover at least five of these eight categories: (1) specialized encyclopedias; (2) specialized subject dictionaries (*not* language dictionaries); (3) subject or general field bibliographies (e.g., *Guide to Resources in Journalism* or *Index of Literary Criticism*); (4) biographical reference books (e.g., *Who's Who in Criminal Law*); (5) directories of firms, foundations, professional organizations; (6) specialized handbooks; (7) specialized annuals, yearbooks, almanacs; (8) guides to government publications. Be prepared to explain the reasons for your particular choices to your classmates.

Indexes and Abstracts

As you know, there are many indexes, both online and in print, that provide information on articles in journals, magazines, and newspapers. Some indexes include *abstracts* or short summaries of the articles, and some even offer full-text versions of the articles themselves. Like reference books, some indexes, such as the *Readers' Guide to Periodical Literature* or *InfoTrac*, are general and multidisciplinary; others narrow their focus to special fields of study. Knowing which indexes to use can save you a lot of time. For instance, a researcher in early childhood development would probably consult the *Education Index* or *ERIC (Educational Resources Information Center)* rather than wade through all the entries in *ArticleFirst* (a database of over 12,500 journals in a wide variety of fields). And someone writing about computers could focus her search by using the *Applied Science and Technical Index* or the *Computer Database*.

You can find an extensive list of periodical indexes in every field, from the Library of Congress, at www.loc.gov/rr/main/ab_index.html. The Internet Public Library also provides a list of directories of periodicals: www.ipl.org/div/subject/browse/ref60.00.00.

Writing Activity

Using the online catalog or perhaps one of the disciplinary guides to research listed in Table 6.1, find out what specialized indexes and abstracts are available in your college library, both electronically and in print. Identify at least three that are appropriate to your field of study. Describe each one by giving the following information: full name of the index/abstract, its location in the library or how to access the electronic version, and the dates the index covers. For printed indexes, provide a brief sampling of the topics or subject areas listed; for the electronic form, indicate some of the keywords or phrases that you used to search the index successfully.

Specialized Professional Journals

Scholars and professionals use journals to share their ideas with one another and to report their research findings to other members of their discourse communities. Unlike popular magazines or public newsletters, which are nonspecialist publications directed toward a diverse readership, scholarly journals contain specialized information intended for readers in a particular field. Students who want to participate and succeed in their chosen fields need to know about the leading journals in the discipline. A political science student, for example, should become acquainted with the *Political Science Quarterly, Politics and Behavior,* and *Political Theory;* and someone working in marketing would want to be familiar with the *Journal of Marketing,* the *Journal of Marketing Research, Direct Marketing,* and the *Journal of Marketing Education.*

Writing Activity

Locate five specialized professional journals in your field that are currently held by your college library. Describe the ones in print form by giving the call number, location in the library, and the dates of available issues (e.g., 1945 to 1960 and 1970 to present). For those in electronic form (for example, journals available via the Project Muse collection), give the steps used to access the journal on the library terminal and the dates of available issues (e.g., 1980 to present). Select an issue from one of the journals and write a brief analysis of how it—and the journal in general—might be useful to a student in your major.

The World Wide Web

You can also use the World Wide Web to find materials that relate specifically to your field of research. As you probably know, there are dozens of search engines available to help you locate information on the Web. These search devices all work a little differently and have different strengths and weaknesses. You will probably want to explore your topic on more than one search engine to see what you can find. For advice on search engines, as well as for tips on searching techniques, consult Appendix A (pp. 274–277).

You can also join electronic communities called *newsgroups*, through which members exchange information about a common interest or affiliation by posting questions and answers to online sites. Or you can become a member of an Internet discussion list, frequently called a *listserv*, by which subscribers use e-mail to converse on a particular subject. You will find searchable indexes of e-mail discussion lists at www.tile.net/lists.

Writing Activity

Use a search engine on the Web to do the following:

1. Locate a *professional organization* appropriate to your field. Provide the name and Web address for the organization.
2. Find a *listserv* to which people in your major or profession might belong. Provide the name and method for subscribing to the listserv.
3. Identify a general Web site that you think would be interesting or useful to students in your major or to people in your profession. Supply the address and a brief description of the site.

Researching for Public Writing

Doing research for public writing has the same goals as doing research for professional or academic writing: you want to find reliable, up-to-date information that will help you to explain your ideas and support your opinions. In public writing, however, you want your message to be accessible to the general reader, someone who may know something about your topic but lacks the expertise to follow a specialized presentation. In addition, public writing often involves current events and social issues. For these reasons, material from scholarly publications and technical sources might not be very helpful, especially if you need to educate yourself as well as your readers about the topic. It would be more efficient to use research tools that will guide you to recent nonspecialist sources intended for diverse readers. The following is a list of indexes and resource sites that you might want to consult when working on a public writing project:

Readers' Guide to Periodical Literature. Indexes articles in general-interest magazines. Available at most libraries in chronologically bound volumes; may also be available in a computer database. 1901 to present.

Readers' Guide Abstracts. Electronic database with citations and abstracts of articles on current topics published in popular general-interest periodicals. May be available through your library. 1983 to present.

Magazine Index. Indexes 370 popular American periodicals. Extremely useful for very current topics. Appears in microform; your library may also have it on CD-ROM. 1978 to present.

WilsonSelectPlus. Electronic database with citations, abstracts, and complete articles from 1400 periodicals covering subjects in the general sciences, humanities, current events, and business. Available in many college libraries. 1994 to present, updated weekly.

Facts on File. A weekly world news digest with cumulative index; issued in loose-leaf format for updating. Available in most libraries. Indexed online in its entirety by NEXIS. 1940 to present.

Issues and Controversies on File. From Facts on File News Services. Provides articles that highlight important issues in the news. Available to subscribers online at www.facts.com/online-icof.htm; your library may subscribe.

Gallup Poll News Service. Summaries and analyses of current opinion poll results. Includes a searchable archive. Available online at www.gallup.com/poll/.

PAIS International. Database from Public Affairs Information Services (PAIS). Citations for articles and documents about important political, economic, and social issues. Available online at www.pais.org.

Public Agenda Online. Research studies, surveys, forum guides, and other resources on public opinion and policy issues. Available online at www.publicagenda.org.

Evaluating Sources

With all the material available today, your challenge as a researcher isn't so much finding sources but deciding how reliable or trustworthy they are. Just because an article or book appears in print or online doesn't mean that its opinions are credible or that its information is accurate. You'll want to approach all your sources somewhat skeptically and look into their credentials and connections.

Recognizing Bias

One of the most important goals of evaluating a source is to identify any bias in its treatment of the topic. The fact is that most writing is not neutral or objective and doesn't try to be. Almost all authors and publications have political, social, economic, generational, and religious points of view that influence their presentation and determine what information they include—and exclude—especially when they deal with controversial subjects. These viewpoints don't make the sources unusable or unreliable, but you need to be aware of such biases and take them into account when deciding what to use and how to use it. For example, if you were researching the topic of home schooling, you might come across a journal called *Growing without Schooling*. With a little investigation you would find that this publication is by and for home schoolers who write about why they chose home schooling and what they like about it. You might find a lot of valuable material in such a source, depending on your purpose and audience; but if you were looking for something about the shortcomings and objections to home schooling, you would have to go to other sources.

Here are some specific questions to pose when trying to identify the strengths and limitations of a source:

- What are the author's credentials and reputation? Is the author's point of view clear and relevant?
- Was the material published by a commercial publisher, a corporation, a government agency, an educational institution, a professional organization, or a special interest group?
- What interests does the source represent? What interests does it seem to ignore?
- What is the publication's political slant?
- Who supports or advertises in the source?
- What is the tone of the writing? Does it use loaded words or confrontational language?
- Do you know a trustworthy expert in the field who would recommend this source?
- Is the information in this source verified or contradicted by other sources?

These two reference works can help you find information about periodical sources:

Gale Directory of Publications and Broadcast Media (1990–, updated yearly). A useful source for details about newspapers and magazines. Entries often indicate intended audience or political slant. The *San Diego Union,* for example, is described as a "newspaper with a Republican orientation."

Magazines for Libraries (1997–, updated regularly). A listing of periodicals arranged by academic discipline. Entries give publication data, describe intended audience, and evaluate content and editorial focus.

For provocative online assessments of media bias, you can take a look at these two sites:

FAIR (Fairness and Accuracy in Reporting) at www.fair.org offers a liberal take on balance and fairness in the news.

The Media Research Center (America's Media Watchdog) at www.mrc.org presents a conservative perspective.

Assessing Electronic Resources

You should, of course, be concerned about the credibility of any source you cite in your writing. With scholarly books and journal articles, you can generally consider the information credible because it has been reviewed and edited; the authors are often recognized authorities and their claims are documented. Popular books and periodicals are not as reliable and often have political biases, but they have probably been reviewed and edited by publishers, editors, and librarians. Books are also reviewed after publication by specialists in the field, and magazines and journals frequently include letters to the editor from readers who question or support an article's findings or conclusions.

But materials from the Internet are a different story. With newsgroups and the World Wide Web, you have the widest possible participation in creating and disseminating information: everyone's ideas and opinions are there for you to consider. Web sites sponsored by well-known institutions and companies depend on the credibility—and the interests—of their supporting organizations. Material posted by the U.S. government or by colleges and universities, for example, can usually be trusted. But listservs and individual Web pages are rarely reviewed for accuracy and completeness. Given this wide assortment of unmonitored sources and unedited information, you have to judge for yourself the quality and reliability of electronic resources. Here are some points to guide you in making your evaluations:

Look for credentials. What do you know about the people supplying the information? What's the basis of their expertise? Has their work been funded by an organization? Do they have a personal agenda?

Track down affiliations. Who sponsors the online site? Is it a reputable group that you can easily identify? Is the information influenced by commercial or political sponsorship? Does the site include links to other resources? Does it provide a means for asking questions?

Analyze motives. What purpose does the site serve? Many online postings are trying to buy or sell something; they don't usually make good sources for research. Others are promoting a favorite cause; you might get some general ideas from such advocacy sources, but you'll want to check the information you get from them very carefully. Personal postings vary widely in their usefulness; it's probably better to search elsewhere for more clearly reliable information.

Consider currency and stability. Is the material updated regularly? Is there an archive for older information? As you know, many online sources quickly become obsolete or disappear overnight. You'll want to check for dates of the original posting and the most recent updates.

Confirm your information. Can you find other sources to verify what you've found online? Ideally, you want to have several different kinds of sources to achieve a credible balance of material. Remember, too, that erroneous information circulated in a listserv or newsgroup is often challenged by other participants. So don't accept the first posting; wait to see if others support or dispute it.

For more details about evaluating online resources, see the discussion on pp. 276–277 in Appendix A. You might also visit one of these sites:

Evaluating Web Sites: a comprehensive and instructive guide to judging information resources for reliability and accuracy, at www.lesley.edu/library/guides/research/evaluating_web.html.

LibrarySmart: an online guide to "smart information"; created and maintained by the Washington State Library as part of its information literacy program, at www.librarysmart.com/working/LSPublic/01_evaluate.asp.

Writer's Workshop

Choose a topic of importance to your major or profession. Familiarize yourself with the topic by reading the information available from an online encyclopedia such as www.encyclopedia.com or a specialized encyclopedia such as the *Encyclopedia of Television* (at www.museum.tv/archives/etv/index.html). After you've finished this introductory reading, locate information about your topic by using the same series of keywords on four different search engines. What similarities and differences do you see in the listings from the four search engines? Which sites appear on all four lists? Which sites appear on only one list? Are the same sites listed higher or lower on different lists? Can you tell why? Finally, evaluate several of the sites, using the guidelines given in the previous section. Choose the two that you think would be the most useful and reliable. Justify your choices.

Documenting Your Sources

The most obvious reason for documenting your sources is to avoid plagiarism and its consequences. But there are less tangible, more important reasons for providing the details of your research. Documenting your sources will build credibility with your audience, establish the background for your writing, enable readers to follow up on your work, and give credit to the people whose ideas and knowledge have informed your writing. Acknowledging your sources also places you within a community of writers and readers who share common ideas—or at least common grounds for dialogue and debate.

What to Document

The conventions of research writing require that you document information that originates in someone else's work. All of the following materials should be accompanied by a reference to the original:

- direct quotations
- paraphrases and summaries
- facts that are debatable or not widely known
- statistics, graphs, charts, diagrams, figures, and other kinds of "hard evidence"
- opinions, claims, or assertions of others, particularly when controversial or questionable

You don't have to document what is called "general knowledge"—that is, information that could be found in a variety of sources, particularly in an encyclopedia or dictionary—although you should use your own phrasing to convey these facts and ideas. And you don't need to document your own thoughts, observations, and personal experiences. Sometimes, however, it is difficult to determine what falls into these last two categories. How do you know where your sources end and your own thinking begins? Which facts and ideas can you claim as your own and which ones should you attribute to others? One way to decide is to ask yourself, "Did I really know this information before I began researching the topic?" You might also consider how you'd like your own work to be credited, and use that as a guide. Finally, using a project notebook will assist you in distinguishing original insights from researched materials.

Styles of Documentation

A documentation style is a standard approach for citing your sources. As you know, different discourse communities, especially academic disciplines, use different documentation styles. Most documentation styles require both an in-text citation (like parenthetical references or footnotes) and end documentation (like a Works Cited list or a References list). These two components work together to give your readers the full bibliographic details about your sources.

There are four commonly used systems of documentation. You may already be familiar with one or more of them.

- MLA (Modern Language Association) style involves brief in-text citations that refer readers to a list of Works Cited (with full publication information) at the end of the paper; it is widely used in the arts and humanities (e.g., English, philosophy, art).

- APA (American Psychological Association) style also involves brief in-text citations that refer to a References list (with full publication data) at the end of the document; it is used in many of the social sciences (e.g., anthropology, education, home economics, linguistics, political science, psychology, sociology).
- CMS (*Chicago Manual of Style*) presents two forms of documentation: author-date citations in the text paired with a reference list (much like MLA and APA) and numbered endnotes or footnotes. This style is often used in history, art history, and other humanities.
- CSE (Council of Science Editors) style presents two methods for documenting references: a name-year system similar to the APA's and a citation-sequence system that lists sources in the order of their use. This is the basic guide for most writing in the life sciences and medicine.

Some of these styles may appear similar, especially MLA and APA, but there are numerous specific differences—differences that reflect the special concerns, interests, and values of each discipline. In MLA style, for instance, the parenthetical in-text citations are usually placed at the end of a sentence or paragraph, where they don't interrupt the flow of the writing. But in APA style these citations, which are used more frequently, can be placed anywhere within a sentence, a practice that emphasizes the research rather than the fluency of the prose. Another difference is that APA in-text citations include a date: scientific knowledge must be current, so the date of publication is important to both writer and reader. But MLA citations don't contain a date, probably because the observations and opinions of literary scholars can remain relevant and valuable for a long time.

It is not necessary, or even possible, to learn all the conventions of a particular style of documentation, although you may want to familiarize yourself with the main features of any system that you'll be using frequently. But it is important to know which style your readers expect and where to find directions and guidelines for using that style. If you are not sure which method is appropriate for the writing you are doing, check with your teacher, your editor, your project manager, or an expert in the field. In Appendix B (pp. 287–313) we provide a description of the four major documentation styles—MLA, APA, CMS, and CSE—along with sample citations and bibliographic entries. We also tell you how to locate the official style manuals for these four systems as well as for other styles used in a number of subdisciplines and professions.

Informal Documentation

A detailed, academic approach to citing sources is not always appropriate for some genres of professional and public writing. Journalists, for example, routinely work source details into the text of an article, as seen in these examples from "Stop That Face!" by Linda Rothstein (pp. 104–107):

Face-recognition technology got even more attention when it was demonstrated by British comedian John Cleese on a BBC television special, "The Human Face," which was shown on The Learning Channel on August 27.

And according to Julia Scheeres's September 5 report for *Wired News,* the "biometrics" industry, of which faceprinting is only a part, is now trying to find a few heart-warming "Good News Biometric Stories" to counteract opposition.

These references don't follow the precise requirements for MLA or APA in-text citations, and the article doesn't include footnotes or a list of works cited. The author clearly knows the value of identifying her sources of information, but she also recognizes that a formal documentation style would be inappropriate for the audience, purpose, and tone of the genre.

In the casebook readings in Chapters 4 and 5, you will find a number of writers who cite their sources informally.

The Project Notebook

In many ways, the process for writing a research paper is the same as for any other writing project. You still need to narrow the topic to fit the limitations of time, space, and audience; and you still have to generate content, organize your materials, prepare a draft, get feedback, revise the draft, and edit and format the final version. But in researched writing your task is further complicated by the need to find, read, and assimilate the findings and opinions of others. You then have to incorporate this information into your own writing and document the sources for your readers. You will be greatly aided at all the stages of this process by a *project notebook.*

Keeping Track of Your Research

Like the notebook used in ethnographic studies, your secondary research notebook is a history of your actions and thinking for the project. (See Chapter 3, pp. 58–60.) It's a device for keeping all your materials in one location. It is also a place where you can summarize and analyze readings as you construct your own working thesis and arguments. If you work on computer, you can create a folder in which to keep your research notebook.

You might want to begin your research notebook with these entries:

1. Write down your topic and record your thoughts about it. Why are you interested in the topic? What do you want to learn about it? Do you know of any unresolved problems or disagreements among the experts that you need to address?

2. Talk over the proposed topic with others who might be involved in the project (teacher, supervisor, editor, group members, co-workers, etc.) and record their reactions. Using their feedback, explain how you plan to limit the scope of the topic to make it more manageable.

3. Using your topic analysis and conversations, formulate several questions that you will try to answer with your research. For example, if you were writing on identify theft, you might ask: Why is identity theft on the increase? What are businesses and governmental agencies doing about the problem? What can the average person do to protect against identity theft?

4. Outline your research plan. Where are you likely to find information? Given your audience and assigned genre, what kinds of sources will you probably need to consult? Which ones will you look at first? Which indexes and databases should you use? Will you need to do any primary research (interviews, surveys, or observations)? You might also want to work out a tentative schedule for the entire research project.

Reading and Analyzing Sources

After narrowing the topic, posing research questions, and defining a search plan, you are ready to locate sources and start reading them. At this stage your research notebook will be an invaluable tool. We strongly recommend that you use the divided-page format described in Chapter 3 (pp. 59–60) as you read and take notes. On one side of the page, summarize your reading of the source material and write down the complete bibliographic data and URLs. On the other side, comment on your sources, noting their importance to your topic and their relationship to other sources; you can also include an assessment of your source's credibility (who is the author? why should I consider using this resource?).

This method of conducting your research is more efficient than starting with index cards because you can keep all the information in a single convenient place and you don't end up with a stack of cards you don't need. More important, the response side of the divided notebook shows the evolution of your thinking and lets you articulate questions that arise as you read and process the information. This procedure steers you away from a cut-and-paste style of research writing because it encourages synthesis and analysis throughout the project. At the same time, it also helps you to identify which ideas are your own and which ones you picked up along the way—an important distinction that guards against inadvertent plagiarism and allows you to claim your own contributions with confidence.

You can also use your research notebook for analyzing your audience and purpose, answering your research questions, developing a central thesis, and working out a tentative outline or organizational plan. By the time you get to the drafting stage, you should have a clear picture of where your research has taken you and some good ideas about how to put your research into finished form. At this point, you can return to the sources that are most relevant to your narrowed thesis and outline to make note cards for use while writing your first draft.

Writing Project: Critique of a Published Professional Essay

In this writing assignment you will begin the research process by reading and analyzing a documented article on a current topic in your field or profession. This topic will become the focus for the researched writing you do in the next chapter. At this point you will be evaluating the article's success or failure as an example of its genre, withholding your appraisal of its thesis or argument until you complete your research for the assignment in Chapter 7 and have read more widely on the topic. Your critique will be two to four typed pages, and your audience will be other students in your academic discipline or professional area.

Step 1:   Using the specialized indexes that reference professional journals in your discipline or area, select a published article that discusses a central question or concern about which well-meaning professionals in the field disagree. It does not have to be a controversial topic, just a complex one. Some topics that students have recently investigated for this assignment include handgun control (pre-law), inclusion of students with disabilities in general classes (special education), the problem-based approach to math instruction (secondary education), teaching *Huckleberry Finn* in a multiethnic classroom (English), the impact of population growth (environmental studies), and term limits for congressional representatives (political science). The article you choose to analyze should be four to ten pages long.

Step 2:   Read the article several times and prepare an informal summary of its main points. This step will reinforce your understanding of the article and focus your thinking. Your goal is to sum up the gist of the piece, its key ideas and its line of argument. Use your own words but don't insert your own ideas or opinions. Your instructor may ask you to turn in this summary with the final version of your critique.

Step 3:   Determine how you would like to focus your critique of the article: an extended analysis of a single feature such as *persona,* in which you explore several facets of the feature; an evaluation of three or four of the strongest or weakest elements; or a balanced assessment of both strengths and weaknesses. You don't need to cover more than three or four issues. For example, one student focused on three components of persona—credibility, tone, and voice—in analyzing the strengths of an article on teaching *Huckleberry Finn* in a multiethnic classroom. The analysis began with credibility:

> Ann Lew [the author] shows in several ways that she is a knowledgeable source in the debate over *Huck Finn*'s place in the classroom. The most important factor is her experience as a high school teacher. Lew makes it clear that she has taught the book to classes of primarily nonwhite students

many times over the years. She writes: "I had to be absolutely convinced that Twain had important things to say to my classes of multiethnic, multi-lingual teenagers, some of whom were culturally and linguistically re-moved from life in the Mississippi Delta" (17). This information is significant because the article is aimed at other teachers. More importantly, it shows that Lew has had to make hard decisions in evaluating and teaching this book.

Another student chose to examine the style, organization, and attention to audience in an article entitled "The Population Explosion." She made this analysis of the organization:

> The author opens his discussion with a simple one-sentence thesis: "High population growth is making poor people poorer, the hungry hungrier, and an already fragile environment too weak to support its proliferating inhabitants" (9). This statement sets up the main points that the reader ex-pects to see discussed in the article. Next, the author uses a problem-solution arrangement to advance his argument. This approach consists of explaining the impact of population growth on one part of the environ-ment (such as food production) and then, in the next section, discussing the possibilities for reducing the environmental stress in this area. This method of stating the problem and then offering a solution carries the reader through the article with ease.

Review the writing activities you completed in Chapters 1 and 2 about au-dience, purpose, persona, genre, style, design, and discourse communities to reinforce your understanding of the features you might consider in your critique.

Step 4:   Construct a working thesis (a claim that centers your analysis of the article), and map out an organizational plan of some sort for presenting your analysis. Here, for example, is the working thesis that a student constructed for her analysis of an article on whole language in-struction:

> Much of the success of this article stems from the strong, authentic voice that conveys the arguments. There is clearly a real person behind this arti-cle, an experienced teacher who truly cares about whole language learning.

Step 5:   Go back to the article and use the divided-page system to take notes on details that will support your judgments. Use these notes to pre-pare a draft of your critique.

Steps 6, 7, and 8: Solicit feedback on your draft from your writing group or other appropriate readers; revise the draft; write up a final version to submit to your teacher.

Chapter 7
Argument

Chapter Preview

In this chapter you will first investigate the options for writing an effective argument within a discourse community. This investigation will introduce you to specialized resources, help you to evaluate these materials, and show you how to use and document them. You will then apply your research skills to produce an argumentative position paper within your chosen field.

Much of the writing you have done in college is persuasive or argumentative in nature. On essay tests, for case studies, in research reports, and in other writing assignments you are often asked to take a stand or support a conclusion. In the workplace and in public writing, you want your readers to accept your opinion, solution, recommendation, plan, or complaint as their own. Even an informational report can be said to "argue" or "persuade" in the sense that it attempts to establish the writer's facts and explanations as true or believable.

Persuasion and Argument

In classical rhetoric, the word *persuasion* refers to attempts to sway the readers' emotions, while the word *argument* refers to tactics that address the readers' reasoning. In everyday language, *persuasion* means influence over the audience, whether emotional or rational. Many writers mix the two types of appeal. A personal plea from an accident victim to use seat belts persuades through emotional identification. A list of statistics showing injury rates before and after seat-belt laws went into effect argues the point through logic. A combination of the two tactics could be quite effective—for example, in a report to Congress or an op-ed column.

Your writing situation, of course, will determine which approach you take. In professional business and technical communities, for example, a direct appeal to emotion might seem out of place and suspect. In the humanities and social sciences, on the other hand, a writer's personal involvement with a topic can be an integral part of the argument.

In persuasion and argument you deal with **issues**—points that are undecided or in dispute. These lie somewhere between verifiable facts and subjective opinions. Verifiable facts don't need to be argued. If a manufacturer says a package weighs three pounds, you need a scale, not an argument. If someone hates the taste of cauliflower, an advertiser's claims about good nutrition and cancer prevention probably won't persuade that person to eat cauliflower. But an adjustment in thinking can often make the topic arguable. For example, you might argue that the weight of a new package deceives the consumer because it offers fewer pounds for the same price. Or you could argue that even people who hate cauliflower can benefit from eating more fruits and vegetables.

Making Assumptions

Good arguments do not, of course, exist in the abstract. Your argument is effective only if it accomplishes what you want it to with the audience you are addressing. For this reason, you need to decide what assumptions you can make about your readers' knowledge and attitudes on the subject. In an article in favor of increased spending for education, for example, you might advance the argument that more money is needed to reduce class size. If you are writing for a group of educators, you probably don't have to explain that smaller classes mean better instruction and more learning. You can assume they understand these correlations—and accept them. But if you are writing for readers—such as legislators or general citizens, who don't want to raise taxes and don't necessarily agree that small classes are more productive—then you may need to argue the point further by summarizing the research on the issue and explaining how the reduction of class size will benefit students. In short, your understanding of the writing situation and the discourse community you're writing for will help you to decide what to include, what to leave out, and how to handle the issues.

If you look at "Technology as Security" (pp. 81–90), you can see some of the assumptions that the author, Declan McCullagh, has made about his audience. One of the things you'll notice is the language McCullagh uses. He makes many references to computer technology, such as "public key encryption," "dc-nets," "Linux," "Adobe's eBooks," and "Google search," apparently assuming that he doesn't need to explain these terms to people who have come to hear a speech about technology and the law given by the Washington Bureau Chief for *Wired News.* (The essay is a revised version of an address McCullagh made to a symposium at Boalt Hall School of Law.) The author also assumes his audience is familiar with the relevant case law, as evidenced by his frequent citations of statutes and court decisions. This same awareness of the legal background of his listeners is apparent in the way he develops his argument. He doesn't assume his audience will necessarily agree with his main claim—that technology has begun to supplant the law as a means for protecting privacy rights—so he spends some time critiquing the present legal system, pointing out, for example, that "the law, standing alone, has not been able to protect copyrighted works effectively" and that "the effective degree of privacy that Americans enjoy is directly related to the current views of legislatures, judges, and bureaucrats."

It is not always easy to analyze your readers and their opinions on a specific issue. Many of the assumptions McCullagh made about his audience were probably not conscious. He relied on experience and intuition to guide him in choosing his language and his tactics. As you become familiar with a discourse community and its methods of argument, you too will develop a sense of your readers' expectations and how you can appeal to them. The journalist questions offered in Chapter 3 (p. 43) can help you to develop the necessary instincts and knowledge.

Here are some questions to help you construct an argument for a particular readership:

- What do my readers already know about the issues? What do I need to explain to them? What questions will they have?
- What common values can I appeal to? What prejudices or preconceptions are they likely to have?
- What approach is most appropriate? Will my readers expect me to be formal and objective? Or will they respond more favorably to an informal, personal style? Will they be looking for a particular format or arrangement?
- What level of language should I use? Will I need to use common terms, or will my readers prefer the specialized jargon of the discipline?

You also need to be aware of any conflicts or controversies within a profession or discipline. Sometimes there are competing theories or opposing schools of thought that you have to take into account when writing for a particular discourse community. In the field of counseling psychology, for example, there is a huge debate between common factors therapies and empirically supported therapies. One side claims that certain common factors (namely, a working alliance with the client, a healing setting, and a coherent rationale and procedure) are part of any successful psychotherapy, no matter what treatment is used; the other side contends that only treatments supported by empirical research are valid. This controversy is so central to the discipline that it affects almost everything written within the community. Whether you're writing a case history or a report on procedures for relieving stress, your findings will be judged, at least to some extent, by which school of thought they follow.

Writing Activities

1. Using the questions given above identify the assumptions made in "Talk Show Telling versus Authentic Telling" by Evan Imber-Black (pp. 108–113), the "American Nursing Association Action Report"

(pp. 98–102), or "Is Privacy Still Possible in the Twenty-First Century?" by Berman and Breuning (pp. 72–79).

2. Find a piece of public writing that advances an argument (like a letter to the editor or an op-ed column). What assumptions has the writer apparently made about the readers he or she is addressing? Do you think those assumptions were accurate and useful? What revisions would you recommend to make the piece more persuasive?

Reviewing the Elements of Argument

Although there are a number of ways to construct an argument, the basic building blocks are claims, evidence, and refutation. You must understand them in order to write persuasively and effectively.

Claims

The "engine" that propels any argument is its **claim.** In various communities and genres, claims are also called propositions, premises, conclusions, hypotheses, or recommendations. They fall into three categories:

Claims of fact assert, state, or validate that something is indeed true. "Women currently do not receive equal pay for equal work."

Claims of value approve or disapprove of something related to a system of values. "Leaning to appreciate diversity is more important than learning calculus."

Claims of policy state that certain conditions, courses of action, or policies should prevail. "A six-month maternity leave policy ought to be federally mandated."

For any argument to be effective, it must be grounded in a claim that is significant to the audience, consistent with a group's accepted beliefs or with well-reasoned premises, and backed up by the available evidence.

Evidence

Evidence can come in many forms. Some of the most frequently used kinds of evidence are these:

Personal observation or experience: "I visited prisons across the country and can personally attest to their negative impact on inmates." In most genres, this is the least widely accepted form of evidence because it is derived from a narrow band of experience and may be unrepresentative. But it can be very persuasive in communicating the human significance of an issue.

Facts: "Every state in the country has enacted mandatory sentencing laws in the past decade." Facts are noncontroversial pieces of information that can be verified through observation or by generally accepted sources; they are persuasive to the extent that they are relevant to the statement they support.

Relevant examples: "Louisiana has one of the highest lockup rates in the country and imposes some of the most severe penalties, yet it also has the highest murder rate in the nation." Like facts, examples are most persuasive when they are objective and clearly relevant to the argument and the audience.

Testimony: "Eminent sociologist Oscar Teufelmeister refers to the American penal system as 'graduate school for crooks.'" Testimony should come from sources that the readers will accept as credible; it carries its greatest weight when the meaning of the facts or data is not self-evident and some judgment or interpretation is required to reach a conclusion.

Data: "Sixty-three percent of all federal prisoners are repeat offenders." This is probably the most readily accepted form of evidence because of its apparent objectivity and scope.

To be persuasive, evidence in support of a claim must meet certain standards:

1. It must be reasonably up-to-date;
2. It must be sufficient in scope;
3. It must be relevant to the claim.

Thus, you wouldn't use 1990 unemployment data in support of a 2002 policy decision (recentness). Neither would you rely on unemployment data from only one month to formulate a long-term unemployment policy (scope). Nor would you use employment data from Canada to comment on the American unemployment picture, unless your argument involved an overall comparison of the two countries' economies (relevance).

The kind of evidence you use will be determined by the nature of your topic and the expectations of your readers. As you read and analyze the kind of arguments you want to write, you will learn what constitutes evidence in the discourse community you are writing for. In scientific discourse, for example, you'll be expected to support your hypotheses with objective observations, experimental findings, and quantifiable data. In writing for business and the social sciences, you're likely to use case studies, surveys, interviews, focus groups, personal observations, and statistical analyses to support your conclusions or recommendations. If you are writing in the humanities—as a critic, philosopher, or historian, for example—you will probably support your thesis by citing other experts, explaining your insights, providing illustrations of your thinking, and giving accounts of close readings of a text.

Writing Activities

1. The following claims are taken from the article *Is Privacy Still Possible in the Twentieth Century?* What kind of claim is each one? What evidence is used to support each claim?

   > Without question, the growth of government and commercial transactions and the increase in technological developments over the last fifty years have heightened threats to privacy. (p. 72)

   > Encryption tools provide an easy and inexpensive way for a sender to protect information. . . . (p. 77)

   > [B]aseline legislation to address the collection of consumer data is a critical resource that would assure individuals consistent application of principles of fair information practices and an effective redress mechanism. (p. 78)

2. Examine the *Eating Disorders Information Sheets from the BodyWise Handbook* (pp. 117–123), and find a claim of fact, a claim of value, and a claim of policy. What kinds of evidence are offered to support each of these claims?

3. Examine the following excerpts and identify the kinds of evidence used in each one. Then classify the kind of writing for the excerpt: what field or discipline does it come from?

   a. We did a series of laboratory experiments that indicated that the loss of color in *A. elegantissima* in the field was the result of loss of zooxanthellae (Engbertson and Martin 1994). Bleached anemones taken from Leo Carillo State Beach had significantly reduced numbers of zooxanthellae (Fig. 1). We hypothesized that the bleaching was caused by excessive exposure to freshwater runoff. Healthy anemones from another site were placed into several different dilutions of sea water for time periods ranging from several days to several weeks. These *A. elegantissima* lost their symbiotic zooxanthellae and bleached rapidly, proportional to the strength and duration of the hyposaline exposure (Fig. 2). The anemones remained closed and did not feed while in hyposaline water.

   b. Among the fears advertisers have exploited over the years, I find the fear of not having a posh enough burial site the most arresting. Advertisers usually avoid any mention of death—who wants to associate a product with the grave?—but mortuary advertisers haven't much choice. Generally, they solve their problems by framing cemeteries as timeless parks presided over by priestly morticians, appealing to our desires for dignity and comfort in the face of bereavement. But in one television commercial for Forest Lawn we find a different approach. In this ad we are presented with the ghost of an old man telling us how he might have found a much nicer resting place than the rundown cemetery in which we find him had his wife only known that Forest Lawn was so "affordable." I presume the ad was supposed to be funny, but it's been pulled off the air.

c. A [possible] rival theme is that the non-Mormon adolescents were as reluctant or more reluctant than the Mormon adolescents to date outside of their group. The evidence does not appear to support such a statement in that fewer non-Mormons (47%) than Mormons (83%) were able to offer barriers to dating those of the other group. As shown in Table 1, 42% of the Mormon subjects thought that unacceptable beliefs, values, standards, and moral conduct of non-Mormon adolescents were barriers to dating. None of the non-Mormons adolescents raised such concerns in respect to the Mormon adolescents. Further, more Mormons (31%) than non-Mormons would not advise any dating between members of the two groups and more non-Mormons (45%) than Mormons (22%) would advise dating between the two groups.

Refutation

Arguments always presume that other points of view are possible; otherwise, there would be no reason to argue. You may feel so strongly about an issue that you want to attack those who disagree with you and express contempt for their opinions, but that strategy can be counterproductive, especially if you are trying to influence readers who are undecided. Your case will be strengthened if you treat opposing views with respect and understanding.

This acknowledgment of and response to the opposing views is called **refutation.** There is no best place in an argument to refute the opposition, though some genres require a particular arrangement. Sometimes you will want to bring up opposing arguments early and deal with them right away. Another approach is to anticipate objections as you develop your own case point by point. Many writers add a refutation section after they have presented the evidence and reasoning on their own side. Wherever you decide to include your refutation, your goal is to point out problems with the opponents' reasoning and evidence. You can refute opposing arguments by showing that they are unsound, unfair, or flawed in their logic. Frequently, you will present contrasting evidence to reveal the weakness of your opponents' views and to reinforce your own position.

When an opposing argument is so compelling that it cannot be easily dismissed, you should concede its strength. This approach will establish that you are knowledgeable and fair-minded. You can sometimes accept the opponents' line of thought up to a certain point—but no further. Or you can show that their strong point addresses only *one* part of a complex problem.

Writing Activity

1. Reread Roger Ebert's review of *Shallow Hal* (pp. 141–143). Why does he include the "heartfelt message" from a moviegoer? How does he refute her objection? How effective is this strategy? Is this approach appropriate for a newspaper review? Would it work as well in a different context, such as a film journal?

2. Find an argument in a discipline or a discourse community you are familiar with. What kinds of claims are made? What sorts of evidence are used? How are opposing views handled? As far as you know, is this a typical of way of presenting arguments in the discipline?

Strategies for Arranging Arguments

Genres often dictate an argument's organization, but a conventional argument usually involves five tasks.

1. State the *issue* you will address, and put it in a context—why is it controversial or problematic? Why do people care about it? Why do people disagree about it?

2. State your main point or thesis. What point of view, solution, or stance do you wish the readers to adopt? This is your *claim.*

3. Provide well-developed *evidence* on your own side of the issue. You can develop your point through facts, statistics, examples, testimony of experts, and logical reasoning (cause and effect, analogy), just to name a few strategies. This is the longest part of a conventional argument, and each piece of evidence will probably take a paragraph or more to develop.

4. Respond to opposing viewpoints. This is called the *refutation* section. Especially when arguments against your own are widely known, you need to acknowledge them and deal with them, or your case will have an obvious weakness in it. You might minimize the importance of opposing views, demonstrate that they are not logical or factual, or offer alternative ways of thinking about them.

5. Close by reminding your reader of your main point and the strength of your evidence. You might also include a call to action, encouraging the reader to do something—change a rule, make a contribution, picket city hall—in support of your cause.

Writers often alter this conventional plan, especially tasks 3 and 4. You can tailor your written argument to fit your topic, audience, purpose, and the nature of your evidence.

The Counterargument

One way to present your position is to anticipate what people on the other side of the issue would say and to organize your argument as a point-by-point refutation. This approach works well for tackling controversial topics and for clearing up common misconceptions. The following outline of a political science article entitled "Five Myths about Immigration" demonstrates the process:

Major claim: Passion, misinformation, and short-sighted fear often substitute for reason, fairness, and human dignity in today's immigration debates.

Myth 1: America is being overrun with immigrants.

- In one sense this has always been true: we are a nation of immigrants.
- The first-generation immigration share of population is not growing: 8 percent in 1990 as compared to 15 percent from 1870 to 1920.
- Almost 80 percent of immigrants are refugees or immediate relatives of U.S. citizens.

Myth 2: Immigrants take jobs from U.S. citizens.

- Numerous studies have shown that immigrants create more jobs than they fill.
- Immigrants are often highly productive, run their own businesses, and employ both immigrants and citizens.

Myth 3: Immigrants are a drain on society's resources.

- Most studies have found that immigrants generate significantly more in taxes paid than they cost in services received.
- Some subgroups impose a net cost in the short run, but from a long-term perspective the economic advantages of immigration are undeniable.

Myth 4: Aliens refuse to assimilate and are depriving us of our cultural and political unity.

- Cultural separatism rarely survives a generation.
- Many groups once viewed as separatist and alien—Irish Catholics, Jews, Italians, Eastern Europeans, Cubans—have become mainstream Americans.
- Besides, our society is built on the values of pluralism and tolerance.

Myth 5: Noncitizen immigrants are not entitled to constitutional rights.

- The Constitution extends the fundamental protections in the Bill of Rights to all people, limiting to citizens only the right to vote and run for federal office.

Conclusion: We will be judged by how we treat others. If we are collectively judged by how we have treated immigrants—those who appear to be "other" but will in a generation be "us"—we are not in very good shape.

The Pro and Con Argument

Another way to present an argument is to look at the pros and cons of an issue. These may also called advantages and disadvantages or strengths and weaknesses. This format is commonly used in making proposals and recommendations. The following outline from a Department of Energy booklet illustrates the pro-con approach:

> Advantages of earth-sheltered houses
>> Less vulnerable to temperature extremes than conventional homes
>> More stable inside temperatures: interior rooms seem more comfortable
>> Not as much outside maintenance
>> Has natural soundproofing
>> Protected from storms and natural disasters: often cost less to insure
>
> Disadvantages of earth-sheltered houses
>> Higher initial construction costs: as much as 2% more
>> More care to avoid moisture problems
>> Sometimes difficult to re-sell
>
> Conclusion: Despite some drawbacks, earth-sheltered homes are energy efficient and provide a comfortable, tranquil, weather-resistant living space.

The Problem-Solution Argument

Problem solving is a basic objective in most disciplines and professions. Educators help students with learning problems; medical researchers look for cures to disease; sociologists investigate ways to alleviate troubling social problems; engineers work out how to build bridges and improve computers; counselors enable clients to resolve their personal problems. The problem-solution approach to argument will help you to organize your thinking in a form that's both clear and easy to follow. It's primarily a method for proposing change, one that works in a number of writing situations.

Problem solving follows a standard sequence of steps:

1. *Identify the problem.* Many topics are complicated and contain a number of problems. You have to decide which you want to focus on.

2. *Demonstrate that the problem exists and is serious.* Some problems are so obvious that your readers will quickly agree with you. But other times you will need to make your audience aware of a problem they have overlooked or underestimated.

3. *Explain why current methods for dealing with the problem aren't working.* This is a key step, especially if the topic is controversial. People usually don't like to alter the status quo if they can avoid it. Your criticisms of the present system will lead logically to the next step.

4. *Propose a solution.* Sometimes you will merely call people's attention to a problem without offering a solution, but most of the time you will present a remedy, a plan, or a course of action to eliminate or reduce the problem.

5. *Show how the proposed solution will work.* If you offer a solution, explain how it solves the problems. Your readers will want to know if the solution is practical and affordable. You may also need to anticipate alternate solutions and explain how your proposal is more effective.

Writing Activities

1. Rewrite the outline for "Five Myths about Immigration" (p. 245) as a pro and con argument. Do you think the pro-con format would work for this argument?
2. Write a brief analysis of "Making Age Irrelevant" (pp. 164–166), explaining how it follows a counterargument strategy.
3. Reread "Let's Solve S.F.'s No. 1 Problem" by Mike Sullivan (pp. 196–197). Then evaluate how closely Sullivan follows the problem-solution format. Does he define the problem? Does he help readers realize the seriousness of the problem? Does he show that the present system doesn't work? Does he propose a solution? Does he attempt to convince readers that the solution will solve the problem and can be implemented? Does he anticipate alternate solutions? Does he urge readers to take specific action?
4. Think of a change that you would like to see made at your school or workplace. Using the five problem-solution steps given above, outline a proposal that argues for making the change.

Finding a Middle Ground

An argument, by definition, involves a difference of opinion. But not all arguments are heated exchanges between adversaries who are determined to prevail. In many situations, argument can be a form of dialogue, a means of resolving differences and drawing people together. If, for example, you were asked to write a memo recommending ways to improve efficiency in your business, you would want to avoid alienating your audience, which would probably include your boss and your co-workers. You would try to build rapport with your readers and show them how your recommendations would benefit the company as a whole. Instead of insisting that your suggestions are the only workable ones, you would try to help others feel that their ideas also have value and that some compromise can be achieved. You would emphasize the importance of concession rather than refutation and attempt to depict a win-win situation for all parties involved in the final decisions.

Consider these guidelines for writing an argument that finds some middle ground between competing positions:

1. Early on, outline the core issue and the controversy surrounding it.
2. Summarize your own position—its claims and primary evidence—and explain why this argument has merit.
3. Point out the elements of the other views—their claims and primary evidence—and explain why these arguments have merit.

4. Indicate your own willingness to negotiate and identify what you see as the major differences separating the two (or more) sides.

5. Explain how accepting a middle ground can benefit everyone involved in the disagreement.

6. Offer a solution that appeals to the interest of both (or all) sides.

However you choose to structure your argument, it is important to treat your opponents with respect. If you show that you are fair minded and that your own position is clear, sincere, and well supported, you open the way for creating long-term solutions based on mutual understanding and shared beliefs.

Writing Activity

1. Re-read Jonathan Rauch's review of *The Adonis Complex* (pp. 147–151). Explain how the author proposes a middle-ground solution to the problem of "body obsessions."

2. What problem does Brent Staples discuss in "Just Walk On By" (pp. 168–171)? What middle ground solutions has he worked out for this problem?

Writer's Workshop

The following excerpts present arguments about the effects of human activity on global warming. The first selection is taken from *Climate Change 2001: The Scientific Basis*, published by the Intergovernmental Panel on Climate Change. The second is a release from the U.S. Department of Energy. Compare and contrast the use of argumentation in the two selections: What sort of claims do they advance? What kinds of evidence are used? How are opposing views handled? What discourse community is each one apparently written for? What efforts are made to reduce the threat of the arguments? What role does arrangement play? Which one do you find more convincing?

Climate Change 2001: The Scientific Basis

Human beings, like other living organisms, have always influenced their environment. It is only since the beginning of the Industrial Revolution, mid-18th century, that the impact of human activities has begun to extend to a much larger scale, continental or even global. Human activities, in particular those involving the combustion of fossil fuels for industrial or domestic usage, and biomass burning, produce greenhouse gases and aerosols which affect the composition of the atmosphere. The emission of chlorofluorocarbons (CFCs) and other chlorine and bromine compounds has not only an impact on the radiative forcing, but has also led to the depletion of the stratospheric ozone layer. Land-use change, due to urbanisation and human forestry and agricultural practices, affect the physical and biological properties of the Earth's surface. Such effects change the radiative forcing and have a potential impact on regional and global climate.

For about a thousand years before the Industrial Revolution, the amount of greenhouse gases in the atmosphere remained relatively constant. Since then, the concentration of various greenhouse gases has increased. The amount of carbon dioxide, for example, has increased by more than 30% since preindustrial times and is still increasing at an unprecedented rate of on average 0.4% per year, mainly due to the combustion of fossil fuels and deforestation. We know that this increase is anthropogenic because the changing isotopic composition of the atmospheric CO_2 betrays the fossil origin of the increase. The concentration of other natural radiatively active atmospheric components, such as methane and nitrous oxide, is increasing as well due to agricultural, industrial and other activities. The concentration of the nitrogen oxides (NO and NO_2) and of carbon monoxide (CO) are also increasing. Although these gases are not greenhouse gases, they play a role in the atmospheric chemistry and have led to an increase in tropospheric ozone, a greenhouse gas, by 40% since pre-industrial times. Moreover, NO_2 is an important absorber of visible solar radiation.

Chlorofluorocarbons and some other halogen compounds do not occur naturally in the atmosphere but have been introduced by human activities. Beside their depleting effect on the stratospheric ozone layer, they are strong greenhouse gases. Their greenhouse effect is only partly compensated for by the depletion of the ozone layer which causes a negative forcing of the surface-troposphere system. All these gases, except tropospheric ozone and its precursors, have long to very long atmospheric lifetimes and therefore become well-mixed throughout the atmosphere.

Human industrial, energy related, and land-use activities also increase the amount of aerosol in the atmosphere, in the form of mineral dust, sulphates and nitrates and soot. Their atmospheric lifetime is short because they are removed by rain. As a result their concentrations are highest near their sources and vary substantially regionally, with global consequences. The increases in greenhouse gas concentrations and aerosol content in the atmosphere result in a change in the radiative forcing to which the climate system must act to restore the radiative balance.

Global Climate Change

Perhaps no single environmental issue is as complex or holds such potentially profound implications for the world's inhabitants than the issue of global climate change.

There is little question that human activity is changing the make-up of the atmosphere that surrounds our planet. As world economies have become more industrialized over the last century, we have begun emitting more greenhouse gases into the air than natural processes can remove. Deforestation and clearing land for agriculture have accelerated the buildup of greenhouse gases in the atmosphere, both by releasing significant quantities of these gases and by reducing the capacity of green plants to absorb carbon dioxide, one of the chief greenhouse gases.

In 1995, a panel of more than 2,000 of the world's top climate scientists concluded that the Earth was indeed warming and that the "balance of evidence suggests a discernible human influence" on climate. Yet, there are still large gaps in the scientific data. The warming in the last century—about 1 degree Farenheit—is still small enough to fall within the range of normal climatic changes for a planet that has fluctuated in and out of ice ages for at least the last 200,000 years. A small part of that single degree of warming may have come from variations in the sun's intensity which can raise or lower the Earth's temperatures in ways not yet fully understood.

Nonetheless, the bulk of recent evidence—from rising sea levels and retreating glaciers to freak storms and floods—appears to be falling within the boundaries of scientists' predictions of greenhouse warming.

Writing Project: Researched Position Paper

This writing assignment continues your investigation of the central question or concern in your field that you decided to pursue in the previous writing project (pp. 234–235). Using your critique of a published professional essay as a starting point, you will research the literature in your field on this issue, summarize the major schools of thought on the question or controversy, and then present your own position. Your paper will be eight to ten pages long and contain at least eight documented sources. Because of their interest in the field and the level of expertise you will develop through your research, your audience will be students in your academic major or professional area. You should use the research notebook approach when doing this assignment (see Chapter 6, pp. 232–233).

Step 1:   Review your critique of a published professional essay. Then write in your project notebook a statement of the controversy or question you are going to research. Also write out your own starting questions for this project and outline your research plan.

Step 2:   Using the databases and indexes that reference journals and books in your field or discipline, locate sources that will help you provide an informed overview of the nature and current status of the debate about the issue, with fair and adequate representation of all schools of thought.

Step 3:   For each source, record the bibliographic date needed for documentation, and use the divided-page system to summarize your reading of the source materials and comment on their importance and relevance. As you progress, use your notebook entries to refine your starting question and shape a thesis that asserts your understanding of the debate within your field. You should summarize and analyze a minimum of twelve sources in your research notebook. (You will use at least eight of these sources in your final essay.) These sources should all be journal articles or chapters from books: essays written by professionals for other professionals in the field.

Step 4:   Based on the questions raised by your research and the conclusions reached in your project notebook, begin writing your draft. Your goal in the first section of the essay will be to help your readers see the extent and nature of the debate, to describe the basic positions taken by professionals in the field, and to sum up the arguments and evidence used to support these points of view. Avoid simply describing the issue or stringing together quotations which reflect the judgments of others. Use the sources to support the analytical generalizations you have identified as being central to the controversy.

Step 5:   Having reviewed and analyzed the debate, you can now begin drafting your position. You should take a stand on the question by using one of the arrangements described earlier in this chapter: the conventional argument, the counterargument, the pro and con argument, or the problem-solution argument that provides a resolution to the controversy. The first sample student research paper that follows takes a middle-ground approach. You might want to consider using the kind of argument you observe in the research conducted for the project.

Step 6:   Revise your draft and prepare your list of references or works cited. Follow the documentation style appropriate for your major. See Appendix B for examples and further information about documenting your sources.

Step 7:   Solicit feedback on the revised draft from your writing group, your instructor, or other appropriate readers. Prepare the final version of your essay, paying particular attention to the details of documentation.

Sample Student Research Papers

The following documented essays, written by students at Eastern Illinois University, illustrate the writing project for this chapter. In the first paper, a third-year Special Education major investigates the division of professional opinion about the inclusion of special-needs students in regular classrooms. She follows the conventions of the 2001 revision of the American Psychological Association (APA) documentation style, which recommends the use of italic type instead of underlining. In the second paper, a fourth-year Political Science major examines the debate about the reasons for the fall of the Soviet Union and explains his position on the issue. He uses the documentation style of the Modern Language Association (MLA).

Full or Partial Inclusion:

A Look at the Debate about Where and How to
Educate Special-Needs Students

Toni Spainhour

English 3001

Dr. Coleman

April 29, 2002

The Debate about Inclusion 2

Abstract: Two schools of thought exist concerning inclusive education—
full inclusion and partial inclusion. The best educational experience,
however, can be achieved only when each child is evaluated individually
and when collaboration takes place among parents, teachers, and school
administrators.

Nearly three decades have passed since the federal government
passed The Education for All Handicapped Children Act of 1975. This act
was supplemented by the 1990 Individuals with Disabilities Education
Act (IDEA) and its amendments of 1995 and 1997. The IDEA requires
that special-needs children be put in "the least restrictive environment"
possible (Individuals). According to Marie Thompson (1997), this means
that "the school must try as hard as it can to help the child fit in with
the rest of the students" (p. 25). Today, our education system is experiencing what some may call the second generation of inclusion (Lowenthal, 1999). While still in its infancy, the first generation of inclusion
brought the disabled child into the regular educational setting. According to the U.S. Department of Education, "three-fourths of all students
with disabilities are currently fully or partially integrated in general education classrooms" (Leyser & Tappendorf, 2001, p. 751). The second
generation now bears the responsibility of deciding how, where, and to
what extent a child with disabilities should be included.

Full Inclusion

Proponents of fully inclusive education believe that a child with
disabilities ought to be educated in the regular classroom regardless of
the severity of the child's disabilities and needs. This approach means
the child stays in the general education setting for 100% of the school
day. As reported in "Educating Students with Special Needs" (1997),
"many people now see these students possessing what was commonly
known as a disability as students who are capable, but in different areas"
(Thompson, p. 38). Promoting social interaction and academic achievement are two key elements of the full inclusive view.

Advocates of full inclusion argue that a child's self-concept and social interaction skills will benefit when he or she is included in the general education classroom on a full-time basis. They claim the child will
experience a "normal" mode of behavior by observing his or her peers.
"Normal" is best defined as acceptable or appropriate behavior. Intervention programs can be put into place to teach all students self-control and
discipline. As Taylor and Baker (2001) point out, "All students deserve
well-disciplined learning environments that are fun, focused, and full of

The Debate about Inclusion 3

creative energy" (p. 30). Proponents also maintain that full inclusion brings about many positive effects in the general education classroom and in the community as a whole. A bulletin published by the National Center on Educational Restructuring and Inclusion (NCERI) (1996) states that "research documenting positive outcomes for all students is to be found in a growing body of research and reports from districts implementing inclusive education programs" (p. 1). General education students, administrators, teachers, and even parents tend to lose their fears and misconceptions about the disabled through interactions with them; friendships and a sense of community begin to form when inclusion is implemented at an early age. Villa and Thousand (1995) sum up the point this way: "Inclusion assumes that living and learning together is a better way that benefits everyone, not just children who are labeled as having a difference" (p. 8).

Additionally, full inclusion advocates believe that the pull-out programs offered to special-needs students have not shown enough significant change in the student's academic progress (Berger, 1997). They also believe these programs tend to isolate the child by taking him or her from the regular class and thereby making others feel that something is wrong. Advocates claim that these same specialized services can be administered in the regular classroom and that both sets of students stand to benefit. Lastly, several courts have ruled in support of this argument. In *Oberti v. Board of Education of the Borough of Clementon School District* (1993), the court held that "Many of the special education techniques used in the class could be successfully imported into a regular class and that the regular teacher could be trained to apply these techniques" (NCERI, p. 4).

Partial/Optional Inclusion

Those who advocate partial or optional inclusion "believe that they are more realistic about what models can be embraced given teacher skill levels and personnel resources in most schools" (Bergen, 1997, p. 160). Partial inclusion advocates are concerned that full inclusion fosters a "one size fits all" approach and may bring about "a return to conditions of the past in which children who needed learning assistance will be overlooked" (Bergen, 1997, p. 161). They also argue that full inclusion has created a fallacy that a special-needs student should be able to operate at the same level as the rest of the students in a regular class (Kluth, Villa, & Thousand, 2001). Supporters of partial inclusion feel, therefore, that a variety of options for placement are needed and that

The Debate about Inclusion 4

specialized services should be given in resource rooms, in self-contained classrooms, and in some instances in a fully inclusive environment through one-on-one assistance. These advocates also believe that because some educators tend to gear their curriculum to the typical learner, specialized programs are necessary to enhance the academic potential of special-needs students (Kluth, Villa, & Thousand 2001).

Partial inclusion advocates also believe that a student's self-concept may develop better when working alongside other students of the same level (Bergen, 1997). A sense of achievement, not failure, is more likely to be managed best in a specialized program. When appropriately implemented, pull-out services do not have to make the student feel isolated. For example, reverse inclusion may be used where a few of the general education students accompany the special-needs student to a different classroom. Although social skills are developed when modeled by peers in a general education setting, friendships don't just happen for a special needs child. Programs may be needed to teach self-control and discipline so the child is accepted more readily within the regular classroom (Taylor & Baker, 2001). Lastly, partial advocates contend that some specialized services may not be conducive to the regular education class, such as providing physical or occupational therapy or instructing self-help skills (Bergen 1997).

Common Ground

Supporters of both full and partial inclusion recognize problems within their respective models. Both sides realize there is still much work to be done and that each special-needs child should be given the opportunity to reach his or her highest learning potential. An inclusion restructuring facilitator (1999) expressed the point this way:

> What I'm hoping to see it evolve to, is when you go to anybody's classroom . . . you will not be able to tell which child is which. . . . You know you won't be able to pick out a special-needs child from [anybody else's] child. They'll all be working together and working as a group. (Mamlin, p. 49).

Regular education and special education professionals do not entirely agree as to the how, where, and when inclusion policies are to be implemented. But they do believe that collaboration is the key. Administrators, teachers, students, and parents must be willing to work as a team in order for an inclusive environment to have a chance, for as Lowenthal (1999) points out, "The objective of inclusion is to meet the needs and develop the strengths of all the children in the group, whether or not they have disabilities" (p. 18). Finally, proponents on both sides agree that some level of inclusion benefits both the disabled student and the general education student, which will in turn also benefit the community.

Evaluation and Collaboration

Like all children, special-needs children are individuals and have particular problems to be met and diverse skills to be enhanced. Evaluation of each child's needs will provide a quality education for all students. Educators must realize that inclusive education is a system of trial and error. It should provide a continuum of change to best fit each student's requirements. Collaboration between administrators, general teachers, special education teachers, and parents is vital to any successfully inclusive environment. Administrators must take leadership roles in helping implement either full or partial inclusion based on the child's assessment. In a discussion group study of sixty-one principals, their comments referred to what others might do to make inclusion work, but did not mention what they were currently doing. There was no plan of action for training teachers, planning time, or increasing parent involvement (Brotherson, Sheriff, Milburn, & Schertz, 2001). Administrators must educate themselves with regards to the law (the school's rights as well as the student's) and become familiar with the research and methods of inclusion. By accepting this responsibility, administrators set a positive tone for inclusion within the classroom. They must provide training for general education teachers who feel unprepared to teach a special-needs child. Additionally, districts will need to encourage collaboration between staff members and realize that it takes time to examine and review each student's needs. The general and special education teachers should be given time to plan and implement appropriate curricula—and to make as many changes and adaptations as they deem necessary. Administrators need to encourage these collaborative efforts and support both sets of teachers, as well as remind them to make these efforts on behalf of each child. It is also a teacher's responsibility to become educated about the research and methods used in successful inclusion. For many years, both sets of teachers have felt that their classroom was their turf and the students were simply "theirs" (Krmpotich, 1995). For each child to experience a positive learning

The Debate about Inclusion 6

experience, these teachers must be willing to work together. Neither the classroom teacher nor the special education teacher should focus on who is in charge, but rather learn to work together while learning from each other. What better example can be given to students to work together and accept each other than having the teachers themselves put these same principles into practice?

Teachers measure success by the progress their students make; therefore they must recognize the time and effort needed to be successful in their teaching methods. Educators must learn creative ways to teach these children and broaden the scope of their practices. Collaboration is also required when defining the goals for a child's Individual Education Plan (IEP). The methods for achieving these goals become the responsibility of the group involved. The general and special education teachers, other service providers, and administrators also need to be willing to investigate new methods in order to provide a positive, successful learning experience.

Lastly, teachers and administrators need to involve all parents in the education system. Keeping an open line of communication is key to getting parents involved. Parents should be able to get information about their child's progress and the teaching methods being used so they can be reinforced at home. Likewise, teachers must be able to get from parents all the information essential for the education of the student. Parents of nondisabled students also play an important role in successful inclusion. These parents and their children need to learn that being different is not a bad thing. They need to be invited into the classroom to observe the methods used and to participate in activities that involve all students. Educators possess the ability to build the foundation for acceptance of diversity. As Stahl (2000) points out, the "skills that are learned are that everyone is different, everyone deserves respect, and everyone should be accepted" (p. 131).

The debate over how and where a special-needs child is to be educated may never entirely be resolved. The fact remains, however, that school districts must evaluate the needs of each child in order to answer these questions. Administrators, general and special education teachers, and parents have no choice but to be involved and work together in order to provide the best educational experience for all children.

References

Bergen, D. (1997). Perspectives on inclusion in early childhood education. In J. Isenberg & M. Rench Jalongo (Eds.), *Major trends and issues in early childhood education* (pp. 151–171). New York:
Teachers College Press.

Brotherson, M. J., Sheriff, G., Milburn, A. P., & Schertz, M. (2001). Elementary school principals and their needs and issues for inclusive
early childhood programs. *Topics in Early Childhood Special Education, 21*(11), 31–45. Retrieved March 25, 2002, from EBSCO Professional Development Collection database.

Individuals with Disabilities Act of 1990, PL. 101-476. *Federal Register 57,*
44794–44852. Retrieved March 27, 2002, from Nexis-Lexis database.

Kluth, P., Villa, R., & Thousand, J. (2001–02). Our school doesn't offer
inclusion and other legal blunders. *Educational Leadership, 59*(4),
24–27. Retrieved March 25, 2002, from EBSCO Academic Search
Elite database.

Krmpotich, J. (1995). *Inclusion: A classroom teacher's perspective.* Minnesota: HBK Publishing Company Inc.

Leyser, Y. & Tappendorf, K. (2001). Are attitudes and practices regarding mainstreaming changing? A case of teachers in two rural
school districts. *Education, 121,* 751–760.

Lowenthal, B. (1999). Early childhood inclusion in the United States.
Early Child Development and Care 150, 17–32.

Mamlin, N. (1999). Despite best intentions: When inclusion fails. *The
Journal of Special Education, 33,* 36–49. Retrieved March 26, 2002,
from InfoTrac Expanded Academic ASAP database.

National Center on Educational Restructuring and Inclusion. (1996). An
inclusion talkback: Critics' concerns and advocates' responses.
NCERI Bulletin, 3(1), 1–3.

Stahl, J. (2000). What can teachers do? *Academic Exchange Quarterly,
4,* 131. Retrieved March 26, 2002, from InfoTrac Expanded Academic ASAP database.

Taylor, J. A. & Baker, R. A. (2002). Discipline and the special education
student. *Educational Leadership, 59*(4), 28–30. Retrieved March 30,
2002, from EBSCO Academic Search Elite database.

Thompson, M. (1997). Educating the student population with special
needs. In N. R. Jacobs, M. A. Siegel, & M. Mitchell (Eds.),
Education: Is it improving or declining? (pp. 25–32). Wylie, TX: Information Plus.

Villa, R. & Thousand, J. (1995). *The rationale for creating an inclusive school.*
Virginia: Association for Supervision and Curricular Development.

The Decline and Fall of the Soviet Union

By
Marty Ruhaak

Professor Coleman
English 3001

29 April 2002

The Decline and Fall of the Soviet Union

Modern historians look upon communism during the twentieth century as a prolonged experiment that went awry and ended with the fall of the Soviet Union in 1991. The experiment began in 1871 when Frederick Engels and Karl Marx issued their *Communist Manifesto* to the world. This work depicted a political and economic system that was the exact opposite of capitalism. Marx and Engels believed that every citizen of a nation deserved the same amount of goods and services as everyone else. This goal could be achieved through heavy government regulation, and everyone would be in the same economic class, thus solving problems of poverty and injustice. The *Communist Manifesto* influenced many people and eventually resulted in the establishment of the Union of Soviet Socialist Republics (USSR) in 1917. What followed were nearly seven decades of isolation and cold war between the two preeminent superpowers of the world—the United States with its capitalistic society and the Soviet Union with its socialist economy. According to Vladimir Batyuk, "[i]deologically the Cold War began in 1917. After 1945 it was transferred to the sphere of geopolitics" (29). During this time the United States and the Soviet Union engaged in a standoff using propaganda and political maneuvering to fight each other. The standoff came to an abrupt halt in 1991 when the Soviet Union fell and communism in Europe died.

This question still remains, however: How and why did the Soviet Union collapse so quickly in the late 1980s and early 1990s? Two major schools of thought have emerged among historians. The first suggests that the faulty socialist economy could not sustain itself and was the main cause of the country's social and political demise (Laqueur 389). The second school of thought points to the democratic reforms that Mikhail Gorbachev, the Soviet General Secretary, introduced into Soviet society. Proponents of this school of thought claim that the Soviets and the Communist Party were not prepared to face democratic reforms and were not able to return to their Communist doctrine after Soviet citizens received a sample of self-rule (Strayer 375–76). Each school of thought concedes some validity to the other, but each believes its theory holds the key to the decline of the USSR.

Failure of Socialist Economics

All Cold War historians agree that from the beginning the Soviet economy was inherently inadequate to sustain the welfare of the nation. Initially, the Soviet system of socialism was able to keep pace with capitalist nations in the Western Hemisphere. In fact, by 1970, most economists claim, the Soviet Union had surpassed the United States in total economic growth and Gross National Product (Laqueur 391). But the success of the socialist economy in the USSR was short-lived. Careless defense spending in the 1970s and early 1980s crippled any hopes for sustained economic growth. At one point during the Brezhnev era, Soviet defense budgets consumed almost 40 percent of the nation's Gross Domestic Product (Aslund 21). By contrast, the United States under the administration of Ronald Regan effectively restructured its nuclear arms and began to rebuild the military from the ground up. Reagan called for defense to consume over 20 percent of the American budget in the 1980s. The Soviets, on the other hand, could barely supply all their soldiers. Although the Soviet military received nearly 40 percent of the national budget, this amount was insufficient because the Soviet's total resources were so meager (Aslund 22).

Economic problems were not limited to the Soviet military alone. The socialist economy also created wasteful spending on subsidies for production surpluses. Socialism requires that the government subsidize farmers and industries for any overproduction so that the producers do not lose profits. Farming in the Soviet Union during the late 1970s and early 1980s was a good business to be in; harvests were usually plentiful and sales were good. But such success had its downside: by the time that Gorbachev took office in 1985, the Soviet Union was spending billions to subsidize farmers for overproduction (Aslund 38). Profits from the Gross National Product were quickly spent on agriculture subsidies or defense build up. Soon the Russian ruble collapsed and inflation skyrocketed because of lack of money in the Soviet market (Elliot 31).

By 1985 the Soviet's socialist economy looked as if it might soon fail. In fact, Robert Strayer claims, the Soviet Union underwent an "economic decline that surpassed even that of the Great Depression, and had no parallel in southern Europe or Latin America" (386). Michael Ellman and Vladimir Kontorovich point out that by the mid 1980s inflation and lack of economic growth placed the Soviet Union on the brink of bankruptcy (285). Gorbachev took office near the end of 1985 and faced an economic crisis that most nations would never encounter. By November of 1985, the Soviet government announced that it could no longer effectively subsidize farmers or farm workers (Laqueur 390). Essentially, the government was too far in debt to further support the agricultural industry. Soviet farmers, also in economic distress, could not pay for planting or harvesting and, as a result, lost their land. The country soon found itself with massive food shortages. What food could be found was extremely expensive because of inflation.

According to Robert English, the economic crisis prompted many Soviets officials to call for new economic policies: "By the mid-1970s, many economists, scientists, and foreign affairs experts were actively promoting policy alternatives [in the Soviet Union]" (284). Gorbachev agreed with these demands. He assumed the position of General Secretary in 1985 with many liberal policies in mind, and he believed that unless the policies were instituted the economy would eventually fail. Gorbachev had every intention of preserving the Soviet Union and its socialist system, but he knew that it could not be done in a conservative manner. He turned to western policies of economic theory to prevent the "ruthless centralization that would inevitably lead to economic and social degradation and crisis" (English 292). The policies of *perestroika* and *glasnost* were the cornerstones of his attempts to reform the economic system. Historians in the economic school of thought claim that these reforms were too late to halt the economic disintegration of the Soviet Union. By 1985, the economy was so stagnant that it was bound to crumble. No single person could prevent its collapse.

Gorbachev and Liberal Reforms

The second school of thought focuses on Gorbachev and the political climate his political and social reforms gave to the Soviet Union. The policies of *perestroika, glasnost,* and other democratic procedures opened the doors for democratization of the Soviet Union and its satellite nations. *Perestroika* was Gorbachev's attempt to use neo-capitalist reforms to modernize the Soviet economy and preserve the future of the Soviet Union. *Glasnost* was a Western democratic measure used to curtail censorship, gain feedback about the impact of *perestroika,* and open the public to the history of the Soviet Union. Much of this history was secret and illegal to talk about before *glasnost.* But, as Marshall Goldman explained, "[f]or Soviet General Secretary Mikhail Gorbachev, economic reform or *perestroika* is the number one priority. As important as *glasnost* and democratization are, they are merely facilitators toward the goal of economic revitalization" (313).

Gorbachev entered 1985 with a full agenda. Soviet citizens looked
to him to fix their economic problems, raise morale, and revive a dying
political system. Within six months, Gorbachev met with President Reagan to discuss nuclear disarmament and economic solutions. At this
meeting in Reykjavik, Gorbachev proposed to Reagan that the two countries end the nuclear arms race (Uhler 40). Gorbachev decided that if he
could convince Reagan that total disarmament was a good idea, then he
could save billions on his defense budget for the next fiscal year. He
hoped that this move might solve the Soviet economic crisis. Originally,
Reagan agreed to this total disarmament, but at the end of the conference the two sides disagreed on the deployment of Reagan's Strategic Defense Initiative. The two sides left Iceland in 1986 without an agreement,
and Gorbachev had to devise a new plan to rejuvenate the Soviet economy (Uhler 44). Gorbachev did devise a new plan shortly after the Reykjavik conference. He ordered deep cuts in the military budget and
returned more than 500,000 Russian soldiers to civilian life (Uhler 45).
In 1986, Gorbachev instituted his most radical and controversial system
to invigorate the Soviet economy—*perestroika*. This new economic policy
called for "marketizing the Soviet economy by opening it to the West":

> Foreign trade should not be a central monopoly, but the decision of
> each self-managing, self-financing enterprise; joint ventures and
> foreign investment should be sought; currency convertibility
> should be achieved, followed by membership in the World Bank,
> IMF, and GATT. (English 291)

The new liberal Communists were excited and truly believed that this
policy would save the Soviet Union and return the country to the international status it had under Stalin and Kruschev.

Despite Gorbachev's insistence that he was a staunch Marxist-
Leninist economic thinker, he knew that the only way to mend the economy was to institute capitalist policies. During the 1980s, many Western
nations experienced economic booms. For example, the United States reduced inflation and increased their Gross Domestic Product (GDP) by billions of dollars each year. If the Soviet Union hoped to stay afloat in the
world economy, it had to follow the lead of the Western nations. Conservative Communists, however, greatly resisted any new reforms, especially
perestroika, because they went against all prior doctrines of the Soviet
Union. Ellman and Kontorovich explain that "the country was cynically
led to financial and economic collapse in the calculation that escape from

this crisis would require those same structures of state exploitation and arbitrariness which *perestroika* had attempted to leave behind" (266). But Gorbachev and his supporters found enough backing in the Soviet Politburo for the economic reforms and consequently sidestepped the conservative opposition.

Shortly after Gorbachev announced his plans to use *perestroika* to reform the Soviet economy, he also announced his plans to institute *glasnost* or "openness" into Soviet society. This new policy would enable people to freely critique government actions of the past and the present. People were able to learn about their history and discover the truths about many of their former leaders, such as Joseph Stalin. Citizens were also allowed to assemble and freely protest or assert their political views. Gorbachev saw *glasnost* as an opportunity to gain support for *perestroika*. If the people approved of *perestroika*, Gorbachev could use them to sway conservative Communists to support him as well (Aslund 39). Through *glasnost*, Gorbachev did gain the popular support he needed to combat the right-wing Communists and push his reforms through the Politburo.

By 1988–1989, however, the new economic plans started to break down and began to damage the Soviet economy more than they helped. When Gorbachev instituted his open market system in 1987, he hoped that it would revitalize the Soviet economy and drive down inflation. Then agricultural workers and the Soviet farmers could begin to make a profit and the national production rate would rise, causing an economic revival. What Gorbachev and his liberal economists did not take into account was the fact that the socialist system did not allow for a market system to inflate prices on a long-term scale. It was virtually impossible to change prices in the Soviet Union through market fluctuations (Goldman 341). From that point on, historians claim, the Soviet Union entered a two-year period of stagnation and deterioration that eventually lead to the collapse of the Soviet economy in 1991. Later that year, the Soviet Union itself crumbled. In looking at this series of events, the proponents of the Gorbachev school of thought agree that the weak economy caused the overall collapse of the Soviet Union, but they contend it would not have happened without Gorbachev's liberal reforms (Laqueur 418).

Personal Position

The Soviet Union's collapse is one of the most significant and intriguing events of the twentieth century. It is important to understand the

Ruhaak 6

reasons why the Soviet Union ended because it still has tremendous implications for international relations. The two schools of thought that historians have developed and still write about today present effective and convincing arguments. Each side has plenty of evidence to support its conclusions. The Gorbachev school of thought credits the Soviet leader and his liberal reforms with inadvertently destroying the Soviet Union. The economic school of thought presumes that the failure of the Soviet economy, which extended back into the 1970s, was too much for the Soviet Union to overcome and the nation collapsed, despite Gorbachev's efforts. Although Gorbachev made great strides in reforming the Soviet economic and political system, he did not attempt to break up the Soviet Union.

Therefore, it seems clear to me that the defective socialist economy was the main cause of the Soviet Union's collapse.

During the late 1970s every major nation in the world experienced some sort of recession or stagnation of economic growth. The United States, for example, saw high unemployment rates and extremely high inflation rates. The Soviet Union experienced the same events, so most Soviets believed that they were going through a simple recession caused by a downturn in the economic cycle. In the mid-1980s when major nations such as the United States regained economic prosperity, the Soviet Union did not. As the GDPs of other countries grew, the Soviet's plummeted. For example, between 1986 and 1989, the Soviet Union's GDP fell over three percent, which resulted in billions of dollars lost by the Soviets in the world market. Coupled with domestic inflation and food shortages, this loss crippled the economy so badly that it could not sustain itself.

Soviet economists also seemed to be somewhat incompetent in assessing measures to solve economic problems. For years, even when in excessive debt, the government earmarked 40 percent of the nation's budget and resources to upgrading defense. Thus, the military absorbed billions of dollars that should have been used to repair the country's domestic conditions. Moreover, when Gorbachev instituted his open market policy, his economic advisors overlooked the fact that open market operations could not change price indexes in a socialist economy. Administrative measures and price fixing were the only ways to solve the problem. Gorbachev took extreme measures to overcome these difficulties, yet his efforts were too late. Personally, I will agree that Gorbachev hastened the dissolution of the Soviet Union, but the end was inevitable because of a failing socialist economic system. Many important and significant conditions had to exist for the Soviet Union to fall. The economic system had to be in dire straits and the political groups in the Soviet Union had to be at odds over the economy. These conditions did exist in the Soviet Union throughout the 1970s and 1980s. During this time the Soviet political system broke into factions. The right-wing conservative Communists wanted to keep the status quo and slowly work through the economic crisis. New liberals, led by Mikhail Gorbachev, wanted to institute radical reforms to get the Soviet Union back on its feet quickly. For the next six years, the Soviet Union endured factional fighting and radical change, and this situation resulted in the fall of the Soviet Union.

Works Cited

Aslund, Anders. "Gorbachev, Perestroika, and Economic Crisis."
    <u>Problems of Communism</u> 40 (1991): 18–41.

Batyuk, Vladimir. "The End of the Cold War: A Russian View." <u>History
    Today</u> 49.4 (1999): 28–36.

Elliot, John E. "Disintegration of the Soviet Politico-Economic System."
    <u>International Journal of Social Economics</u> 22.3 (March 1995):
    31–45. <u>Expanded Academic Index ASAP</u>. InfoTrac. Eastern Illinois
    U Lib. 4 April 2002.

Ellman, Michael, and Valdimir Kontorovich. "The Collapse of the Soviet
    System and the Memoir Literature." <u>Europe-Asia Studies</u> 49 (1997):
    259–79.

English, Robert D. "Sources, Methods, and Competing Perspectives on
    the End of the Cold War." <u>Diplomatic History</u> 21 (1997): 283–94.

Goldman, Marshall. "Perestroika in the Soviet Union." <u>Current History</u>
    87 (1988): 314–16, 340–41.

Laqueur, Walter. "Gorbachev and Epimetheus: The Origins of the Russ-
    ian Crisis." <u>The Journal of Contemporary History</u> 28 (1993):
    387–419.

Strayer, Robert. "Decolonization, Democratization, and Communist Re-
    form: The Soviet Collapse in Comparative Perspective." <u>Journal of
    World History</u> 12 (2001): 375–406.

Uhler, Walter C. "Gorbachev's Revolution." <u>The Nation</u> 31 Dec. 2001:
    40–45. <u>Wilson Select Plus Advanced Search</u>. OCLC FirstSearch.
    Eastern Illinois U Lib. 3 April 2002.

Guidelines for Making an Oral Presentation

At some time in your education or your professional career, you will be asked to speak before a group. Although oral presentations are stressful, even for experienced speakers, you can use your knowledge as a writer to help you in a speaking situation. But you also need to consider some techniques that apply only to oral presentations.

Writing and Speaking

Effective writing and successful speaking have a lot in common. They both entail a thorough understanding of topic, audience, purpose, and other related practices of the appropriate discourse community. You can use many of the activities and strategies from your writing process—audience analysis, invention, outlining—to prepare for an oral presentation. But you must be aware that writing for readers is not the same as speaking to an audience. Your listeners have one chance to grasp your meaning; they can't go back and reread what you've said. So to be an effective speaker, you have to adapt your presentation to the audience's listening abilities.

Here are some points to help you do that.

1. *Define your purpose.* What exactly do you want your audience to get from your presentation? You should focus on a few key points; three is often enough, even for a long talk. A well-known acronym for giving a speech is KISS: Keep it simple, stupid.

2. *Think about your audience.* Why have people come to hear you? Are they interested in your topic or have they been required to attend? Obviously, it will be more difficult to engage and hold people who have to be there. Concentrate on getting your audience interested and showing them why your ideas are important.

3. *Consider the setting.* How large is the audience and where will you speak? Try to match your style and approach to the setting. You can be casual with a small group of listeners who are familiar to you. If you're speaking to a large number of strangers in an auditorium, you may have to use a public address system and adopt a more formal mode of speaking.

4. *Organize carefully.* How can you arrange your points to keep your audience interested and involved? An effective presentation needs to have a recognizable shape: a clear beginning, middle, and end. In the opening you want to gain your listeners' attention and interest, so you might begin with a challenging question, an unusual example, or a brief anecdote. You also want to introduce and preview your topic and purpose, but don't try to pack too much into the opening—just give a quick peek at what's to come. And whatever you do, *don't apologize* ("I'm not feeling well today" or "I didn't have a lot of time to spend on this presentation"). In the middle section, plan to include some humorous or emotional moments: a witty quotation or a brief story, true or fictional, to illustrate a

point. You should also try to vary supporting materials; too many statistics, for example, will be boring and difficult to remember; too many anecdotes may obscure the point. In the conclusion, remind listeners of your main ideas and connect them, if you can, to your audience's interests and needs.

Presentation and Delivery

Once you've determined your purpose, analyzed your audience and setting, and organized your ideas, you will have to decide how you're going to present your material. Here are some pointers about the methods and techniques of oral presentations. Some suggestions may not apply to all speaking situations, but they will work most of the time. Studying the techniques of other presentations in similar circumstances will provide additional ideas.

Delivery Style

- *You should talk, not read.* You'll connect more easily with your audience and communicate with them more informally.
- *Use notes, don't memorize.* You'll appear more relaxed and be better able to make genuine contact with your listeners. If you memorize, you risk forgetting your place or leaving out whole sections.

Physical Delivery

- *Dress appropriately.* Your dress is the first thing your audience will see. If you're not sure what style is suitable for the occasion, ask someone whose opinion you trust, someone who's familiar with the situation.
- *Stand, don't sit.* People will see you better, and you'll be better able to see them and adjust to their reactions.
- *Move around and gesture.* You want to appear dynamic and lively. Step out from behind a podium or desk; cross to one side of the room and then the other; gesture appropriately, as you would in conversation. Try to use natural movement and gestures to draw attention to important points.
- *Make eye contact with your audience.* Look around the room, settle your gaze on one person, then move on to someone else.

Vocal Delivery

- *Speak loudly and confidently.* Breathing deeply is important for volume. Also try to use the lower range of your voice; it's the loudest and most authoritative. And don't be afraid to ask for feedback from the audience: "Can you hear me back there?"
- *Speak slowly enough to be understood.* Although most audiences prefer a moderately fast pace (about 150 words per minute), they will have difficulty following a rapid-fire delivery (more than 180 words per minute).

- *Vary the pitch of your voice.* A monotone is deadly. Even if you speak in a lively way, you still need to change the pitch of your voice. Taping yourself when you practice your presentation will help spot this problem.

Visual Aids

- *Use them selectively.* Contemporary audiences are visually oriented; they expect visual aids of some sort. Charts, posters, graphs, illustrations, overhead transparencies—they can help to focus attention and improve understanding. But too many or overly complex aids will bury your ideas and confuse your listeners.
- *Use them as supplements.* Don't expect visuals to do the work for you. They can reinforce a point, but you have to tell your listeners what they are looking at and what it means.
- *Choose appropriate media.* A small audience may be able to see a photograph or a chart, but a larger group will need projected images. Also keep in mind that the more technology you use, the more things can go wrong.
- *Consider a computer-based program.* Presentation software like PowerPoint or Keynote can be a great help. Such programs are effective tools for organizing your presentation, creating visuals, and even projecting those visuals during your talk. In fact, PowerPoint and other kinds of presentation software have become an almost obligatory part of business and professional communications. Be sure to make arrangements for required equipment well in advance of the presentation.

Time Limits

- *Don't go over your time limit.* The average audience's attention span is forty minutes at the most. After that, you're just talking to yourself.
- *Leave time for questions.* It's always a good idea to interact with your audience and find out what they're thinking.

Practice, Practice, Practice

The single most important thing you can do for an oral presentation is *practice.* All of the pointers we've given you require practice to make you appear confident and comfortable. You need to practice to check your timing; you need to practice to find out if you're speaking loudly and slowly enough; you need to practice making eye contact; you need to practice movements and gestures; you need to practice using visual aids; you need to practice the wording and to improve fluency; you need to practice to reduce anxiety and build your confidence.

You won't accomplish much by going over your presentation silently in your head. You need to rehearse out loud, with the notes and visual aides you will be using. At first you can practice in private, perhaps in front of a mirror. You can also videotape yourself and watch the results with a critical eye. But the best kind of rehearsal is with a live audience. Try to get some friends and colleagues to listen to your presentation and give you feedback. This process is analogous to giving a draft of an essay to a writing group; the same advice and guidelines apply (see pp. 31–32). You may also want to conduct a separate run-through with the visual aids, just to make sure there aren't any glitches (like a missing slide or an incomplete chart).

Activity

Prepare an informal ten-minute talk in which you present the main ideas from your researched position essay to your instructor and your classmates. Draw up a plan for your presentation, including, for example, a statement of purpose, a brief analysis of the audience and setting, an outline of key points, a set of note cards, and a description of the visual aids you intend to use. After getting feedback on your plan, practice your presentation and then deliver it to your audience.

Appendix A
Using and Designing Web Sites

In a very short period of time, less than a decade really, the Internet resource known as the World Wide Web has come to serve an increasing number of our professional and personal needs as readers, consumers, researchers, citizens, and writers. We read the news, watch sports, research ideas and products, share information and opinions, sell and promote goods and services. Being fully and ably prepared for these activities requires the same care and planning that you need when using the equivalent print and other media—with the added complexities of blending the mediums and understanding and mastering the associated technologies. This Appendix will provide basic advice and several resources for successfully using, researching, and composing on the Web. As you read, if you need additional information on a topic, you can visit one of these helpful general Web reference sites:

> The Librarians' Index to the Internet
>   http://lii.org/search/file/netsearch
> The WWW Help Page
>   http://werbach.com/web/wwwhelp.html
> Matisse's Glossary of Internet Terms
>   http://www.matisse.net/files/glossary.html

Before You Start: Protecting Your Privacy

You have probably heard the warning, "Don't send any e-mail that you wouldn't want your mother to read." The Internet is a very public place and thus many of your communications and activities can be monitored by the people who operate and interact with your system (your employer, a Webmaster, your service provider, the people who operate the sites that you visit, or even a malicious computer hacker). There are ways to limit or at least become aware of this surveillance or intrusion.

First, consider adding *firewall* and *virus* protection programs that automatically detect and deflect unwanted activity or viruses. These are available

273

commercially or may be downloaded through your school's technology center. Also, depending on your *browser* (Netscape, Explorer, AOL, for example), you will find tools that allow you to "manage the cookies" that Web sites place on your computer. *Cookies* are chunks or pieces of information that can be very useful and even necessary to efficient and complex Web surfing. They allow sites to download pages to and collect information from your computer. Without the cookies, you may be denied access to a site or receive only a limited version of the site's resources. If you accept cookies from Amazon.com, for example, the next time you visit the site it will remember your name and perhaps even suggest products based on a set of preferences established during your previous visit.

Browsers usually allow you several options for handling cookies. Use the Help function of your browser to access specific instructions. Generally, though, you can accept all, reject all, or be prompted to accept or reject each attempt to place a cookie. You can also erase cookies after you visit a site so that you are not recognized on subsequent visits. Your choices depend on how much privacy and control you want. A good starting point is the site-by-site prompting which will allow you to observe the cookie process. You may be amazed by the number of cookies sent by a single site—and the notifications may make you think twice about sharing personal information with unfamiliar sites. For additional information on Web privacy, visit the Electronic Frontier Foundation fact sheet at http://www.eff.org/Privacy/eff_privacy_top_12.html.

Successful Surfing

Accessing the Web through your system's browser can begin with simply entering the **URL**, or address, of a site you wish to visit and clicking *Go*. More often, though, you will sit down at the computer with a question or idea rather than a set destination. It's like walking into the library to begin a research project and heading to the reference room.

Getting There: Search Engines

The Web's "reference room" contains an array of *search engines* that help you to identify relevant sites. As you may already know, there are two major types of search engines: *crawlers* and *directories*. In the first type, the search engine surveys the Web or even other search engines (these types are called *metacrawlers*) for sites containing your *keywords* or phrases. It then arranges the results by the most likely keyword or phrase matches, most popular sites, and sponsored (paid) sites. Directories, on the other hand, are compiled by people, not machines, according to various criteria established by the search engine company. Some, for example, are based on quality while others favor paid subscriptions to the search engine. Increasingly, these distinctions are blurring and directory engines now include crawler options to expand individual searches. Below is a list of popular search engines. Each has distinct search approaches and features. Try several to find the ones that work best for you, and consider using more than one for any substantial research projects.

Crawlers:
> www.google.com (Google, by the way, has become such a popular search engine that "googling" is now a commonly used verb for conducting an Internet search.)
>
> www.alltheweb.com
>
> www.teoma.com
>
> www.lycos.com

Directories:
> www.yahoo.com
>
> www.askjeeves.com

Given how quickly things change, you should also consult these useful reference sites for up-to-date lists and reviews:

> SearchEngineWatch.com (with a latest "Top Choices" list)
> http://searchenginewatch.com/
>
> Search Engine Showdown (with a comparative "Features Chart")
> http://www.searchengineshowdown.com/

Conducting Your Search

Efficient searches begin with well-defined questions and **keywords** (specific and commonly used subject terms). The broader your topic, the greater the number of possible sites you will have to evaluate for their relevance. If you simply enter "World Wide Web" into a search engine, you will generate hundreds to thousands of **hits,** or sites. On the other hand *"Writing" + "World Wide Web,"*—or, even more narrowly, *"Writing" + "HTML" + "World Wide Web"*—will focus the search, limit the hits, and get you to your resources more quickly. Notice that the terms are in quotation marks and are joined by a plus sign. Each search engine has a particular system for shaping its searches, but for most engines, the quotation marks will limit searches to sites relevant to the full phrase rather than to sites that contain the individual words in the phrase. The plus sign requires a site to have both, not just either, of your suggested terms. Other common codes include a NOT or minus sign to exclude a keyword (Homelessness NOT families) and OR to expand a search with similar terms (gay OR lesbian). It pays to take a few minutes to study the "How to Use" section of your favorite sites, where they will explain how to conduct advanced searches.

A second way to approach defining your topic is through a directory engine that gives you a subject directory. Two good starting points are the Internet Public Library at http://www.ipl.org/ and BUBL Link at http://bubl.ac.uk/link/. These sites are organized in the same fashion as a library—BUBL even uses the Dewey Decimal System—and provide an overview of topics in the way an encyclopedia or annotated bibliography might. In addition, they include up-to-date, credible links to other sites on your topic. You'll find commercial subject directories at some of the general search engine sites such as Yahoo.Com.

For a more complete discussion of how to conduct searches, visit one of the many tutorials available on the Internet, such as

> UC Berkeley—Teaching Library Internet Workshops at http://www.lib.berkeley.edu/TeachingLib/Guides/Internet/SubjDirectories.html, and Learn the Net.Com at http://www.learnthenet.com/english/index.html.

Evaluating Sites

Determining the credibility of sources on the World Wide Web can be challenging. Anyone can create and publish a Web site. That's part of what makes it such an exciting new technology. When you use information from a site, however, you want to be confident that it is sound and comes from someone with the appropriate authority.

In addition to the advice for evaluating sources that was offered in Chapter 6 (pp. 226–229), here are some specific questions you can ask to start your evaluation of a site:

- *Did you arrive at the site via a* **link** *(an electronic reference) from a site whose credibility is already known to you? Does the site provide links to other credible sites?*

- *Is the site associated with a university? A recognized corporation or nonprofit organization? A government agency?* The ending of the URL can provide some of this information. Look for the <.gov> <.com> or <.edu> ending. You can also truncate a long URL to its core *server* address to connect to the originating or sponsoring site. For example, if you go back to the server for the site "Deciding to become a lawyer: Make an informed choice" at http://www.skidmore.edu/tschmeli/decide.html, you arrive at the Skidmore University Homepage www.skidmore.edu. Although personal sites (usually published through a commercial server) can be valuable in many cases, you want to be especially cautious in your use of them.

- *Is there a name and e-mail address for the site creator and/or* **Webmaster?** This and other basic site information is often in a header, a sidebar, or at the bottom of the Homepage.

- *Is there an "About Us" or "About the Site" link that provides useful biographical or company information?* What relevant or appropriate credentials are offered?

- *Is the site well designed and carefully maintained?*
  - Does it have a clear purpose?
  - Does the information appear to be accurate, given what you know or have read elsewhere?

- Is the information presented in an objective voice?
- Does the site clearly give credit for information taken from other sites or sources?
- How does the style compare to what you are used to reading in comparable print genres?
- Are the links usable and up-to-date?
- How recently was the site updated?

When you have doubts, try using search engines to gather additional details about the site, its creator, the Webmaster, and the information provided on the site. For example, does the site appear in one of the established directory-style search engines (p. 275)?

One additional word of caution on using a personal or questionable site: If you plan to make a critical point or take a major step based on such a Web site's representation of someone else's ideas, locate the original source to confirm the accuracy of the quotation or representation.

Constructing and Maintaining Your Own Web Site

Web sites can be as simple as a single page and as complex as a university's collection of pages related to their programs and activities. The advice that follows provides guidance for planning a basic site—from the technology you will need to the design decisions you must make. Should you wish to tackle a larger, more complex project, these two resource sites will be especially useful:

> Web Style Guide: Basic Design Principles for Creating Web Sites (considered the standard style sheet for Web Design)
> http://www.webstyleguide.com/
> The Web Developer's Virtual Library (including free tutorials)
> http://wdvl .internet.com/Authoring/Tutorials/

Tools for Construction: HTML and Servers

The two essential tools for Web site creation are *HTML* and a server. HTML is Hypertext Markup Language, a system of codes that allow you to create a combination of texts and images that can be read by a browser in the Web medium. Many of the functions we take for granted in word processing programs, such as putting a word in bold, must be coded in HTML for a Web page: <B>word</>. If you would like to see the code that goes into writing a Web page, visit any site and do a right click with your mouse. Select "View Source Page" and it will show you the HTML version of the page you are on.

Your instructor may offer an introduction to HTML, and campus technology centers often provide workshops on the topic. In addition, tutorials and advice can be found on many of the sites discussed in the "Successful Surfing" section of this appendix. Increasingly, though, both casual and professional Web creators are turning to Web composing programs that enact the code for them, much as Word or Word Perfect might when you word process. These programs work on the WYSIWYG principle—"What You See Is What You Get." Simple pages can be completed using free and easily available programs like Netscape's Composer. Other fee-based commercial products, such as Micromedia's Dreamweaver or Microsoft's FrontPage, offer more complex options, such as using frames to design your pages. Most Web designers find that a basic understanding of HTML can be a valuable tool for fine tuning and editing even when using a composing program. There are additional programming languages, like Javascript, that are useful for Web construction, but a simple site can be constructed with HTML alone.

Once a page is completed, it must be uploaded to a server to place it onto the World Wide Web. A server is the computer and associated software that connect your pages to the Internet. For school or professional projects, you may have access to a server through the university's or company's technology services. Personal or public pages can be published using commercial server space, which is often packaged for a fee with other Internet services.

Your site will have unique URLs that contain information about your server as well as a unique name for each page of your site. Your Homepage name is especially important. Within the guidelines set out by your server and your Web composing program, use a simple but distinct address that clearly identifies the content of your site. For example, www.lsp.com/Jackson tells you that this is a commercial site (.com) on the lsp server. Using Jackson, the creator's name, for its unique address is simple and easy to remember; however, this address gives Web surfers little information about the site's content. But www.lsp.com/jacksonspoodles, by contrast, gives a clearer sense of the site's business. A linked page on the site might be www.lsp.com/jacksonspoodles/litters.html. Notice, too, that the entire URL is lowercase. This makes typing in the URL much easier.

Designing a Web Site

Much of what you have learned about good composing practices is applicable to Web construction as well. As you prepare the content of the site, you need a clearly articulated purpose and a strong awareness of your persona and audience in order to focus and hone your message. For example, do you want to provide information about an organization or recruit new volunteers? Will most visitors be familiar with your group's accomplishments or need to be convinced of the organization's value to its community? Will users be novice Web surfers or experienced site designers?

To accomplish your goals and to prepare for the design phase of the project, you will need to thoroughly analyze the discourse practices in both your own and the site user's communities. Users in an education community, for example, accept more text-heavy page designs than do visitors to commercial sites. In addition to using the research techniques you learned in Chapter 3 for completing your analysis, you should add the practice of surfing the Web for sites created for purposes like your own and for users like the ones you hope to reach, looking for both positive and negative models of content and design.

Many Web design issues are unique to the medium because of the technology and the users' genre expectations. Few successful Web pages are simply print documents posted on the Internet.

Ways of Reading: Print versus Hypertext

The most basic contrast between print and electronic publishing comes from the different ways texts are read and images are viewed. Authors of articles or books can expect a reader to pick up a text and, most often, to read through the material in the linear order it was printed. Even reference texts (such as encyclopedias and almanacs) and magazines contain discrete selections that are intended to be read from beginning to end, if not in the order that they appear in the collection. This magazine or reference-book format is perhaps closest to what we experience when visiting a Web site. A "site" is usually a collection of several associated or linked pages with a center, or Homepage, from which these sites spin off like satellites. A link is a technology that allows readers to click on a word or image and move immediately from the place where they are to another place on the page, to another page, or to a different site. This *hypertext* approach to reading means the reader, not the author, is given responsibility for the order in which information is read and images are seen. The Web page creator can still influence the way information is received, but the organization must be carefully planned and the designs thoughtfully set out.

Visual Complexity: Adding Images

A majority of Web sites make significant use of graphics, such as pictures, graphs, and logos. Visitors expect interesting graphics to be integrated into the design of most Web genres, even those that are Web versions of print resources. Accomplishing this goal can be as simple as designing a graphic with text, color, and font or as complicated as adding animated graphics. The rhetorical uses for graphics are varied: a recurring logo or picture on all site pages provides a site identity; graphs or photographs can make, elaborate on, or illustrate points; a visually interesting or unusual graphic can draw user attention to a particular point on the page; and the combination of text and graphics can set the site's tone. On the I Spy site in Chapter 5 (p. 178), for example, the campaign's logo is a bright pink bull's eye that draws the reader to the summary paragraph and becomes the unifying element among the campaign pages. The shocking pink may also resonate with some readers and challenge their association of pink with passive femininity.

If you plan to include your own digital photographs, you will need to use photo manipulation software such as Photoshop to prepare them for site use. Clip art can also be incorporated, though you want to ensure in this and all cases of borrowing that you do not violate copyright. The Librarian's Index to the Internet offers several suggested sites for understanding copyright issues. To borrow safely, you can use any of the search engines to identify free online clip art; in other cases you may need to request permission from site Webmasters.

Navigating: Overall Site Organization

Movement within a Web site is called *navigating.* The metaphor, like many used to describe life on the Web, accurately captures the control the site visitor expects of a Web site. It also suggests the responsibility of the site author to establish a terrain that is easily understood and traveled.

A first step to success is organizing the primary material you wish to share into manageable and logical parts. Except for academics, few site readers are comfortable reading long, dense, and complex pages of Web text. The medium seems to foster shorter attention spans and a desire to surf rather than read without interruption. This means the overall body of information must be carefully divided into meaningful units or chunks that can be understood independently. The most common models for this approach are the hierarchical outline and the hub, depending on the creator's desire to convey a useful sequence or simply to cluster related elements efficiently. Once you decide on a plan, you can set up topics on a Homepage, with links that will take site visitors to each point in the outline or each component of the hub.

The outline style, for example, is equivalent to a table of contents in a book or magazine and is laid out in sequential pages that either develop subtopics or lead to additional subtopic pages:

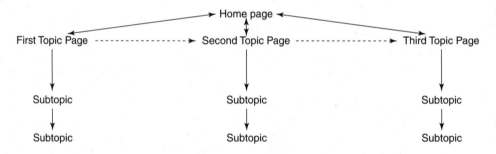

The hub approach, by contrast, uses topical clusters without prompting a particular linear progression. Links on each of the hub pages may be repeated, taking users from one page to one another or to common resource links.

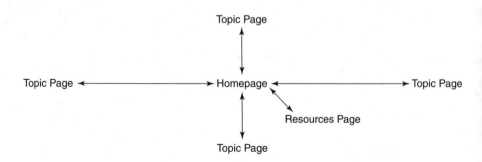

On many sites, you will find a combination of these approaches on the Homepage, used to manage different types of information, perhaps an outline for the core material and a list or hub for site-use or site-related information. Use your favorite sites as models or a quick Web search to locate several sites that offer sample templates for designing pages.

Page Layout

Individual page layout is the next concern for a site planner. At this point, other significant contrasts between print and Web design must be considered, such as how layout and color affect the images and text. Depending on the genre (the product sales site versus organizational fact-sharing site, for example), users expect an appropriate design with a visually pleasing and easy-to-read appearance. Your instincts for what might work on a print page, even one including graphic images, may not always help with Web page layout. The computer screen, for example, presents a horizontal or landscape view of the page, as opposed to the vertical or portrait print page.

Consider these suggestions as you design your pages:

- *Plan for user variation:* Not all site visitors will have fast Internet connections, large monitors, or the same browser as the one you use to design the site.
  - Different browsers show Web pages in different ways. Always evaluate your site using a variety of browsers.
  - Special attention should be given to making your site accessible to people with disabilities, in line with the Federal Communications Commission's regulation. For example, people with hearing difficulties may use technologies that read text on a site, thus requiring text explanations of images or perhaps a text-only alternate download (which will also be useful to any user with slow download times). Information on making your site accessible is available on many of the Web sites listed in this appendix. A well-respected fee-based evaluation of your site is available at Bobby: http://bobby.watchfire.com/bobby/
- *Layout the page using a grid plan:* Most Web pages are arranged in sections on the page. The simplest approach is to use the column and grid functions of your word processing or Web composing program. Each section of the grid should be planned carefully for a meaningful and visually appealing organization (using headers, text, and graphics). And, of course, the grid sections within a page must be visually complementary. More complex approaches such as frames and cascading pages add sophistication but they also make basic functions, such as bookmarking and printing, more difficult for the average user.
- *Simple is usually better:* Although early sites were often composed using the many exciting bells and whistles that the technology makes available, most

experts now suggest keeping the design simple and using the technology, instead, to assist visitors in effective site use. Animated graphics and sound files, for example, require significant download time, can't be seen or heard by some users, and are often distracting and even annoying to some viewers. You can have a unique page identity without visually shouting at the visitor. Your core goal should be a pleasing balance of easy-to-read text and easy-to-view graphics.

- *Make your style straightforward and concise:* Because visitors' habits and progress are unpredictable, page creators want to use all available tools to sustain interest and provide information in the most efficient manner. You can achieve these goals by arranging material with a clear up-front summary that previews material within a section and by providing concrete topic sentences within each paragraph or chunk for the same purposes.

- *Try to strike a balance between too much and too little information on each page:*
  - Except when using sites intended as the electronic equivalent of a printed text (for example, an online journal), few readers expect to read long pages of text as they would on a page. If your site will have long sections of text, divide the material into sections, with clear and logical headings. Then use a linking device (an outline at the beginning of the page or a button bar list at the top or along the side) to allow the reader to access the sections at will. Another useful tool is the side scroll bar, though users often tire of an overly long section that depends on the scroll bar for navigation, so keep its use to a few pages.
  - Visitors also get frustrated when too little information is provided on each page, requiring a long sequence of steps to get them where they want to go.

- *Make each page independently usable yet clearly linked to the rest of the site:* Repeating a side bar of site links on each page is one way to ensure page to page consistency. Also include a link to the Homepage and a forward and back link on each page.

- *Make readability a priority:* Tools such as page resolution, color, and font style and size allow you to present ideas, convey a tone, and create a personality for your site; but you should always test to be sure that your choices allow your site to be easily read. The computer page requires different choices frm the print page in most cases. Here are a few common options:
  - A standard *resolution* or page density for Web pages is 800 × 600 because it allows most monitors to display the entire page as designed. Whatever you decide upon, be consistent from page to page.
  - A multitude of colors are available to you but most designers recommend sticking with just a few colors selected from the 216 "browser safe" scheme (a subset of the 256 color monitor option). Dark text on a lighter or muted background is generally most easily read. It is also a good idea to use the same color for a function (headers, for example) on

every page and to stick with the Web's conventional colors for functions, such as blue for an unused link and purple for a link once it's been used).

- Commonly recommended fonts are Times New Roman, Helvetica, Georgia, and Verdana. These display best on the low resolution offered by a computer screen. For design purposes, you might combine two of these fonts in a few different sizes for use in different sections of the page. Your font size should be at least 12 point, but avoid overuse of a large font, except in headers or to draw attention to a page section. Finally, use text enhancements such as bold, italics, and underlining with the same constraint and purpose (for book titles, for example) that you would in print texts.

- To read a computer screen easily, viewers need more white space than they do for reading printed materials. Use such space and a consistent text arrangement (section style or paragraph format, for example) to highlight your organization and to guide your user's eye and progress.

- *Use the standard formats for photographic images:* The two options are the standard GIF (the Web standard using the 216 color scheme) and the JPEG format (24 bit color); select a 1:1 display ratio. Not all browsers will display JPEG images. Also, remember that large, high-resolution photographs will be more difficult for some users to download.

Homepage: Core Information

Your Homepage is perhaps deserving of the most attention as you design your site. It should include, at the least:

- An introduction to your site—its purpose and content
- An indication of the site's organizational plan (outline or hub, for example)
- A summary of the site's additional resources (a site search engine or suggested links, for example)
- An "About Us" link and a "Contact the Webmaster" link (a link that takes the user to the Webmaster's e-mail address), along with information on how regularly correspondence will be read
- A "Last Updated" area to assure visitors of the site's currency

Looking at a Sample Design

This National Service Learning Clearinghouse (www.servicelearning.org) site illustrates several effective choices in organization and design. The page is simply designed using three columns (not separate frames) with a distinctive header. Color, font size and style, and graphics are simple, appealing, and consistent (for example, green is used for all links in the two dense columns); they are also appropriate to an educational site (showing groups of students and teachers, for example).

The national site for service-learning information

Search
Sitemap
Contact
Support
Home

National Service-Learning Clearinghouse

nslc
etr associates

Higher Education | K-12 | Community-Based | Tribal

Search

Home

Welcome to
Service-Learning

NSLC Library

Resources & Tools

Events & Jobs

Who We Are

What's New

Mentoring and Focus on Health
Four Historically Black Colleges and Universities
(HBCUs) in Florida are participating in a new
AmeriCorps mentoring program designed to help
struggling freshmen and sophomores stay in college.
HBCUs are also receiving Learn and Serve America
support to address minority health issues. Read more
at the Corporation for National & Community Service,
National Service News site.

The John Glenn Institute **has named** Frank Aquila,
Professor of Educational Administration at Cleveland
State University, as a **John Glenn Scholar in
Service-Learning** in the academic outcomes
area. The program, funded by the W.K. Kellogg
Foundation, recognizes scholars from any discipline
whose scholarship contributes to advancing the
understanding of or adoption of service-learning in
K-12 classrooms. View award details.

New Quick Guide: Funding for K-12 Service-Learning
Programs is the latest quick guide from the National
Service-Learning Clearinghouse. This new resource
was created by the NSLC senior program advisor for
K-12 service-learning, RMC Research Corporation.
View all thirteen quick guides.

LSA-News Electronic Newsletter
Welcome to the July issue of Learn and Serve America
News! This newsletter is published on a quarterly basis
and is distributed to members of all the NSLC listservs.
Subscribe or unsubscribe to LSA-News.

Submit Your Service-Learning Effective Practice.
The National Service-Learning Clearinghouse (NSLC)
is collaborating with the National Service Resource
Center Effective Practices Collection to collect and
share best practices for service-learning projects. We
are particularly looking for practices on key
service-learning topics such as student orientation,
community partnerships, funding, assessment,
reflection, civic education, and program strategies and
ideas. Every person who submits a service-learning
effective practice between June 30 and July 31 will
receive an NSLC apple or NSLC clip dispenser. Submit
a practice. For ideas, see all 88 service-learning
effective practices. If you need help, please call
Magdalena Montagne at 831-438-4060 ext. 100.

Featured Library Item

Serve and Learn: Implementing and
Evaluating Service-Learning in
Middle and High Schools, by
Florence Fay Pritchard and George
I. Whitehead, III (2004), provides a
framework grounded in theory and
best professional practice,
which middle and high school
teachers, their students, and
community partners can use to
design, implement, and evaluate
service-learning projects that
address authentic community needs. View previously
featured library items.

**Are you new to service-learning? A
service-learning expert?** We have picked some of
our best fact sheets, quick guides, bibliographies, and
hot topics for beginners and experts. As always, you
can also explore our resources by **sector**: K-12, HE,
CBO, and Tribal; by **type**: NSLC Library, Resources &
Tools, Events & Jobs; and by using our site-wide
search. Individual reference assistance is available
toll-free at 1-866-245-SERV (7378) or
info@servicelearning.org

Conference Resources Service-learning resources
on assessment, partnerships and more from the recent
2004 National Conference on Community Volunteering
and National Service.

**Recent Dissertations on Service and Service-Learning
Topics: Volume III (2001-2003)** (129 p., 500K pdf) is
now available. Completely online, Volume III provides
over 125 dissertation abstracts and was produced by
Katrina Norvell for the National Service-Learning
Clearinghouse. Volume I (1899) and Volume II (2001)
are in the NSLC Library and print copies are available.

New and updated resources on the National
Service-Learning Clearinghouse website that you
might find useful include updated Sector pages: Higher
Education, K-12, Community-Based, Tribal; new and
updated Bibliographies; new Featured Library Items
page; updated LSA Grantee page; and new virtual
Library Corner.

Service-Learning At-A-Glance: Selected Resources is
one of eight **new bibliographies** from the National
Service-Learning Clearinghouse. See all NSLC
bibliographies, including an updated CBO bibliography
from senior program advisor Points of Light
Foundation.

"Students in Service to America": Engaging
America's students in a lifelong habit of service" can
now be shipped to you for $1.50, with discounts on
orders over 15 copies. Order your copy online, or call
(toll free) 1-866-245-7378, ext. 272. You may also view
or download the guidebook online.

Starter Kits

* K-12 Starter Kit
* **HE Starter Kit**
  Coming soon!
* **CBO Starter Kit**
  Coming soon!

Hot Topics

* Citizenship
* Risk Management
* Statistics
* ...and more!

From the Field

Updates

President's 2005 budget would engage
record number of Americans in service.

Promoting the health of older adults is the
focus of the new National Clearinghouse
on Service-Learning for Healthy Aging.

The latest news from the Corporation for
National and Community Service.

Funding
The **Ruddie Memorial Youth
Foundation** has funding available to
evaluate and disseminate innovative
youth programs. Applications are due
September 1, 2004. More information and
online application.

Learn and Serve America announces
$4 million for 10 grants to support
activities that teach students about and
engage them in homeland-security
related efforts. More information.

HUD announces $37 million in funding for
eight FY 2004 grant programs and
graduate fellowships through the Office of
University Partnerships. More information.

The **Constitutional Rights Foundation**
is now accepting applications for the
2004-2005 Robinson Mini-Grant awards
of up to $600 for K-12 service-learning
projects designed to address serious
community issues. Deadline is October
15, 2004.

The Campaign for the Civic Mission of
Schools invites **Requests for Proposals**
from state-level coalitions for grants in two
categories: large grants (194K pdf) of
$150,000 over two years (due June 18),
and small grants (185K pdf) of $20,000
over two years (due August 2).

Reading is Fundamental (RIF) and
Nestlé USA will grant twenty-five Nestlé
and RIF's Very Best in Youth awards to
young people ages 10-18 who have made
reading a priority, put the needs of others
before their own, and contributed
significantly in creating healthy
communities. Nominations are due by
November 1, 2004.

More funding resources.

More awards, fellowships & scholarships
resources.

Conferences

Enroll in one of over 25 **Summer
Institutes on Service-Learning** offered
across the nation. More information.

Register by August 13 for the First
National Urban Service Learning Institute
scheduled for August 19-20, 2004 in Saint
Paul, Minnesota.

The Conference on Civic Education
Research will be held Sept. 26 - Sept. 28,
2004, in Reno, NV, sponsored by the
Centre for Policy and Practice.

Attend the NSEE/ICEL Joint Conference
2004: Exponential Learning: Sustaining
Global Partnerships in a Changing World
Sept. 28 - Oct. 2, 2004, in Miami, FL.
More conference information.

Grantees

Visit the LSA Grantee Information Page for
highlights and resources.

Website Tips

How to Borrow Items From Our Library.
How to Order Publications.
Search for Other Service-Learning
Programs.

Corporation for
NATIONAL &
COMMUNITY
SERVICE ★★★

USA
Freedom Corps
Make a Difference. Volunteer

The Homepage uses a hub to categorize the primary site information into six broad informational areas: "What's New," "Starter Kits," "Hot Topics," "From the Field," "Grantees," and "Website Tips." More specific subtopics are listed within each category. This manages a great many topics by placing them into easily negotiated clusters. Along the left sidebar, in the least textually dense column, is a linked list of important site-related information, including a helpful description of the organization. This sidebar is available at each of the linked pages on the site and allows users to quickly return to this Homepage. There is also a navigation bar under the header that takes specific types of users directly to the page of most interest to them: "Higher Education," "K–12," "Community-Based," and "Tribal." Finally, in the upper right-hand corner, a visitor finds a simple list of links for quick access to site resources and information. This varied and thoughtful arrangement allows a substantial amount of information to be presented in a flexible and visually manageable fashion. It also serves the needs of the casual visitor in search of an understanding of the site's purposes or goals, as well as the more advanced and focused needs of a K–12 teacher in search of materials to use in the classroom.

Editing and Maintaining Your Site

Your final editing of a Web site should include testing with multiple browsers, monitors, and download options. You don't have to design for clearly outdated technologies, but a 15-inch monitor and telephone modem downloads are still common. Sites such as Search Engine Tutorial for Web Designers (http://www.northernwebs.com/set/) offer useful advice for designing for different browsers.

With most print projects, an author's role is usually finished when the text is published. But site creators have a responsibility to regularly update and revise pages on their sites. Links, for example, must be checked to ensure that they remain active. Correspondence generated by the site also needs to be answered. Each site has a Webmaster who assumes these responsibilities. This person may or may not be the site creator but must be someone capable of handling the technical challenges of the task. If the site is a collaborative project, for example, the best advice is for one person to assume responsibility for oversight of the pages, even if this simply means orchestrating revisions by a number of people.

Appendix B
Styles for Documenting Sources

Every time you make use of the words, facts, or ideas of others, you need to document the source—that is, provide a reference telling your readers where you found the material you have included in your writing. Readers in most professions and academic disciplines expect a specific documentation style (or format) in the scholarly books and articles they read. Styles of documentation differ markedly in citation form, arrangement of source information, and other details. Each style reflects the expectations of its practitioners for particular kinds of information presented in particular ways.

You will need to find out which style is preferred in the field for which you are writing. Your instructor, editor, or supervisor will probably specify which documentation system to use and which style manual to consult. Another way to find out this information is to examine the form of the notes and the bibliography entries in scholarly journals of your field. Karen Honeycott, for example, is a social scientist who used the American Psychological Association (APA) style to document "Fat World/Thin World" (pp. 125–139). Marty Ruhaak used the Modern Language Association (MLA) format for his history paper "The Decline and Fall of the Soviet Union" (pp. 260–268). And Evan Imber-Black followed the Chicago Manual Style (CMS) endnote system in documenting her sources (pp. 108–114).

This appendix describes four commonly used systems for documenting sources: MLA style, used in English, foreign languages, and some other humanities; APA style, used in psychology and the social sciences; Chicago style (CMS), used in history, art history, philosophy, religion, and some other humanities; and CSE style, used in biology and other life sciences. At the end of the appendix is a list of style manuals used in a variety of disciplines; this list also includes links to Web sites that explain and supplement many of the manuals.

Documenting Sources Using MLA Style

The documentation style of the Modern Language Association (MLA)—used in English, foreign languages, and some other humanities—requires that source citations be given in the text of the paper rather than in footnotes or endnotes. This in-text style of documentation involves *parenthetical references.*

Throughout this section, titles of books and periodicals are underlined (a printer's mark to indicate words to be set in italic type). If you have italic lettering on a computer, you can use italics instead of underlining, as long as your instructor, editor, or supervisor approves.

In-Text Citations

a. You will usually introduce the cited material, whether quoted or paraphrased, by mentioning the name of the author in your lead-in and giving the page number (or numbers) in parentheses. Put the parenthetical reference near the cited material, but preserve the flow of your writing by placing the citation where a pause would naturally occur, preferably at the end of the sentence, as in this example:

   Edmund Wilson tells us that the author of <u>Uncle Tom's Cabin</u> felt "the book had been written by God" (5).

b. Your readers can identify this source by consulting your Works Cited at the end of your paper (see pp. 289–295). The entry for the source cited above would appear like this one:

   Wilson, Edmund. <u>Patriotic Gore: Studies in the Literature of the American Civil War</u>. New York: Oxford UP, 1966.

c. If you do not mention the author in your lead-in, include his or her last name in parentheses along with the page number, without an intervening comma, like this:

   One of the great all-time best-sellers, <u>Uncle Tom's Cabin</u> sold over 300,000 copies in America and more than 2 million copies world wide (Wilson 3).

d. If you have to quote indirectly—something from another source not available to you—use "qtd. in" (for "quoted in") in your parenthetical reference. This example refers to a book written by Donald Johanson and Maitland Edey:

   Richard Leakey's wife, Maeve, told the paleoanthropologist David Johanson, "We heard all about your bones on the radio last night" (qtd. in Johanson and Edey 162).

e. If you are using a source written or edited by more than three people, use only the name of the first person listed, followed by "et al." (meaning "and others") in your lead-in.

   Blair et al. observe that the fine arts were almost ignored by colonial writers (21).

f. If you refer to one of two or more works by the same author, put a comma after the author's last name and include a shortened title in the parenthetical reference.

> (Gould, <u>Mismeasure</u> 138).

g. If the author's name is not given, use a shortened title instead. Be sure to use at least the first word of the full title to send the reader to the proper alphabetized entry on your Works Cited page. The following is a reference to a newspaper article entitled "Environmental Group Calls DuPont's Ads Deceptive":

> The Friends of the Earth claimed that, despite DuPont's television ads about caring for the environment, the company is the "single largest corporate polluter in the United States" ("Environmental Group" F3).

Preparing the List of Works Cited

On a separate page at the end of the paper, alphabetize your Works Cited list for all sources mentioned in your paper. Format the list according to the these rules:

- Center "Works Cited" at the top of the page.
- Arrange your sources in alphabetical order by the last name of the author. If the author is not given in the source, alphabetize the source by the first main word in the title (excluding *A, An,* or *The*).
- Double space the entire list, both within and between entries.
- Use hanging indention: put the first line of each entry flush with the left margin and indent any subsequent lines in the entry one-half inch (five spaces).
- In both titles and subtitles, capitalize the first and last words and all other words *except* articles (*a, an, the*), prepositions, coordinating conjunctions, and the *to* in infinitives.
- Omit any use of the words *page* or *pages* or *line* or *lines*. Do not even include abbreviations for these terms. Use numbers alone:

> Kinsley, Michael. "Continental Divide" <u>Time</u> 7 Jul. 1997: 89–91.

- Shorten publishers' names: for example, use Prentice instead of Prentice Hall or Norton instead of W. W. Norton and Co. or Oxford UP instead of Oxford University Press or U of Illinois P instead of University of Illinois Press. See sample entries 1 through 14.
- For nonperiodical works, include the city of publication, usually given on the title page of the work cited. If you find two or more cities, use only the first. For cities outside the United States, add an abbreviation of the country (or of the province for cities in Canada) if the name of the city may be unclear or unknown to your reader:

> Waterloo, ON
> Manchester, Eng.

- Use *lowercase* roman numerals (ii, xiv) for citing page numbers from a preface, introduction, or table of contents; use roman numerals in names of monarchs (Elizabeth II).
- Abbreviate months and titles of magazines as shown in the sample entries.

Sample Entries for a List of Works Cited

The following models will help you write Works Cited entries for most of the sources you will use. If you use a source not illustrated in these examples, consult the more extensive list of sample entries found in the *MLA Handbook for Writers of Research Papers*, 6th ed., or ask your instructor, editor, or supervisor for guidance. The MLA's Internet home page includes a list of frequently asked questions (FAQs) that address a number of thorny citation issues: www.mla.org/www_mla_org/style/style_faq.

Books

1. Book by one author

   Chused, Richard H. <u>Private Acts in Public Places: A Social History of Divorce</u>. Philadelphia: U of Pennsylvania P, 1994.

2. Two more books by the same author

   Gould, Stephen Jay. <u>The Mismeasure of Man</u>. New York: Norton, 1981.

   ---. <u>The Panda's Thumb: More Reflections in Natural History</u>. New York: Norton, 1980.

   [Give the author's name in the first entry only. Thereafter, use three hyphens in place of the author's name, followed by a period and the title.]

3. Book by two or three authors

   Anderson, Terry, and Donald Leal. <u>Free Market Environmentalism</u>. Boulder: Westview, 1991.

   McCrum, William, William Cran, and Robert MacNeil. <u>The Story of English</u>. New York: Viking, 1986.

4. Book by more than three authors

   Medhurst, Martin J., et al. <u>Cold War Rhetoric: Strategy, Metaphor, and Ideology</u>. New York: Greenwood, 1990.

   [The phrase *et al.* is an abbreviation for *et alii*, meaning "and others."]

5. Book by an unknown author

   <u>Literacy of Older Adults in America: Results from the National Adult Literacy Survey</u>. Washington: Center for Educ. Statistics, 1987.

6. Book with an editor

   Gallegos, Bee, ed. <u>English: Our Official Language?</u> New York: Wilson, 1994.

   [For a book with two or more editors, use "eds."]

7. Book with an author and an editor

> Whorf, Benjamin. <u>Language, Thought, and Reality: Selected Writings of Benjamin Lee Whorf</u>. Ed. J. B. Carroll. Cambridge: MIT P, 1956.

8. Book by a group or corporate author

> National Research Council. <u>The Social Impact of AIDS in the United States</u>. New York: National Academy P, 1993.
>
> [When a corporation, organization, or group is listed as the author on the title page, cite it as you would a person.]

9. Work in a collection or anthology

> Gordon, Mary. "The Parable of the Cave." <u>The Writer on Her Work</u>. Ed. Janet Sternburg. New York: Norton, 1980. 27–32.
>
> [Include page numbers for entire work, not just pages quoted in the paper.]

10. Previously published article reprinted in a collection or anthology

> Sage, George H. "Sport in American Society: Its Pervasiveness and Its Study." <u>Sport and American Society</u>. 3rd ed. Reading: Addison-Wesley, 1980. 4–15. Rpt. in <u>Physical Activity and the Social Sciences</u>. Ed. W. N. Widmeyer. 5th ed. Ithaca: Movement, 1983. 42–52.
>
> [First give complete data for the earlier publication; then add "Rpt. in" and give the reprinted source.]

11. Multivolume work

> Blom, Eric, ed. <u>Grove's Dictionary of Music and Musicians</u>. 5th ed. 10 vols. New York: St. Martin's, 1961.

12. Reprinted (republished) book

> Jespersen, Otto. <u>Growth and Structure of the English Language</u>. 1938. Chicago: U of Chicago P, 1980.

13. Later (second or subsequent) edition

> Gibaldi, Joseph. <u>MLA Handbook for Writers of Research Papers</u>. 6th ed. New York: MLA, 2003.

14. Book in translation

> Grmek, Mirko D. <u>History of AIDS: Emergence and Origin of a Modern Pandemic</u>. Trans. Russell C. Maulitz and Jacalyn Duffin. Princeton: Princeton UP, 1990.

Journals and Magazines

15. Article from a journal with continuous pagination throughout the whole volume

> Potvin, Raymond, and Che-Fu Lee. "Multistage Path Models of Adolescent Alcohol and Drug Use." <u>Journal of Studies on Alcohol</u> 41 (1980): 531–42.

16. Article from a journal that paginates each issue separately or that uses only issue numbers

> Holtug, Nils. "Altering Humans: The Case For and Against Human Gene Therapy." <u>Cambridge Quarterly of Healthcare Ethics</u> 6.2 (Spring 1997): 157–60.
>
> [This notation means volume 6, issue 2.]

17. Article from a monthly or bimonthly magazine

> Lawren, Bill. "1990's Designer Beasts." <u>Omni</u> Nov.-Dec. 1985: 56–61.
>
> Rosenbaum, Dan, and David Sparrow. "Speed Demons: Widebody Rackets." <u>World Tennis</u> Aug. 1989: 48–49.

18. Article from a weekly or biweekly magazine (signed and unsigned)

> Coghlan, Andy. "Warring Parents Harm Children as Much as Divorce." <u>New Scientist</u> 15 Jun. 1991: 24–28.
>
> "Warning: 'Love' for Sale." <u>Newsweek</u> 11 Nov. 1985: 39.

Newspapers

19. Signed newspaper article

> Krebs, Emilie. "Sewer Backups Called No Problem." <u>Pantagraph</u> [Bloomington] 20 Nov. 1985: A3.
>
> [If the city is not part of the name of a local newspaper, give the city in brackets, not underlined, after the newspaper's name.]
>
> Weiner, Jon. "Vendetta: The Government's Secret War Against John Lennon." <u>Chicago Tribune</u> 5 Aug. 1984, sec 3:1.
>
> [Note the difference between "A3" in the first example and "sec. 3:1" in the second. Both refer to section and page, but each newspaper indicates the section in a different way. Give the section designation and page number exactly as they appear in the publication.]

20. Unsigned newspaper article

> "No Power Line-Cancer Link Found." <u>Chicago Tribune</u> 3 Jul. 1997, final ed., sec. 1: 5.
>
> [If an edition is specified on the paper's masthead, name the edition (late ed., natl ed., final ed.) after the date and before the page reference. Different editions of the same issue of a newspaper contain different material.]

21. Letter to the editor

> Kessler, Ralph. "Orwell Defended." Letter. <u>New York Times Book Review</u> 15 Dec. 1985: 26.

22. Editorial

> "From Good News to Bad." Editorial. <u>Washington Post</u> 16 Jul. 1984: 10.

Other Sources

23. Book review

> Emery, Robert. Rev. of <u>The Divorce Revolution: The Unexpected Social and Economic Consequences for Women and Children in America</u> by Lenore Weitzman. <u>American Scientist</u> 74 (1986): 662–63.

24. Personal interview or letter

> Ehrenreich, Barbara. Personal interview. 12 Feb. 1995.

> Vidal, Gore. Letter to the author. 2 Jun. 1984.

25. Anonymous pamphlet

> <u>How to Help a Friend with a Drinking Problem</u>. American College Health Assn., 1984.

26. Article from a reference work (unsigned and signed)

> "Psychopharmacology." <u>The Columbia Encyclopedia</u>. 5th ed. 1993.

> Van Doren, Carl. "Samuel Langhorne Clemens." <u>The Dictionary of American Biography</u>. 1958 ed.

> [Treat a dictionary entry or an encyclopedia article like an entry from an anthology, but do not cite the editor of the reference work.]

27. Government publication

> United States Dept. of Labor, Bureau of Statistics. <u>Dictionary of Occupational Titles</u>. 4th ed. Washington: GPO, 1977.

> [GPO stands for Government Printing Office.]

28. Film or videotape

> <u>Citizen Kane</u>. Dir. Orson Welles. Perf. Orson Welles, Joseph Cotton, Dorothy Comingore, and Agnes Moorehead. RKO, 1941. 50th Anniversary Special Edition videorecording: Turner Home Entertainment, 1991.

29. Lecture

> Albee, Edward. "A Dream or a Nightmare?" Illinois State University Fine Arts Lecture. Normal, IL. 18 Mar. 1979.

For other sources (such as televised shows, performances, advertisements, recordings, works of art), include enough information to permit an interested reader to locate your original source. Be sure to arrange this information in a logical fashion, duplicating as much as possible the order and punctuation of the entries above. To be safe, consult your instructor for suggestions about documenting unusual material.

Electronic Sources. If you get material from a full-text database or online source, you need to indicate that you read it in electronic form. You will probably use a service to which your library or corporation subscribes. Many of the items you access have also appeared in print. Give the print information first, and complete the citation by giving the name of the database (underlined), the name of the online service (such as InfoTrac or Lexis-Nexis), the library you used, and the date of access.

30. Article from a searchable database

Wells, Walter. "John Updike's 'A & P': A Return Visit to Araby." Studies in Short Fiction 32.2 (1993): 127–34. Expanded Academic Index ASAP. InfoTrac. Eastern Illinois U Lib., 6 Mar. 2001.

You might also consult journals, magazines, and newspapers that are available independently on the Internet. For these sources, cite the author, title, and publication data for the printed version as usual; then give the number of pages, paragraphs, or other sections of the electronic version, if provided on the site—followed by the date of access and the electronic address, or URL (Uniform Resource Locator), in angle brackets.

31. Article from an online journal

Dorval, Patricia. "Shakespeare on Screen: Threshold Aesthetics in Oliver Parker's *Othello*." Early Modern Literary Studies 6.1 (May, 2000):15 pars. 5 Sept. 2003 <http://purl.oclc.org/emls/06-1/dorvothe.htm>.

[*Pars.* stands for paragraphs. Pages, paragraphs, or other sections are sometimes numbered in electronic publications. Include these numbers in the Works Cited list and the in-text citations.]

32. Article from an online magazine

Yeoman, Barry. "Into the Closet: Can Therapy Make Gay People Straight?" Salon.com 22 May 2000. 23 May 2000 <http://www.salon.com/health/feature/2000/05/22/exgay/html>.

33. Review from an online newspaper

Ebert, Roger. Review of Real Women Have Curves, dir. Patricia Cardoso. Chicago Sun-Times Online 25 Oct. 2002. 2 Feb. 2003 <http://www.suntimes.com/ebert/ebert_reviews/2002/10/102510.html>.

34. Article from an online reference book or encyclopedia

Daniel, Ralph Thomas. "The History of Western Music." Britannica Online: Macropaedia. 1995. Online Encyclopedia Britannica. 14 June 1995 <http//www.eb.com:180/cgi-bin/g:DocF=macro/5004/45/O.html>.

35. Material accessed on a CD-ROM

Shakespeare. Editions and Adaptations of Shakespeare. Interactive multimedia. Cambridge, UK: Chadwick-Healey, 1995. CD-ROM. Alexandria: Electronic Book Technologies, 1995.

"Silly." The Oxford English Dictionary. 2nd ed. CD-ROM. Oxford: Oxford UP, 1992.

36. Internet site

> *Voice of the Shuttle.* Ed. Alan Liu. 1994. Dept. of English, U of Califor-
> nia, Santa Barbara. 17 Sept. 2004 <http://vos.ucsb.edu/>.

37. Message posted to a discussion list

> Morris, Richard. "Teaching Cause-Effect Thinking." Online posting. 10
> Aug. 2001. Writing Discussion List. 15 Aug. 2001
> <news:comp.edu.writing.instruction>.
>
> [Include a title or description of the posting, the date of the posting, the
> name of the discussion forum, the date of access, and the URL or e-mail
> address of the list's moderator or supervisor in angle brackets.]

Documenting Sources Using APA Style

The guidelines of the American Psychological Association (APA)—used in many
of the social sciences—require parenthetical citations in the text for all quotations,
paraphrases, summaries, and other material from a work used in your research.
These in-text citations correspond to the full bibliographic entries found in an alphabetical reference list placed at the end of your paper.

The APA recommends using italics for titles of books, periodicals, and micro-
film publications. If you are using a typewriter instead of a computer with an italics function, you should underline the titles to be italicized. Do not underline or
use quotation marks around the titles of articles.

In-Text Citations

a. In most cases you will use the author-date method of citation: mention the
   surname of the author to introduce the material and place the date of the
   work in parentheses immediately after the author's name.

> Bordin (1979) conceptualized the therapeutic alliance as including the emo-
> tional bond between client and therapist.

Your readers can identify this source by consulting your References list at
the end of your paper. The entry for the source cited above would appear
like this one:

> Bordin, E. S. (1979). The generalizability of the psychoanalytic con-
> cept of working alliance. *Psychotherapy: Theory, Research, and
> Practice, 16,* 252–260.

b. If you do not mention the author in your text, give the name and the date,
   separated by a comma, at the end of cited material, as shown in these examples:

> The average client who gets counseling is better off than 79 percent of simi-
> lar people who do not receive counseling (Wampold, 2001).

Children's problems stemmed from an inability to cooperate with society and from feelings of inferiority (Utay, 1996), the same sources of adult problems.

c. Include page number(s)—preceded by "p." or "pp."—for all direct quotations. (The APA also recommends them for paraphrases.) Separate the elements with commas, and position the reference so that it is clear what material is being documented.

> In the view of one linguist (Pinker, 1998), language is "a distinct piece of the biological makeup of our brains" (p. 18).

> Pinker (1998) believes that language is "a distinct piece of the biological makeup of our brains" (p. 18).

> Many people overestimate the value of studying formal grammar because they fail to realize that "language is not a cultural artifact that we learn the way we learn to tell time or how the federal government works" (Pinker, 1998, p. 18).

d. For a work with two authors, cite both names every time the reference occurs in the text. Connect the authors' names with "and" when you mention them in the text, but use an ampersand (&) in a parenthetical citation:

> Masling and Bronstein (1993) claim that Freud's psychoanalytic theory is largely untested and accepted uncritically by its adherents.

> Some of Freud's detractors claim that his psychoanalytic theory is largely untested and accepted uncritically by its adherents (Massling & Bronstein, 1993).

e. In the first citation of a work with three to five authors, name all the authors; but in subsequent references, include only the first author's name, followed by "et al." (not italicized and with a period after "al").

> Stockwell, Schachter, and Partee (1973) divide simple sentences into four major syntactic types.

> According to Stockwell et al. (1973) the four types of syntactic structures are associated with four major classes of discourse functions.

For a work with six or more authors give only the first author's name, followed by "et al."—even in the first citation of the work.

> One study (Weaver et al., 1996) found that status-marking dialect features seldom occur in students' writing by the time they reach age seventeen.

f. For an anonymous or unsigned work, use the first two or three words of the title in place of an author's name. Use double quotation marks around the title of an article or chapter, and italicize the title of a periodical, book, brochure, or report. Capitalize the significant words in all titles cited in the text.

> Several supporters of the new general education requirements questioned the need for numerous courses in professional majors ("New Curriculum," 2001).

> The guidelines in *Making Age Irrelevant* (2003) emphasize the need for older workers to maintain a positive attitude in their job search.

g. In citations of one of two or more works by the same author(s), the date will tell the reader which source you mean. But if your reference list contains two or more works by the same author(s) with the same publication date, use lowercase letters in the reference list (1988a) and in parenthetical citations in your text to distinguish the sources.

> Adler stressed that children can be better understood as integrated individuals, each with a social history that fashions his or her personality in a unique way (1930a).

h. Personal communications—such as interviews, electronic mail, and nonretrievable online postings—should be cited only in your text and not in the list of references.

> At least one member of the evaluation team expressed concerns about the validity of the competency testing procedures (S. Day, personal communication, November 8, 2003).

Preparing the References List

On a separate page at the end of the paper, alphabetize a list of References for every source cited in your paper. Format the list according to the these rules:

- Center the title "References" at the top of the page.
- Arrange your sources in alphabetical order by the last name of the author. If the author is not given in the source, alphabetize the source by the first main word in the title (excluding *A, An,* or *The*). When citing two or more works by exactly the same author(s) but not published in the same year, arrange the sources in order of their publication dates, earliest first.
- Double space the entire list, both within and between entries.
- Use *hanging indention:* put the first line of each entry flush with the left margin and indent any subsequent lines in the entry one-half inch (five spaces).
- Place the publication date in parentheses after the author's or authors' names, followed by a period.
- Separate the parts of the entry (author, date, title, and publication information) with a period and one space. Do not use a final period in references to electronic sources that end with an electronic address.
- In titles of books and articles, capitalize only the first word of the title, the first word of the subtitle, and proper nouns. In titles of journals, capitalize all significant words.

- Italicize the titles of books and journals, along with any comma or period that follows the title. Do not italicize or put quotation marks around the titles of articles.

- For nonperiodical sources, give the publishers' location: city and state for U.S. publishers; city, province, or state, if applicable, and country for publishers outside the United States. Use the two-letter postal abbreviation for U.S. states. Major cities that are well known for publishing can be listed without a state abbreviation or country. If more than one city is listed on the work's title page, give only the first one.

- Shorten publishers' names and omit terms like "Co.," "Publishers," or "Inc." For example, use Prentice instead of Prentice Hall or Norton instead of W. W. Norton and Co. However, give full names of associations, corporations, and university presses, and do not omit "Books" or "Press" from a publisher's name.

- Use the abbreviation "p." or "pp." before page numbers in books and in newspapers, but *not* in other periodicals. For inclusive page number include all figures: pp. 215–216.

Sample Entries for a List of References

The following models will help you write the entries in the References list for most sources. If you use a source not illustrated in these examples, try to find one that comes close and provide enough information for readers to find the source. You can also consult the more extensive list of sample entries found in the *Publication Manual of the American Psychological Association,* 5th ed., or ask your instructor or editor for guidance. The APA's Web site also provides answers to frequently asked questions about style (http://ww.apa.org).

Books

1. Book by one author

    Deacon, T. W. (1997). *The symbolic species: The co-evolution of language and the brain.* New York: Norton.

    [The initial "T" is used instead of the author's first name, even though his full first name (Terrence) appears on the source.]

2. Book by two or more authors

    Anderson, T. & Leal, T. (1991). *Free market environmentalism.* Boulder: Westview.

    [Use an ampersand (&) to separate authors' names. Invert all authors' names.]

3. Book with an editor

    Burbank, P. M., & Riebe, D. (Eds.). (2002). *Promoting exercise and behavior change in older adults.* New York: Springer.

[For a book with one editor, use "(Ed.)." Note the periods before and after the second parenthesis.]

4. Book by an unknown author

   Literacy of older adults in America: Results from the national adult literacy survey. (1987). Washington, DC: Center for Educ. Statistics.

5. Book with a translator

   Grmek, Mirko D. (1990). *History of AIDS: Emergence and origin of a modern pandemic* (R. C. Maulitz & J. Duffin, Trans.). Princeton, NJ: Princeton University Press.

6. Book with a group author

   National Research Council. (1993). *The social impact of AIDS in the United States.* New York: National Academy Press.

   [When a corporation, organization, or group is listed as the author on the title page, cite it as you would a person.]

7. A later edition

   Patterson, C. H. (1980). *Theories of counseling and psychotherapy* (3rd ed.). New York: Harper & Row.

8. Two or more works by the same author(s) published in the same year

   Adler, A. (1930a). *The education of children.* South Bend, IN: Gateway.

   Adler, A. (1930b). *Problems of neurosis.* London: Kegan Paul.

   [Works by the same author published in the same year are arranged alphabetically by the first main word of the title and distinguished by adding a lowercase letter to the date.]

9. A work in more than one volume.

   Kaslow, F. W. & Lebow, J. (Eds.). (2002). *Comprehensive handbook of psychotherapy* (Vols. 1–4). New York: Wiley.

10. Encyclopedia or dictionary

    McArthur, T. (Ed.). (1992). *The Oxford companion to the English language.* New York: Oxford University Press.

11. An article or chapter in an edited book.

    Day, S. X. & Rottinghaus, P. (2003). The healthy personality. In W. B. Walsh (Ed.), *Counseling psychology and optimal human functioning* (pp. 1–23). Mahwah, NJ: Erlbaum.

Journals and Magazines

12. Article from a journal with continuous pagination throughout the whole volume

    Lorge, I. & Chall, J. (1963). Estimating the size of vocabularies of children and adults: An analysis of methodological issues. *Journal of Experimental Education, 32,* 147–157.

[Capitalize only the first words of the article's title and subtitle; don't put quotation marks around it. But italicize the journal title and capitalize all significant words in it. The volume number is separated from the journal title with a comma and is italicized.]

13. Article from a journal that paginates each issue separately

Holtug, N. (1997) Altering humans: The case for and against human gene therapy. *Cambridge Quarterly of Healthcare Ethics, 6*(2), 157–60.

[Place the issue number in parentheses after the volume number with no intervening space; do not italicize the issue number.]

14. Article from a magazine

Coghlan, A. (1991, June 15). Warring parents harm children as much as divorce. *New Scientist, 151,* 24–28.

[Give the date shown on the publication—the month for monthlies or the month and day for weeklies. Include the volume number.]

Newspapers

15. Signed article in a daily newspaper

Schwartz, J. (1993, September 30). Obesity affects economic, social status. *The Washington Post,* pp. A1, A4.

[If an article appears on discontinuous pages, give all the page numbers, separated by commas. Use *The* in the newspaper title if the paper itself does.]

16. Unsigned article or editorial in a daily newspaper

No power line-cancer link found. (1997, July 3). *Chicago Tribune,* sect. 1, p. 5.

17. Letter to the editor (weekly newspaper)

Burrowbridge, C. (2003, November 7). Students who have attention disorders [Letter to the editor]. *The Chronicle of Higher Education,* pp. B4, B14.

Other Sources

18. A review

Holt, J. (2003, November 3). To infinity and beyond [Review of the book *Everything and more: A compact history of ∞*]. *The New Yorker,* 84–87.

[If the review is untitled, use the material in brackets as the title, keeping the brackets.]

19. A government publication

United States Department of Energy. (1997). *Global climate change* (Publication No. 97-0370-P). Washington, DC: U.S. Government Printing Office.

20. Videotape, recording, or other audiovisual source

> Poe, K. L. (Producer). (1991). *Alzheimer's disease* [Videotape]. New York: American Journal of Nursing.

Electronic Sources. Most researchers now use aggregate, searchable databases to find articles and other resources. Because these databases are available from a variety of sources and suppliers, the APA recommends that you follow the format appropriate to the work retrieved and add a statement that gives the date of retrieval and the name of the database. You can also provide an item or accession number, but it is not required.

21. Online version of a journal article retrieved from a database

> Rahman, Q., Abrahams, S., & Wilson, G. D. (2003). Sexual-orientation-related differences in verbal fluency. *Neuropsychology, 17,* 240–246. Retrieved October 23, 2003, from PsychARTICLES database.

You might also consult journals, magazines, and newspapers that are available by searching the Internet. For these sources, use the format appropriate to the work retrieved followed by a retrieval statement that includes the URL.

22. Newspaper article, online version available by search

> Mills, S., Armstrong, K., & Holt, D. (2000, June 11). Flawed trials lead to death chamber. *Chicago Tribune.* Retrieved November 14, 2001, from http://www.chicagotribune.com/

23. Message posted to an online forum or discussion group

> Maltz, R. (2003, May 22). Women's strength, body image, and masculinity. Message posted to WMST-L electronic mailing list, archived at http://research/umbc.edu/~korenman/wmst/bodystrength.html

Documenting Sources Using Chicago Manual Style

Many publications in the humanities, particularly those in English and foreign languages, follow the MLA style of documentation, which is discussed and illustrated earlier in this appendix (pp. 288–295). But publications in some other disciplines rely on the source-citation procedures outlined in *The Chicago Manual of Style,* while some college instructors use the student reference adapted from it, *A Manual for Writers of Term Papers, Theses, and Dissertations* by Kate Turabian (known simply as "Turabian").

Both the fifteenth edition of *The Chicago Manual of Style* (2003) and the sixth edition of Turabian (1996) provide detailed descriptions for two styles of documentation. One style, the author-date system, is used mainly in the physical, natural, and social sciences. It closely resembles the style of the American Psychological Association, which is covered on pages 295–301 of this appendix.

The other style, the notes-bibliography system, is often used by writers in history, literature, and the arts. This second system is described in the following sections.

Using the Chicago Notes and Bibliography Style

a. In the Chicago note style, bibliographic citations are provided in notes (either footnotes or endnotes), usually supplemented by a bibliography, or list of works cited. You need to find out from your instructor, editor, or supervisor whether you should use footnotes or endnotes and whether you should also include a bibliography.

b. A raised number (superscript) in your text refers the reader to source information in endnotes or footnotes. In the notes themselves, the numbers are full size, not raised, and followed by a period.

"A modifier is restrictive when it is needed to identify the referent of the headword."[1]

1. Martha Kolln, *Rhetorical Grammar*, 4th ed. (New York: Longman, 2003), 301.

c. Notes, whether footnotes or endnotes, should be numbered consecutively, beginning with 1, throughout the article or chapter. If you use footnotes, separate them from the text with a short line. You can use your word processor program to position footnotes at the bottoms of appropriate pages and to number the notes automatically through your text. If you use endnotes, place them on a new page directly after the text.

d. If your bibliography includes all the works cited in the notes, the note citations—even the first citation of a source—can be brief, as in examples 3 and 4 below, since readers can consult the bibliography for the publication details. The *Chicago Manual* recommends this practice as "user-friendly and economical." If you don't include a bibliography, give all the publication details in the first note for a source, as in examples 1 and 2 below; then use shortened citations in subsequent notes (examples 3 and 4).

1. Julie Roy Jeffrey, *Frontier Women: The Trans-Mississippi West 1840–1860* (New York: Hill and Wang, 1979), 145–47.

2. John Lagone, "Acupuncture: New Respect for an Ancient Remedy," *Discover* 5 (1984), 70–71.

3. Jeffrey, *Frontier Women*, 62.

4. Lagone, "Acupuncture," 72, 74.

e. In notes and bibliography entries, follow these stylistic conventions:
   • For the titles and subtitles of books, articles, periodicals, and chapters, capitalize the first and last words and all other major words in the title.
   • Italicize the titles of books and periodicals.
   • Put quotation marks around the titles of articles in periodicals or parts of books (such as chapters).

- Do not shorten publishers' names, but omit "Inc.," "Co.," and similar abbreviations.
- Do not use "p." or "pp." before pages.

f. In notes, the Chicago style recommends using a shortened form for subsequent citations of a source you have already cited. You may use the Latin abbreviation "ibid." (meaning "in the same place") to refer to the same source in a preceding note. For any source already cited in your notes, but not immediately before, you may use the author's name; if you have cited more than one work by the same author, then include a shortened form of the title.

g. In the bibliography, or list of works cited, arrange the sources alphabetically by the authors' last names. For more than one work by the same author, give the author's name in the first entry only; thereafter, replace the name with a dash (not a hyphen), followed by a period.

Sample Entries for Notes and Bibliography Entries

In these samples, notes and bibliography entries appear together for easy reference. You will notice key differences in the two forms:

NOTES	BIBLIOGRAPHY ENTRIES
Begin with a number that corresponds to the note number in the text.	Do not begin with a number.
Use regular indention (the first line indented five spaces).	Use hanging indention (the second and subsequent lines indented five spaces).
Give the author's name in normal order.	Begin with the author's last name.
Use commas between elements (such as author's name and title).	Use periods between elements, followed by one space.
Enclose publication information in parentheses.	Put a period before publication information; don't use parentheses.
Include specific page number(s) for the material cited.	Omit page numbers for books; cite inclusive page numbers for periodical articles and parts of books.

If you use a source not illustrated in these examples, consult the more extensive list of sample entries found in *The Chicago Manual of Style*, 15th ed.; or ask your instructor, editor, or supervisor for guidance. The University of Chicago Press Web site also provides answers to frequently asked questions about style (http://www.press.uchicago.edu/Misc/Chicago/cmosfaq/cmosfaq.html).

Books

1. Book by one, two, or three authors

1. Richard H. Chused, *Private Acts in Public Places: A Social History of Divorce* (Philadelphia: University of Pennsylvania Press, 1994), 27.

Chused, Richard H. *Private Acts in Public Places: A Social History of Divorce.* Philadelphia: University of Pennsylvania Press, 1994.

    1. William McCrun, William Cran, and Robert MacNeil, *The Story of English* (Viking Press, 1986), 216–17.

McCrum, William, William Cran, and Robert MacNeil. *The Story of English.* New York: Viking Press, 1986.

2. Books by more than three authors

    2. Martin J. Medhurst and others, *Cold War Rhetoric: Strategy, Metaphor and Ideology* (New York: Greenwood Press, 1990), 187.

Medhurst, Martin J., Robert L. Scott, Robert L. Ivie, and Philip Wander. *Cold War Rhetoric: Strategy, Metaphor, and Ideology.* New York: Greenwood Press, 1990.

3. Book with an editor

    3. Jeffrey Abramson, ed., *Postmortem: The O. J. Simpson Case* (New York: Basic Books, 1996), 136.

Abramson, Jeffrey, ed. *Postmortem: The O. J. Simpson Case.* New York: Basic Books, 1996.

4. Book with an author and an editor

    4. Benjamin Whorf, *Language, Thought, and Reality: Selected Writings of Benjamin Lee Whorf,* ed. J. B. Carroll (Cambridge: Massachusetts Institute of Technology Press, 1956), 37.

Whorf, Benjamin. *Language, Thought, and Reality: Selected Writings of Benjamin Lee Whorf.* Edited by J. B. Carroll. Cambridge: Massachusetts Institute of Technology Press, 1956.

5. A translation

    5. Mirko D. Grmek, *History of AIDS: Emergence and Origin of a Modern Pandemic,* trans. Russell C. Maulitz and Jacalyn Duffin (Princeton: Princeton University Press, 1990), 233–34.

Grmek, Mirko D. *History of AIDS: Emergence and Origin of a Modern Pandemic.* Translated by Russell C. Maulitz and Jacalyn Duffin. Princeton: Princeton University Press, 1990.

6. A later edition

    6. Randolph Quirk, *The Use of English,* 2d ed. (London: Longman Group, 1968), 203-04.

Quirk, Randolph. *The Use of Engish.* 2d ed. London: Longman Group, 1968.

7. Work in a collection or anthology

    7. Mary Gordon, "The Parable of the Cave," in *The Writer on Her Work,* ed. Janet Sternburg (New York: W. W. Norton, 1980), 29.

Gordon, Mary. "The Parable of the Cave." In *The Writer on Her Work,* edited by Janet Sternburg, 27–32. New York: W. W. Norton, 1980.

Periodicals: Journals, Magazines, Newspapers

8. Article from a journal with continuous pagination throughout the whole volume

>8. Raymond Potvin and Che-Fu Lee, "Multistage Path Models of Adolescent Alcohol and Drug Use," *Journal of Studies on Alcohol* 41 (1980): 539.

>Potvin, Raymond, and Che-Fu Lee. "Multistage Path Models of Adolescent Alcohol and Drug Use." *Journal of Studies on Alcohol* 41 (1980): 531–42.

9. Article from a journal that paginates each issue separately

>9. Nils Holtug, "Altering Humans: The Case For and Against Human Gene Therapy," *Cambridge Quarterly of Healthcare Ethics* 6, no. 2 (1997): 158.

>Holtug, Nils. "Altering Humans: The Case For and Against Human Gene Therapy." *Cambridge Quarterly of Healthcare Ethics* 6, no. 2 (1997): 157–60.

10. Article from a weekly or monthly magazine

>10. Malcolm Gladwell, "The Trouble with Fries," *New Yorker*, March 5, 2001, 54.

>Gladwell, Malcolm. "The Trouble with Fries." *New Yorker*, March 5, 2001, 52–57.

11. Article from a newspaper

Newspapers are more commonly cited in notes or parenthetical references in the text than in bibliographies. No bibliographic entry would be needed for the following citation:

>In an article on the unexpected outbreak of influenza (*Chicago Tribune*, December 4, 2003), Judith Graham explained that the H3N2 virus mutated into a variety called the Fujian strain, unknown in the United States.

If, for some reason, you wanted to include an entry for this source in your bibliography, it would appear as follows:

>Graham, Judith. "Vicious Flu Strain Hits Nation Early." *Chicago Tribune*, December 4, 2003, midwest edition, 1, 16.

12. A review

>12. Carlin Romano, "Was It as Bad for You as It Was for Me?" review of *Just Being Difficult?: Academic Writing in the Public Arena*, ed. by Jonathan Culler and Kevin Lamb, *Chronicle of Higher Education*, October 24, 2003, B11.

>Romano, Carlin. "Was It as Bad for You as It Was for Me?" Review of *Just Being Difficult?: Academic Writing in the Public Arena*, ed. by Jonathan Culler and Kevin Lamb. *Chronicle of Higher Education*, October 24, 2003, B11.

Other Sources

13. An interview

    Cite an unpublished interview in your text or in notes, although your instructor or editor may want you to also include it in the bibliography. Give the names of both the person interviewed and the interviewer, a brief identification (if appropriate), and the place and date of the interview (if known).

    > 13. Ken Burns (producer and director of documentary films), interview with the author, September 1998, Illinois State University.

    Cite a published interview as you would a periodical article or a chapter in a book.

    > 13. Mikhail Gorbachev, interview by Amitabh Pal, *The Progressive*, December 28, 2003, 30.

    > Gorbachev, Mikhail. Interview by Amitabh Pal. *The Progressive*, December 28, 2003, 28–31.

14. Article from a reference work

    Cite well-known reference works, such as major dictionaries and encyclopedias, in notes rather than in bibliographies. Omit the facts of publication, but specify the edition (if not the first). For an alphabetically arranged work, cite the item (not the volume or page number) preceded by *s.v.*, which is Latin for *sub verbo*, "under the word."

    > 14. *The Columbia Encyclopedia*, 5th ed., s.v. "psychopharmacology."

    > 14. *The Dictionary of American Biography*, s.v. "Clemens, Samuel Langhorne."

15. Government publication

    > 15. House Committee on Science and Technology, *Procurement and Allocation of Human Organs for Transplantation*, 106th Cong., 1st sess., 1999, H. Rep. 409, 9–10.

    > U.S. Congress. House. Committee on Science and Technology. *Procurement and Allocation of Human Organs for Transplantation*. 106th Cong., 1st sess., 1999. H. Rep. 409.

Electronic Sources. To cite online journals and magazines, follow the relevant examples presented above, add the URL (Uniform Resource Locator) and, if your discipline or publication requires an access date, include it in parentheses at the end of the citation.

16. Article from an online journal

    If page numbers are not available, add a descriptive locator to note citations to help readers.

16. C. Sheldon Woods and Laurence C. Scharmann, "High School Students' Perceptions of Evolutionary Theory," *Electronic Journal of Science Education* 6, no. 2 (2001), under "Implications for Instruction," http://unr.edu/ homepage/crowther/ejse/woodsetal.html.

Woods, C. Sheldon, and Lawrence C. Scharmann. "High School Students' Perceptions of Evolutionary Theory." *Electronic Journal of Science Education* 6, no. 2 (December 2001): 121–38. http://unr.edu/homepage/crowther/ejse/woodsetal.html.

17. Article from an online magazine

17. Sheerly Avni, "Geezers Know Best," *Salon,* May 2, 2003, http://www.salon.com/mwt/feature/2003/05/05/elder/html (accessed May 10, 2003).

Avni, Sheerly. "Geezers Know Best." *Salon,* May 2, 2003. http://www.salon.com/mwt/feature/2003/05/05/elder/html (accessed May 10, 2003).

18. Article from a searchable database

To cite sources obtained by searching a third-party Internet database, whether by subscription or otherwise, follow the relevant examples of journals and other periodicals given above. Then add the URL of the main entrance to the service and, if required by your discipline or publication, include an access date in parentheses at the end of the citation.

18. David E. Nye, "Technology, Nature, and American Origin Stories," *Environmental History* 8, no. 1 (2003): par. 31, http://www.historycooperative.org/journals/.

Nye, David E. "Technology, Nature, and American Origin Stories." *Environmental History,* 8, no. 1 (2003): 8-24. http://www.historycooperative.org/journals/.

19. Article from an online newspaper or news service

19. Associated Press, "More Women Aspiring to Be Doctors," *CNN.com,* December 8, 2003, http://www.cnn.com/2003/EDUCATION/12/08/medical.school.ap/index.html.

20. Original content from a Web site

If there is no author per se, the sponsor or owner of the site may stand in for the author.

20. The Bahá'í of the United States, "Advancement of Women," *The Bahá'í World,* http://www.bahai.org/section8.html.

The Bahá'í of the United States. "Advancement of Women." *The Bahá'í World.* http://www.bahai.org/section8.html.

21. A retrievable online posting

Citations to electronic mailing groups and discussion groups should generally be limited to text and notes. Include the name of the list, the date of the individual posting, and the URL. Also give an access date, if your discipline or publication requires it.

>   21. Russ Hunt, e-mail to Teaching Composition Digest mailing list, December 6, 2003, http://mailman.eppg.com/pipermail/teaching_composition/2003-December/001713.html.

Documenting Sources Using CSE Style

Writing in the natural and applied sciences is specialized and technical, and the details of documentation vary slightly from discipline to discipline. For more information about writing in the following fields, you should consult one of these style manuals.

- Chemistry: American Chemical Society, *The ACS Style Guide: A Manual for Authors and Editors,* 2d ed. (1997). Web site: http://pubs.acs.org/index.html.
- Geology: U.S. Geological Society, *Suggestions to Authors of Reports of the United States Geological Survey,* 7th ed. (1991). Web site: http://www.agu.org/pubs/contrib.html.
- Mathematics: American Mathematical Society, *A Manual for Authors of Mathematical Papers,* Rev. ed. (1996). Web site: http://www.ams.org.
- Medicine: American Medical Association, *AMA Manual of Style,* 9th ed. (1998). Web site: http://healthlinks.washington.edu/hsl/styleguides/ama.html.
- Physics: American Institute of Physics, *Style Manual for Guidelines in the Preparation of Papers,* 4th ed. (1990). Web site: http://www.aip.org/pubservs/style/4thed/toc.html.

The most thorough and widely used manual for scientific writing is *Scientific Style and Format: The CBE Manual for Authors, Editors, and Publishers,* 6th ed. (1994). *The CBE Manual* was published by the Council of Biology Editors, but in January 2000, the organization changed its name to the Council of Science Editors, so the style is abbreviated either CSE (as here) or CBE (www.councilscienceeditors.org/).

CSE style itself includes two methods for documenting sources used in research: a *name-year* system that resembles the APA style and a *citation-sequence* system that lists sources in order of their use. In this appendix, we describe the basics of the second system.

Using the CSE Citation-Sequence Style

> a. When you need to cite a source in the text of your paper, insert a raised number immediately after the word or phrase which refers to the source. Citations are numbered in the order you use them.

Coyotes are becoming increasingly common in human modified habitats throughout North America.[1] According to Atkinson and Shackleton,[2] one possible explanation is that human-dominated areas produce abundant food sources.

These raised numbers in the text refer to a numbered list of references at the end of the paper.

b. If you use a source you have already cited and numbered, refer to it by its original number.

MacCracken's[3] description of the annual diet of coyotes in residential habitat was based on a small number of scats collected during a single month. Atkinson and Shackleton[2] described the diet of coyotes in an area that was mostly agricultural, and Shago's[4] description of urban coyote diet was based on 22 scats.

This reuse of numbers is the major difference between the CSE citation-sequence system and numbered references to footnotes or endnotes. In CSE style, each source has only one number, which is determined by the order in which the source is cited.

c. When you refer to more than one source in a citation, put the numbers in sequence and separate them with a comma but no space.

Coyotes living in urban habitats have relatively small home ranges,[1,3] which may indicate abundant food resources.

Using a CSE References List

On a separate page at the end of the text of your article, provide a list of all the sources you have cited. These sources are numbered: source 1 in the text will be listed in the first entry on the References page, source 2 in the text will be entry 2 in the list, and so on. The References list is *not* alphabetical. You should follow these guidelines when preparing your References list:

- Arrange entries numerically, in order of their citation in the text. Put a period and a space after the number for each entry.
- Single-space within each entry, but double-space between entries.
- Use hanging indention—that is, begin the first line of each entry at the left margin and indent subsequent lines.
- List each author's name with the last name first, followed by initials for first and last names. Do not put a comma after the last name or use periods or spaces with initials. But do use commas to separate names of different authors.
- Put the date of a book after the publication information; put the date of an article in a periodical after the title of the periodical.

- Book and article titles: do not underline, italicize, or put quotation marks around the titles of articles or books; capitalize only the first word and any proper nouns.

- Journal titles: do not underline or italicize the titles of journals. For titles of two or more words, abbreviate words of six or more letters and omit most prepositions, articles (*a, an, the*), or conjunctions. For example, *Journal of the National Cancer Institute* becomes J Natl Cancer Inst, *Scientific American* becomes Sci Am, and *Annals of Medicine* becomes Ann Med. Capitalize all the words in journal titles.

- Leave a space after the title of a journal and give the year followed by a semicolon, the volume number followed by a colon, and the inclusive page numbers of the article: J Reprod Fertil 1982;64:485–9. If the journal has an issue number, put it in parentheses after the volume number: 98(3):26–40.

Sample Entries for a References List

The following examples show the forms for common entries in a References list. For more information, consult the detailed descriptions in *Scientific Style and Format.*

Books

1. A book with one author

    1. Horne J. Why we sleep: the functions of sleep in humans and other mammals. New York: Oxford Univ Pr; 1988. 319 p.

    [Total pages (319 p.) are given for a whole book.]

2. A book with two to ten authors

    2. Franklin JF, Dyrness CT. Natural vegetation of Oregon and Washington. Corvallis: Oregon State Univ Pr; 1984. 452 p.

    [For books with more than ten authors, list the first ten and add "and others."]

3. A book with an editor

    3. Chapman J, Feldhamer G, editors. Wild mammals of North America. Baltimore: Johns Hopkins Pr; 1982. 1147 p.

4. Chapter or article in an edited book

    4. Ziem E. True foxes. In: Keienburg W, editor. Grizmek's encyclopedia of animals. New York: McGraw Hill; 1990. p 118–29.

    [Inclusive pages (p 118–29) are given for the article or chapter.]

Periodicals: Journals, Magazines, Newspapers

5. Article from a journal with continuous pagination throughout the whole volume

    5. Jokiel PL, Coles SL. Response of Hawaiian and other Indo-Pacific corals to elevated temperatures. Coral Reefs 1990;8:155–62.

6. Article from a journal that paginates each issue separately

> 6. Holtug N. Altering humans: the case for and against human gene therapy. Cambr Quart Health Eth 1997 Spr;6(2):157–60.

7. Article from a weekly or monthly magazine

> 7. McClintock J. The secret life of ants. Discover 2003 Nov:56–9.

8. Article from a newspaper

> 8. Levathes L. A geneticist maps ancient migrations. New York Times 1993 Jul 7;Sect C: 1 (col 1).

Other Sources

9. A government publication

> 9. Committee on Environment and Public Works, Senate (US). Implementation of environmental treaties: joint hearing with the committee on foreign relations. 107th Cong., 2d Sess. Senate Doc. Hrg 107–807; 2002.

10. Thesis or dissertation

> 10. Quinn T. The distribution, movement, and diet of coyotes in urban areas of western Washington [dissertation]. Seattle: Univ of Washington. 1992. Available from University Microfilms, Ann Arbor, MI; AAG9312734.

Electronic Sources. You will find only a few samples for citing electronic sources in *Scientific Style and Format.* For additional models, the CSE Web site refers authors to the revised supplement of the *National Library of Medicine Recommended Formats for Bibliographic Citation,* which is available at www.nlm.nih.gov/pubs/formats/internet.pdf.

The following sample entries are based on the National Library of Medicine formats.

11. An electronically published book

> 11. Baker C. Your genes, your choices: exploring the issues raised by genetic research [Internet]. Washington, DC: American Assn for the Advancement of Science; 1997 [cited 2003 Dec 12]. [about 89 p.]. Available from: http://ehrweb.aaas.org/books/yourgenes.pdf.

12. An article in an online journal

> 12. Williamson I. Internalized homophobia and health issues affecting lesbians and gay men. Health Educ Res [Internet] 2000 [cited 2003 Dec 11];15(1):97–107. Available from http://her.oupjournals.org/cgi/content/full/15/1/97.

13. A source from a searchable database

> 13. Megner T, Maurer C, Peterka RJ. A multisensory posture control mode of human upright stance. Prog Brain Res 2003; 142:189–201. In: PubMed [Internet]. Bethesda (MD): National Library of Medi-

cine; [cited 2003 Dec 10]. Available from: http://www.ncbi.nlm.nih.gov/PubMed;PMID:12693262.

[After "In," provide information about the database: title, place of publication, and publisher. Record the date of publication or copyright date if one is given. Add the date of your access, preceded by "cited," in brackets. If the database gives an identifying number to the source, add it at the end of the citation.]

List of Style Manuals and Supplementary Internet Sources

Anthropology: *The Chicago Manual of Style,* 15th ed., 2003.
American Anthropological Association site: www.aaanet.org/pubs/style_guide.htm
University of South Dakota instructional site: www.usd.edu/anth/handbook.bib/htm

Biology and Life Sciences: *Scientific Style and Format: The CBE Manual for Authors, Editors, and Publishers,* 6th ed., 1994
Council of Science Editors site: www.councilscienceeditors.org/
Ohio State University instructional site: http://library.osu.edu/guides/cbegd.html

Chemistry: *The ACS Style Guide: A Manual for Authors and Editors,* 2nd ed., 1997.
American Chemical Society site: http://pubs.acs.org/index.html

English and the Humanities: *MLA Handbook for Writers of Research Papers,* 6th ed., 2003.
MLA site: www.mla.org/www_mla_org/style/
Westfield State College Ely Library instructional site: www.lib.wsc.ma.edu/mlastyle.htm

Engineering: *Institute of Electrical and Electronics Engineers Standards Style Manual,* 7th ed., 2000.
IEEE site: www.ieee.org/organizations/pubs/transactions/information.htm
Computer Society Press guidelines: www.computer.org/authors/style/index.htm

Geology: *Geowriting: A Guide to Writing, Editing, and Printing in Earth Science,* 5th ed., 1995; *Suggestions to Authors of the Reports of the United States Geological Survey,* 7th ed., 1991.
American Geophysical Union publications site: www.agu.org/pubs/contrib.html

Government Documents: *The Complete Guide to Citing Government Information Resources: A Manual for Writers and Librarians,* Rev. ed., 1993; U.S. Government Printing Office, *Style Manual,* 2000.

Memphis State University instructional site: http://exlibris.memphis
.edu/resource/unclesam/citeweb.html

History: *The Chicago Manual of Style,* 15th ed., 2003.
Chicago Manual site: www.chicagomanualofstyle.org/cmosfaq.html
University of Wisconsin instructional site: www.wisc.edu/writing/
Handbook/DocChicago.html

Journalism: *Associated Press Stylebook,* 35th ed., 2000.
Associated Press site: www.ap.org
Utah State University instructional site: www.usu.edu/~communic/
faculty/sweeney/ap.htm

Law and Legal Studies: *The Bluebook: A Uniform System of Citation,* 17th ed., 2000.
Harvard Law Review site: www.legalbluebook.com/
Cornell University instructional site: www.law.cornell.edu/citation/

Linguistics: Linguistic Society of America, "LSA Style Sheet." Published annually in the December issue of the *LSA Bulletin.*

Mathematics: *The AMS Author Handbook: General Instructions for Preparing Manuscripts,* Rev. ed., 1996.
American Mathematical Society site: www.ams.org

Medicine: *AMA Manual of Style: A Guide for Authors and Editors,* 9th ed., 1998.
American Medical Association site: www.ama-assn.org
Long Island University Library instructional site: www.liu.edu/cwis/
cwp/library/workshop/citama.htm

Music: *Writing About Music: A Style Sheet from the Editors of* 19th-Century Music. 1998.

Physics: *AIP Style Manual,* 4th ed., 1990.
American Institute of Physics site: www.aip.org/pubservs/style.html
[Manual may be downloaded free of charge.]

Psychology and other Social Sciences: *Publication Manual of the American Psychological Association,* 5th ed., 2001.
APA site: www.apastyle.org
University of Southern Mississippi instructional site: www.lib.usm.edu/
research/guides/apa.html

Political Science: *Style Manual for Political Science,* Rev. ed., 1993.
American Political Science Association site: www.aspanet.org
University of Wisconsin instructional site: www.wisc.edu/writing/
Handbook/DocAPSA.html

Science and Technical Writing: *Science and Technical Writing: A Manual of Style,* 2nd ed., 2001.
Virginia Tech instructional site: http://writing.eng.vt.edu

Social Work: *Writing for SASW Press: Information for Authors,* Rev. ed., 1995.
National Association of Social Workers site: www.naswpress.org/
resources/tools/01-write/guidelines_toc.htm

Index